POST-COLONIAL AND AFRICAN AMERICAN WOMEN'S WRITING

Post-Colonial and African American Women's Writing

A Critical Introduction

Gina Wisker

St. Martin's Press, Scholarly and Reference Division, 175 Fifth Avenue, New York, N.Y. 10010

First published in the United States of America in

This book is printed on paper suitable for recycling and made from fully managed and sustained forest sources.

Printed in China

ISBN 0–312–23287–X cloth bound
ISBN 0–312–23288–8 paper back

Library of Congress Cataloging-in-Publication Data
Wisker, Gina, 1951–
    Post-Colonial and African American women's writing: a critical introduction / Gina Wisker.
        p.   cm.
    Includes bibliographical references (p.   ) and index.
    ISBN 0–312–23287–X (cloth)—ISBN 0–312–23288–8 (paper)
    1. Commonwealth literature (English)—Women authors—History and criticism.   2. Women and literature—Commonwealth countries—History—20th century.   3. American literature—Afro-American authors—History and criticism.   4. Women and literature—United States—History—20th century.   5. American literature—Women authors—History and criticism.   6. Commonwealth countries—In literature.   7. Decolonization in literature.   8. Postcolonialism—History. I. Title.

PR9080.5. W57   2000
820.9′9287′09171241—dc21   99–059202

For Alistair, Liam, Kitt, my parents and my students

Contents

Acknowledgements

I would like to thank Alistair, Liam and Kitt for their support, tolerance and enthusiasm, not merely during the writing of this book but also when we have all flown off (most enjoyably) to international destinations to seek out books, writers, critics and performances. Thanks to Anglia Polytechnic University for financially underpinning these working visits, and to my students, particularly on the 'Black and Asian women's writing' module at Anglia, and at Madingley, who have worked with the texts with me. Many other people have generously given their advice, books, conversations and e-mail discussions including Carole Ferrier and Bronwen Levy (Brisbane), Teresia Teiawa and Helu Konai Thaman (Fiji), Roger Landbeck (Brisbane and Fiji), Dorothy Driver (South Africa), Ruth Kashishian and Niki Marangou (Cyprus). Thanks are due to Deborah Madsen and the unknown reader for sensitive and tough advice on drafts, to Isabel King for her stalwart administrative assistance and to Margaret Bartley at the publishers for her invaluable commitment, support and openness to discussion throughout the book's development.

G. W.

1

Introduction

Post-Colonial and African American Women's Writing: A Critical Introduction aims to unite a concentration on twentieth-century post-colonial and African American writing, with a gendered focus on women's writing, its contexts, forms and concerns. Toni Morrison once said that she wrote the books she wanted to read but could not find published. This project springs from a similar impetus. A book which provided a critical introduction to two increasingly popular, related areas of writing, African American and post-colonial, and which concentrated on women's writing, was what I and others constantly sought for our reading and teaching, and could never find. There are a number of very good, useful critical books and text selections in the field of post-colonial writing, African American writing and women's writing (see below). There is, however, a dearth of books concentrating on, and relating to the critical concerns and the textual study of twentieth-century post-colonial and African American writing by women. Writing such a book, to try and fill such a gap, bringing together overlapping areas of study – post-colonialism and African American, with the focus on women – has raised many issues of scope and definition, as well as providing me with great pleasure. I hope it will provide pleasure and also be useful for readers. Engaging with the contested critical areas of both feminism and the post-colonial is bound to be fraught with difficulties and selection necessarily means much is omitted, largely because it does not fit the dual concentration on the post-colonial and gender issues, or for reasons of space and cohesion, and I apologise for this. But I hope readers will find here a comprehensive, useful and rich source for their reading and work, and a stimulus to further reading.

In my focus on post-colonial writing I have been careful to include both Black and white writers, basing this selection on their parallel concerns with issues of identity, race and women's lives. The decision to include white writers is in alignment with similar choices in other post-colonial selections and critical works such as Rutherford, Jensen and Chew's *Into the Nineties* (1994), Thieme's *The Arnold*

Anthology of Post-Colonial Literatures in English (1996) and Walder's *Post-Colonial Literatures in English* (1998). The decision recognises both Black and white writers who are genuinely taking a critical, post-colonial perspective, some while still under colonial rule, though for the most part subsequent to its formal removal.

What has been achieved, I hope, is an accessible introduction to: major critical concerns and issues in post-colonial and African American women's writing; feminist critical practice in the reading of the selected texts, and a consideration of writing by a range of women writers, some well established and available, others well known in their countries of origin, and now gaining wider recognition, and still others who I have categorised as 'emergent' because of the current lack of exposure and critical discussion of their works outside their countries of origin.

There are some very good *collections* of post-colonial writing, such as John Thieme's (1996), and of African-descended women's writing, such as Margaret Busby's *Daughters of Africa* (1992). There are some fine critical introductions to, or engagements with, the issues involved and the range of the field, such as Chrisman and Williams's *An Introduction to Post-Colonial Theory* (1993) or Mongia's *Contemporary Post-Colonial Theory* (1996). *Into the Nineties* (1994) is one of the very few collections of both primary and critical materials focusing on women's writing, with an Australian emphasis. There are also some most useful books exploring the terms and range of, and providing critical introductions to, post-colonial writing (however it is defined, and this is certainly contested), such as Ashcroft, Griffiths and Tiffin's *The Empire Writes Back* (1989), Tiffin and Adam's *Past the Last Post* (1993) and Tiffin and Lawson's *De-scribing Empire* (1994). There are also some good books on post-colonial women's writing, such as *Black Women, Writing and Identity* (Davis, 1994), and *Motherlands* (Nasta, 1991), as well as my own *Insights into Black Women's Writing* (1993). Students, academics and other readers will find much to complement their use of *Post-Colonial and African American Women's Writing: A Critical Introduction* by referring to these texts.

The critical focus of *Post-Colonial and African American Women's Writing: A Critical Introduction* springs from a concern with the twentieth-century post-colonial, with critical perspectives developed from African American writing and with feminist critical practice. These concerns influence choices of texts, approaches and tone. Gender is a very important issue in the specific choice of texts to discuss, for there are many psychoanalytical, political and economic similarities in the ways in which women have been and are constructed and enabled in society, represented in discourse and the breadth of the arts. Silencing and subordination have been a shared experience for colonial and African American peoples, and for women in particular. Speaking out and back in one's own terms is a shared development.

My own subject position is ex-colonial. I grew up in the colonies post-independence and since have spent much of my intellectual energy and my imaginative leisure time on working with the post-colonial. This governs my desire both to work in the field and to write about it, to think back over my childhood in colonial settings (Egypt, Cyprus, Malta, Singapore) and return to these and others (Malaysia, Australia, New Zealand, Fiji, South Africa), and their literatures (and those of the Americas) through travel and reading. My impetus and my choices here are governed by a mixture of the personal and the academic, as well as space.

THE SHAPE OF THE BOOK

Post-Colonial and African American Women's Writing: A Critical Introduction begins by looking at the contested definitions of post-colonialism and critical questions which surround this, whether temporal, based on resistance, or in relation to critical discourse. It indicates the range of writers to be looked at, some as representative, and all as individually distinctive, noting differences in definition between post-colonial, other indigenous, diasporan and settler writers.

After the critical introduction, three sections follow: the first section concentrates on African American women's writing, looking specifically at the work of Alice Walker and Toni Morrison. It introduces critical perspectives developed by African American women's writing which are then drawn from in the book as a whole to discuss women writers from a diversity of cultural contexts, recognising both their contextual differences and their different approaches to feminism. In the next two sections, each chapter considers a different country, continent or group of islands/countries, using established cluster terms such as Pacific Rim/Oceania, and South-East Asia.

The second section of the book looks at established and newly rising writers from well known, fully critically documented and anthologised contexts – the Caribbean, Africa, South Africa, India, Australia and Aotearoa, Canada and Britain (arguably the newest post-colonial context).

The third section looks at emergent women writers or those who have written within post-colonialism more recently, and includes South-East Asia, Oceania and Cyprus.

In each chapter, some historical background and cultural context is sketched in, and the conditions of women's writing are explored, establishing, where it exists, a legacy in earlier writing by women. The main focus is on writing in *English* by contemporary or later twentieth-century post-colonial women writers, from a *British* post-colonial context. What unites the women's writing considered here is not merely the economic, political and psychoanalytic constrictions and influences on gendered experience, but also themes and concerns which arise out of these experiences: motherhood, an interest in the mother tongue; identity and subjectivity as a woman, Black or white; relationships; families; sexual politics.

Post-colonial and African American women's writing is now read and studied by people all over the world. Some of the writers discussed here have blazed the way for the recuperation and recognition of the work of others – Toni Morrison, Alice Walker and Margaret Atwood, for example. For other women writers – Aboriginal, Maori, from the Pacific Rim, Cyprus and South-East Asia – critical appreciation is still largely absent. This book sets out to redress this imbalance and tentatively fill in some of the gaps and silences, making available entrances, critiques and celebrations of a very wide range of women's writing from twentieth-century post-colonial and African American contexts. It considers a number of writers, enabling a cohesive discussion of key gendered issues, specifically motherhood, language, mother tongue, relationships, cultural and gendered identity, and different modes of expression. The selected women writers, white, Black, indigenous, settler or migrant (forced or by choice), speak from a variety of cultural contexts. While each chapter focuses on women writers from a particular location, some now writing in the post-colonial diaspora are considered in the context of where they have settled.

My main aim is to discuss writers using culturally and gender inflected critical reading practices. There are of course many difficulties and dangers, as a white reader and teacher, to be writing about largely Black and Asian writers' texts: avoiding appropriation, selection itself, and avoiding claims both of homogeneity and of the construction of an alternative canon to the established white male middle-class European and American (but one perhaps potentially just as exclusive). There are dangers, but I hope they are outweighed for readers as they are for me by the many excitements and pleasures of critically engaging with and enjoying reading the selection of texts included here.

COLONIALISM, IMPERIALISM AND POST-COLONIALISM

These three terms are often used confusingly so I will attempt to simplify and clarify their use here. Imperialism is usually taken to mean, literally, 'of the empire'; authority assumed by a state over other states or peoples. It is often accompanied by symbolism, pageantry as well as military power, and Roman imperialism was a prime example of this – military power and ways of life, symbols and beliefs taking over from those of indigenous peoples, absorbing difference under the power of empire. We are looking, in relation to texts considered here, at the expansion of European nation-states in the nineteenth century. Not all imperialism involves settling or colonising.

Colonialism involves settlement, governing indigenous people, exploiting and developing the resources of the land, and embedding imperial government. *Colonial* literature is that produced under colonial rule, by both the settlers and the indigenous people, while *colonialist* literature is that supporting colonial rule, springing from the viewpoint of the colonialists, those supporting imperialism. *Post-colonial* describes a period of time, after colonialism, but it is also taken to mean (here) 'in opposition to the colonial'. There are numerous arguments about whether post-colonial literature can be produced during the colonial period, because of its oppositional nature, or whether, strictly speaking, it only develops once colonialism, colonial rule, has ended and independence has been achieved (see Boehmer, 1995, pp. 2–3). Here it will be taken to mean writing in opposition to colonialism, which has been written after colonial rule has ended; but roots prior to this ending will be mentioned. A more detailed discussion of the applicability of the terms to different locations, and most specifically of the contested term 'post-colonial', appears below.

DEALING WITH DIFFERENCE

A very great number of the women writers discussed in this book
are Black or Asian in origin – Toni Morrison (US), Alice Walker (US),
Buchi Emecheta (Nigeria), Bessie Head (South Africa), Jean Binta
Breeze (Caribbean/UK), Sally Morgan (Australia/Aboriginal), Teresia
Teaiwa (Fiji), Patricia Grace (Maori), Suniti Namjoshi (India/Canada).
Some, including those of slave origins in the US, Caribbean and
Africa, live permanently in countries to which their families moved
historically and where they have lived for generations. Others live
now in the diaspora, moving between families and friends, work
and homes. Others are indigenous to the countries in which they
write – Aboriginal, Maori, Cypriot, African, Indian, South-East Asian,
Pacific Rim, etc., writers – their ancestors perhaps having arrived in
these countries so long ago that only the paintings and myths of
their arrival remain. Even African American women's writing,
which I have separated off as distinct, is post-colonial in the broadest
sense (the US was an early colony, after all). Some, of mostly European origins rather than African, Black or Asian, write from settler
societies such as Australia, Canada and New Zealand. The choice is
certainly an ideological, politicised one, and deliberately so. I explore
varying arguments around the term 'post-colonial' below.

The creative success of African American women has itself been a
liberating model for many other Black and Asian women writers. As
Marie Evans notes:

> Afro-American woman remained an all pervading absence until
> she was rescued by the literary activity of her black sister in the
> latter part of the twentieth century.   (Evans, 1985, p. 4)

Their success, the critical structures and frameworks which they
have helped to establish, have provided a real stimulus to confirming
a sense of identity, to writing, publishing and reading around the
world for women.

Dealing with difference springs from political, gendered, philosophical and psychoanalytical positions and is critical to the enterprise of this book:

> In our work and in our living we must recognise that difference
> is a reason for celebration and growth rather than a reason for
> destruction.   (Lorde, 1984, p. 101)

Audre Lorde's point is powerful and liberating. It makes a challenge to Westernised polarised thought processes which would categorise as 'Other' all that is not 'self', separating and hierarchising – Black/ white, male/female, good/bad, passive/active. This kind of hierarchical thinking leads to both racism and sexism. But the premise of binary difference is flawed. French feminist Hélène Cixous in 'The Laugh of the Medusa' (1981) inveighs against such diminishing and destructive rigid polarities, denouncing them as originating in patriarchy. They also originate in imperialism: once difference has been defined, in this cracked logic, there seems to have been a reason for domination and hierarchy. This need not be so.

CULTURAL CONTEXTS AND CRITICAL PRACTICES – READING POST-COLONIAL AND AFRICAN AMERICAN WOMEN'S WRITING IN CONTEXT

Celebrating difference is not enough in itself. It must lead, as Cora Kaplan points out, to acquainting ourselves with the specificity as well as any similarities of cultural contexts, the 'being in the world', the world view and experience from which diversity of work springs. Knowledge of cultural context is crucial, or, more broadly, knowing where writers are located psychologically, politically, culturally, geographically, historically and in terms of gender and race, in order to avoid cultural imperialism:

> Unless we are actually specialist on the area from which these foreign anglophone literatures come, and teaching them in that context, our more than usually fragmented and partial knowledge of the history, politics and culture in which they were produced and originally read, frequently leads us into teaching and thinking about these texts through an unintentionally imperialist lens, conflating their progressive politics with our own agendas, interpreting their versions of humanism through the historical evolution of our own.   (Kaplan, 1986, p. 185)

The post-colonial 'imaginary' (the way we and others see the world, how it appears in our imaginations, which influence thoughts and actions), and the discourses available to us, mesh with our experiences as readers, students, teachers. 'Location' as a notion and phenomenographical whole is much richer merely than that of the cultural, historical and geographical context of writing and reading, which it includes. Location and the 'loci of enunciation' are the places or contexts from which we experience and speak, where we place ourselves ideologically, spiritually, imaginatively. In everyday language, it answers the question 'where are you coming from?' and so gives us, as readers, a sense of the differences we need to negotiate, the information and feelings we need to find out about in order to gain a better understanding of writing by those who come from and speak from contexts different from our own. Mignolo, using this language of poetics, points out:

> Despite all of its ambiguities and potential hazards, however, the notion of the 'post colonial' ultimately foregrounds the politics and ethics of location in the construction of knowledge: first, because it clarifies the theorizing of colonial experiences as non-neutral with respect to where the act of theorizing is (ethically and politically, not necessarily geographically) located or performed, and second, because it inserts the personal signs of the understanding subject (her or his ability 'to be from' and 'to be at') into an imaginary construction.   (Mignolo, 1994, p. 508)

As readers we need to negotiate our own expectations and imaginary versions of the lives and meanings of others in order to make contact with and begin to understand them. Lauretta Ngcobo reduces the chances of a superficial white response of genteel liberalism to texts by Black and Asian, African American and post-colonial writers, noting:

> We as Black writers at times displease our white readership. Our writing is seldom genteel since it springs from our experiences which in real life have none of the trimmings of gentility. If the truth be told, it cannot titillate the aesthetic palates of many white people, for deep down it is a criticism of their values and their treatment of us throughout history.   (Ngcobo, 1987, p. 4)

Often the tone and subject matter of Black and Asian women's writing specifically focuses on Black/white relations and the effects of racism, indicting white societies. Sometimes in a direct, overt fashion and sometimes in a covert fashion, it records the ways in which racism, or a history of genocide – slavery, the mass extinction of Aboriginal peoples in Australia, apartheid in South Africa – have operated. This indictment should produce neither avoidance nor merely stunned, speechless guilt from white readers who confusedly recognise some inherited complicity in such terrible racist histories (and their contemporary legacies). Critical response is an important way to articulate and negotiate communication. Merely celebrating and recording, without critical response, is insulting, and 'speaking for' other people's experiences should be avoided.

However, writing about the writing of others hitherto marginalised, hidden and silenced raises the issue of the potential for appropriation, and for arrogant liberal assumptions that *our* recognition of texts by Black writers puts them on the reading and studying map. These responses replicate the cultural imperialism against which many African American and post-colonial authors write.

Similarly problematic is an approach which essentialises all Black and Asian women's writing as if the variety of experiences of these diverse people was largely a product of being 'Other' than European (and specifically Other than British) and, additionally, somehow always characterised in the main by speaking out against oppression. Cypriot women, for instance, do not seem to need to identify themselves Against a monolithic British or European identity, nor do they write from positions of colonial oppression. Rather they tend to concentrate on identity, relationships, women's roles, as do many of the women from other contexts, and specifically on the pain of political division of their island home. These issues of post-colonial critical practice: avoiding essentialising and Otherising; avoiding seeing all women writers solely in terms of speaking from a subaltern position, speaking out against oppression, among others, will be explored in discussing the texts. It is, however, crucial to my own need when working with students and others to enable them to overcome the desire to stand back in awe at difference, or remain silenced with an inherited guilt at the huge weight of history. Our reading of writing by many post-colonial women is imbricated with historical colonial guilt. It is a fraught position. But silencing and absence are no solutions:

> The problems of speaking *about* people who are 'other' cannot, however, be a reason for not doing so. The argument that it's just too difficult can easily become a new form of silencing by default.... But whites can never speak *for* Blacks. (Spivak and Gunew, 1986, p. 137)

Gayatri Spivak offers a speaking position for white audiences reading texts by Black and Asian, African American and post-colonial
writers:

> Why not develop a certain degree of rage against the history that
> has written such an abject script for you that you are silenced?
> (Spivak and Gunew, 1986, p. 137)

Culturally informed critical appreciation gives us a voice.

POST-COLONIALISM – WHAT IS IT?
WHAT ARE THEY?

Post-colonialism is a contested term. Even taking a post-colonial
perspective is itself an imperialist or colonial assumption: i.e. that
British colonialism and imperialism (in this instance) had such a
huge effect that its end is the most notable historical marker in the
history of so many peoples and their writing. Clearly this is only
partly true. Ideologically, epistemologically and in terms of literary
critical appreciation, however, it does mark a key moment for our
purpose here in looking at a breadth of women's writing when
women, it could be argued, are in a double or triple position of colonial subordination through gender, race and economic position, and
write out against this as a post-colonial response.

Colonialism has operated very differently in different countries,
and the spread of colonialism was vast and varied in the relations it
inspired:

> Modern European colonialism was distinctive and by far the most
> extensive of the different kinds of colonial contact that have been a
> recurrent feature of human history. By the 1930s, colonies and ex
> colonies covered 84.6 percent of the land surface of the globe. Only
> parts of Arabia, Persia, Afghanistan, Mongolia, Tibet, China, Siam
> and Japan had never been under formal European government.
> (Fieldhouse, 1989, p. 371)

The extent of this makes it difficult to theorise; colonialism operated
throughout the world in different ways, however it can, if simpli-
fied, be defined as: 'the conquest and control of others' land and
goods' (Loomba, 1998, p. 2), with a two-way flow of money, goods

and politics: essentially an economic situation. Imperialism has attached to it the meaning of 'command', and the *Oxford English Dictionary* defines its use as relating to the rule of an emperor or royalty – although royalty has not always been part of the equation and Lenin, Loomba tells us, saw in the spread of Western capitalism a kind of global imperialism – a capitalist economic dominance subordinating other countries' economies. Colonialism needs colonies, people settled in new lands. While imperialism does not necessarily settle its people, it can rule many other peoples from a distance, economically as much as politically, as does the US colonialism:

> covers all the culture affected by the imperial process from the moment of colonisation to the present date … there is a continuity of preoccupations throughout the historical process initiated by European imperial aggression. (Tiffin et al., 1989, p. 2)

'By 1914 the annual rate [of colonial domination] had risen to an astonishing 240,000 square miles, and Europe held a grand total of roughly 85% of the earth as colonies, protectorates, dependencies, dominions and commonwealth' (Said, 1993, p. 6). The reach of British colonialism was historically the most widespread and various. Vijay Mishra and Bob Hodge, considering the different experiences of colonialism, comment:

> in the Indian subcontinent the colonial experience seems to have affected the cities only; in Africa it worked hand in hand with evangelical Christianity; in Southeast Asia the use of migrant labour – notably Chinese and Indian – mediated between the British and the Malays. In the West Indies slave labour, and later Indentured Indian labour, again made the relationship less combative and more accommodating. (Hodge and Mishra, in Chrisman and Williams, 1993, p. 282)

We also find representation of the effects of colonialism and imperialism in many literary texts, although this is rarely the major focus of such texts. So, for example, Jane Austen's *Mansfield Park* (1814) has Sir Thomas Bertram travelling to visit one of his colonial plantations, leaving the party to indulge in a minor revolt (a play) unparalleled in the slave population whose labour provided the Bertrams with their wealth, as it did (off-stage) for so many landed families in the nineteenth century.

Post-Colonialism

America was an early colony whose independence (1783) preceded the full development of nineteenth-century imperialism, and even the arrival in 1785 of the First Fleet at Botany Bay, New South Wales, Australia. India, in which British rule was first established in 1757, became in 1947 both independent and partitioned, to form India and Pakistan. If the nineteenth century was the great era of expansion, the 1950s and 1960s was the great era of Independence, involving:

> various campaigns of anti colonial resistance, usually with an explicitly nationalist basis. These took forms ranging from legal and diplomatic manoeuvres – opposing the colonisers on their ideological high ground of principles and procedures – to wars of independence, as in Kenya and Algeria in the 1950s – opposing the colonisers in what many would regard as the real ground of colonialism: military power.   (Chrisman and Williams, 1993, p. 3)

Jamaica achieved self-government in 1944, the first assembly of the United Nations was held in 1946, Burma and Ceylon gained Independence in 1948, the Sudan in 1956, Ghana in 1957, Nigeria in 1960, Tanzania in 1961, Algeria, Jamaica, Trinidad and Tobago, Cyprus, and Uganda in 1962, Malawi, Zambia, and Malaya in 1964, Zimbabwe in 1980. However, Independence was not necessarily the greatest spur to writing; often opposition proved most inspirational. Many other events took place which are of equal or greater significance in terms of recognition of cultural identity, such as the organisation of the anti-Pass laws by the ANC in South Africa in 1952 and students' revolts in Soweto in 1976, the Vietnam war in the 1960s, the Biafran war (Nigeria) in 1967, the murder of Martin Luther King in 1968 coinciding with student uprisings in Paris, Australian Aboriginals gaining the vote in 1973. Not every colony sought Independence. Bermuda, for example (which figures in *The Tempest* and *Robinson Crusoe*), Britain's oldest colony, rejected Independence in 1995.

   Nor are all post-colonial contexts and post-colonial texts necessarily similar, this would be a naive and culturally simplistic, essentialist assumption which ignored the very different geographical, historical, social, religious, economic, etc., contexts of the different ex-colonies. Some of these are small islands – Cyprus, Malta, Singapore – chosen for their military locations and trading significances, others are islands developed for their plantation economy such as in the Caribbean, and still others, huge lands such as Australia and different African countries. Post-colonial discourse analysis (in this context, discourse analysis indicates analysis of verbal structures functioning within texts – the language, expression and arguments of texts which convey representations conditioned by culture and enabled by linguistic structures) also often groups together ex-colonial peoples and the texts they have produced as if there was everything in common in their experience and situation, which itself accords immense significance and importance to the colonial influence when, as Boehmer points out:

> Moreover, as Gayatri Spivak, Ben Okri, Kwame Anthony Appiah, and others have stressed, indigenous religious, moral, and intellectual traditions in colonized countries were never as fully pervaded by colonialism as the authorities might have desired. (Boehmer, 1995, p. 245)

The ending of colonial rule created a short-lived hope in many newly independent countries that a properly post-colonial era would result. However, continuing Western economic, political, military and ideological influence predominated, labelled 'neo-colonialism' by Marxists.

Interpretations of post-colonialism often depend largely upon the speaking position of those defining it. I will attempt to represent the debate but also to state clearly how I interpret and use the term here. Post-colonial writing here is taken to mean (far from unproblematically) writing which resists colonialism and its power politics, produced both during and, mainly, after the colonial period. The book concentrates on British colonialism rather than, for instance, that of Latin America or the US.

Ashcroft, Griffiths and Tiffin in *The Empire Writes Back* (1989) establish probably the first, but rather too broad, interpretation for my purposes, identifying post-colonial or resistance impulses as far back as seventeenth-century settler societies. However, it is not so simple to recognise resistance writing as post-colonial. Not all of it will be concerned with colonial power issues such as establishing identity and, in the case of women's post-colonial writing, family/kinship, motherlands and mother tongue. Nor is it straightforward to concentrate simply on writing produced from the moment of the official end of colonial rule. Not all such writing resists or criticises colonialism, and much of it is tinged by neo-colonialism. In Chapter 10, for instance, New Zealand/Aotearoan women writers argue that theirs is still very much a colonial country in terms of values and behaviours. The term post-colonialism can be understood more clearly according to the interpretation of Stephen Slemon, who sees it as referring to a set of anti-colonial cultural practices, attitudes and behaviours:

> it locates specifically anti or *post*-colonial *discursive purchase* in culture, one which begins in the moment that colonial power inscribes itself onto the body and space of its Others and which continues as an often occulted tradition into the modern theatre of new-colonialist relations.   (Slemon, in Tiffin and Adam, 1991, p. 3)

A country can be post-colonial, i.e. independent, and yet also neo-colonial, i.e. still economically dependent on the relations and links with those who operate colonial rule over it. It is sometimes debatable whether once-colonised countries can be seen as properly post-colonial because their ideas and economies are still tied to the coloniser (McLintock, 1992).

Hybridity and Settler Societies

Other terms which deserve attention, particularly because of the post-colonial focus of this book, are 'hybridity', and 'settler societies'. In the Caribbean, for example, much intermixing of peoples and languages has taken place resulting in hybridity. There are also societies which rarely intermixed, such as the settler societies of Australia and New Zealand or Canada. As Mishra and Hodge (1991) have noted, there is much difference between these countries and their peoples, even though they might wish to be called post-colonial too, since 'the experience of colonisation was more similar across all the white settler colonies than in the non settler colonies' (Mishra and Hodge, 1991, p. 282). Settlers, although living under colonial rule, have different experiences from colonised indigenous peoples:

> white settlers were historically the agents of colonial rule, and their own subsequent development – cultural as well as economic – does not simply align them with other colonised peoples... white populations here were not subject to the genocide, economic exploitation, cultural decimation and political exclusion felt by indigenous peoples.   (Loomba, 1998, p. 9)

Not all settlers are white, of course. If the position of settler societies is different, so too is their literature, which sits uneasily in either of the categories of First or Third World writing and, as Slemon (1990) argues, cannot be ascribed unproblematically to the category of the literature of empire (the First World), precisely because its position sits ambivalently, neither quite First World nor Third World, coloniser or colonised. Much Second World or settler writing is actually resistance writing, not empire writing, and excising it from the post-colonial, resistance debate actually undersells it:

> Slemon maintains that the settler communities have been excised from many analyses of resistance strategies and yet their writings articulate the dominant concerns of post-colonial theory: an ambivalent position between oppressor and oppressed plus a complicity with colonialism's territorial appropriations in the process of forging a resistance to its foreign rule – such that resistance has never been directed against a wholly external force.   (Chrisman and Williams, 1993, p. 81)

For a major example of exactly this problematic, Thea Astley's *It's Raining in Mango* (1987, see Chapter 9) explores an Australian settler family's response over time to the horrors of Aboriginal genocide caused by the intrusion of the very diggers whose long-term work helped settle Australia, and from which the more contemporary land-owning branch of the family benefits. The family is consistently concerned as they see the dominant remnants of racism against Aboriginals in the Queensland society in which they live.

Post-Colonialism, Post-Structuralism, Post-Modernism...

There are other theory issues here too, quite apart from the different readings of what post-colonialism is taken to 'be'. There have been critical declarations against the alignment of post-colonialism with post-structuralism and post-modernism, often themselves seen as identical (for definitions, see Belsey, 1980; Eagleton, 1991). In this conflation, post-colonialism is seen, on the one hand, to favour fragmentation and diffuseness, but on the other, to recognise so many similarities in different post-colonial situations and experiences that, problematically, differences are elided, experiences and peoples homogenised. On the one hand then, a major argument for similarity of experience arises from recognising that people and places involved in post-colonialism can all be seen to be connected today by international capitalist activities (for definitions, see Jameson, 1971). In the opposite scenario, if the myriad cultural contextual differences between post-colonial peoples are asserted one might become embroiled in hierarchising the suffering, the different experiences of subordination and marginalisation, which is an insidious divisiveness. This is a contradictory and rather absurd situation, the flip side of Lorde's celebration of difference. But merely acknowledging that there is so much diversity produces the same kind of shapelessness of which post-feminism is criticised (see Faludi, 1992). The world is 'seemingly shapeless' (Dirlik, 1994, p. 355).

The Diaspora, Migrant Writers – Colonisation in Reverse

Caribbean poet Louise Bennett once referred to the move of colonial and ex-colonial peoples to the diaspora as 'colonisation in reverse' (Childs and Williams, 1997, p. 13). David Dabydeen (1991) identifies Britain as the last colony, the last outpost of colonial unsettlement and racially motivated discord. Post-colonial people have migrated from the margins to the centres, they have settled in the US and the UK and form an integrated group in those ex-imperial powers or in other ex-colonies – Canada, South Africa, Australia, Aotearoa/New Zealand:

> The idea that post-colonial groups and their histories, far from being alien or Other to carefully constructed and guarded Western identities are in fact an integral part of them, derives ultimately from Said's insights on the colonial period in *Orientalism*, but it is even truer in the post-colonial period when the Other comes home.   (Childs and Williams, 1997, p. 13)

Post-colonial migrants both unsettle and enrich what was thought of as the centre of imperial powers. Diasporan and migrant writers reflect on, record, imagine beyond, and articulate newly changed, merged, differently focused perspectives on their adoptive cultures, and their position as writers with multiple roots in the history of several cultures. Some critics see post-colonialism as not always resistant but collusive; a state of being and thinking which involves siding with the forces of imperialism. These have been formed *from and by* the colonial situation and attitude rather than *in opposition to* it. This is not the reading of post-colonialism which I have used to inform my work here.

MAJOR POST-COLONIAL CRITICS – APPROACHES

Edward Said

Said has been described as the originator of Anglophone post-colonial theory. A Christian Arab, he was born in Palestine and partly educated at Columbia University, USA. His background straddles East and West and he is uniquely placed to analyse the ways in which the West has constructed those from the East as Other, defining Orientalism as a discourse which has enabled the West to recognise itself by defining itself against the East, the Oriental. In psychoanalytic theory, this is similar to Lacan's arguments that children grow to a sense of identity, as subjects, through recognising the difference between self and Other, me and not me, in what he has termed 'the mirror phase' (Lacan, 1977). In *Orientalism* (1978) Said makes significant contributions to our understanding that there is a varied object – colonialist discourse – which we can discover and analyse. Foucault (1976) explores the ways in which discourse controls, silences or enables the expression of knowledge and sexuality, including gendered identities, in relation to structures of power. His work on discourse and power feeds into Said's writing, particularly in terms of the implications of power and knowledge. Western power, especially that to enter or examine other countries at will, enables the production of a range of knowledge about other cultures, and knowledge feeds the will to power. What then seems to happen is that this knowledge and power produce both stereotyping and dominance based on the recognition of difference:

> Colonial discourse analysis and post-colonial theory are thus critiques of the process of production of knowledge about the Other. As such they produce forms of knowledge themselves, but other knowledge, better knowledge it is hoped. (Tiffin and Lawson, 1994, p. 8)

Said's arguments in *Orientalism* see colonial texts as literary sites of conflict. His *Culture and Imperialism* (1993) provides a post-colonial re-reading of some canonical texts, including Austen, Dickens, and Conrad, thus opening them up to different perspectives in the context of the history of imperialism from which they were written and with which they engaged. These perspectives (he calls them 'contrapuntal') avoid mere blame and rejection of the earlier texts, and enable readings which perceive embedded in the texts the reflection of the influences (and sometimes therefore potential critiques or at least contradictory elements) of the colonial systems from which they spring.

Tiffin and Lawson also argue that discourse and textuality have controlled by representation (and of course by silencing of alternative representations in other discourses):

> Imperial relations may have been established by guns, guile and disease, but they were maintained in their interpellative phase largely by textuality, both institutionally...and informally. Colonialism (like its counterpart racism) then, is a formation of discourse, and as an operation of discourse it interrelates colonial subjects by incorporating them into a system of representation. (Tiffin and Lawson, 1994, p. 3)

When we use colonial discourse analysis and post-colonial criticism we consider how through other writing, discussion and behaviour, the Other – different peoples – were denigrated, stereotyped, disempowered, silenced, rendered invisible, etc., and in so doing we open up new understandings of the subject position of the Other.

Frantz Fanon and the 'Other'

Fanon is a Martinique-born psychiatrist and activist for the Algerian National Liberation Front. *Black Skin, White Masks* (1952), *The Wretched of the Earth* (1963), and two collections of essays critique the construction of 'Negritude' (developed in the 1930s by, for example, Aimé Césaire) as a concept mirroring the racism and colonial dynamics of colonialism itself. Fanon recognises culture as being a product of both nationhood and the anthropological. In 'On National Culture' (1961) he argues that colonialism does not seek merely to shape the present and future of colonised peoples but to also reshape their past, carrying out a cultural estrangement: 'By a kind of perverted logic, it turns to the past of the oppressed people, and distorts, disfigures and destroys it' (1990 [1961], p. 265) leaving only distorted dregs. For colonialism the 'vast continent was the haunt of savages', and all Black people were homogenised into 'the Negro' (1990 [1961], p. 266), a savage, so what the contemporary Black person needs to do is rediscover history and reaffirm African identity and culture. Today's natives (his label), delving back into history are probably wonder struck at the 'dignity, glory, solemnity' that they find there (1990 [1961], p. 266). Fanon identifies the movement towards culture as reclaiming a version of parts of the past, which the Negro intellectual, in particular, will laud, arguing that it is important to fight for the nation first and see culture as one part of it. As colonialism shakes off its stranglehold on the history and culture of its subjects and ex-subjects, what has brought culture up-to-date is the updating of narratives, establishing a history. Within post-colonial studies the issue of subject formation converges with that of the colonial and post-colonial. Fanon starts by reworking the Lacanian mirror stage when the infant, seeing himself or herself in the mirror, constructs a version of self, or subject, as opposed to that of Other, not-self. In gendered terms, this identity recognition results in woman being seen as the Other (the norm taken, in both Freudian and Lacanian psychoanalysis, is that of the male), and in terms of culture and ethnicity, it results in the Black person being defined as the Other. However, Fanon does not deal with the experience of women in particular, subsuming any interest under a generalising concern with men. In terms of ethnicity, Fanon argues:

> When one has grasped the mechanism described by Lacan, one can have no further doubt that the real Other of the white man is and will continue to be the black man. And conversely, only for the white man is the Other perceived on the level of the body image, absolutely as the not-self – that is, the unidentifiable, the unassimilable. For the black man ... historical and economic realities come into the picture. (1967, p. 161)

As Ania Loomba has pointed out (1998, p. 144), the Black man then becomes defined by his 'limitless sexuality' (the notion that Black men are more highly sexed than white presumably related to the racist argument that animal nature is more predominant in a Black than a white man, thought to be inevitably 'civilised', i.e. in control of his libido, because of his pale skin colour). For 'the black subject' however, the white Other serves to define everything that is desirable, everything that the self desires. This desire is embedded within a power structure, so 'the white man is not only the Other but also the master, real or imaginary' (Fanon, 1967, p. 138, quoted in Loomba, 1998, p. 144). Therefore 'blackness confirms the white self, but whiteness empties the black subject' (Loomba, 1998, p. 144).

Faced with the ostracism and Otherness of the image of the Negro, in Fanon's terms, the Black person attempts to cope by adopting white masks. Fanon's work is divided – *Black Skins, White Masks* is concerned with the psychologies of the oppressed, and *The Wretched of the Earth* with the revolt of the oppressed. While there are divided responses to his work, many see continuity and figure him as an author of revolutionary fervour who argues for recognition of a unified Black self released by valuing the cultures colonialism denigrates and subordinates.

Fanon's insistence on nation is ultimately not insular, although this is not always so true of every such nationalist identity. He asserts that at the heart of national consciousness, international consciousness lives and grows. Moving on and making national identity and culture relevant for today is crucial. Nationalism and a nostalgia for idealised roots can themselves cause difficulties, however. One result of the Negritude movement, which Fanon found problematic, was an uncomplicated, celebratory Negroism, and unconditional affirmation of African cultures which succeed that of the European. Fanon's work enables engagement with debates about how ex-colonial subjects develop and seize their own identities and slough off the destructiveness of the colonial experiences which represent them in a negative light. His revolutionary fervour is seen by some in contradistinction to his post-structuralist angst (Loomba, 1998, p. 147).

Problems with Fanon's theories circle around the relationship between the psychoanalytic and the material – how does his psychoanalytic understanding relate to the material revolutionary action? and over gender? Although women (see above) have also been figured as Other in identity formation, just as is the Black man, Fanon makes no connections between gender and ethnicity. Fanon's Black subject, like that of Lacan and Freud before him, is always male, and gendered hierarchies tend to be reinforced by the projection of this newly unified subject.

POST-COLONIALISM AND WOMEN – SPIVAK AND SULERI

Overall, not merely in the case of Fanon, there are many problems in relation to feminism's dealings with psychoanalysis because, as Loomba argues, issues of race and ethnicity have not yet been properly theorised. If Fanon's psychoanalytic concerns with subject identity formation concentrate on Black men, feminism's concerns concentrate on women without raising issues of cultural difference: 'Kalpana Sheshadri-Crooks accuses feminism of reproducing the existing problems of mainstream psychoanalytic discourse' (Loomba, 1998, p. 149):

> by not raising the question of racial difference with regard to irrational and mysterious 'others' (African and Orientals) in theories of subject formation . . . we mark a moment of departure for postcolonialism from the political and theoretical intentions of First World feminism. (Sheshadri-Crooks, 1994, pp. 175–218, quoted in Loomba, 1998, p. 149)

I would argue that there are certainly beginnings to this in the theories of the post-Lacanian French feminist psychoanalytic critic Julia Kristeva, particularly in *Strangers to Ourselves* (1991). Here she equates response to the Other as being both to women and to Black people, and argues that we need to recognise the stranger *in ourselves* as a product of ourselves, part of our formation of identity. If we manage that, she argues, we will come to terms with the Other in/of ourselves and no longer need to subordinate, abject or eradicate it.

Gayatri Chakravorty Spivak and Sara Suleri both develop theoretical perspectives which relate ethnicity and gender, concentrating on Third World women (women from developing countries, indicating states distinct from the West, or First World, and the Second World, which was the name applied to the Soviet bloc – the term is both geographical and economic, signifying the relative poverty and debt-dependence of the Third world on the First). She looks at women speaking from what has been called the 'subaltern' position (initially a Forces term meaning subordinate officer, used here to suggest a secondary or subordinate role, often expected to be silent), in which these women are constructed and constrained, which they can learn to challenge and from which they can learn to speak. Women's roles as carriers of the race, she argues, position them in a complex primary role in enculturation and in both academic and popular representations of gender, sexuality and ethnicity. The control of women is crucial to national and ethnic processes (see Nira Yulal-Davis and Floya Anthias, in Spivak and Suleri, 1989).

Indian-born, US-based Gayatri Chakravorty Spivak considers the silencing and speaking of the 'subaltern' subordinated woman, in a

South Asian context. She combines Marxism, feminism and deconstruction in a dialogue showing that women are contradictorily controlled by patriarchal society and by colonialism, both silencing
them. In this she highlights two things: how complex the history of
colonialism is; and how women are the symbols of an economic
control through silencing.

Spivak's work is central to consideration of the relationship
between post-colonialism and feminism. Like Chandra Talpade
Mohanty, she argues against an essentialist Third World 'woman'
with a uniform life and outlook. She also criticises the tendency to
reject all critical method when talking of Third World women's
writing, arguing that critics and readers do writers an injustice
when they rely on a non-critical response of report and record. The
critical argument against scholarship and critical attention ran
something like this: 'as the subaltern is *not* elite (ontology), so must
the historian not *know* through elite methodology (epistemology)'
(Spivak, 1988, p. 253):

> Such thinking bases the possibility of 'knowing' on 'being', a view
> that results in attempts to 'identify' with the other, when, for a
> post-structuralist such as Spivak, knowledge is only achievable
> through attention to difference (the 'Third World' cannot be 'known'
> in itself but in relation to the 'First World,' and vice versa). One
> example of such confused practice is the decision to apply theory to
> Western texts but not to Third World texts, when a non-theoretical
> 'information retrieval' approach is taken.   (Childs and Williams,
> 1997, pp. 166–7)

Spivak points out that to define diverse women as some kind of
composite entity is to replicate labelling found under colonial paternalism (see Chandra Talpade Mohanty, 1988, in Chrisman and
Williams, 1993). She cautions, too, against the interpretation of Third
World women's texts as examples of irony, individualism, and other
terms more suited to European models of writing. Women are, she
argues, forced to negotiate a variety of different and difficult subject
positions under patriarchy and imperialism, and their lives and writings cannot be read with the lens of Western feminism in a straightforward manner. Her essays chart a course between opposed
positions that either homogenise the Third World within radical
readings, placing all texts in the context of nationalism and ethnicity
(universalism), or automatically apply the Western orthodox approach

to literature (individualism) (Childs and Williams, 1997, p. 169). While Western reading practices have tended to centre on the authority of the author and the experience of the reader, Spivak's practice is different, aiming 'to focus on the different representations of the subaltern within subject positions constructed through discourses of race, class, gender and imperialism' (Childs and Williams, 1997, p. 170). The intersection of gender and ethnicity is potentially problematic in post-colonial academic practice and critique. Many feminist critics have pointed out the similarity between the marginalisation and silencing, the objectification and patriarchal oppression afforded to both women and subordinated peoples under colonialism, seeing men as colonisers, women as colonised. This straightforward analogy, however, ironically helps many of us to bridge gaps in our understanding and experience when confronting and trying to understand racial discriminatory practices. Mohanty recommends care, using a sensitive mixture of historically specific generalisations which can still be responsive to complex realities (Mohanty, 1988, in Chrisman and Williams, 1993, pp. 199–200).

In 1975 Barbara Smith castigated the 'racist pseudo-scholarship' of feminist critics who marginalised, ignored or misinterpreted Black women's experiences. Despite the usefulness, for reading post-colonial women's writing, of the development of a body of critical work based on recognition of the interrelation between ethnicity and gender in African American women's writing, it is dangerous to elide African American women's experience and writing with that of all Black, Asian and post-colonial women. Their conditions of living and expression are often as enormously different from the African American as they are, one from the other. Assumptions of a homogeneous Black or post-colonial woman and her life, or our impositions of Western feminism's individualism on the many different Black or post-colonial women's lives, are all dangerous, replicating a kind of patriarchal appropriation.

THE POST-COLONIAL AND DISCOURSE

The struggle for the power to name oneself and one's state is enacted fundamentally within words, most especially in colonial situations. So a concern for language, far from indicating a retreat, may be an investigation into the depths of the political unconscious. (Kiberd, 1995, p. 615)

Discourse is a key issue in the construction, limitation, expression, representation and articulation of experience. Those who hold language hold the power. Throughout colonial histories the language of British-ruled colonies has been English, which itself relies upon certain ways of constructing knowledge of the world, and upon certain underpinning beliefs. Language not only constructs and colours our experiences of the world, it can also be used to marginalise, to constrain, or to enable. It is mainly for this reason that the right opportunity to speak and write out, to publish and to express in creative writing, is so powerful for all peoples. It is particularly so for those whose colonised experience has rendered them absent, silenced, marginalised, and for whom the discourse of imperial and colonial rule has been one relegating their own experiences to a subordinate position. Those in power ensure that language controls others, enabling or preventing, translating where necessary, and maintaining certain hierarchies. It is with this in mind that looking at historical and contemporary discourse is so important.

The English leaving India, for example, left it their language but, more importantly, the values and hierarchies which that language maintained, and in so doing they empowered colonised peoples to become involved in the very large part of the world whose activities involved articulation in English, but they disempowered national identity and expression. Asserting nationhood and difference is one element in independence, but it is not the only element. Avoidance of deterioration into stressing national difference for its own sake is an important step towards recognition of differences between all peoples, and recognition of a common humanity.

The control of language, it has been argued, could be worse for women who are secondary, and silenced. In the context of colonial production which favours white over Black, male over female, subaltern women cannot speak. Spivak's 'Can the Subaltern Speak?' (1988) directly confronts the ignoring of women's different economic and social positions and lives. Spivak points out that an epistemic violence has been carried out on colonial peoples, devaluing their language, history and ways of seeing and expressing the world during the process of categorising native languages hierarchically, beneath the scientific and Westernised. In this way she offers 'an explanation of how the narrative of reality was established as a normative one' (1988, p. 76), taking for her example Hindu law and its British codification. Spivak questions how, doubly disempowered and secondary, women can speak out against such oppression: 'the possibility of collectivity itself is persistently foreclosed through the manipulation of female agency' (1988, p. 78).

In *Colonialism/Post Colonialism* (1998, pp. 95/6), Ania Loomba warns against the dangers of relying solely on discourse and text for interpretations of the daily realities, historical and contemporary, of colonialism, and the post-colonial. Inscribing post-colonial objects in (specifically literary) discourse reduces the lived experience – blurring the relationship between material reality and ideologically charged representation in text. Boehmer warns:

> discussions of text and image mask this reality of empire: the numbers who died in colonial wars and in labour gangs, or as the result of disease, transportation and starvation.
>
> (Boehmer, 1995, p. 20)

Alternatively:

> in calling for the study of the aesthetics of colonialism, we might end up aestheticizing colonialism, producing a radical chic version of raj nostalgia.　(Dirks, 1992, p. 5)

There is a problem where post-colonial studies are situated in English studies, not merely because the writings we read are limited to those in English or in translation, but also because of reduction to a textual analysis. Colonialism as text avoids the monstrosity of genocide, daily racism, disempowerment and grand theft. It can be argued, however, that a broader take on cultural studies enables a clearer picture of the lived reality to emerge. Analysis of the language of colonialism and post-colonialism by using the tactics of cultural studies, also looking at images, artefacts, visiting, interviewing, etc., can help situate the textual more usefully as a crucial historical element of control. It can highlight what is represented and how, and what is silenced, misinterpreted. The misrepresentation of Aboriginal, Maori and Pacific Islander women (Chapters 9, 10, 14) in the discourses of reports of first ships landing on their shores is a case in point. Through the misrepresentation of discourse we sense ways in which ideology, philosophy and world view operated to excise and subordinate peoples. Different forms are chosen by people to express their lived realities and these must be sought out, such as Aboriginal women's life and family testimonies (Chapter 9) and oral performance poetry in South Africa (Chapter 7).

WHAT IS FEMINISM IN POST-COLONIAL AND
BLACK AND ASIAN CONTEXTS?

Many Black and Asian and post-colonial women have argued that feminism is a largely white, Westernised construct which ignores the daily experience of race and economic hardship (see Talpade Mohanty in *Feminist Review*, 1988), and which also makes certain assumptions about motherhood, sexual and gendered relationships, and women's ability or desire to ironise or speak out critically. Several of the chapters in this book take up this issue (Chapter 2, on African American, and Chapter 6, on African writing, for instance). Alice Walker (Chapter 4), among others, has been criticised for asserting women's rights rather than subsuming these beneath an overall insistence on racial equality (which would yet again marginalise the issue of challenging women's subordinated position). There are several strands to this argument.

Susheila Nasta comments on the development of Black and Asian women's 'feminism' in the context of more general struggles for racial equality:

> In countries with a history of colonialism, women's quest for emancipation, self-identity and fulfilment can be seen to represent a traitorous act, a betrayal not simply of traditional codes of practice and belief but of the wider struggle for liberation and nationalism. Does to be 'feminist' therefore involve a further displacement or reflect an implicit adherence to another form of cultural imperialism?   (Nasta, 1991, p. xv)

On the one hand, Trinh Minh-Ha in *Woman, Native, Other* (1989) questions where women of colour can recognise their loyalties, to race or to gender, as if there were a hierarchy. On the other hand, Sara Suleri insists that a concern for colour above that for gender produces a constrained sense of identity, a feminism merely 'skin deep in that the pigment of its imagination cannot break out of a strictly biological reading of race' (1992, in Chrisman and Williams, 1993, p. 251). She worries about the importance accorded the voice of a rather heterogeneous post-colonial woman when feminism argues, under the influence of post-structuralism, about identity and subjectivity, essentialism and constructivism, i.e. the biological argument on the one hand that all women are basically the same, essential 'Woman', or that we are differently constructed in our lived roles, products of different cultural situations. Feminism:

is still prepared to grant an uneasy selfhood to a voice that is best described as the property of 'post colonial Woman'. Whether this voice represents perspectives as divergent as the African American or the post-colonial location, its imbrications of race and gender are accorded an iconicity that is altogether too good to be true.... The embarrassed privilege granted to racially encoded feminism does indeed suggest a rectitude that could be its own theoretical undoing.

(Suleri, 1992, in Chrisman and Williams, 1993, p. 457)

A privileging of the term 'post-colonial woman' as if everyone was the same, iconic, idealised, always good, is just another simplifying gesture which ends up absurdly homogenising, idealising and marginalising Black women of different backgrounds and cultures:

The coupling of *post colonial* with *woman*, however, must inevitably lead to the simplicities that underlie unthinking celebrations of oppression, elevating the racially female voice into a metaphor for 'the good'. Such a metaphicity cannot exactly be called essentialist but it certainly functions as an impediment to a reading that attempts to look beyond obvious questions of good and evil.

(Suleri, 1992, in Chrisman and Williams, 1993, p. 457)

An alternative problem to homogenising Black women, however, is that of no-one ever being able to speak about anyone else without inside experience of their subject position, which is doubly disempowering:

The claim to authenticity – only a Black can speak of a Black; only a post-colonial subcontinental feminist can adequately represent the lived experience of that culture – points to the great difficulty posited by the 'authenticity' of female racial voices in the great game that claims to be the first narrative of what the ethnically constructed woman is deemed to want. (Suleri, 1992, in Chrisman and Williams, 1993, p. 247)

FORMS OF WRITING – IDENTITY AND SUBJECTIVITY

The forms in which post-colonial and Black women write have been debated by many critics also, some of whom take an ideologically related position. bell hooks in *Talking Back: Thinking Feminist, Think-ing Black* (1989) argues that personal narrative is the only form possible, while Suleri questions the authentic record of lived experi-ence as the only valid writing format. When you allow the 'native' to speak and use their subjectivity as a basis for information, Suleri argues, you are left with the problem of how subjectivity can provide truth. Lived experience uses realism, does not have to be first-person, but shows experience in action (such as laws governing rape, and women's value) (1992, in Chrisman and Williams, 1993, p. 255). This debate continues in and over the work of many women writers considered below, particularly indigenous writers. Interest-ingly, many Black women writers choose realism and testimony (Aboriginal women, Chapter 9, some African American women, Chapter 2, etc.), but still others choose to write complex symbolic poetic works. Limiting critical appreciation to testimonial realism is an arrogant cultural imperialist act, but so too is insisting that using symbolism and the poetic is an indication of (preferable, advanced) sophisticated writing (see reviews of Toni Morrison's work, Chapter 3). Another complication is that of post-structuralist problems over claiming unique selfhood, subject identity, a critical focus which has developed just when many post-colonial women writers have started to speak out, and claim such identity and difference.

Much writing by Black women writers breaks down categories of public and private, speaking 'in tongues' which connote both the pre-symbolic mother tongue described by Kristeva (1977) and the diversity of voices, discourses and languages described by Bakhtin (1981). Kristeva adds a feminist and linguistic dimension to psycho-analytic theory. She argues that the infant communicates with the mother using the 'semiotic', a science of signs, and a form of com-munication which precedes the development and constraint of 'the symbolic', the language structures imposed by society, most notably by the father and patriarchy. The symbolic can also be seen as a lin-guistic constraint imposed by imperialism which limits the expres-sion of colonised people, particularly women, while also offering entrance into language understood by men (but constructed and controlled by those in power). (See the introduction to Kristeva, 1980.) Bakhtin in *The Dialogic Imagination* (1981) argues that the novel sets up dialogues between many voices (polyphony) and points of view; it allows debate and negotiation. Elleke Boehmer (1995, p. 206) argues that this polyphony and dialogue exist in many post-colonial texts where formerly marginalised peoples speak. Jamaica Kinkaid's

Annie John (mentioned in Chapter 5) is a case in point, while different perspectives on women's behaviour are negotiated in writing by African and South African women, notably Flora Nwapa and Buchi Emecheta (Chapter 6) and Bessie Head (Chapter 7). Suleri notes two meanings in privileging Black women's writing, the first connoting polyphony, multivocality and plurality of voices, and the second signifying intimate, private, inspired utterances. Through their intimacy with the discourses of others, Black women writers weave into their work complementary discourses – that seek both to adjudicate competing claims and to witness common concerns. They negotiate many positions in writing of women's relationship to oppression and to speaking out:

in their works, black women writers have encoded oppression as a discursive dilemma, that is, their works have consistently raised the problem of the black woman's relationship to power and discourse. (Suleri, 1992, in Chrisman and Williams, 1993, p. 263)

The hierarchical gender relations between (white) men and (Black) women are reproduced in the patriarchal discourse of master texts conspiring to exclude female 'minor' forms from the (scribal, written) literary canon. For subordinated women, making any kind of creative or critical statement is making a stand. If tradition decides to hierarchise creative forms, women tend to write back, revaluing what has been marginalised, writing semi-fictionalised autobiographies (see Sally Morgan and Ruby Langford, Aboriginal writers in Chapter 9; Bessie Head and Zoe Wicomb, South African writers in Chapter 7). They write down oral poetry and storytelling forms (see Chapters 5, 6, 7, 10, 11), using dialogic forms to negotiate the kind of debates found in communities and families (see Alice Walker, Chapter 4, and Toni Morrison, Chapter 3):

Feminised literary forms such as letters, diaries, and the literature of romance have had the same relationship to the 'Great Tradition' as marginalised oral texts: beyond the pale. (Cooper, 1993, p. 7: using Zora Neale Hurston from *Their Eyes were Watching God*: 'Well, you know what dey say 'uh white man and uh nigger woman is de freest thing on earth. Dey do as dey please.')

Mae Gwendolen Henderson's discussion of language use is based on Barbara Smith's work on Black feminist criticism (1975), arguing that perspectives of race and gender intermix in Black women's writing, overcoming problems of homogeneity, the repression of individual differences (of heterogeneity). Instead, she says: 'I propose a model that seeks to account for racial difference within gender identity and gender difference within racial identity.' (Henderson, in Chrisman and Williams, 1993, p. 258). She, too, identifies a dialogic character as characteristic of Black women's writing – in dialogue with the Other outside the self, and with several selves:

> What is at once characteristic and suggestive about black women's writing is its interlocutory, or dialogic, character reflecting not only a relationship with the 'others', but an internal dialogue with the plural aspects of self that constitute the matrix of black female subjectivity. The interlocutory character of black women's writings is, thus, not only a consequence of a dialogic relationship with an imaginary or 'generalized Other', but a dialogue with the aspects of 'otherness' within the self. (Henderson, in Chrisman and Williams, 1993, pp. 258/9)

Helen Carr illuminates the ways in which sexual and colonial domination are paralleled:

> In the language of colonialism, non-Europeans occupy the same symbolic space as women. Both are seen as part of nature, not culture, and with the same ambivalence: either they are ripe for government, passive, child-like, unsophisticated, needing leadership and guidance, described always in terms of lack – no initiative, no intellectual powers, no perseverance; or on the other hand, they are outside society, dangerous, treacherous, emotionally inconsistent, wild, threatening, fickle, sexually aberrant, irrational... lascivious, disruptive, evil, unpredictable. (Carr, 1985, p. 50)

The sexuality of Black people, and particularly of women, becomes related to the animal and the deviant, otherised, and so all Black women become labelled primitive: 'the primitive is black, and the qualities of blackness, or at least of the black female, are those of the prostitute' (Carr, 1985, p. 248; Gilman, 1992, pp. 223–61). While Westernised feminist racism has been indicted (see Davis, 1982; Mohanty, 1988; Parmar and Amos, 1997), Susheila Nasta comments on the development of Black and Asian women's 'feminism' in the context of more general struggles for racial equality:

In countries with a history of colonialism, women's quest for emancipation, self-identity and fulfilment can be seen to represent a traitorous act, a betrayal not simply of traditional codes of practice and belief but of the wider struggle for liberation and nationalism. Does to be 'feminist' therefore involve a further displacement or reflect an implicit adherence to another form of cultural imperialism? (Nasta, 1991, p. xv)

It is vital that we avoid jumping on the bandwagon of a transient popularity, and that we ensure that the merit of these works and their contribution to literature (and popular literature) is never ignored again. Barbara Burford points to the short-livedness of earlier recognition, the Negritude movement in France, the Harlem Renaissance: 'This time we must not allow ourselves to be turned on and off, and we must not disappear quietly, when it is decided that we as an "issue" have suffered from over exposure' (Burford, 1987, p. 37). For many, the ability to read, write, have some economic stability, recognise a legacy in previous writers and artists has been immensely liberating. Perhaps often the first task is to speak out against inequality.

CONCLUSION: DEBATES

Readers usually meet African American women's writing and Black feminist criticism first after their own canonical texts. What follows, as it does also in this book, is writing by very different women from very different contexts. Many of these writers are white settlers, themselves caught in the intersection between First World feminist criticism, which often excludes or ignores them, and Third World experience, in relation to which their communities are often indicted as culpable in perpetuating colonial power divisions. But as women, the writers considered here often align themselves through their post-colonial experiences with the Black, Asian and indigenous peoples among whom they live and work. What the white writers included in the book have in common with Black, Asian and indigenous women is their concern with living at the intersection of race and gender, and their shared, if different, experiences of being post-colonial subjects, and women.

In looking at different women writers from different cultural contexts, we need to ask questions about what effects those different contexts of geography, race, ethnicity, religion, economy and sexual choice can have on their writing, and what they might have in common. In common we find such things as an interest in exploring family relationships, mothering and motherhood, the role of women in family and economic life, and a search for identity with all the complexities of race, religion, sexual choice, myth, family position, unique experiences. Some of the themes running through the book engage with the different treatments of similar themes in the work of different Black and Asian women, African American and post-colonial writers. Some other elements in the book encourage critical thinking about our position as readers in the face of such a wealth of diversity of writing, and our own ability to respond and comment.

Women writers speak out not only against the triple burden of race, class and gender, but against a history of colonialism which has silenced and subordinated them. Bringing together critical studies of a broad, individualised and also representative selection of women writers from African American and post-colonial contexts enables the appreciation of their similarities in concerns (motherhood, mother tongue, identity, gendered and sexual relationships, family, etc.) and of their differences in context and creative expression.

Part I
African American Women's Writing

2

African American Women's Writing

Afro-American woman remained an all-pervading absence until she was rescued by the literary activity of her black sisters in the latter part of the twentieth century.

(Evans, 1985, p. 4)

This chapter begins by tracing a historical and critical background to African American women's writing and moves on to consider some of the main themes and key writers. In their work, African American women writers concentrate on issues of race, colour, roots, motherhood, relationships, identity, women's roles and representations, community, the supernatural and the spiritual, recuperating and revivifying hidden histories, and sexism as much as racism. Work by Anne Petry, Gloria Naylor, Gwendolyn Brooks, Zora Neale Hurston, Nella Larson, Ntozake Shange and Maya Angelou is discussed, and other writers are mentioned in passing.

Early 1980s criticism of and by African American women writers concentrated on recuperating the silenced writers of the past, and speaking out against racism and sexism. Issues of determining specific African American women's language and expression were also central. A very common theme was that of suffering and silencing, the 'triple burden' of which Zora Neale Hurston speaks (1986 [1937]) and a task for writers and critics alike was to rediscover hidden foremothers, their own, and their literary foremothers, in order to trace relationships and developments in African American women's writing (Greene and Kahn, 1985; Perry, 1976; Smith et al., 1982; Tate, 1985).

The necessity for the rediscovery, common in all women's critical writing of the seventies and eighties, has largely been superseded by an interest in exploring the work of well established women writers such as Alice Walker and Toni Morrison, considering the forms of a Black feminist criticism and the angles and discourse this might develop, and relating some of the concerns of African American women, in their writing, with those of post-colonial women writers (Wilentz, 1992; Wisker, 1992).

We are likely to be most familiar with African American women's writing largely due to its availability, and its relatively long history. Anne Lucy Terry, who wrote 'Bars Fight' in 1746, was the first African American woman to be published, and only the second woman published in America. She was followed by Phillis Wheatley, also a Black female slave, just nine when she arrived in America, who produced her first volume of poetry in 1773. In 1861 Harriet Jacobs authored *Incidents in the Life of a Slave Girl*, the first slave narrative by a woman. This followed several Christian testimonies to the struggles of womanhood by free born African Americans, notably by Jarena Lee and Zilpha Law. Jacobs' slave narrative is a record of injustices experienced by women under slavery. The slave narrative's first-person account ensures realism and authenticity, and for that reason later African American women writers have adopted the form. As with Aboriginal women's narratives (see Chapter 9) an editor, Lydia Maria Child, helped with Jacobs' publication, and verified the authenticity of this first-hand 'testifying' as Child retained the correspondence between the two of them. The formal legacy of testifying guarantees authenticity and encourages the recognition of identity, and has remained a feature of African American women's writing, including that of Maya Angelou. One of its dangers, however, is the potential substitution of authenticity for narrative technique (Gates Jr and McKay, 1997), i.e. celebrating the truthfulness of a testimony over its literary merit.

The first novel, *Our Nig; Or Sketches for the Life of a Free Black* by Harriet E. Wilson, came out in 1859 (see Allen Shockley, 1988, p. 4). Writers such as Toni Morrison and Alice Walker, who each have a separate chapter in this book, have featured in the syllabi of universities, colleges, adult classes and schools for several years now, introducing new generations of readers to the issues and pleasures of Black women's writing. It is just such a global statement which represents a kind of comfortable danger, however, for their inclusion is possibly the only step made towards the recognition of Black women's writing and diversity, in many cases. One of the great achievements of their wide popular and academic recognition is hopefully that reading their work will encourage readers to look at other African American writers, and then proceed to other Black and Asian women's writing, looking not merely for similarities, but also for differences and individuality.

Literary activity has rescued silenced, disenfranchised and invisible Black women from the margins, enabling them to speak and to be seen and heard. Alice Walker's *The Color Purple* (1983), and the fictionalised autobiography sequence of Maya Angelou, grow from the slave narratives and testimonies so that:

> If the slave narratives began by positing the 'I', they do it to dramatically wrest the individual black subject out of anonymity, inferiority, and brutal disdain. The 'I' stands against and negates the perception of the black person as indistinguishable from the mass, as slave, as animal. The 'I' proclaims voice, subject, and the right to history and place.   (Greene and Kahn, 1985)

and:

> In speaking of great matters, your personal experience is considered evidence.   (Nelson, quoted in Gwaltney, 1980, p. 8)

One of the problems for African American women when they started writing was the triple burden of their class, race and gender. Lorraine Bethel comments:

> The codification of Blackness and femaleness by whites and males is seen in terms of 'thinking like a woman' and 'acting like a nigger' which are based on the premise that these are typically Black and female ways of acting and thinking. Therefore, the most pejorative concept in the white/male world view would be that of thinking and acting like a 'nigger woman'.   (Bethel, 1982a, p. 178)

There were many African American women writers in the late nineteenth century, though they were neither as well known nor as well distributed as the twentieth-century women writers, because of limited publishing and distribution opportunities, let alone the availability of a reading public. Edythe Mae Gordon, Gladys Ciseley Hayford, Ida Rowland, Lucy Mae Turner, Georgia Douglas Johnson, Clarissa Scott Delaney, Ethel Caution Davies, Angelina Weld Grimke and others found publishing difficult and readership confined to a close circle.

AFRICAN AMERICAN WOMEN IN THE TWENTIETH CENTURY

The major development period for Black writers bringing them to a wider readership was during the Jazz age, in the 1930s, the period of the Harlem Renaissance, and it is from this time that both Zora Neale Hurston and Nella Larsen spring. Other writers of the period are Jessie Fauset, Dorothy West (prose fiction), Anne Spencer, Georgia Douglas Johnson, Gwendolyn Bennett, Helene Johnson – all poets (see Perry, 1976). Other writers have been recuperated in Roses and Randolph (1997).

When we look at the best known contemporary African American women writers such as Alice Walker, Toni Morrison and Maya Angelou, we find self-awareness, an educated and highly developed discourse and narrative style, integrated with a politicised engagement with issues of racism and sexism. Their asserted aim is to bring light to periods of history untold and hidden:

> I think my whole programme as a writer is to deal with history just so I know where I am.   (Walker, in Tate, 1985, p. 185)

> to bear witness to a history that is unrecorded, untaught in mainstream education and to enlighten our people.   (Morrison, in Tate, 1985, p. 124)

Writing is seen as a historical act of reclamation, a way of recognising and charting roots and identity. It is a political act of breaking silence for women from a diversity of backgrounds to explore that contextual diversity. As Audre Lorde puts it, writing enables women to speak out, step out and value their lives. It is empowering and creative: 'In our work and in our living we must recognise that difference is a reason for celebration and growth, rather than a reason for destruction' (Lorde, 1985, p. 101). Barbara Smith defines characteristics typical of African American women writers, arguing that their similarities spring from:

> the specific political, social and economic experience they have been obliged to share. The way for example that Zora Neale Hurston, Margaret Walker, Toni Morrison and Alice Walker incorporate the traditional Black female activities of rootworking, herbal medicine, conjure and midwifery into the fabric of their stories is not mere coincidence, nor is their issue of a specifically

Black female language to express their own and their characters'
thoughts accidental.   (Smith, 1982, p. 164)

Particularly notable is the deliberate development of expression
which enables the articulation of experiences, thoughts, feelings and
arguments unrecorded or marginalised in the discourse of male and
particularly white male writers:

> The use of Black women's language and cultural experience in
> books by Black women ABOUT Black women results in a mira-
> culously rich coalescing of form and content and also takes their
> writing far beyond the confines of white/male literary structures.
> (Smith, 1982, p. 164)

Lorraine Bethel adds:

> Women in this country have defied the dominant sexist society by
> developing a type of folk culture and oral literature based on the
> gender solidarity and female bonding as self affirming rituals.
> Black women have a long tradition of bonding together in a com-
> munity that has been a source of survival information and psychic
> and emotional support. We have a distinct Black woman-identified
> folk culture based on our experience in this society: symbols, lan-
> guage and modes of expression that specifically reflect the realit-
> ies of our lives as Black females in a dominantly white/male culture.
> Because Black women rarely gained access to iterary expression,
> Black women-identified bonding and folk culture have often gone
> unrecorded except through our individual lives and memories.
> (Bethel, in Wilentz, 1992, p. 179)

This interest in reclaiming both individual and community leads in
part to the adoption of the vernacular and oral storytelling modes:
circling, repeating motifs, spiralling narratives. The interest in herbalism and rootworking aligns itself with the use of spirituality, magic
and the metaphorical in the content and language of much work by
African American women writers. Confronting and dealing with a
history of racism and sexism is a powerful motive for writing. Writers, moving through and beyond their articulated rage, celebrate difference. Alice Walker (1983b) explains why it is important to deal
with racism, the most extreme example of which is slavery. Not to do
so silences, prevents truth and constrains development:

In large measure, black Southern writers owe their clarity of vision to parents who refused to diminish themselves as human beings by succumbing to racism. Our parents seemed to know that extreme negative emotions held against other human beings for reasons they do not control can be blinding. Blindness about other human beings, especially for a writer, is equivalent to death. Because of this blindness, which is above all racism the works of many Southern writers have died. Much that we read today is fast expiring. (Walker, 1983b, p. 19)

One of Walker's important achievements has been to rediscover and celebrate Zora Neale Hurston, Harlem Renaissance writer and foremother of today's novelists in terms of style and concerns for women's identity and independence.

Zora Neale Hurston

Zora Neale Hurston was born in Eatonville in Florida in 1891 or 1901 (she changed the dates). She was fortunate in being brought up in an all Black township, where seeing Black people holding local office and varied jobs as normal prevented her from developing a sense of subordination current among writers of the Southern States where racism lingered longest. Her mother's insistence that Black people should speak out freely, and the abandonment by her preacher father upon remarriage, encouraged her to invest in her own abilities and to fend for herself. Hurston supported herself at 14, worked her way through school, and in 1925 won a major literary contest, after which she entered Barnard College. There she began studying anthropology with Frederick Boas, concentrating on African American folklore. She spent some time living among groups of people (including loggers) as a participant observer, to study their ways, and her research produced material feeding into later writing, particularly *Mules and Men* (1935), a unique treasury of voodoo and folklore. Part of her anthropological work included photographing a zombie in Haiti.

Zora Neale Hurston was fashionable, lively and sociable. She became a leading figure in the Harlem Renaissance, and her works show an engagement with 'porch life', the local community which gathered on the front porch to exchange information, beliefs and views. Hurston writes a mixture of standard American English and sometimes a slang dialect used by the groups of people of whom she writes. Her best known novel is the influential *Their Eyes were Watching God* (1937), in which the protagonist (Janey)'s Nanny points out the balances of power she has observed, against which Janey decides to strive:

> Honey de white man is de ruler of everything as fur as Ah been able tuh find out. Maybe it's some place way off in de ocean where de black man is in power, but we don't know nothin' but what we see. So de white man throw down de load and tell de nigger man tuh pick it up. He pick it up because he have to, but he don't tote it. He hand it to his womenfolks. De nigger woman is de mule uh de world so fur as Ah can see.   (Hurston, 1986 [1937], p. 29)

Their Eyes were Watching God establishes many of the patterns of concern and voice, of technical and narrative form, and of engagement with the gritty realities and imaginative escapes, the dreams and the metaphorical formulations which help African American women to speak out against oppression and develop a sense of individual identity in the face of silence and absence. Yet, interestingly, this early, hugely influential work in Zora Neale Hurston's *oeuvre* does not spend its energies in a politicised attack on racism and sexism and for this she has attracted criticism from contemporary writers, initially being accused by the novelist Richard Wright of trivialising Black people's lives. In ideological terms she played down the importance of actually being Black as regards her own success as a writer, arguing that she did not just want to write about 'the race problem'.

Since then, her great legacy to African American women has been reclaimed and developed by Alice Walker. Many of the themes and interests of her work – the community, the individual women, folk culture and oral storytelling – have continued by those she has influenced, including Alice Walker, Toni Morrison and Ntozake Shange.

Hurston and the Harlem Renaissance

What was the Harlem Renaissance like? It was a flowering of the work and skills of Black people, in New York in the 1930s. Duke Ellington played in the Cotton Club, Bessie Smith sang the blues, there was the Charleston and gin drinking; it was the heady Jazz age. Zora Neale Hurston landed in Harlem in 1925 and was described as 'bodacious', big boned and brave (Russell, 1990). She had one dollar fifty, a bag of manuscripts and a determination to 'wrassle me up a future or die tryin' (Hurston, 1930, letter to Mrs Mason, 25 November). She said she had 'the map of Florida on her tongue' and was steeped in folklore: 'folklore is the arts of the people before they find out there is such a thing as art' (Hurston, 1938, in Russell (1990) p. 35).

Her literary reputation soared in the 1930s with the publication of *Jonah's Gourd Vine* (1934), her acclaimed first novel, followed by *Mules and Men* (1935). *Their Eyes were Watching God* (1937) was produced out of the end of a love affair with a much younger man, 'AWP', who did not like to play second fiddle; the novel focuses on the quest for self-realisation of a young Black girl, Janie Crawford. Janie initially believes she can escape from the limitations of her confined life through marriage, but discovers she is just being constrained in different ways within marriage, this time by her two husbands. The first expects hard domestic work, and is rather dull; later, the second expects her to act the lady wife. Both marriages design, define and limit her. Life, she believes, holds more than this and so, jettisoning all the material gains, she runs away with Vergible Teacake Woods. He is sensuous, unpretentious and loves her for herself but, even in the context of a loving relationship, Janie has to teach him about respect when initially he copies other men, and beats her. Equal and happy together, they work 'on the muck' doing manual agricultural work. Janie's life becomes fulfilled when she can follow her real feelings with Teacake. Hers is a love story which avoids the unrealistically romantic:

> Love is lak de sea. Its uh movin' thing, but still and all, it takes its shape from de shore it meets, and it's different with every shore. (Hurston, 1986 [1937], p. 284)

Zora Neale Hurston's settings and tales record the everyday life of township people. Hers is an oral storytelling style: she picked up experiences and the lilt of people's language on porches, listening to and then capturing in writing the thoughts and expressions of local folk:

> It was a time for sitting on porches beside the road. It was the time to hear things and talk. These sitters had been tongueless, earless, eyeless conveniences all day long. Mules and other brutes had occupied their skins. But now, the sun and the bossman were

gone so their skins felt powerful and human. They became lords of sound and lesser things. They passed nations through their mothers. They sat in judgement. (Hurston, 1986 [1937], pp. 9–10)

In *Their Eyes were Watching God*, the porch folk are the first we meet, judging Janie in her return to their community and evaluating the mistakes she made in their (rather superficial) opinion. They feel that she has been taken up by Teacake for her money and that, being younger than her, he must have left her. Unable to 'place' her because of her challenge to dress, hair and behavioural codes (she keeps her hair in a plait down her back and wears men's clothes), they criticise Janie for being radical and non-conformist. However, while some might gossip speculatively, Janie's friends, particularly Phoebe, are happy to sort out food for her at the end of the day and to support the deliberately non-conformist choices she has made.

Janie's tale asserts the importance of being an individual in the face of the strains of working in a poor Southern agricultural community. It shows how an individual can rise above these constraints and achieve her own sense of self-actualisation. Unravelling as if a porch tale to enlighten community folk, Janie's story is based on her achievement of both independence and a love which enables her to flourish rather than be kept down emotionally, psychologically, physically or socially. As an experienced storyteller, Janie provides a frame to her tale which encompasses even the sadness of Teacake's death. She pulls it all together into the meshes of her life story, which she describes as hauling in a catch:

> She pulled in her horizon like a great fish net. Pulled it from around the waist of the world and draped it over her shoulder. So much of life in its meshes! She called in her soul to come and see. (Hurston, 1986 [1937], p. 286)

But she does not merely record and invent stories, she also uses symbolism and imagery to explore feelings, events, meanings. Hurston's novel is based on journeying and life's journey. The symbol of a pear tree represents a loving marriage of two equal souls, and Teacake is compared to a bee visiting pear-tree blossom in Spring. The novel's climax and end are also symbolic. A flood washes away all of Janie's life with Teacake. Later in court, her oral powers enable her to defend her action of shooting him to put him out of the misery of rabies resultant from being bitten by a rabid dog. Janie returns to Eatonville a whole woman, having experienced life and love for herself.

Zora Neale Hurston and the women who follow her are part of a matrifocal kinship system, passing on cultural values and personal history from generation to generation of women. Building on the form of the slave narrative, Hurston tells a story, makes a moral social comment and places the reader into a living, lively community. By finding a female voice with values other than the merely material, Janie, re-telling her story to Phoebey, establishes a female speech community, repudiating the kind of oppressive mothering (or absent mothering – Janie's own mother was raped and turned to drink, and her Nanny, though nurturing, repressed her spirit) she has experienced. Janie reasserts her voice among a community of speechmakers who decide the truth or versions of it and judge using their voices, but she can refuse to formalise matters or express them as people would wish when it suits her own form of expression. When Janie meets Teacake she says she really loves him, 'he dun taught me de maiden language all over'. She turns the damaging, boasting stories he tells of conquering and beating her, against him, achieving equality. When faced with a white set of jurors and judge, Janie just re-tells her story of Teacake's death, in her own words. She wins the day, and eventually learns to be able to seize language to determine truth for herself – her own knowledge. She tells big stories on the porch too. The novel was called a 'rich and racy love story' when received, the sensuality of Hurston's work being compared to that of D. H. Lawrence. However, not everyone liked it. Richard Wright said it carried 'no theme, no message', while Alain Locke, a long-time friend, reacted against the oral nature, the dialect and porch talk. He demanded that she stop writing about 'those pseudo primitives who the reading public still loves to laugh with, weep over and envy', and start writing 'motive fiction and social document fiction'. They wanted her to have written something else entirely. *Their Eyes were Watching God* is not a directly polemical piece, but a great imaginative work of sexual politics. It explores and enacts women's challenges to the dominant order of social control and versions of relationships. It also dramatises the lively spirit of successful African Americans seizing their own values and lives and their own ways of telling them.

By 1940, having never earned enough of a living by her writings, Hurston responded to her publisher's suggestion that she write her autobiography. *Dust Tracks on a Road* appeared in 1941/42, recalling her childhood in Eatonville and the Harlem Renaissance experiences. Although it received criticism for breaking with the tradition of identification with racial oppression, and seemed to hide more than it revealed about Hurston's development, it made a positive contribution to the development of Black women's writing by breaking with the tradition of slave narrative testimony:

> Hurston was the first Black women writer to venture on the uncertain path of creating a self outside of the group framework in which black autobiography had existed since the late eighteenth century.   (McCay, 1990, p. 266)

The reception of Zora Neale Hurston's work by women writers and critics has been more favourable than that of the men and, after Alice Walker's recuperation of her works and name, she has been accepted as the great foremother of contemporary women novelists. Wilentz says of her:

> Zora Neale Hurston, the spiritual and literary foremother of many modern African American women writers drew from the orature of her African culture turned slave culture in her tales, novels and short stories. Contemporary African American women writers have had to take their search one step further to envision their African foremothers, and now sisters, whose use of oral traditions and storytelling to impart cultural values has been passed down from generation to generation. As Zora Neale Hurston says 'If I see you no'mo' on earth, Ah'll meet you in Africa'.   (Wilentz, 1992, p. 241)

Nella Larsen

The work of Nella Larsen (1891–1964) is also an important feature of the period. Born in Illinois, of mixed race descent, her subject is frequently the complexities and difficulties of colour. Her *Quicksand* (1928) concentrates on conflicts resulting from mixed ancestry, while *Passing* (1929) focuses on a middle-class African American woman whose colour enables her to 'pass' for white. The result is a loss of her earlier friends and culture, and she is in permanent danger of being recognised as non-white. The book highlights the suffering caused by prejudices based on skin colour, an issue which re-emerges in Walker's *The Color Purple* (1983) and in the work of many African and African American women writers. The whiter someone's skin, the more likely, it seems, they are able to align themselves with the opportunities open to white people, and blackness is, even within Black society, considered a stigma. Pecola, in Morrison's *The Bluest Eye* (1970), similarly suffers from being a Black Black girl. Larsen hits a note of constant sensitivity in the Black community.

Ann Petry

Ann Petry (born 1908/1911) was born into relative poverty in one of the few African American families in Old Saybrook, Connecticut, USA. She studied pharmacy, graduated in 1931, and worked in the family drugstore. She married in 1938 and moved to New York, combining newspaper reportage for the Harlem paper *The People's Voice* with social work in slum areas, then studied creative writing at Columbia University (1946). Out of her mixed experience came her first stories, published in *Crisis* and *Phylon*, including 'Like a Winding Sheet' (1945) and her famous novel, the first by a Black woman to sell over a million copies, *The Street* (1946), followed by *Country Place* (1947). *The Street* highlights the harsh realities of urban African American women's lives, concentrating on how Lutie Johnson, who survives in Harlem with her young son although crippled, is exploited and driven to murder by her experiences of racism and misogyny. Lutie circles the street, where 'the dark passages were like ovens' in summer. Its bar, the 'Junto', offers the lure of muted lights, music and companionship (and danger) from 'sleek, well dressed men' who earned their living as tipsters, pimps and hustlers. Gritty in its historical realism, Petry's work marks the struggles of Black women's lives and sets a trend for writing about local communities in urban settings.

Gwendolyn Brooks

Gwendolyn Brooks was born in Kansas, USA, in 1917, and lives in Chicago. She was the first Black writer to win a Pulitzer Prize, for *Annie Allen* (1949). In a period when Black women writers were largely ignored in the literary world, Brooks' many honours and her genius made her the exception, breaking ground for future writers. Her poetry for ordinary people, including *A Street in Bronzeville*

(1946) and *The Bean Eaters* (1956), has made her famous. *Maud Martha* (1953), her novel, illustrates the imaginative stoicism of an ordinary Black American woman. *Report From Part One* (1972) (comparable to Hurston's *Dust Tracks on a Road*), shows how she was supported by her family in her writing. Brooks was proud of her blackness and writes very positively about the natural beauty of Black women:

> When I was a child it did not occur to me, even once, that the black in which I was encased (I called it brown in those days) would be considered, one day, beautiful . . . I always considered it beautiful. (Brooks, 1972, p. 37)

The autobiography is a prose poem, a fragmented text of short sections including travel, autobiography, and introductions by other Black, male writers in the tradition of authentication from slave narrative, history, letters, book reviews, etc. Family and community voices speak out from these fragments. Brooks' is an essentially urban and widely travelled history. In both her poetry and her autobiography she celebrates Black women:

> Sisters,
> Where there is cold silence –
> No hallelujahs, no hurrahs at all, no handshakes,
> No neon red or blue, no smiling faces –
> Prevail
>   ('To Black Women', in Busby, 1992, p. 268)

Gloria Naylor

Gloria Naylor was born in New York to working-class, Southern migrant parents. She worked as a telephone operator, gained a BA in English, and an MA in African American Studies at Yale, and has been writer-in-residence, lecturer and winner of a National Endowment for the Arts grant. Naylor has written three novels exploring the harsh everyday experience of African American urban ghetto women, drawing from the influence of Ann Petry. The most famous, *The Women of Brewster Place: a Novel in Seven Stories* (1982), received an American Book award for best first novel. Linked stories focus on Black women's lives, sisterhood and support. The sixth tale explores heterosexual women's fears about, and rejection of, lesbians. Lorraine and Theresa, in 'The Two', are lesbian professionals in a loving but claustrophobic relationship. They try to camouflage their sexuality by moving to the end of a slum block, but meet suspicion and prejudice. Each responds differently to being discovered, emphasising the splits faced by lesbian couples in society. One wants to fit in, the other to remain defiantly an outsider:

> Why should she feel different from the people she lived around? Black people were all in the same boat – she'd come to realise this even more since they had moved to Brewster – and if they didn't grow together, they would sink together.   (Naylor, 1982, p. 40)

It is a story of homophobia, leading to violent rape and near murder, and has shocked many, particularly lesbian readers. *Linden Hills* (1985) focuses on the problems that African Americans inherit when buying into the American Dream's materialistic offer. Naylor's treatment of African American gay and lesbian lives is cautionary, pessimistic, but an enlightened critique of destructive homophobia.

Paule Marshall

Paule Marshall has published several novels and short story collections, inheriting from Petry and Naylor an interest in women's street lives in *Brown Girl, Brown Stones* (1959), and *Praisesong for the Widow* (1983). Marshall's family emigrated from Barbados and in her work there is a focus on Caribbean identity and links. Selina, in *Brown Girl, Brown Stones*, is caught between the different values of her mother and father in a New York Barbadian community. Her mother needs security. Her father's pride in his manhood overrides everyone else's needs and Selina has to interpret their demands and find her own way, her own identity. As with the work of Morrison, Paule Marshall seeks answers to questions of how to live with and transform the past but move into the future. Several people including Suggie, who has many lovers, and Miss Thompson the hairdresser, help her but all suffer from racism. Selina has the support of her mother to develop her own identity. She comes to recognise the importance of aligning herself with her community, its vitality and contradictions. At the novel's end Selina dances, celebrating her selfhood and pride at being a Black American, and a woman.

IDENTITY AND SELFHOOD – THE FICTIONALISED
AUTOBIOGRAPHY: MAYA ANGELOU

Maya Angelou writes about and for women of all colours and, in particular, for the otherwise ignored Black women who need a voice:

> So many young Black women are not spoken to by white women. Are not spoken to by Black men. Are not spoken to by white men. And if we don't speak to them, there will be no voice reaching their ears or their hearts.   (Angelou, conversation with Rosa Guy in 1988, in Elliott, 1989, p. 240)

She has lived a very full life and travelled widely, seeing this as enlightening in terms of difference:

> Perhaps travel cannot prevent bigotry, but by demonstrating that all peoples cry, laugh, eat, worry, and die, it can introduce the idea that if we try to understand each other, we may even become friends.   (Angelou, 1995, p. 12)

Angelou's use of the fictionalised autobiography aligns her work with many other Black women writers, notably the Aboriginal women writers such as Sally Morgan and Ruby Langford (Chapter 9), and the South African Bessie Head (Chapter 7). As a powerful way of writing about and through your own life, women have chosen this very female of forms, self-expression, autobiography, to testify and to recognise themselves. In the cases of the Aboriginal women writers, many actually began by recording their lives through the amanuensis role of another, usually a white woman, but African American women writers belong to a very long tradition of testifying, writing and publishing and a third party is culturally unnecessary. The desire to seize identity through speaking out and forming versions of self, and to suggest to others that they too might do the same, is a similar venture, however. Maya Angelou uses the 'I' figure throughout her five volumes of autobiography. She tells her tale to record her own life, to explore her experiences, and also to provide models, and in using the autobiographical 'I' figure, she is imposing form and providing expression of herself as a member of the Black community, not merely recording her own life. She provides a public statement as much as a private one, and she empowers other readers who can relate to this record.

Criticism of the autobiographical form is itself critically naive. The 'I' figure is a mode of discovering and celebrating identity, but even when the experiences and feelings recorded have a basis in the author's life, the 'I' figure is necessarily distanced from that life. It is not merely a record of personal experience. The 'I' is a speaking subject created by the act of writing, a space where culture and ideology meet and are inscribed, and in which certain choices of expression are made. The 'Maya figure' in Maya Angelou's works provides a voice for herself, and a model of expression and embodiment of self, for other Black women. Depending on her memory, she records her childhood from a mixed vantage point. There is the innocence and ignorance of youth, of a young girl who, for example, does not realise that her mother's boyfriend is first about to, and then does, rape her. After this incident she spent years mute. The silence into which she was shocked was very real, but it can also be seen as a concrete metaphor for the depersonalisation and trauma caused by such an extreme denial of an individual's wholeness and value as a human being. The boyfriend was subsequently beaten to death by her uncles.

Part of Maya Angelou's analysis of racism focuses on the importance of establishing and maintaining identity against a backdrop of hundreds of years of enforced adoption of others' names, under slavery:

> Every person I knew had a hellish horror of being 'called out of his name.' It was a dangerous practice to call a Negro anything that could be loosely construed as insulting because of the centuries of their having been called niggers, jigs, dinges, blackbirds, crows, boots and spooks.   (Angelou, 1970, p. 106)

Misnamed 'Mary' as a servant, Maya insists on recognition of her own name, dropping Mrs Cullinan's best china for effect:

> 'You mean to say she broke our Virginia dishes?' . . . Mrs. Cullinan cried louder, 'That clumsy nigger. Clumsy little black nigger.'
> Old speckled-face leaned down and asked, 'Who did it, Viola? Was it Mary? Who did it?'
> Everything was happening so fast I can't remember whether her action preceded her words, but I know that Mrs. Cullinan said, 'Her name's Margaret, goddamn it.'   (Angelou, 1970, p. 107)

In later years her insistence that white shop assistants call her 'Miss Johnson' causes potential racist reprisals. In a state where the Klan are an everyday nightmare, asserting equality through naming yourself is a dangerous act. Maya packs up with her son, Guy, and leaves. White racism is consistently exposed throughout Angelou's five-part autobiography. Though Joe Louis, the 'Brown Bomber', wins the world title, and though in the war Blacks fought alongside whites, in the South there is no equality. When Maya's brother Bailey is late home, Momma fears for his safety:

> Her apprehension was evident in the hurried movements around the kitchen and in her lonely fearing eyes. The Black woman in the South who raises sons, grandsons and nephews had her heartstrings tied to a hanging noose. (Angelou, 1970, p. 110)

It is an everyday humiliation. Despite her comfortable position as store owner, Momma still has to pay respect to the 'po-white trash' children who taunt her and when Maya goes to the white dentist who owes Momma money, his refusal to treat her emanates from centuries of race hatred:

> 'Annie, my policy is I'd rather stick my hand in a dog's mouth than in a nigger's.' (Angelou, 1970, p. 184)

Maya Angelou's own life is a fascinating history of the acclaiming of African American voice, identity and power in the twentieth century. In the 1920s she toured Africa in *Porgy and Bess*, joined the Harlem Writers Guild in New York and earned her living as a night club singer. She became involved in Black struggles in the 1960s:

> Often this black artist is the first in his family and possibly his environment to strive to write a book, to strive to paint a painting, to sculpt, to make being an artist a life work. So the black writer, the black artist probably has to convince family and friends that what he or she is about is worthwhile. Now that is damned difficult when one comes from a family, an environment, a neighbourhood or a group of friends who have never met writers, who have only heard of writers, maybe read some poetry in school. (Angelou and Chrisman, 1977, in Elliott, 1989, p. 54)

Hers is a celebratory, life-affirming model for other African American women aspiring to be creative:

I try to live my life as a poetic adventure, everything I do from the way I keep my house, cook, make my husband happy, or welcome my friends, raise my son; everything is a part of a large canvas I am creating, I am living beneath. (Angelou and Chrisman, 1977, in Elliott, 1989, p. 5)

WRITING THE BODY: MYSTICAL AND EROTIC WRITING – NTOZAKE SHANGE

> i found god in myself
> & i loved her/i loved her fiercely
> (Shange, 'for colored girls who have considered
> suicide when the rainbow is enuff',
> 1992 [1975], p. 63)

I believe in honor, color and good sex.   (Shange, 1995, p. 16)

Ntozake Shange is a gifted, sensual, African American writer of prose fiction, drama and poetry. Her much acclaimed choreopoem 'for colored girls who have considered suicide when the rainbow is enuff' (1975) has been widely performed in the USA and UK and this, along with her novel *Cypress, Sassafrass and Indigo* (1977), helped establish her reputation as an engaged, lyrical writer of issues of race and gender. The choreopoem concentrates on the lives of seven women, each represented by a colour, who move through the 'dark phases of womanhood' (1992 [1975], p. 3), sexual activity, love and loss and finally find their own identity and self worth. *Cypress, Sassafrass and Indigo*, a poetic novel incorporating recipes and songs with fictional prose, looks at the development of awareness, identity and relationships, the magical and sensuous experiences of three sisters. In *Liliane* she continues her evocation of the imaginative and sensuous lives of Black women. The novel is concerned with identity, self-actualisation and relationships in a context of entrenched racism and sexism. Shange's subject is frequently the pain of relationships which deteriorate when the man denies the woman identity and self-worth. Liliane realises: 'the freedom you wage your most serious battle for is your very own mind' (1995, p. 44). Her women suffer, but essentially they are powerful, positive, sensual and creative, and many are artists. Her work celebrates the ability of African American women to survive despite often brutal relationships. Shange's quest is a poetic celebration of the magic of life and the body and her writing reclaims women's bodies; reclaims the erotic for Black women set against racist and sexist society's structures and male/female relationships which consistently shut out women's feelings, sensitivities and creative self-awareness. *Liliane* is concerned with communication and speaking out: 'I paint. I don't talk too much. The world overwhelms me' (1995, p. 45) says Liliane, isolated. It alternates between third/first-person narration from Liliane and friends and lovers, and dialogue between Liliane and her analyst helping her reconstruct a positive version of her past, relationships and self. Flashbacks and discussions build up versions of responses to relationships and the intrusiveness of racism which invades everything: parties of middle-class aspiring Black people such as her father, a judge, and everyday life. Violence is a constantly lurking threat which invades her life when her friends suffer: Roxie is harmed by her mad lover, and Sawyer is shot in the head.

Shange also concentrates on the important issue of recuperation of the past and of a women's tradition. Liliane needs to come to terms with and re-establish her once positive relationship with her politically aware, orchid growing, beautiful, outspoken mother, S. Bliss Lincoln. Her actions are confusing to her daughter and need unscrambling. On the one hand, she rejects white power, calling the invading Ku Klux Klan (racist extremists who wear white robes and pointed hats, carry burning crosses, and have been responsible for lynchings and violence against Black people, on the grounds of colour) 'white trash in used cars' (1995, p. 47), and champions Civil Rights, but she then elopes with a white partner. Liliane's greatest suffering is a result of an oppressive love affair. A crushing silence was imposed on her by her former lover's rejection. His envious, destructive influence shut off the music, enforced silence and denied her art while simultaneously denying the value of Black women. His is a racist attack on her, emphasising her sense of disadvantage because of her colour and her gender. No-one wants Black women, he insists, and her art (which he cannot recognise) is inferior. Denigrating her erotic art of 'labia boxes', he argues that all Black men prefer Chicana, Latina or white women. Another politically active, destructive macho lover, wrapped up in his own male self-image, needs to have total power over women and his insistence relates language and body: 'Now I'm a nice fella,' he insists, 'but had to get her to where she spoke my language' (1995, p. 66). Language and expression are keys to her own articulation of self-worth, and through recalling the positive expressions of her mother, Liliane starts to regain her own self-worth. Her mother dancing, loving her body, said 'that's like mastering the "turn" of a phrase, don't you think?' (1995, p. 58). Eroticised language helps Liliane recall sensual relationships with a lover in Casablanca. She needs to develop a positive image about being Black: 'I needed to see Negroes and mulattos, bona fide free, or somebody who looked like me win for a change' (1995, p. 35).

This is frequently a painful book. It indicts the vicious, crass racism of much of white society and, as with Walker's novels, and some of the comments of Angelou's autobiographical works, the humiliating sexism of many Black men. Speaking out and breaking silence has always been a powerful insistent force in African American women's writing, and eventually Liliane literally breaks the enforced silences which have denied her own joy of self and body. She learns that 'loving and grieving don't cancel each other out' (1995, p. 84), and moves on to a positive recognition of different feelings and experiences, learning to love her own baby, her father, mother, status and context, and of course herself and her art. The novel ends in an artistic and imaginative way, in a blaze of celebration and colour at a wedding. At this wedding, this celebratory moment, the spirits of dead friends join a lively party with photos, laughter and flowers. Liliane is at its centre promising to paint it all for them.

Shange contributes to the political, race and feminist debates we find in many works by African American women writers, but her particular gift is her lyrical writing and her reclaiming of the value of the body, and of the erotic. She instates a celebratory erotic writing. It is a painful, rather beautiful and ultimately positive novel.

Jewelle Gomez

Other erotic writing, this time lesbian erotic writing, is produced by Jewelle Gomez who is best known for her vampire novel *The Gilda Stories* (1991), in which a young escaped slave girl joins with two older women vampires in a vampire community, inheriting the name Gilda from one, and establishing a relationship with the other, Bird. The book is affirming, sisterhood is positive throughout, and the vampires are not predatory for the sake of it. Jewelle Gomez's novel is part of a contemporary lesbian interrogation of genres including vampire and horror writing, and it develops a positive representation of African American women.

Whether developing the testimonial form originating with slave narratives or experimenting with choreopoems and fantasy, African American women writers consistently confront sexism and racism, celebrating strong, articulate, Black women.

3

Toni Morrison

I think that all good art has always been political. None of the best writing, the best thoughts have been anything other than that.

(Morrison, 1994b, p. 3)

This chapter concentrates on Toni Morrison, Nobel Prize winner and major voice in Black writing, who says that she sets out to write the novels which she wanted to read; novels which dealt with Black lives and Black history. Essentially dialogic, her works present many voices and perspectives which place the reader at the centre, probably of a community, able to measure versions of experiences, perceptions and representations. Her work springs, in part, from oral storytelling, using repeated motifs, circularity and variation, producing the sounds and voices of the people and concentrating on how, at different historical moments in different contexts, the strategies of representation construct, control and constrict people's lives.

Morrison values the influence and power of her heritage, recuperating historical, lived moments in African American history to fill in the blanks, give voice to voiceless people hidden largely from official history. Her work concentrates also on gendered relations, on women's lives, motherhood, sisterhood, the community, and sexual politics. She has written several novels and critical works including: *The Bluest Eye* (1970); *Sula* (1973); *Song of Solomon* (1977); *Tar Baby* (1981); *Beloved* (1987); *Jazz* (1992); *Playing in the Dark: Whiteness and the Literary Imagination* (1992), and *Paradise* (1998).

Toni Morrison is an artist and an intellectual, a publisher and teacher who declares herself a 'Black woman writer'. She balances the polemical with style. Her work is always both political and beautiful.

One major trend in African American women's writing is that of mixing magic and history. History provides the opportunity for testimony and a record of the uncharted times and lives of Black people ever present but virtually invisible in social and literary terms until they started to be written of and by – mostly from the 1970s onwards. Toni Morrison's fine blend of the magical/supernatural/ spiritual, imaginative and metaphorical with the historical and realistic has caused some criticism among those who would seek to limit Black women's writing to testimony and record alone. This kind of restraint upon form and language is yet another covert example of racism: subordinating others' voices and expression. Embarrassing critical comments, such as Sara Blackburn's review of *Sula*, are evidence of such limited, imperialist thinking:

> Toni Morrison is far too talented to remain only a marvellous recorder of the Black side of provincial life, might easily transcend that early and unintentionally limiting classification 'Black woman writer' and take her place among the most serious, important and talented American novelists.   (Blackburn, 1973, p. 3)

Toni Morrison followed this in an interview about *Beloved*:

> I refuse to let them off the hook about whether I'm a Black woman writer or not, I'm under a lot of pressure to become something else. That is why there is so much discussion of how my work is influenced by other 'real' writers, for example white Southern writers, whom I'm constantly compared to.
> (Morrison, 1988, interview with Stuart, p. 15)

Her engaged aim is a full record which recreates and revitalises history through factual testimony and a re-creation of the imaginative world:

> What I wanted to do in my writing is to create an intimacy, share something with the reader. But I also wanted to write a book where your literary history wouldn't help you. So there are other voices in my work, like the folkloric, rather than the literary voices we are used to, and my language though in a sense seductive isn't there merely to make you feel good but to make you feel....
> I wanted to make a novel, with a pattern but not one that was regimental. That's about patronising the reader, and I can't patronise Black people. So your criteria changes. You can't play the same literary games....

Writing is about danger for me; it's like life – you can go under. Like all art it has to be political and it has to be beautiful – and no subject, not even slavery, should be beyond its reach.   (Morrison, 1988, interview with Stuart, p. 15)

Morrison creates a sense of history in the periods of which she writes by blending both the factual historical details, some specific, some generalised, to suggest everyday life, and a supernatural, imaginative, spiritual, magical and mythical element. In her re-creation of people's lives in historical moments she presents us with the lived reality, comprising both the actions and the imaginative constructions, the thoughts, feelings, perceptions, and what myths and constrictions form and influence these. She speaks of her main aim:

the tone in which I could blend acceptance of the supernatural and a profound rootedness in the real time at the same time with neither taking precedence over the other. It is indicative of the cosmology, the way in which Black people looked at the world, we are a very practical people, very down to earth, even shrewd people. But within that practicality we also accepted what I suppose could be called superstition and magic, which is another way of knowing things. But to blend these two works together at the same time was enhancing not limiting. And some of those things were 'discredited' only because Black people were 'discredited' therefore what they knew was 'discredited'. And also because the press upward towards social mobility would mean to get as far away from that kind of knowledge as possible. That kind of knowledge has a very strong place in my world.   (Morrison, in Evans (ed.), 1985, p. 342)

Beloved (1987) focuses on another historical era, the most painful in Black history, that of slavery, the time when some States had free Black residents while others continued with an inhuman regime. It is a powerful and painful story which involves us from the inside, building up to the horrifying climax at the novel's centre. The supernatural lives side by side with the detailed realistic, and for the reader this involves a suspension of disbelief, and involvement:

To make the story appear oral, meandering, effortless, spoken – to have the reader feel the narrator without identifying that narrator, or hearing him or her knock about, and to have the reader work with the author in construction of the book – is what's important. What is left out is as important as what is there. (Morrison, in Evans (ed.), 1985, p. 341)

THE NOVELS

The Bluest Eye (1970)

Identity is a major issue in Black women's writing, particularly the assertion of the value of the individual woman's identity and women's rights to construct their own identities rather than having them imposed against a host of negative stereotypes, representations and dehumanising practices. Much African American women's writing asserts the right to speak out and reverse the devaluing and silencing of hundreds of years of racial and gendered subordination (cf. Zora Neale Hurston's Janey's response to the triple burden of race, gender and class in *Their Eyes were Watching God*, see Chapter 2). By exploring different individuals as part of different communities in all their variety, at different points in history, Morrison can fill in everyone's knowledge and understanding, appreciation and empathy with the diverse lives of African Americans. This is a positive recuperative project. But her earlier works, particularly her first novel, *The Bluest Eye*, necessarily, it seems, deliver a depressingly negative message in their investigation of the lived realities of racial prejudice.

The damaging internalisation of negative representations of beauty and Blackness are Toni Morrison's major focus in *The Bluest Eye*, set in 1940s Ohio, which opens with the familiar schoolbook fantasy of Dick and Janey. Their ideal middle-class white family and home, subsequently increasingly scrambled, translated, is rendered most unrepresentative of the lives of Pecola Breedlove and her family. Morrison's naming is always significant: the last thing this family do is breed love. Pecola's father, Cholly, was conditioned to relate the sexual act with humiliation, a mechanical show which rendered him vulnerable and a figure of fun, the woman an object of disgust causing his sense of vulnerability. This particularly negative self-image came about when, stealing off for some love-making, he and his girl, Darlene, were the butt of jokes, forced to complete their 'show' while he was being called 'coon' and 'nigger' by a bunch of laughing white men. The blind victim of racial hostility and dehumanisation, he acts 'with a violence born of total helplessness' (1987 [1970], p. 137). He, in turn, directs his negative self-image and disgust at women onto his daughter Pecola, whom he rapes. Attempting to keep the white household where she works in total order, keeping up a certain face, responding to stereotypes which help pay their way, Pecola's mother is immensely unloving to her children – rejecting them for the pretty white ones she brings up in her work role. The ultimate victim is the unattractive, uneducated little Black girl. Pecola has only a Shirley Temple doll, icon of fairytale whiteness, and the image of blue eyes, something which should provoke love, she has been told (however, no-one can describe how to persuade someone to love you prior to the making of babies). This she adores as a visual representation of what girls should be, one she aspires to with an ironically desperate pointlessness. Subject to the overwhelmingly negative stereotype of Black women and the overwhelmingly positive, idealised stereotype of white woman, Pecola can only see herself as a hopeless, absurd failure. Her vulnerability is the tragedy of centuries of internalising negative perceptions constructed by the oppressors, in her case both white people and men. She is neither culpable nor guilty; how could she do otherwise? But the horror of her complete destruction makes this a highly negative novel. Claudia, Pecola's companion, rejects the stereotypes – they don't fit. She would like to dismember the Shirley Temple doll. She requires other representations and alternatives, but in their absence she will learn to lie, pretend to love. Claudia comments:

> It had begun with the Christmas and the gift of dolls. The big, the special, the loving gift was always a nice blue-eyed Baby Doll. (Morrison, 1987 [1970], p. 22)

> Adults, older girls, shops, magazines, newspapers, window-signs – all the world had agreed that a blue-eyed, yellow-haired, pink-skinned doll was what every girl child treasured. (Morrison, 1987 [1970], p. 22)

Not finding it beautiful, she investigates its working parts and dismembers it, to the horror of the adults. She 'destroyed baby white dolls' (1987 [1970], p. 22). The impulse to transfer 'to little white girls' is clearly far too dangerous, ultimately self-destructive. Collusion is a good decision for self-preservation. Thus she moves from pristine sadism to fabricated hatred, to fraudulent love:

> It was a small step to Shirley Temple. I learned much later to worship her, just as I learned to delight in cleanliness, knowing, even as I learned, that the change was adjustment without improvement. (Morrison, 1987 [1970], p. 25)

In Pecola's life there is nothing of hope or worth. She is the victim of her upbringing, ignorance, disorder, lack of love, and of the reception her Blackness produces. Geraldine, one of the Mobile girls, controlled and cold, on returning home to be greeted with the lie that Pecola (who would hurt nothing) has killed her cat, characterises Pecola as ragged detritus, absurd disorder. When Pecola becomes pregnant after her father's rape, gossips blame her (she is not quite twelve) and everyone wishes the baby dead. It is bound, they say, to be as ugly as both Pecola and Cholly.

Sula (1973)

> I wrote *Sula* and *The Bluest Eye* because they were books I had wanted to read. No-one had written them yet, so I wrote them. My audience is always the people in the book I am writing at the time, I don't think of an external audience. (Morrison, in Tate, 1984, p. 122)

Sula concentrates on the unconventional Black woman Sula Peace, whose life of unlimited experiment is unusual, outrageous, evil. Evil preoccupied Morrison in *Sula*, and one of her main aims was to testify to the ways in which Black people accept evil as a part of their lives, rather than feeling that they need to destroy it, as white people do. They have, then, a different concept of the 'Other':

> Black people never annihilate evil. They don't run it out of their neighbourhoods, chop it up, or burn it up. They don't have witch hangings. They accept it. It's almost like a fourth dimension in their lives. They have to protect themselves from evil, of course, but they don't have the puritanical thing which says if you see a witch, then burn it. (Morrison, 1994a, in Taylor-Guthrie (ed.), p. 8)

White reactions are to 'Otherise' Black people: 'White people's reaction to something that is alien to them is to destroy it. That's why they have to say Black people are worthless and ugly' (Morrison, 1994a, p. 8). Sula herself is a 'classic type of evil force' (Morrison, 1994b, p. 190, interview with Robert Stepto), focusing on the pariah figure. The Black community is also a pariah community living apart from others. So in one respect Sula, representing what unsettles and is considered evil, represents the community and its conscience:

> it was interesting to me that Black people at one time seemed not to respond to evil in the ways other people did... they thought evil had a natural place in the universe; they did not wish to eradicate it. They just wished to protect themselves from it, maybe even to manipulate it, but they never wanted to kill it. They thought evil was just another aspect of life.   (Morrison, quoted in Tate, 1984, p. 129)

Sula is a violent book of drowning and fires, mysterious suffering and loss and one which is, Morrison argues, honest about the existence and reception of evil: 'Evil is not an alien force, it's just a different force' (Tate, 1984, p. 129). The imaginary of these people, Morrison argues, has a place for evil. They need to off-load their doubts and discordance onto Sula, who is then seen as the cause. By exploring this dichotomising impulse, Morrison actually explores the way in which society itself can construct versions of values and reality which polarise people, emphasising and attempting to destroy what is different. This polarisation is nothing if not a negative, destructive and harmful response, even if it makes those who buy into it feel (falsely) secure in their sameness. Her project here with *Sula*, through investigating the pariah, is to also investigate the social forces which create one person or a group (Black Americans, women) as pariahs and as 'Other', onto which to off-load hostility, fear and disgust. If this impulse can be deconstructed and overcome, the basis for racial prejudice and for abjecting those who are not like a supposed or established 'norm' would ideally be eroded.

Barbara Christian sees *Sula* as a community novel: 'The novel is not only about Nel Wright and Sula Peace, it is most emphatically about the culture that spawns them' (Christian, 1984, p. 153). It has a compelling focus on women's friendships. Even when Sula sleeps with her best friend Nel's husband, Nel eventually realises Sula's worth. Morrison stated: 'I knew I was going to write a book about good and evil and about friendship' (Morrison, in Tate, 1984, p. 128), arguing that their friendship enables them to share everything and everyone, and this is a most positive force in the novel. The novel adopts oral storytelling forms, '*Sula* is more spiral than circular' (Morrison, in Tate, 1984, p. 124), has a rhythm, takes shape, records the end of the community before the story begins, events before they happen, spiralling round to fill in the details and thus creating both a sense of oral history, and lived reality. The form of the novel draws us in as participants in an oral history:

> My writing expects, demands participatory reading...it is about involving the reader. The reader supplies the emotions. The reader even supplies some of the colour, some of the sound. (Morrison, quoted in Tate, 1984, p. 125)

Toni Morrison says she wanted to make the neighbourhood, Medallion, Ohio, strong without making it quite a character. The novel spirals from 1910 to 1940 with a postscript in 1965. Time collapses and events come before and after years specified. Like an African folk tale, myths come to life and the past seems today, the teller 'spins ever intricate webs of connectiveness' (1984, p. 125). Death introduces each section, epitomised by Shadrack, a shell-shocked First World War veteran who establishes 'National Suicide Day'. The townspeople's attitude to life is to get in the hand of God.

The forces of nature are essential in the novel. Fire, water, earth and wind pervade it and Sula is often seen in relationship to water (by accident Morrison lighted on a name which in Tui means water). Sula is different, aligned with the natural. She has a birthmark like a plant, like water; she assumes whatever shape she likes and doesn't make a set thing of herself; she sleeps with all the men, has curiosity and a gift for metaphor. Nel is both her opposite and her compatriot, each deciding to react positively to their subordinate, gendered and racial position: 'Because each had discovered years before that they were neither white nor male, and that all freedom and triumph was forbidden to them, they had set about creating something else to be' (1980, p. 152):

> In one of the most haunting novels of African-American literature, Toni Morrison considers the thwarted freedom of a Black woman, a community's fear of change and experimentation, and above all the importance of female friendship. (Russell, 1990, p. 99)

Song of Solomon (1977)

Song of Solomon recuperates the mid-twentieth century when materialism took over some people's lives. Morrison concentrates on Macon Dead and his family, who own a big car but only ride out, slowly, formally and impressively in it on important occasions and Sundays. Their son, Milkman, is a slickly dressed, valueless young man at odds with his more politicised friend, Guitar, the radical. Names are always important in Morrison's novels. The family is called Dead and individuals, for example Pilate, Corinthians, are named inappropriately, blindly, from the Bible. There is a loss of spirituality and roots for all but Macon Dead's root-working (using roots for healing), herbalist, alternative lifestyle sister, inappropriately named Pilate. Pilate has no navel – significant of the fact that she has made herself, owns her own identity in the face of all the shaping and constricting forces which would restrict her. As Milkman, with a self that 'lacked coherence' (1980 [1977], p. 73), retraces his family's steps through history out from the urban environment back into the rural, he literally comes into contact with his roots. His white shoes and city slicker clothes are dirtied, but he meets those who remember his grandfather, his family.

His relationship with his cousin Hagar starts when he is 17, and at 31 he decides to call it off. Her ideal, waiting for a prince charming, had turned into a need, with duty at the centre of their relationship, but his arrogant rejection of her after so long destroys the sense of identity which she has constructed for herself. At the heart of this destruction is the internalisation of the belief that only with a man like 'prince charming' can she be herself and develop. Hagar's beliefs in the cultural myths of romantic fiction destroy her. She falls for cosmeticised lies, believing, if she has a total make-over, that her man might come back. How could he find her attractive, she thinks, looking at herself in the mirror, without her making all those expensive efforts that adverts tell her to make: 'Look at how I look, I look awful. No wonder he didn't want me, I look terrible' (1980, p. 309). Buying into this lie, she loses her sense of self worth and her hold on life. The scene of Hagar impulse-shopping in a systematic and overwhelming way is culturally resonant for all women who have bought these lies, believed they could construct versions of identity with which they felt comfortable when in fact they were buying pre-packaged images. It kills her. She dissolves as the complex artificial make-up dissolves in the rain and the parcels leak onto the floor:

She bought a Playtex garter belt, 1. Miller No Color hose, Fruit of the Loom panties and two nylon slips – one white, one pink – one pair of Joyce Fancy Free and one of Con Brio ('Thank heaven for little Joyce heels'). She carried an armful of skirts and an Evan-Picone two-piece number into the fitting room. (Morrison, 1980, p. 311)

She is too big for most of the clothes she tries on – sold on an image of perfect womanhood. When she reaches the cosmetics department she is overcome by the promise, the exotic names suggesting erotic power, and money: 'Fracas, and Calypso and Visa and Bandit' (1980, p. 312):

Peachy powders and milky lotions were grouped in front of poster after postcard board poster of gorgeous grinning faces. Faces in ecstasy. Faces sober with achieved seduction. Hagar believed she could spend her life there among the cut glass shimmering in peaches and cream, in satin. In luxe. In love. (Morrison, 1980, p. 312)

She wants a 'beauty that would dazzle him' (1980, p. 313). Buying into an artificial culture which denies the self, is destructive, the language warns, especially for women whose vulnerability is more psychologically charged than that of the men (Milkman fights his opponents – Hagar internalises them and believes they are part of her self-identity, to her cost):

At last she opened the door and presented herself to Pilate and Reva. And it was in their eyes that she saw what she had not seen before in the mirror: the wet ripped hose, the soiled white dress, the sticky, lumpy face powder, the streaked rouge and the wild wet shoals of hair. All this she saw in their eyes, and the sight filled her own with a warmer water and much older than true rain. Water that lasted for hours, until the fever came, and then it stopped. The fever dried her eyes up as well as her mouth. (Morrison, 1980, p. 315)

Discovering a damaged rouged doll of a self in the eyes of her mother and sister, Hagar self-destructs. Milkman's imagined gaze has helped her construct this image – the absurdity and inappropriateness of which indicts both Milkman and material society. Hagar, like Pecola in *The Bluest Eye*, is the victim of internalising and believing in vacuous representations, based on racial and gendered power structures. The novel also confronts racism and the dangers of violent response. Down South, Milkman discovers a history of embedded racial difference so taken for granted that when his grandfather, Macon Dead, was killed because his land was in a developer's way, no-one investigated. Although they knew the white family who owned most of the land were guilty, neither Black nor white were bothered: 'Arrested for what? Killing a nigger? Where did you say you was from?' (1980, p. 233), is the Reverend's question. The Reverend himself, marching in the Armistice Day parade, was run down by a horse, so great was the white rejection of the right of Black soldiers to take part. When four little Black girls are killed, Guitar and the other vengeful young men, the Seven Days, intend to kill white people to even the odds: 'There are no innocent white people, because every one of them is a potential nigger killer' (1980, p. 157). His view is seen as an extremist response to the sufferings and absurdities of racial inequalities.

Beloved (1987)

Toni Morrison's *Beloved* articulates and embodies a history and experience which has been ostensibly, literally and 'safely' recuperated but is actually still raw. The final page claims 'it was not a story to pass on' (1987, p. 275), using an established literary trick: creating a readership *ensures* it will be passed on. *Beloved* directly confronts racism in a novel which combines lyrical beauty with an assault on the reader's emotions and conscience. It traces, embodies and focuses on the legacy of slavery, using forms derived from a traditional Black folk aesthetic. Both content and form are controversial for the reader or teacher/student. *Beloved* provides a paradigm for critical issues related to our reading of Black women's writing.

Beloved engages with racism, and the most disturbing part of African American history, slavery. Its exposure of the pathology and the legacy of slavery directly confronts the reader. It is a mixed mode, containing both historical realism and the magical. The story is based on the factual account of the killing by escaped slave Margaret Garner, of her young children, in the face of recapture. This mixed mode raises particular difficulties of reader response, but yields particular richness also. The combination is disturbing: social and historical realism; overt political impetus in its confrontation of both racism and sexism; the supernatural; a dead baby ghost who returns as a young woman, Beloved, disrupting relationships and nearly destroying the mother whose mother-love caused her to be sacrificed in the face of re-enslavement.

One warning, of the care we must take in reading and studying this text not to misappropriate it for our own ends, emerges from our consideration of its indictment of the slave owner, School-teacher, the intellectual whose dehumanising cruelty to his slaves dresses up denial of human rights in the cloak of academic author-ity. Schoolteacher's pupils are told to study Sethe and the other slaves, drawing up lists with their animal characteristics on the one hand, their human on the other. This misuse of knowledge gives Schoolteacher and the white man power over those designated as only fit for scientific categorisation rather than human relationships and respect. Study in itself is not devalued. Later, herself not an object for formal study, Denver's own studying provides her with an opportunity to develop insight and articulacy. *Beloved* focuses on the all-pervading dehumanisation of slavery and, in a dramatic and concrete form, its legacy which is made manifest in the figure of Beloved herself.

As readers, teachers and students of this novel, we need to discover the context of the history of slavery, the torture, murder, and the economic sources and descriptions of the institution, the treatment of slave women used by slave owners, denied family lives yet forced to be breeders of future slaves, and the historical changes which the period of the novel focuses on, when the free States gave homes to freed slaves, but they were unprotected from slave-catchers crossing to recapture those who had escaped. In 1855 slave owners could cross into free States to recapture escaped slaves. Margaret Garner, who had escaped with her family, saw the slave-catchers coming and tried to kill her four children. The baby girl died, the boys lived. She was convicted of escaping (a property issue) rather than murder. The novel dramatises the incident, which starts, apocalyptically 'When the four horsemen came' (1987, p. 148). The fugitive slaves are described as if they are children playing guilty games. Dehuman-ised, they are also described as wild animals:

> Caught red-handed, so to speak, they would seem to recognise the futility of outsmarting a white man and the hopelessness of outrunning a rifle. Smile even, like a child caught dead with his

hand in the jelly jar, and when you reached for the rope to tie him, well, even then you couldn't tell. The very nigger with his head hanging and a little jelly-jar smile on his face could all of a sudden roar, like a bull or some such, and commence to do disbelievable things . . .   (Morrison, 1987, p. 148)

They are considered valuable only as property, and of less use than an animal when dead: 'Unlike a snake or a bear, a dead nigger could not be skinned for profit and was not worth his own dead weight in coin' (1987, p. 148).

In the face of such 'humanity', the 'crazy' mother, Sethe, murders her child to save her. It is a stark description:

Inside, two boys bled in the sawdust and dirt at the feet of a nigger woman holding a blood-soaked child to her chest with one hand and an infant by the heels in the other. She did not look at them; she simply swung the baby toward the wall planks, missed and tried to connect a second time.   (Morrison, 1987, p. 149)

The 'pickaninnies' are now considered worthless, and Sethe's anguished act a mere product of the nephew's 'mishandling' of her, as one might mishandle a dog: 'Suppose you beat the hounds past that point thataway. Never again could you trust them in the woods or anywhere else' (1987, p. 149). The viewpoint and tone of the slave-catcher provide a fallible narrative voice against which to measure our own horror that the dehumanisation of slavery could result in such suffering.

Beloved is essentially a novel about the vitality and intrusiveness of memory, the memory of racial oppression under slavery. Memory or 'rememory' is acknowledged as present, solid, vital:

If a house burns down, it's gone, but the place – the picture of it – stays; and not just in my rememory, but out there in the world...it's when you bump into the rememory of someone else.   (Morrison, 1987, p. 36)

This suggests that history is a tangible, visible existent that a community can experience, bump into. In this novel, the insanity and absurdity upon which a capitalist society dependent on slavery is founded, translates itself into the lived madness, the haunting of the past within no. 124, the house where first Baby Suggs, the grandmother, then Sethe, the mother, and Denver, her daughter, live. It is over the issue of this tangible history that readers face a problem. *Beloved* is an historically situated, politically focused novel, but it is equally a novel essentially based on an acceptance of the supernatural and magic. We suspend our disbelief when we are told that the baby whose throat Sethe cut to save her from the slave-catchers haunts the house on Bluestone, no. 124; whose red aura provides a presence, however, occasionally malevolent and spiteful; and whose presence effectively isolates Baby Suggs from the community. Previously the centre of community root-working, herbal medicine and mystical powers, as a lay preacher Baby Suggs represented the socially acceptable face of the supernatural's place in shared society. Like the community around her, however, we have problems as readers, when Beloved actually appears, right at the moment of a new family harmony and sexual unity for Denver, Sethe and Paul D., one of the last of the 'Sweet Home' men who has come to stay in Sethe's life. Footsore and weary from a long journey, confused in her memories about who gave her clothes, taught her ways, Beloved intrudes on family harmony, upsetting Sethe's sexual relationship with Paul D. by sleeping with him and forcing him to recognise her. She demands: 'call me by my name' and 'touch me on the inside'. Sexuality, here as elsewhere in Toni Morrison's works, is used, as Susan Willis points out, as a register for the experience of change: 'sexuality converges with history and functions as a register for the experience of change, i.e. historical transition' (Willis, 1984, p. 263).

Through her new sexual relationship with Paul D., Sethe begins to be able to reopen and cope with the memories of the slave past, as did Paul D.; Beloved challenged her sexually, and won, her past literally refusing to be so easily laid. At the novel's close Sethe and Paul are reunited, with a return of the honesty which recognises that much must be left unsaid, cannot be fully faced if sanity is to be possible. Beloved is a succubus. She drains the house of love and vitality both spiritual and physical, then forms a strong bond of dependency with Denver, finally turning to Sethe when her mother recognises her as the daughter she sacrificed. She grows fast as Sethe shrinks and shrivels, and she causes the whole house to be united in a crazy bond. Too much recognition drives Paul D. away, drains Sethe of life as she both serves and battles with the ghost-made-flesh. Beloved is manifest history, the guilt and pain of slavery as it enters personal lives causing brutal, dehumanised actions in self-defence from those denied human rights. For the community this is too much to face, jealous of the celebrations they failed to warn Sethe of the slave-catcher's arrival. They feel culpable. Here as elsewhere in Morrison's work there is a focus on the relationship of the individual to the community:

> Rather, these individuals, struggling to reclaim or redefine them-selves, are portrayed as epiphenomenal to community and cul-ture; and it is the strength and continuity of the black cultural heritage as a whole which is at stake and being tested.   (Willis, 1984, p. 270)

The role of the community response is crucial, as the events at no. 124 are a metaphor for the sufferings, memory and guilt of the Black community.

Silence and breaking silence are central issues. The bit which Paul D. is forced to wear dehumanises him, reducing him in his own eyes below the level of Mister, the liberated rooster:

> Mister was allowed to be and stay what he was. But I wasn't allowed to be and stay what I was. Even if you cooked him you'd be cooking a rooster named Mister. But wasn't no way I'd ever be Paul D. again, living or dead. Schoolteacher changed me. I was something else and that something was less than a chicken sitting in the sun on a tub.   (Morrison, 1987, p. 72)

Paul D. is silenced, his heart holding its secrets tight like a tobacco tin, and finally there is a debate about hiding the unmentionable histories of slavery. The women of the community finally return to exorcise Beloved from no. 124, utilising a pre-linguistic community humming sound, denying the dehumanising language of the white man, coping with, recognising and placing the ghost of slavery, rid-ding Sethe's house of the draining succubus of lived guilt and pain, Beloved:

> They stopped praying and took a step back to the beginning. In the beginning there were no words. In the beginning was the sound, and they all knew what that sounded like.   (Morrison, 1987, p. 259)

The noise unlocks Sethe's mind, reunites her with the community:

For Sethe it was as though the Clearing had come to her with all its heat and summer leaves, where the voices of women searched for the right combination, the key, the code, the sound that broke the back of words . . . it broke over Sethe and she trembled like the baptised in its wash.   (Morrison, 1987, p. 259)

'This is not a story to pass on' ends the novel (1987, p. 261). But it is crucial to pass on the tale in the shape of the novel, not let its horror undermine the ability to confront, live with and move on from memories of slavery and everyday racism. This acknowledgement is ultimately empowering for African Americans, whites, and for Sethe herself: she learns, as Paul points out, 'You your own best thing, Sethe' (1987, p. 259).

Jazz (1992)

Jazz captures and re-visions a historical and cultural moment, restoring and re-writing a hitherto silenced and absent Black history between the wars. The story moves from the Southern countryside to New York, with its juke joints and violence, poverty and promises. It presents a different perspective on Black life, looking at the lies of urban promise, standards of living, rural myths vs. urban myths, suffering, power, boundaries, male–female relationships, the role of music. All three main characters, Violet, Joe Trace and Dorcas, are victims of the lies about urban success, and each has bought into the cosmetic artifice of the period when Black striving seemed to ensure some financial and status success, but actually confined people to ghettoes, falsely bolstered up by glittering hopes, the heat, the vibrancy of the city and its music. For Black folk strap-hanging from the South on trains, the American Dream seemed to be available in the city. Toni Morrison points out that this is deceptive. Equality and freedom are false promises; people are actually ghettoised in working-class Black areas with no escape, sold on the lies and images: 'The City makes people think they can do what they want and get away with it' (1992a, p. 8). However, while streetcars and juke joints predominate, the infrastructure which could enable economic development is missing. They have been sold a lie. The ghetto contains:

the church, the store, the party, the women, the men, the postbox (but no high schools), the furniture store, street newspaper vendors, the bootleg houses (but no banks), the beauty parlors, the barbershops, the juke joints, the ice wagons, the open food markets, the number runner, and every club, organisation, group imaginative. (Morrison, 1992, p. 10)

The city is alive: 'there is no air in the City but there is breath' (1992a, p. 34). It encourages love, desire, dreams, which lead to Joe being hooked on Dorcas, cosmetics ('Cleopatra' – which he sells) and fancy clothes, to Violet's hairdressing. These are all cosmeticised artificial images and actions, representing, like Hagar's shopping spree in *Song of Solomon*, a loss of authenticity and values.

Dorcas is the main victim. She is sold on the cosmeticised image of the city, and on the city slicker, Acton (a town name), whose shoes are ruined by her blood hence Dorcas's death is paradigmatic of the destructive powers of the lies of urban life.

The novel also scrutinises male–female relations, their deceits and their lasting pleasures. While Joe, bored and complacent, their love atrophied, leaves Violet for Dorcas, he eventually returns and their love is bolstered up with a threesome relationship. Dorcas's Aunt Manfred is so repressed and frozen she is a danger, but Dorcas's own sexual longing for Acton is seen as false, she is too easily taken in by his city slicker appearances. The novel scrutinises varieties of relationships, digging back into a legendary past, of myths about a relationship between a Black Wild sexual woman in the rural South and white beautiful boy Golden Gray (product of a rich white woman and a Black man – Hunter). The relationships between Vera Louis Gray, Golden Gray and Hunter, his father, raise issues of race and race history. Golden Gray, the boy of mixed blood, idealised, meets and cares and calls for the Wild woman (a mythic type), their union producing Joe. So the story/Trace is his trace/history. Myth and historical realism combine and through it all the structure and language of the novel run like a jazz tune, with solos and harmonies, themes, repeated motifs.

Jazz music was of the time, the Harlem Renaissance, and promised social improvement to those who succeeded in it, while providing ordinary people with a rhythm and a celebration in their lives. The Jazz music is a structuring device providing a social comment and commentary. Jazz is a mixture of the blues, Black music, South American, Cajun, French, a true social melting pot of music and an expression beyond the pain of the blues, and 'Jazz promised new freedoms, sensuality and romantic love without ties and without

real loss or suffering' (Wisker, 1992, p. 43). *Beloved* was a blues working through the ache of slavery, while '*Jazz* itself gives a voice,
expression, and a form to the searchings, pains and the celebratory
patternings of a specific historical moment' (Wisker, 1992, p. 43). The
music produces desire and anger, it enlivens, lies, lures on, lets steam
out, captures the contradictions of the city, the activities of buying
food, spending money, sitting amongst large numbers, anonymity,
surface values, hope. It also suggests an alternative way of passing
on information and mood, a community tone starting with gossip as
messages pass through community, and through music versus the
news. Black people's lives are not considered newsworthy, hence
Dorcas's murder is not reported. As beliefs and values are upset,
lies predominate and so also forms are undercut. *Jazz* refuses the
mystery of a detective or crime novel, but contains a crime, shows
up the lies of romantic fictions, and mixes history with the imagery
and suggestiveness of the popular imaginary, fuelled by music and
dreams.

Paradise (1998)

With *Paradise* Toni Morrison concentrates on the representation and
treatment of women, focusing on a community, 'the Convent', of
women leading alternative, feminist lives, on the edge of an all Black
pioneering town, Ruby. The established ways of this town make
them fiercely proud of their history and heritage, but their inability
to cope with the role this women's community provides for the
women of the town (escape from abuse, seeking abortion, seeking
someone to talk with), and the challenge that a community of
women seems to pose, just by being there, prove too much. The
essential ossifying conservatism of the town, somehow afraid to
change its ways and move on, leads to the final assault on the community by the young Black men. Fear of the power of the women
leads the men to characterise them as evil, they are witches in the
men's minds and all that goes wrong in this too incestuous, old-
fashioned, patriarchal paternalistic town is blamed on them:

> It was a secret meeting, but the rumours had been whispered for
> more than a year. Outrages that had been accumulating all along
> took shape as evidence. A mother was knocked downstairs by
> her cold-eyed daughter. Four damaged infants were born in one
> family. Daughters refused to get out of bed. Brides disappeared on

their honeymoons. Two brothers shot each other on New Year's day.... So when nine men decided to meet there they had to run everybody off the place with shotguns... the one thing that connected all these catastrophes was in the Convent. And in the Convent were those women.   (Morrison, 1998, p. 11)

Attacking the women, white and Black, the men feel they have God on their side:

Bodacious black Eves unredeemed by Mary, they are like panicked does leaping toward a sun that has finished burning off the mist and now pours its holy oil over the hides of game. God at their side, the men take aim. For Ruby.   (Morrison, 1998, p. 18)

The novel concentrates on recounting the town's history and the parallel history of the women's community, revealing the hidden evils and rot of this paternalistic patriarchal society and the free-thinking, supportive ways of the women whose sexual shamelessness attracts and terrifies the men and so, in time-honoured fashion, must be seen to be punished. The different stories are told of the women who flee from loveless relationships, oppression, excessive religious control, hypocrisy, taking refuge in the alternative ways of the Convent.

That even initially powerful, free-thinking Black communities can lose energy and momentum, turn to oppression and hypocrisy, lose their way, is one warning message of the novel. Another relates very centrally to the ways in which conventional patriarchal beliefs figure questioning and free-thinking women as a threat to be destroyed. The novel ends where it begins, with the raid on the Convent, its message lasting beyond the novel but providing no utopian ending within it.

Beautiful, painful and revelatory of Black lives, Toni Morrison's novels focus on creating and recuperating the pyschological and imaginative lived experiences as well as the historical and the everyday, drawing on the dreams and fears as well as the actions of African Americans in different periods of history, re-writing the partial, received versions of history, as their own.

4

Alice Walker

In Alice Walker's work a legacy from the Southern experience provides a consistent interest and voice:

> What the Black Southern writer inherits as a natural right is a sense of community. Something simple but surprisingly hard these days, to come by. (Walker, 1983, p. 17)

This is true of much Black women's work, including that of Toni Morrison and, like Morrison, Walker is concerned with recuperating history to underpin a sense of her own and her community's identity:

> I think my whole program as a writer is to deal with history just so I know where I am. (Walker, 1983, p. 185)

This chapter concentrates on Alice Walker's contribution to the establishment of a Black women's writing tradition, as an 'apologist and chronicler' of Black women's lives. Her aim is to rescue Black women from silence, recuperate women's lives and myths in different periods of history, confronting racism and sexism through the establishment of sisterhood and the writing of what she terms 'womanist' prose, using quilting, bricolage, the vernacular, myth and storytelling forms. Part of her achievement is also to demythologise the damaging myths of Black women's limitless strength (the powerful Mammy figure) or limitless, excessive, dangerous sexual energies (the figure of the whore). Born in Eatonton, Georgia, and educated at Spelman and Sarah Lawrence colleges, Alice Walker was active in the Civil Rights Movement and taught in several colleges and universities, including the University of California at Berkeley. Along with Toni Morrison's *The Bluest Eye* (1970), her first novel, *The Third Life of Grange Copeland* (1970), set in a Southern agrarian community, established the rebirth of a Black women's writing movement.

Alice Walker is well known for establishing a Black matrilineal tradition which has helped so many women contextualise their own work and read back through that of their grandmothers. This she chiefly did in rescuing the burial place and the writing of Zora Neale Hurston from oblivion, aided by Hurston's biographer, Robert Hemenway. Although her first published work was poetry, which she continues to write, it is for her novels that she is better known: *The Third Life of Grange Copeland* (1970), *Meridian* (1976), *The Color Purple* (1983), *The Temple of My Familiar* (1989), *Possessing the Secret of Joy* (1992), and *By the Light of My Father's Smile* (1998). Her short stories have been collected in *In Love and Trouble* (1973) and *You Can't Keep a Good Woman Down* (1982), and her poetry appears in the collections *Once* (1968); *Five Poems* (1972); *Revolutionary Petunias and Other Poems* (1986 [1968]); *Good Night, Willie Lee, I'll See You in the Morning* (1979), and *Horses Make a Landscape Look More Beautiful* (1984). Important collections of essays have also appeared in *In Search of Our Mothers' Gardens* (1983), and *Living By the Word* (1988). She has also published a significant collection of Zora Neale Hurston's work and a biography of Langston Hughes.

For Walker, among other Black women writers such as the South African Bessie Head and the Caribbean British poet Grace Nichols, the personal is both a political and an artistic statement. The model of the speaking subject is one the construction of which foregrounds the oppressive nature of Black women's lives, their relegation to a position of silence and powerlessness. Black women's oppression is a function of the mixture of sexism, racism and economic deprivation. Alice Walker critiques the roles assigned to women, the myths which represent them. Her characters are famous for speaking out against oppression and refusing to accept as 'natural' institutionalised racism and sexism. Against a context of Black consciousness in America, she deliberately separated the issue of women's subordination, from that of the similarly dehumanising experience of living under white racism's daily humiliations. For this she was criticised by many, specifically Black men. A highly politicised voice, she tackles the ways in which cultural myths perpetuate inequalities for women, in the US, more broadly in the Americas, and in Africa. She confronts the most emotionally charged issues and practices such as rape, incest, wife beating and female circumcision. But her novels are far from bleak. Alice Walker's women are usually of the 'battler' type (an Australian term). They stride head on against tanks (*Meridian*) and hypocrisy, speak out and celebrate their own identity and empowerment as women, mothers, and as sisters. Her 'womanist' (more positive she feels than 'feminist') prose enables a celebration of women-identified relationships and sisterhood. One of her greatest contributions was to rediscover and republish the work of Zora Neale Hurston (see Chapter 2) whose recuperation helped to give Black women writers a sense of a growing literary history in the context of which they could develop their own voices.

Walker critiques and reverses misogynistic stereotypes of Black women in her work: 'When I write . . . I try to make models for myself. I project other ways of seeing' (in Tate, 1984, p. 183).

During the Civil Rights Movement and Black Power Movement, arguments for relegating Black women to their 'natural' inferior role appeared in the writing of Richard Wright and Amiri Baraka, who preached a romanticised vision of woman in the home, while showing brutal scenes of Black men abusing their women. Their outright misogyny perpetuated images of Black women as 'matriarchs, castrators, bitches' (hooks, 1981, p. 102). In *Meridian*, Alice Walker dramatises these conflicts within the Movement. Black men like Truman, Meridian's lover, 'did not want a general beside him', he would prefer 'an attractive woman, but asleep' (Walker, 1982 [1976], p. 107).

It is the strength of Walker's writing that it confronts issues problematised within feminism, and within Black writing. She traces Black women writers from Phillis Wheatley onwards. In her own mother she recognises creativity in her growing of a beautiful garden:

> What did it mean for a black woman to be an artist in our grandmothers' time? . . . Did you have a genius or a great-great-grandmother who died under some ignorant and depraved white overseer's lash? Or was she required to bake biscuits for a lazy backwater tramp, when she cried out in her soul to paint watercolours of sunsets . . . it is to my mother – and all our mothers who were not famous – that I went in search of the secret of what has fed that muzzled and often mutilated, but vibrant, creative spirit that the black woman has inherited, and that pops out in wild and unlikely places to this day . . .   (Walker, 1983a, pp. 233/4)

THE NOVELS

Meridian (1976)

Meridian is a political book which utilises Walker's own Civil Rights experiences. In concentrating on the life of Meridian Hill, a Southern woman, it emphasises the need to assert the importance of civil rights even after their official granting. It opens with Meridian Hill, 'dressed in dungarees and wearing a light-colored, visored cap', like that worn by men on trains, facing down a tank in the centre of the town's square, accompanied by supportive children, black and white, observed by Truman Held, the man who is to become her lover. The tank, bought years ago by the white folk of the town, was painted red, white and blue and set as a signal against problematic marching Black folk. Meridian's gesture, in context, represents a refusal to accept racism. Significantly, the incident takes place overlooking a travelling show which itself represents both sexism and racism. In the show, a repainted, shrunken body of a wife who 'went wrong' (rejecting suburban values), is exhibited by her husband. The townsfolk visit in relays but those working at the 'Po' factory (mostly Black folk, making things out of guana) are only allowed to visit on Thursday. This differentiation, which incorporates their children, is effectively both a race and class segregation. Both Meridian and Walker are actively against the divisions and disempowerments triggered by race, class and gender and throughout the novel Meridian's is a highly significant challenge. In tracing Meridian's upbringing many updated myths and events in Black history align themselves with her own: she momentarily rescues a 'Wild Child'; studies in a college where a tree grows, named after one of the earliest Black women activists and writers – Sojourner Truth (who wrote the famous poem and political statement 'Ain't I a woman', asserting her rights and human dignity); her family unearth Native American treasures, plant their own food, but all is taken away and turned into a theme park. She finds gold but it is ignored. When a house full of Black Americans working for the vote is burned to the ground, Meridian wakes up to politics and action: 'And so it was that one day in the middle of April, 1960, Meridian Hill became aware of the past and present of the larger world' (1982 [1976], p. 67). In a society where 'Black people were never shown in the news' (1982 [1976], p. 67), she witnesses acts of racism, fuelling her sense of political activism. In Atlanta, Georgia, Meridian sees:

> small black children, with short, flashing black legs, being chased by grown white men brandishing axe handles. She saw old women dragged out of stores and beaten on the sidewalk, their humility of a lifetime doing them no good. She saw young Black

men of great spiritual beauty changed over night into men who valued nothing. (Walker, 1982 [1976], p. 92)

Meridian identifies the intermingling of sexism and racism, questioning stereotyping and noting that while Black women are chosen by all men for sexual exploits, white women, smelling of nothing, are wanted by no-one. Black women, even good time girls, gain good jobs, but white women fall into suburban mindlessness. In *Meridian* personal relationships are seen as symptoms of the political situation. Meridian's body, as Christine Hall (1993) points out, is associated with the body politic, and when she is finally restored to health, the body politic has some chance of the same restoration. Walker raises issues of 'the suppression of language, the need to recontextualise, the need for a sense of the self in history, as a prerequisite of spiritual and psychological health' (Hall, 1993, p. 96). The kind of activism possible is also called into question. Meridian, in the face of racism and sexism, reaches the conclusion that direct violent action might, at least in theory, be necessary. This revelation comes in church, where she sees depicted the image of a Clansman holding a guitar and singing, but brandishing a bloody sword at the same time. The congruence of art and political change, the individual's responsibilities in making things happen, all come home to her:

even the contemplation of murder required incredible delicacy as it required incredible spiritual work, and the historical background and present setting must be right. Only in a church surrounded by the righteous guardians of people's memories could she even approach the concept of retaliatory murder. (Walker, 1982 [1976], p. 205)

Although there is much silencing of women in the novel, there is also much giving voice, and revaluing language. Critical comment is essential in terms of political, racial and gender action against inequalities. Meridian concludes that it is by means of art, storytelling performance, music, etc., that history can be transformed to be truly meaningful and to enable action to take place. Walker's own novel is, of course, such an example of art transforming thoughts and actions. In the fragmentary form of the novel folk tale, different versions are juxtaposed. Unlike Truman, who wants a single answer, Meridian, like the novel's form, offers reconciliation between several versions and answers, so what might seem disjointed is actually a multiple perspective. In *Meridian* Walker celebrates the creation and preservation of life, and confronts the political issue of revolution versus violence.

The Color Purple (1983)

Alice Walker's epistolary novel is a powerful, lively and imaginative depiction of the abused life of a young Black woman, Celie. Celie is one of those many whose lives have gone unrecorded, effectively silenced by their race, poverty and gender, which categorise them as victims. The novel's opening is one of the most powerful in literature, giving voice to the voiceless as Celie tries to write to the only person who could possibly listen, God, explaining her confused sense of guilt, shame and innocence, and unfolding for us the pain of her life. Sexually abused by the man she believes to be her father, Celie takes on the household chores, and bears two children stolen away from her. This abuse replicates the experiences of Black slaves: it is a slavery clearly continuing for poor Black girls, but this time at the hands of poor Black men. Walker's indictment of the limitless, off-hand cruelty of the Black men in Celie's life caused a furore among politicised African Americans (such as Richard Wright, and other established figures) who felt she should concentrate on racist abuse. Her project, she insisted, was to attack all abuse and silencing – racist *and* sexist – and the cause would not be furthered by such selectivity. Walker utilises forms of writing open to women, personal autobiographical forms, such as were found in Harriet Jacobs' *Incidents in the Life of a Slave Girl* (1861), testifying to abuse, although Celie would probably have not been literate enough to write letters. This form of testifying (see Maya Angelou in Chapter 2) was considered to be a guarantee of legitimacy and a manner of passing on hidden histories, giving voice to the silenced. It was also, under slavery, a way of claiming one's own identity. Elsewhere, Aboriginal women writers use semi-fictionalised autobiographies to speak out against racism and marginalisation (see Chapter 9). Celie's speaking out, initially confined to God then Nettie, is a powerful first-hand testimony:

> Look at you. You black, you poor, you ugly, you a woman. God-dam, he say, you nothing at all. . . .
> I'm poor, I'm black, I may be ugly and can't cook, a voice say to everything listening. But I'm here. Amen, say Shug. Amen, amen. (Walker, 1983, p. 176)

Celie's assertion of her own identity, and the importance of her existence, is a revolutionary step for one crushed under the triple burden of racism, sexism and class oppression. Alison Light notes of the novel that it offers:

> a paradigm of change through the agency of black women and a fictional celebration of their capacity to assess and affect the social relations in which they find themselves. An ability to survive the brutal exploitation of their bodies and their labour, by both the dominant culture and their own world of social relations. (Light, 1985, p. 25)

Walker speaks for the community through the voice of the individual. Celie's love for her sister Nettie ensures her protection, education, and rescue from 'Mister' and her father's attentions, at her own cost. Nettie, able to read and write, enacts the African American romance with roots by 'returning' to Africa and experiencing life there. Walker's fascination with Africa appears again in *Possessing the Secret of Joy*, where the lives of characters from *The Color Purple* are continued. Her response is enlightened: through Nettie's eyes we see health and white teeth, in a context where Black people are the norm. This is a powerful experience. Nettie also meets imperialism in the form of capitalist development when the village is invaded by railway builders and the Olinka lifestyle is threatened. Sexism is a major issue here too, as it is in the USA. The Olinka practise paternalistic patriarchal ways, the men disempowering as they protect and own the women, an economy which devalues Nettie's freedom.

In *The Color Purple* Walker's imagery of quilting highlights both Black women's creativity and their sisterhood in the face of misrepresentation, abuse and silence. A beautifully crafted quilt in the Smithsonian showed Walker that it is in the everyday creative activities, socially devalued by patriarchy, that she can find work by creative grandmothers whose largely ephemeral craftwork included storytelling, singing in their fieldwork, contributing to the sense of community among Black people. In *The Color Purple* the activity of quilting establishes a sisterly solidarity between several of the oppressed, uneducated women: Celie; Sofia, whose 'uppityness' leads to her incarceration in prison, then more humiliating, virtual imprisonment as the mayor's wife's servant; and Shug Avery, bisexual, fast, colourful and mean night-club singer and

Albert (Mister)'s mistress. These women reject the disempowerment and marginalisation society imposes, and speak out, forming
alliances which free and empower them. Initially Celie advises
Harpo to replicate the oppression meted out to many women by
beating his wife Sofia, then she begins to learn about sisterhood
from Shug, surprising everyone by welcoming rather than rejecting
her husband's mistress. The two women become friends and lovers.
Their lesbian love enables Celie to recognise her own self worth,
and to speak out against Mister's mistreatment, undermining the
basis upon which he maintains his power over her; that of the
necessity of having a relationship with a man to indicate any kind
of worth. A key scene takes place just before she leaves Mister for
Memphis, with Shug:

> Shug say, Albert. Try to think like you got some sense. Why any
> woman give a shit what people think is a mystery to me.
> Well, say Grady, trying to bring light. A woman can't git a man
> if peoples talk.
> Shug look at me and us and giggle. Then us laugh sure nuff.
> Then Squeak start to laugh. Then Sofia. All us laugh and laugh.
> Shug say, Ain't they something?
>
> (Walker, 1983, p. 171)

This liberating laugh changes the course of our reading of *The Color
Purple*, seeing Celie articulate and empowered. Laughing at and
undermining the 'Otherising' of Black people, particularly women,
completely devalues the oppressive hold these beliefs and behaviours have on our minds. Celie and Shug relate like the closeness of
mother and daughter, the closeness of recognition, of similarity. The
lesbian relationship, a challenge to the norms of 'opposites attract',
undermines patriarchal formulations. It is a political and symbolic
act of revolt. The quilt the women make becomes a cooperative
piece stitched with love, appropriately named 'Sister's Choice'.

Identity is a major concern for Black people. In *The Color Purple*,
Squeak, after plucking up courage to act for Sofia, asserts her real
name – Mary Agnes. Her act enables her to claim her own identity.
Through her relationship with Shug, her rejection of her marriage
with Mr...and her self-sufficiency as a maker of a saleable commodity – pants – Celie also finds her own identity. Her growing
appreciation of herself and of living things in the world move her to
consider her relation to God, to whom she has been addressing her

letters for most of the book. She suddenly realises she has envisaged him as the arch white male patriarch:

> the God I been praying and writing to is a man. And act like all the other mens I know. Trifling, forgitful, and lowdown. . . . he big and old and tall and graybearded and white. He wear white robes and go barefooted.   (Walker, 1983, pp. 164/5)

Shug's, then Celie's God is a pantheistic figure, a living spirit in all creation who actually enjoys the celebration of life, so that: 'I think it pisses God off if you walk by the color purple in a field somewhere and don't notice it' (p. 167).

The book is historical, realistic and spiritual, and so it combines realism and the imaginative, confusing some readers. The Utopian ending, with the return of the presumed drowned Nettie and her 'family' of husband and Celie's lost children, was recognised as the stuff of mass-audience dreams by Spielberg in the movie. But the novel actually derives from Utopian African fictional endings, which move away from the constraints of the present and suggest a posit-ive alternative. *The Color Purple* and *The Temple of My Familiar* are written against the dominant white male structural and formal norms for literary production. They are products essentially of Black, politicised, imaginative female folk-culture, and it is against this background, in this context that we need to read them, as Lorraine Bethel points out:

> Women in this country have defied the dominant sexist society by developing a type of folk culture and oral literature based on the use of gender solidarity and female bonding as self affirming rituals. . . . Because Black women rarely gained access to literary expression, this Black women identified bonding and folk culture have often gone unrecorded except through our individual lives and memories.   (Bethel, 1982, p. 179)

The structure, forms and expression of Black women's writing come from their position in the community.

Cora Kaplan suggests that the tale must be seen set against work by Black male writers:

> The utopianism of the Color Purple and its seemingly apolitical model of change as a familial dialectic looks rather less simple

when read as a polemic against the deeply negative imaginary interpretations in Southern Black life in much male Black fiction and autobiography.   (Kaplan, 1986, p. 185)

Spirituality and a sense of the magical, the metaphorical are an important dimension to Walker's writing and, by extension, she suggests, to our lives. In *The Color Purple* an element of the spiritual dimension is the negotiation between the establishment figure of God, and a sense of the need to recognise beauty, harmony and self worth. In many of her other novels, myth and metaphor combine with historical realism to the same ends.

The Temple of My Familiar (1989)

The Temple of My Familiar works on a wide canvas, aligning the experience of African Americans with those of other disinherited, disadvantaged silenced groups including, especially, South American Native Americans. The novel confronts racism and sexism, investigating the legacy of racism before, during and since slavery; charting back through the history of racial oppression to consider Black oppression of Black; the origins of violence among the Pygmies and the Indians; and the origins of sexism. This it does through using memory and myth. Walker's novel explores the memories of various characters, notably Miss Lissie, partner of Uncle Rafe, uncle of one of the protagonists, Sowelo. Miss Lissie represents and physically embodies many women; her diversity an indication of the shifting potential of women. Photographed, she changed on each occasion, representing many different women through time. The exploration of the origins of racism and sexism is articulated in a central myth/ dream scene when Miss Lissie tells of an earlier self, the woman priest who ignored the source of her magic, her feathered familiar. As she succumbed to a white male recording (an actual visitor interviewing her) she lost her powers; the magic disappeared from the temple and from the world. This bright bird escapes, but in the novel the central activity and metaphor of the interweaving of bright bird feathers suggests the interweaving of ostensibly unrelated stories, the intertwining of other textual references and other Walker characters. Zede and Carlotta make and sell cloaks of fine plumage for priests, then for rich rock stars. The creative harmony and cooperation of the essentially female art of quilting is recalled. Barbara Christian notes:

Walker is drawn to the integral and economical process of quilt making as a model for her own craft. For through it, one can create out of seemingly disparate everyday materials patterns of clarity, imagination, and beauty. (Christian, 1984, p. 461)

Both the quilting and the making of feathered robes are signs of communal action, functional and spiritual beauty, challenging convention and suggesting a different kind of radical creative unity.

Essentially, *The Temple of My Familiar*, with its use of race memory, letters, diaries and testimony, explores the origins of racism and sexism, gives voice to the silenced and hidden.

Possessing the Secret of Joy (1992)

'If you lie about your pain you will be killed'

'RESISTANCE IS THE SECRET OF JOY'

Possessing the Secret of Joy is a difficult book to read because of the physical details it contains and the pain it exposes. It has a compelling message about female subordination and collusion in traditionally based male power, which uses myth to mask brutality. Discovering African cultural roots is essential. Walker explores and exposes the political and social complexities of the perpetuation of female circumcision. Her own companion book *Warrior Marks* (1993) helps fill out the picture as does her (1993) *Arena* programme.

There are delicate and difficult issues of cross-cultural writing, opinions and interventions with the book's treatment of a humiliating and potentially fatal ritual, female circumcision or genital mutilation, when the ritual itself is so firmly embedded in another culture's beliefs and practices. For Walker, a very Westernised African American, as for us as readers whatever our position, the critique of an essentially 'tribal' custom can be seen as a form of cultural imperialism.

Possessing the Secret of Joy is a tale told largely by Tashi, who first appeared in *The Color Purple*. It focuses on her reinterpretation of events in her own history from her childhood in the Olinka village in Africa; her political gesture of embracing the customs of her embattled culture; settling in America with her African American husband, Adam, then remembering and reacting. So traumatic are her gradually returning memories of girls maimed by female circumcision, and her own confused and confusing experience of seeking the ritual to assert solidarity with her people, that Tashi needs psychoanalysis to help her reveal, and then heal. Part of her tragedy, however, is that she feels it is essential to take revenge on those who perpetuate and collude with this dangerous and debilitating ritual, based as it is on myths of female disempowerment and male superiority. In her desire to take revenge she seeks out the celebrated national hero, the circumciser herself, M'lissa, and murders her. Walker says Tashi's tale had to be told:

> Tashi... stayed with me, uncommonly tenacious, through the writing of both books, and led me finally to conclude she needed, and deserved, a book of her own.   (Walker, 1992, p. 267)

The story is told largely through Tashi's re-created memories, based on her psychoanalysis by an eminent male doctor (Jung). In recall she understands the dream/myth overheard as the older men discussed controlling women. The myth positions woman as 'Queen Termite', worshipped as vital to the continuation of the community, but rendered powerless and in a static servitude to the drones (males) who appear to be serving her. Tashi's analysis through dream and discussion also emphasises the psychological male dominance embedded in Jungian and Freudian analytical techniques.

Tashi's murder of M'Lissa is a dramatic exorcism for her, making her both the victim and the avenger of the horrors of clitoridectomy. Contemporary French feminist critics and scholars such as Cixous, Kristeva and Irigaray (see Marks and De Courtivron, 1981) point out to us that much male hatred of women is dependent upon their rejection of the 'phallic' or powerful, assertive female, who presents a direct challenge to their power. In *Possessing the Secret of Joy* the myth is the vehicle for an assertion of male power, sanctioned by God:

> At God's approach the termite hill rose up, barring the passage and displaying its masculinity. It was strong as the organ of the stranger, and intercourse could not take place. But God is all-powerful. He cut down the termite hill, and had intercourse with the excised earth.   (Walker, 1992, p. 163)

Here Walker traces among the Olinka the same sort of fears and cultural, myth-based whitewashing noted by the French feminists

Cixous, Irigaray, and Kristeva. Termites and white ants are, of course, not discussed when female circumcision takes place; uncleanness, unnaturalness, and the value a woman must have for her husband, are, however.

Ironically, while women as well as men seek a cultural and political liberation, and a new recognition of their nation land in the twentieth century, their positions are unequal. As Elleke Boehmer points out, the male upholding of national, liberated, cultural values, might not be so welcoming and positive for women:

> gender informs nationalism and nationalism in its turn consolidates and legitimates itself through a variety of political movements . . . the idea of nationhood bears a masculine identity though national ideas may wear a feminine face. (Boehmer, 1991, p. 6)

Tashi's ironic position grows directly out of African culture as expressed, explored and revalued by African and African American women writers. As Gay Wilentz's *Binding Cultures* (1992) so aptly illustrates, writers such as Efua Sutherland, Flora Nwapa and Ama Ata Aidoo expose the same cultural tensions felt by twentieth-century African American women writers. While they wish to write from the community and, by rescuing their cultural history, reinforce the traditions of Africa, they are ironically also reinforcing a subordinate position for themselves. This includes female circumcision, the dominant drive to value women according to their reproductive success, and the maintenance of positions of power within community life which relegate women to second place, keeping them firmly there, bolstered up by reviving the wisdoms of the established myths. Speaking of these African women writers, Wilentz points out some of the tensions:

> The African women see their culture and traditions in both a positive and a negative light – as a life-giving force as well as a restriction of women's rights. (Wilentz, 1992, p. xvii)

Alice Walker, enticed by the need to explore and redefine roots, vividly exposes these gender related contradictions.

Tashi's tale, like Celie's in *The Color Purple*, is a re-creation and revitalisation of the oral literature traditionally passed on by women in Africa. Again, as with Celie, Walker has given voice to the historically and culturally silenced woman through the use of the oral testifying akin to the slave narratives. This is partly achieved by bringing an older Tashi into later twentieth-century America, and through the cultural changes of taking a new name, Evelyn, and living as Adam's wife in a modern city. Walker further empowers her character. Tashi can be expected to become articulate and aware as she acclimatises herself to the rush of the modern, but in herself she combines both the awareness and voice of the *African American*, and the history and experiences of the *African* woman. Tashi bridges that cultural gap, as she bridges the geographical. She embodies and concretises the ironies this exposes: that American racism is based on a simplistic, stereotypical version of the Black woman as the same everywhere. Bringing Tashi into America highlights the critique Walker makes, i.e. that African tribal cultures are driven by the same kind of patriarchal deceptions, power games and culturally infused myths as those operating in America. Arrogance and blindness fuel incomprehension and pain.

One of the central questions of the novel, a kind of mythic conundrum, is about the secret of joy, itself used as an argument by white people to excuse any maltreatment of Black people. It is an argument based on racist assumptions, that Black women are 'natural', to be used like any 'natural resource'. This excuse enables its perpetrators to ignore difference as a basis for equality. Joy is being used here to denote a kind of natural strength in the face of suffering, a salving 'joy' which excuses racism and its evils. Walker herself, of course, when heavy handed, can be accused of preaching. Here she uses a deliberate mixture of a weighty/hallowed and community oriented, chatty tone to critique the origins and results of a racist, sexist misuse of myth.

Mythologising is central to Walker's writing. In *The Temple of My Familiar* the myths and anecdotes she revives are those of Earth mother, Mother Africa, and female goddesses. She:

> sings threnodies over the destruction of the ancient matriarchal worship of Africa: history in Walker's representation achieves meaning insofar as her characters become either avatars or acolytes to the composite, omni-benevolent 'Africa/Mother/Goddess'. (Boehmer, 1991, p. 4)

A celebration of Mother Africa might occur in the earlier novels, but recent work is more paradoxical. The Olinka society colludes to wipe out any image of woman as sexually equal, aware of herself. Africans, villagers, mothers and men erase these traces of a female life force.

In her novels and semi-autobiographical works, Walker provides an alternative version of Black womanhood based on a deconstruction of white racism, Black male sexism, and commodity relations. She has her characters speak of the unspeakable with hope, since what was positive or creative in the past could come again. Her works are powerful, insightful and supportive of a creative sisterhood in opposition to the oppressions maintained and legitimated as a result of racism and sexism.

Part II
Writing by Women from Post-Colonial Contexts

5

Caribbean Women's Writing

[T]here exists among the women of the Caribbean a need for a naming of experience and a need for communal support in that process. In the past silence has surrounded this experience.

(Sistren, 1986, p. xv)

We never saw ourselves in a book, so we didn't exist in a kind of way in our culture and environment, our climate, the plants around us did not seem real, did not seem to be of any importance – we overlooked them entirely. The real world was what was in books.

(Dabydeen, 1988, p. 78)

This chapter explores a brief history of the Caribbean, concentrating on women's roles and writing and sketching in cultural contexts. It moves on to consider the important influence of the work of Jean Rhys, a white Caribbean Creole writer whose *Wide Sargasso Sea* (1966) encouraged interest in Caribbean writing. Several key women writers are discussed, including Louise Bennett, Pamela Mordecai, Lorna Goodison, Marlene Nourbese Philip, Jean 'Binta' Breeze, Jamaica Kincaid and Erna Brodber.

The very term Caribbean (instead of West Indies, the colonial term) is itself an ideological one which indicates a desire to reclaim and restore a voice and identity, traced as :

a desire to decolonize and idigenize imaginatively and to claim a voice for history, a geography and a people who had been dominated by British Victorians – both literally and literarily. Certainly this desire to reclaim and restore alter/native cultural traditions has been a prime motivating factor for many Caribbean writers throughout the twentieth century.   (Donnell and Lawson Welsh, 1996, p. 4)

Identity and finding a voice are important in the English-speaking Caribbean. Women writers explore motherlands, mother tongues, oral storytelling and poetry, nation language, Jamaican language, women's experiences and the importance of telling tales of individuals' lives. It is with Jean Breeze's work that oral performance poetry is discussed in particular, offering, as it does, a chance to hear and see a dramatic representation of examples of the kind of lives of Jamaican women in the everyday kind of language they would use themselves.

INTRODUCTION – IDENTIFYING THE WOMEN WRITERS, DEFINING ISSUES

In considering the writing of the Caribbean we concentrate, here, on the English-speaking Caribbean, including: Jamaica, St Lucia, Grenada, Trinidad, Tobago, Dominica, Antigua, Guyana and other parts colonised by the British. There are many other islands colonised by other European countries, not considered here, such as Cuba, Haiti and Martinique, for example.

Caribbean writing by women is a rich vein brought directly over to the UK where many women writers have visited or settled. Divisions and choices in a book are difficult, but it has been particularly problematic to decide exactly where to 'place' writing by women such as Amryl Johnson, Jean 'Binta' Breeze, Merle Collins, Valerie Bloom and Grace Nichols, whose work is popular and has been published and/or performed both in the UK and the Caribbean. For the most part, I have included in this chapter novelists who remain in the Caribbean, and poets, whether living there or in the UK (Jean 'Binta' Breeze), Canada (Marlene Nourbese Phillip), or elsewhere, whose contribution to the development of oral performance poetry and a politicised focus on the vernacular tradition springs initially from their engagement with Caribbean culture in situ. I hope my rather hesitant decisions will not offend, and indeed, this chapter should be read alongside that on Black British writing (Chapter 12), to further enable consideration of the oral performance poets, in particular.

One of the problems that Caribbean/British women writers have experienced about publication in the past has been a refusal of the 'establishment' press to recognise their work in anthologies of British writing (except for *The New British Poetry*, 1988, where a Black British section is edited by Fred D'Aguiar). The overlap here is a deliberate attempt to remedy that exclusion and to indicate the rich cross-fertilisation between our cultures. Some of my choices here are also to do with where, how and when I met these writers and their work. It is also to do with space so that each can have as full a treatment as possible. Finally, choices are sometimes linked to publication in Cobham and Collins (eds), *Watchers and Seekers: Creative Writing by Black Women in Britain* (1987), one of several of the flowering of books recognising Black women's writing published in the 1980s. Merle Collins, Grace Nichols, Amryl Johnson and Valerie Bloom, all of Caribbean origin and living in Britain, will largely be discussed in the Black British chapter, although Jean Breeze could well appear there too.

Some of the issues which are uppermost in our consideration of writing by women from the English-speaking Caribbean are centred around mothering and mother tongue. These are politicised writers who spring from an established oral tradition, strong women who speak out against the sufferings of their foremothers and the economic difficulties of the present day. The choice of language used reflects not only the origins of the writers but deliberate statements about their relationship to the language of the colonisers and to the everyday language spoken at home. Issues of language choice are important in the expression of identity and nationhood as well as in the desire to depict the lives of everyday people and the ways in which they would express themselves. Their interests also centre on identity and relationships, mothering and motherhood.

Merle Collins, citing Jamaica Kincaid's *Annie John* (1985), Merle Hodge's *Crick Crack Monkey* (1970), Zee Edgell's *Beka Lamb* (1982) and Lorna Goodison's poem *I am Becoming my Mother* (1986), notes the similarity of themes and the importance of women's relationships in both prose and poetry:

> In much of the writing by Caribbean women, the women play a central role in passing on values to young people, either because men have absconded, or because, even when they are there, the women are the ones who concern themselves with such communication. Their relationships between mother and daughter, aunt and niece or guardian and child is a recurring one in Caribbean women's writing.   (Merle Collins, 1988, p. 20)

And:

> For the Caribbean woman, the notion of a motherland is espe-
> cially complex, encompassing in its connotations her island home
> and its unique culture as well as the body of tropes, talismans and
> female bonding that is a woman's heritage through her own and
> her mothers. The land and one's mothers, then, are co-joined.
> (Morris and Dunn, 1991, p. 219)

Women's identity is initially formed through bonding and identifying with the mother, while male identity comes about through
separation. Jean Rhys, Michelle Cliff and Jamaica Kincaid all stress
the importance (and some of the problems) of the mother–daughter
bond, and its nurturing relation to the mother land.

THE HISTORY AND CONTEXT OF WOMEN'S WRITING FROM THE CARIBBEAN

Only relatively recently has there been any major interest in the
literature of the Caribbean, partly due to the fact that the Caribbean
islands are widely dispersed and different, but mainly due to the
difficulties of the domination of colonial literary expression. As the
process of decolonisation continues, the growth of a national identity
(see Frantz Fanon, 1952; 1967, chapter 1) becomes highly important,
particularly in such a geographically divided region. In the pre-1950
period, 'West Indian' as a term indicated a shared experience of
colonial rule, while during the 1950s the term began to represent a
search for a unified regional identity (Blackman, 1949, p. 7; Hearne,
1950, p. 6) and the shortlived West Indian Federation was established in the early 1960s. However, nationalism replaced this as different islands sought independence. Subsequently, the ideologically
conscious term Caribbean has gained acceptance, suggesting a *range*
of experiences and identities and a range of literary production, 'it is
more suggestive of a literature freed from the (re-)centring tenden-
cies of a colonial and Commonwealth framework' (Donnell and Lawson Welsh, 1996, p. 6). Recognition of Caribbean identity is explored
and expressed in and through literature, music and the other arts.

   Historically, the plantation economy produced a multi-racial society. The original Indian inhabitants were not suited to plantation
work so slaves were brought from Africa, and when slavery was

abolished and emancipation began, they were replaced by Asian contract workers. (The abolition of the slave trade occurred in 1807 and the abolition of slavery about 30 years later.) Emancipation did not bring overnight change in terms of the great social gulf between European and African populations and there was little social mobility for free but unskilled Afro-Caribbeans. North American industrialisation entered their lives, demanding skilled workers for oil refineries and bauxite works. Some trained and worked there while others found employment on sugar and banana plantations, in ports or on the Panama Canal. Jamaica achieved self-government in 1944, Trinidad and Tobago in 1962. Bermuda, Britain's oldest colony, rejected Independence in 1995. Impoverished governments did little to improve the infrastructure of their countries and Independence from colonial rule has not necessarily removed the colonial-like controls and effects of the multinationals and of the strong economies of the First World (particularly, in this geographical location, the US and UK).

Still, today, there are distinctions in relation to skin colour and between the international urban community and the poorer classes in slums and rural areas. This polarisation has considerably affected women. Historically, as in the plantations of America, bi-racial women sought a route of improvement through 'passing' as white, and were seen as a threat to European women incarcerated in colonial houses – a prison of Victorian conventions. Erotic rivalry was likely to make these women enemies, not colleagues. In the Caribbean, family patterns which differed from those in the United States, grew up in relation to work. The men had to go away to work, leaving behind partners and families, so a tradition grew of women remaining at home in women-only communities, living on very little money. Rural and slum Black women acted as both parents and were hard working and long suffering, tough, different from the assimilated Black women in the urban situation. Merle Collins sees the issue of colour as one common to many Caribbean women writers. She notes that Caribbean women writing in the UK comment more on race and racism whilst in the Caribbean they are interested in 'shadism' – the shade of colour someone is in relation to their social standing:

> There is, therefore in the poetry and prose written by Caribbean women in Britain a much more overt focus on the theme of race. The Caribbean is more concerned with the 'shadism', the 'pass fe white' phenomenon written of by Louise Bennett in the 1960s.

In England, where racial slurs are an everyday occurrence, the Black woman finds it necessary to claim her identity in a way not considered necessary to the woman in the Caribbean where the woman thinks of herself as *woman* and not as *Black woman*, because there is not the constant presence of a large racist white community. The result is that there is more of a focus on the theme of class and the claim to power of a black or brown middle class. (Collins, 1988, p. 22)

The Development of Women's Writing

Caribbean writers have a difficult task in the face of widespread illiteracy, particularly among women. Writers grow up in a small cultural group exchanging and commenting on each other's work. This fosters development but reduces influence from the outside world. Consequently, much literary production from Caribbean writers, particularly women, has been seen to be limited critically. Mineke Schipper defines some of the ways in which cultural differences lead to the critical dismissal of women writers in particular, saying:

the authors of these works are dependent on the European book market, where literary critics take exception to their 'Caribbean style', which is rather free with the accepted rules of grammar. When these writers attempt to express their experiences in their own way, the wording they choose is often overly emotional. Though they are writing in the European language, their emotional choice of words serves to emphasise precisely those characteristics which are typical of the Caribbean. (Schipper, 1985, p. 172)

In Europe, Caribbean women writers' work is critically acclaimed but, until relatively recently, they had little position or recognition at home.

'Shadism', an interest in being pale coupled with the establishment (particularly in Havana) of women activists concerned with equality, encouraged the development of a version of the female 'mulatto' – beautiful, powerful, essentially tragic – for whom race and appearance were a route to social success, and a problem both culturally and socially. In their novels, Marise Conde and Sonia Schwartz Bart, from Guadeloupe, represent the tragedy of the bi-racial woman, while Astrid Roemer of Surinam challenges colour and class issues and represents bi-racial women in a more positive light. Jean Rhys is a famous Caribbean writer who uses the figure of the tragic bi-racial woman in her great work *Wide Sargasso Sea* (1966) (see below).

POLITICAL INTERESTS AND INVOLVEMENT
MORE RECENTLY – PHYLLIS SHAND ALLFREY, JEAN RHYS, AND MERLE HODGE'S *CRICK CRACK MONKEY*

Women's fiction and poetry have a shorter history than that of the male writers (C. L. R. James, Ralph de Boissiere, more recently Derek Walcott) although a rich oral culture was maintained through women storytellers. Most Caribbean women writers have only been publishing in any significant volume since the 1970s and 80s, with the notable exceptions of Louise Bennett (b. 1919, see below) the performance poet, and Phyllis Shand Allfrey (Dominica and the US) whose novel *The Orchid House* (1953) considers the way of life and emotions of the older Black woman. Notable writers include Olive Senior (Commonwealth Writers' Prize, 1987), Lorna Goodison (Commonwealth Poetry Prize for the Caribbean region, 1986), Merle Hodge, Jean Rhys, Una Marson (Jamaica) and Barbara Ferland (Jamaica). Political activism and ideological connectedness are notable in the work of Marson whose interest in language started to establish Jamaican English as a 'nation language' for writers.

In the 1980s women started to be published in greater numbers, building on their feminist activism and personal involvement in the political and cultural developments of the Caribbean. Erna Brodber, Jamaica Kincaid, Beryl Gilroy and Susan Cambridge are notable novelists, and drama emerged from the working-class drama collective Sistren (Jamaica), who produced *Lionheart Gal: Life Stories of Jamaican Women* (1986). While, earlier in the twentieth century, modernism was enabling for Black men, who transferred the power of utterance from the coloniser to the male colonised, its formal experimentation did not, however, liberate doubly burdened women writers. They have, latterly, turned to the narrative structure of post-modernism – to fragmentation, intertextuality, parody, and doubling, locating gender differences as a site for representing and reconstructing new identities. One way in which women Caribbean writers reject the notion of a subject defined by the dominant patriarchal culture is to produce a shifting subject at odds with dominant language – they experiment with language, producing, as Teresa de Lauretis puts it: 'a multiple, shifting, and often self contradictory identity, a subject that is not divided in, but rather at odds with language' (1986, p. 14).

The Influence and Legacy of Jean Rhys

Jean Rhys was a highly influential Caribbean writer. She was born on Dominica in 1890, left in 1907, and died in 1979, never having returned. Her works include: *The Left Bank and Other Stories* (1927), *Quartet* (1928), *After Leaving Mr Mackenzie* (1931), *Wide Sargasso Sea* (1966), *Sleep It Off Lady* (1976) and *Smile Please* (1981).

The casual reader interested in the Caribbean would most probably have come into initial contact with literature about the Islands through the writing of Jean Rhys. Her sequel to Charlotte Brontë's *Jane Eyre* (1847) – *Wide Sargasso Sea* (1966) – is a starting point for investigating the invisibility of Caribbean writers and the experiences of their peoples. *Jane Eyre* represents a notorious fissure in literature. Bertha Mason, Rochester's mad first wife, connotes the repressed sexuality of nineteenth-century England, designated mad because she is the unknown and uncontrollable. As a Creole, however, she would probably be of mixed race and, as such, her presence represents the whole, complex lumber of society's simultaneous attraction for, and repulsion from the sexualised woman. She is 'Other', woman as nature: powerful, alluring, dangerous, out of control, to be repressed, finally to be destroyed, the dark side of our nature; woman as attractive, passionate, red in tooth and claw, fatal. In Brontë's text Bertha is Jane's alter ego whom she must come to terms with and overcome, in order to relate to Rochester. Bertha is not entirely white (certainly not an English rose) and powerfully passionate (see Gilbert and Gubar's *The Madwoman in the Attic*, 1979, which examines the pathology of nineteenth-century England through her figure). Rhys takes the figure of Bertha and enables the silenced Black woman to speak through Antoinette, the name with which she was born, before Rochester took her over, translated her, confined her, contributed to the destruction of her sense of reality, and called her Bertha, renaming and redefining her. His next move was to ship her to England and incarcerate her in the attic from which she only escaped to hurl herself from the roof in flames and die. Rochester, a second son, has no inheritance, so must marry for money. Marrying hereditarily mentally ill Creole heiresses was not uncommon in those post-slavery days. Jamaica's vibrant colours, and Antoinette's vibrant passion, her difference, her resorting to 'obeah' (magic) to encourage him to develop his love for her, rapidly estrange and disgust him. For Rhys, this novel enabled an exploration of several issues: British inheritance of the legacy of slavery; British racism; and the close linking of representation of the sexualised Other (Creole woman and Black West Indian women) with issues of women's marginalisation and subordination specifically in relation to Black or bi-racial women.

For nineteenth-century England, involvement in the slave trade and wealth produced by the colonial sugar plantations was rarely discussed in the drawing room. Rochester's family income rested upon the labour of slaves in the West Indies (as did Sir Thomas Bertram's in Jane Austen's *Mansfield Park*, 1814). Slavery was a dark secret. So too was the migration and channelling of sexual energies of the colonisers. Colonialism has been recognised by many critics as a way of exporting excess sexual energies, testified to in travel writing of the nineteenth century, which represents the landscapes of Africa and the West Indies as fertile women to be overcome and tamed (see references to 'Mother Africa' in Chapter 6). Colonial landscapes and colonised women represented fertility and wildness to be enjoyed, controlled, plundered and rendered silent. Rhys here, as in other works, investigates the ways in which race, difference and gender affect women's lives.

Literary Production – Who Are the Women Writers?

Caribbean life is a complex interaction of cultures and lifestyles, and race is an important topic in women's writing. The majority of Caribbean writers are of African descent and identify with this cultural inheritance, but there are also writers of Indian and Chinese descent, and Creoles: 'the writers who are most involved with oral performance are strongest in their attachment to particular Creole forms' (Savory, 1989, p. 33). Overseas women write of life on the islands as well as their own sociocultural-specific contexts. Writers use different island dialects, some switching between versions of Creole and international English. Women in particular find it difficult to negotiate the roles of mother/partner/daughter and writer:

> Caribbean women who want to write scarcely ever have an easy time in sustaining a literary career of the kind the major male writers have experienced.... This is for the very obvious reason that the majority of women writers of Caribbean origins have

domestic and family responsibilities as well as an obligation to earn a living (and frequently have to raise their children alone. (Savory, 1989, p. 31)

While Rhys's second husband, Lesley, supported her writing, for Caribbean women, marriage and childbearing often take precedence, and 'the history of Caribbean male writing is also largely a history of female support for it' (Savory, 1989, pp. 31, 32), a support not normally reciprocated. Elaine Savory also comments on parental fears that writing might indicate madness, a fear which often prompts the burning of their daughters' writing. However, political activism and community involvement have fuelled women's writing.

Sistren

The Sistren Theatre Collective is a phenomenon which has grown from the community to respond, reflect and encourage reflection about the lives of ordinary women: 'they are not just playing roles, they are living it. They expose in their dramatic art the realty of their own daily lives and those of their people' (Thomas, 1986, p. 15). The Sistren Theatre Collective began in 1977 as a group of women in a special employment programme. As the group, a mixture of Black and white Caribbean women, grew, they included women with specific cultural skills. They develop their material from real life. *Sweet Sugar Rage*, for example, is based on the lives of women sugar workers. They brought this piece to the city, used improvisation and role play with audience participation, and made it into a film. Sistren have written plays celebrating hidden heroes, and against nuclear arms testing. Their work is socially, culturally and politically engaged and involves people working on materials they have unearthed in relation to colonial policy about women from the 1930s onwards. *Lionheart Gal* (1986) was aided by Honor Ford-Smith, who transcribed along with Sistren, setting up interviews, and a structure, with them; producing a collection of biographies of all the members of the group and of others, both real and typical, written in Caribbean English, embodying the history and mixture of Caribbean peoples. It goes to the heart of how Caribbean women originated and live:

> It is likely to be the most frank and from-the-heart account of the things that our women do not even dare to remember and think, much less to publish! (Thomas, 1986, p. 19)

Humour and historical, mythical and real-life stories can be closely identified with. Motherhood, domestic service, family violence and abuse, and a search for economic independence in an unequal society are popular themes. As Merle Collins notes of them, anyone seeing their performance would have:

> the sensation of sharing in the lives of women who have been held within the grip of poverty, alienated by a brutal neo-colonial political system, brutalised by the police who also brutalise their men, who in turn brutalise them. Their stories are those of women who have learnt to confront life with the same toughness with which it has confronted them, who want love and tenderness and caring but have learnt to carve a niche which ensures their survival in an unyielding atmosphere. Their experiences have given the strength and resilience which make life possible even when it continues to be a constant struggle. (Collins, 1988, p. 20)

A similar sense of community is explored by Olive Senior in such short story collections as *Summer Lightning and Other Stories* (1987) and *Arrival of the Snake Woman, and Other Stories* (1989).

NOVELISTS: MERLE HODGE, JAMAICA KINCAID AND ERNA BRODBER

Merle Hodge, *Crick Crack Monkey* (1970)

Crick Crack Monkey marks a crucial transition from nationalist to post-colonialist writing. It was the first novel by a Caribbean woman to problematise and question notions of difference and quest for voice in a social context that denied social cohesion to the colonised self, cutting it off from liberating forms of self-expression. The idea of establishing a voice against the dominant plantation-owning society is important in a slave or ex-slave culture.

Jamaica Kincaid, *Annie John* (1985)

Annie John charts the growing up of an intelligent young girl, presenting the world from her point of view. Although successful in school, she is no conformist and thus constantly gets into trouble for her rather naively politicised, radical responses. At home, her mother is seen by the adolescent as an aggressor and a spy who 'had suddenly turned into a crocodile' (1997 [1985] p. 84), set against Annie John's growing deceptions, which are largely unimportant (playing marbles instead of studying, walking home a different way, visiting girlfriends). With the passions of love/friendships with first Gwen then 'the Red Girl', she becomes wilder, and is suddenly removed to another island. Each friendship develops her, but must remain largely secret. The point of view changes as she grows, developing from a fear of dying when surrounded by cemeteries and funerals, to adolescent change and distance from her mother, who seems one person in company and another, suspiciously hostile, when alone. The mother/daughter bond is closely scrutinised. It limits and forms Annie John's personality:

> Something I could not name just came over us, and suddenly I had never loved anyone so or hated anyone so, but to say hate – what did I mean by that? Before, if I hated someone I simply wished the person dead. But I couldn't wish my mother dead. If my mother died, what would become of me. I wouldn't imagine my life without her. Worse than that, if my mother died I would have to die too, and even less than I could imagine my mother dead could I imagine myself dead.   (Kincaid, 1997 [1985], p. 88)

Annie John also challenges racism and colonialism through questioning received versions of history, demonising Columbus and transferring a phrase about her grandfather:

> When I next saw the picture of Columbus sitting there all locked up in his chains, I wrote under it the words: The Great Man Can No Longer Just Get Up and Go.   (Kincaid, 1997 [1985], p. 78)

Punished as a radical, Annie John derives her enlightened view from questioning history, identifying the cruel appropriation of her people. She feels none of this would have happened in reverse: her own ancestors would have supported the Europeans' rights to different ways, rather than trying to enslave and change them. Comparing herself to the white girl Ruth, who always sees herself and her ancestors as in the wrong, Annie John feels:

> We could look everybody in the eye. For our ancestors had done nothing wrong except just sit somewhere, defenceless. Of course,

sometimes, what with our teachers and our blood ties, it was hard for us to tell on which side we really now belonged – with the masters or the slaves – for it was all history, it was all in the past, and everybody behaved differently now.... But we, the descendants of the slaves, knew quite well what had really happened, and I was sure that if the tables had been turned we would have acted differently; I was sure that if our ancestors had gone from Africa to Europe and come upon the Europeans, living there, they would have taken a proper interest in the Europeans on first seeing them, and said 'How novel', and then got them to tell their friends about it.   (Kincaid, 1997 [1985], p. 76)

At the end of the novel she sails away, as her mother had left her own home, embarking on a new life and a job, with her own things in her own trunk. It is a voyage through childhood and adolescence, one with which we can all identify, and which is also explicitly that of a Caribbean girl.

Erna Brodber, *Jane and Louisa Will Soon Come Home* (1988)

Erna Brodber's novel is a marvellous post-modernist piece utilising different writing forms and traditions to give a voice to women with differing experiences, distinct from others' versions of their lives:

> Erna Brodber's narrative method exemplifies the interpenetration of scribal and oral literary forms: a modernist, stream of consciousness narrative holds easy dialogue with the traditional teller of tales, the transmitter of Anansi story, proverb, folk song and dance. The casual centrality of the 'supernatural' in Brodber's fiction is also an excellent example of the writer's adaptation of marginalised thematic concepts from the oral tradition which she legitimises in the very process of 'writing them up'.   (Cooper, 1993, p. 3)

In *Jane and Louisa Will Soon Come Home* Brodber chooses to use the novel, a bourgeois construct, as a medium to question the hegemony of the language in which she writes, disrupting the tenets of the genre as modernists do. (See Ann Morris and Margaret M. F. Dunn, 'The Bloodstream of Our Inheritance: Female Identity and the Caribbean Mothers' Land', in Nasta, *Motherlands*, 1991.)

WOMEN POETS: FINDING SELF AND VOICE FOR THE
COLONIAL SUBJECT

Motherlands – Mother Tongue

Caribbean writers are often seen as the inheritors of Caliban (Shake-speare's *The Tempest*) because internalising language brought by Europeans warped the ways in which they thought and felt. English is a language which Marlene Nourbese Philip says 'has sought to deny us' (Philip, 1989, p. 85). The difference between a classical educa-tion – credentialled language – and the non-credentialled language spoken locally made some seem privileged and others barbarians. Lamming and others have attempted to disrupt the colonial langu-age with its claims to linguistic and cultural superiority. There are two main trends in Caribbean poetry – the more classical, literary, and the oral.

The Caribbean is rich in women poets, many of whom also write and live in Britain. They include Louise Bennett (b. 1919, Jamaica); Lorna Goodison (b. 1947); Pamela Mordecai (b. 1942); Valerie Bloom (b. 1956); Grace Nichols (b. 1950, Guyana); Jean 'Binta' Breeze, Elean Thomas and Vivian Usherwood (Jamaica); Merle Collins (Grenada); Amryl Johnson (Trinidad); Gabriella Pearse (Columbia); and Bar-bara Burford (UK). Historically, there are several women poets who have influenced the development and celebration of mother tongue or nation language. Most of these are also performance poets. Miss Lou (Louise Bennett) was the first to formally and deliberately use the mother tongue in her performance poetry. Lorna Goodison and Marlene Nourbese Philip explicitly explore issues around national identity and the use of mother tongue. In considering the work of women poets here we will concentrate on the issues of mother tongue and, most importantly, of orality and performance poetry, looking specifically at Jean 'Binta' Breeze. It is useful to compare Caribbean oral performance poetry with the oral literatures of other countries such as Africa (Chapters 6 and 7) and the Aboriginal culture of Australia (Chapter 10).

Miss Lou (Louise Bennett) (born Jamaica, 1919)

Miss Lou is of middle-class urban origins. It was not until the post-independence seventies that she was rightly recognised, given the title 'Honourable'. Poetry which speaks for and about ordinary, often rural poor people, and uses colloquial language, is deliberately chosen by Louise Bennett, who persisted with 'Anancy' and 'Auntie Roachy' and 'boonoonoonoos' and 'parangle san ting', when she could have opted for more elevated language, that of the colonisers. Her instincts were that she should use the language of her people. The consequence was that for years (since 1936) she performed her work in crowded village halls across the island, but until 1945 could get nothing accepted by the *'Gleaner'*, the oldest established newspaper.

Bennett is a folklorist and performer, deriving much from oral tradition, using stories, proverbs, street chants, children's games and language, voices, intonation, idioms, anecdotes, irony, often in discussions or letters mostly from women, commenting on everyday social and domestic life. Her work employs monologues and dialogues, self-ironising and celebratory expression. Mikey Smith, the performance poet, called her the mother of dub poetry. Her pioneering use of 'nation language' has been augmented by later women poets with a more political tone, and the collective sharing and oral delivery is crucial.

Bennett uses specific personae, often country women travelling to the rather confusing city, which offers fantastic possibilities but excludes or ridicules them. She uses oral literature's techniques – specifically Jamaican proverbs:

> My Aunt Roachy saeh dat Jamaica people have a whole heap a Culture an tradition an Birthright dat han dung to dem from generation to generation. All like de great philosophy of we Jamaica proverbs – dem. Mmmm. (Bennett, in Morris (ed.), 1983, p. 49)

Some of her proverbs are metaphorical, others may be literal statements to educate. She uses the oral tradition's repetition and alliteration, mnemonic devices to aid memory and the power of the proverb (see Walter Ong, in *Orality and Literacy* (1982). In his Introduction to Louise Bennett's *Selected Poems* (1983), Mervyn Morris emphasises the written and oral elements of her poetry:

> Louise Bennett's art is both oral and scribable; the forms are not mutually exclusive. The poem in print is, however, fully available only when readers are in touch with the oral and other cultural contexts the words imply. (Morris, 1983, p. 2)

Rex Nettleford's Introduction to Louise Bennett's *Jamaica Labrish* (1966) warns against underestimating her artistry:

> Those who indulge her rumbustious abandon and spontaneous inducement of laughter will sometimes forget that behind the exuberance and carefree stance, there are years of training – formal and informal – as well as this artist's own struggles to share an idiom whose limitations as a bastard tongue are all too evident. (Nettleford, 1966, quoted in Cooper, 1993, p. 40)

Of the creation of personae, especially 'Aunty Roachy' and the 'doing' of dialect, Bennett comments that people didn't take her seriously:

> From the beginning, nobody ever recognised me as a writer. Well, she is doing 'dialect': it wasn't even writing you know. Up to now a lot of people don't even think I write.   (Interview with Scott, in Markham (ed.), 1989, p. 46)

Part of her legitimising has been to do with writing down. Bennett affirms nativist aesthetic values and the sociopolitical contradictions of Jamaica's history. Her own reading was the English Romantic poets but her ear listened to the people around her, and she discovered and developed a way to record idiomatic, colloquial speech. Commenting on Jamaican proverbs and the dictionary rendition of them, she says:

> Dem-deh is we ole time Jamaica proverbs, an dem got principles gorvernin thoughts an conducts an morals ab-n character, like what dictionary seh. So doan cry dem dung, for what is fi-yuh cyaaan be un-fi-yuh.   (Bennett, in Morris (ed.), 1983, pp. 49, 50)

Louise Bennett uses personae to present a wide variety of women's lives and points of view but chief amongst these is the 'cunny Jamaica Oman' – the crafty cunning woman:

> That cunning Jamaican woman, celebrated and satirised with equal gusto in Louise Bennett's ample corpus, is a composite character – an aggregation of the multiple personae employed by Bennett the ventriloquist, to cover the lives of representative Jamaican women of all social classes. This multifarious heroine–victim of

Bennett's comic/satirical sketches presents us with a diversity of social class values and behaviours that attests to the verisimilitude of Bennett's detailed portraiture. (Morris (ed.), 1993, p. 47)

She gives us market traders like the 'South Parade Peddler', trying to get a sale and abusing a customer even as she is moved on, a lively street figure typical of those found in Jamaica, and now in the markets of London. Amryl Johnson takes up this locale and exchange (see Chapter 5). Louise Bennett reproduces the texture and richness of Jamaican yard and street life, the front porch and the street exchanges between people (also see African American women writers, Chapters 2, 3, 4), representing their enmities and loyalties, those who leave and return, long-standing relationships and crises. In several poems she deals with marriage, for example that following the 30-year courtship of the now toothless, white-haired bride and groom, or sudden, mass, forced marriages.

She was neither represented in collections (for example *Focus*) nor asked to a Poetry League of Jamaica meeting because people thought she would speak in dialect. (Established in 1923, the Poetry League of Jamaica called attention to poetry with a *Year Book*, meetings and prizes, but by the 1930s it had become a little outdated in relation to some of the poetic developments, particulary oral developments.)

At about this time I began to wonder why more of our poets and writers were not taking more of an interest in the kind of language usage and the kind of experiences of living which were all around us, and writing in this medium of dialect instead of writing in the same old English about Autumn and things like that.

For too long it was considered not respectable to use the dialect. Because there was a social stigma attached to the kind of person who used dialect habitually. Many people still do not accept the fact that for us there are many things which are best said in the language of the 'common man'. (Interview with Scott, in Markham, 1989, pp. 47 and 49)

There is both a serious social intent and humour behind her work. Her version of identity is a working-class one, at odds with the middle-class Jamaica Federation of Women satirised in 'Bans O'Ooman!' which attempted to unite all women but only temporarily had space for the working class defined in Bennett's description as 'suspended'. In 'Jamaica Oman' (1983 [1966]) she dramatises the lively confrontational/amusing spiritedness of the cunny/cunning woman, and cites as the archetype the mythical Nanny figure who turned and bared her bottom at the troops' bullets to show defiance and disdain. The irony is that the Jamaica woman is actually powerful and liberated even though neither her men nor the colonisers are aware of this:

> Jamaica oman cunnay, sah!
> Is how dem jinnal so?
> Look how long dem liberated
> An de man dem never know!
> (Bennett, 'Jamaica Oman', 1983 [1966], p. 30)

The streetwise Jamaican woman is 'coaxin/fambly budget from explode', working side by side with, but refusing to be treated as a man, ensuring that she 'gwan like pants-suit is a style'.

Bennett is also articulate on the subject of origins and roots, colonialism and identity, using the lively ironic and realistic tones in both 'Back to Africa' (1983 [1966]) and 'Colonisation in Reverse' (1983 [1966]). In 'Back to Africa' she talks to one of her characters, Miss Mattie, about seeking her African roots. She points out that 'between yuh an de Africans / Is great resemblance' because her grandmother's side is reputedly from Africa, but Jamaica is such a mixture of races and cultures that in her family tree she can count English, French and Jewish also. Recognise that your roots are Jamaican, she advises, and then you can travel but at least return to where you are really from after such periods away:

> Back to Africa, Miss Mattie?
> Yuh no Know what yuh dah seh?
> Yuh haffi some from somewhere fus
> Before yuh go back deh!

In 'Colonisation in Reverse' she jokes about the ironic reversal, the rush to travel to England caused by Independence and cheap flights. The simple-minded sounding narrator/persona focuses on gossip and stereotype as well as straightforward record and highlights the recognition that colonisation in reverse is a neat irony. Settling in England as motherland is an impetus driven by the desire to 'get a big-time job / an settle in de motherlan' while they will possibly end up on the dole. Even those who 'doan like travel' are intent on going just to show how they are loyal to the Empire, as if their travel were both to a promised land, and a gift to England. This highlights her ironic recognition that Jamaicans, who emigrate to many parts of the world (late nineteenth century to Panama, elsewhere in Central America, Haiti, Cuba, Africa, then USA/Canada and to the UK and Europe from the late 1940s), have not always been welcomed:

> What a joyful news, Miss Mattie;
> Ah feel like me heart gwine burs –
> Jamaica people colonizin
> Englan in reverse.
>
> they 'tun history upsid dung!' intent
> Fi immigrate an populat
> De seat a de Empire

Bennett collected folklore work all over Jamaica, won a Black Caribbean scholarship to RADA, produced a Caribbean radio play for the BBC and became a drama specialist for the Jamaica Social Welfare Commission upon her return in 1955. *Jamaica Labrish* (1966) is her most famous collection, and her Selected Works came out in 1983.

Lloyd Brown notes in *West Indian Poetry* (1978) that her characters seem independent of the author's experience:

The woman's experience which so clearly dominates her work remains, paradoxically, unobtrusive rather than explicitly reiterated. No other West Indian writers had dealt at greater length with the West Indian woman. And in no other writer has the world of the Jamaican (and the West Indies as a whole) been presented almost exclusively through the eyes of women, especially the rural women and the poorer women of the city.   (Lloyd Brown, 1978, p. 30)

LANGUAGE AND IDENTITY: MOTHER TONGUE, MOTHERING, MOTHERHOOD

One of the most significant linguistic issues relating to Caribbean women's writing is the ability to use a number of overlapping tongues and the necessity to be understood outside of this society as well as within it to be accessible. Merle Collins comments:

> Throughout the Caribbean, people are more familiar with local languages influenced in some cases by the South American Indian heritage, together with various African language structures and the dynamic development of working language.   (Collins, 1988, p. 19)

The language spoken in Jamaica is Standard English, but most Jamaicans speak Jamaican Creole, a Creole of English lexicon which everyone in the speech community understands. Because of the lexical relationship between Standard and Creole, Jamaicans identify as English speakers. However, there is another complication, the development of Rastafari, the socio-religious group which has produced adaptations through 'Dread Talk' – a lexical expansion within the Creole system with some words said differently. This movement between different versions of language is called *code-switching* and it can be seen in Goodison's poem below, which moves between Jamaican Creole, Rastafari Dread Talk, and Standard English (the first eight and last five words being Standard English, 'no feel now way' Dread Talk, and so on):

> Bless you with a benediction of green rain, no feel no way
> its not that the land for the sea and the sun has failed,
> is so rain stay.
> You see man need rain for food to grow
> so if is your tan, or my yam fi grow? is just so.
>
> PS thanks for coming anyway.
>
> (Goodison, 1986, p. 53)

Goodison has internalised the multilingual nature of the speech community. Mother tongue alone could be seen as quite exclusive because its speech community, i.e. the people who are able to communicate using it, might be harmonious in terms of lifestyle and feel the language really represents their lived experience but, as with practices of communication in other contexts and countries, to get on with and be understood by other communities in Jamaica, people must learn other registers and tongues.

Goodison is one of the best known influences in a mixture of the oral and the scribal (written) tradition. Her work concentrates on women's roles, thinking back through her mother, grandmother and other women in her ancestry, commenting on the passage between Africa and the West Indies, the slave trade, and women finding their identities, freedoms and dignity amid hardship. 'Guinea Woman' tells of her great-grandmother whose beauty, like an antelope, was hidden and denied, her name 'covered' by that of the plantation owner just as she was literally sexually covered by him. Her grace and royal heritage are deliberately rendered strange:

> slender and tall like a cane stalk
> with a guinea woman's antelope-quick walk
> and when she paused
> her gaze would look to sea
> her profile fine like some obverse impression
> on a guinea coin from royal memory
> (Goodison, 'Guinea Woman', in Busby, 1992, p. 722)

She was denied her heritage, memory and her ways. They 'called her uprisings rebellions' but Lorna Goodison shows that the beauty and power of her roots are quietly returning through new generations. In this she celebrates the dark skinned heritage, the beauty of Black womanhood:

> the high yellow brown
> is darkening down.
> Listen, children
> it's great grandmother's turn.
> (Goodison, 'Guinea Woman', in Busby,
> 1992, p. 722)

It is a story, a myth, a family tale.

'Nanny' was a powerful woman too, skilled in herbalism and healing, an Amazon with her breasts flattened, moving to the rhythms of the forest. Her sale to the traders was not loss but a gain. Her mission was to pass on the knowledge and the power, like a trained insurgent and spy, to change the lot of women. This celebratory poem recognises the magic in Black women's lives, re-tells from a positive viewpoint the control women have in passing on gifts and history even within slavery, their continuity power. They:

> ... sold me to the traders
> all my weapons within me.
> I was sent, tell that to history.
>
> When your sorrow obscures the skies
> other women like me will rise
>   (Goodison, 'Nanny', in Busby, 1992, p. 723)

Another poem tells of the meeting of her parents, and yet another of how she is turning into her mother ('I am Becoming my Mother', [1986]). Each celebrates the lineage of powerful women in the family sphere. 'I am Becoming my Mother' is cyclical, beginning and ending with 'I am becoming my mother', only the subtle colour shift of yellow/brown to brown/yellow emphasises the recuperation of the Black women through the developing family. Birth waters, cooking, caring and even the homeliness of onions make this a sensuous poem and link it with the issues of thinking back through one's mothers (see Alice Walker's *In Search of Our Mothers' Gardens*, 1983). Denise Decraires Nerain (1996) has argued that Goodison moves further from writing the body and *écriture féminine* as her three poetry collections develop, and comes to see herself as a poet speaking for people's sufferings. She aligns the continuities and healing powers she has celebrated in her mother, grandmother and other female ancestors with her own powers as a poet to heal and build with words:

> I come only to apply words
> to a sore and confused time
>   (Goodison, 'Heartease', 1988, p. 365)

Her use of 'I' is a testifying found in slave narratives and the fictions of Walker and Morrison. She also uses 'we', speaking for and as part of the voice of the people, as do Aboriginal women poets (Chapter 9):

> The poet's carefully constructed poetic role of healer draws both on the kind of divining traditionally associated with women but also in the linguistic power of the Biblical Word and other patriarchal discourses.   (Decraires Nerain, 1996, p. 435)

In 'My Father Always Promised Me' (1986) Goodison talks about the power of the father to enable her to speak as a woman poet, negotiating her own voice within the space offered by the symbolic order of the father. In the later sequence she speaks for people, not just women, and as a healer for the community. Hers is a mystical role, both as a woman and as a Biblical figure, and the use of Biblical language also links her to Jean Breeze (see Breeze's *Spring Cleaning*, 1992).

Marlene Nourbese Philip

Marlene Nourbese Philip was born in Tobago and lives in Canada. In her poem 'Discourse on the Logic of Language', 'she tries her tongue, her silence softly speaks' (1993 [1989]), she engages specifically with issues of a colonialised discourse and nation language which would enable her to express her roots. This discourse is itself about issues of poetic language, engaging with debates around the use of dialect, Creole, and various forms of English or Jamaican Creole spoken by ordinary people. Valerie Bloom in her performances teaches the audience how to speak Jamaican English, pointing out their lack and enfranchising them as she demonstrates the forms in which the poetry will be articulated so that they can share in the experience and 'overstand' more. Marlene Nourbese Philip talks about dismantling the colonial hold on hers and others' language, to 'deuniversalize' the whole of literature. In the Introduction to *She Tries Her Tongue Her Silence Softly Breaks* (1993 [1989]), referring to 'Discourse on the Logic of Language': 'the poem is sculpted out of the colonial experience – exploitative of people, destructive of mother tongues . . .':

> 'Discourse . . .'
> English
> is my mother tongue.
> A mother tongue is not
> not a foreign lan lan lang
> language
> l/anguish
> anguish
> – a foreign anguish
>
> I have no mother
> tongue
> no mother to tongue
> no tongue to mother

> to mother
>
> tongue
>
> me
>
> (Nourbese Philip, 'Discourse on the Logic
> of Language', 1989, p. 24)

The explicit lack of mother tongue relates, for her, to the loss of a mother's love and yet there is a supposed mother tongue, English, itself a language imposed by imperialist powers, which causes anguish because of its distance from the lived and spoken experience around her.

It is difficult to overturn a language, including a literary language which colours the way you see the world, and reflects a cultural domination. The use of the word 'Black', for example, is derogatory in the English language. Historically, slave plantation owners ensured their slaves came from different language groups in order to prevent insurrection. The ability to discuss and argue could, it was thought, lead to political challenge so language, recognised as power, was thus effectively denied and confused for slaves. Recognising a mother tongue against the imposition of English, then, is a radical awareness and challenge. In the poem sequence 'Universal Grammar' Philip explores grammar rules which led to disenfranchising language speakers through restriction, splitting up the slaves. 'Re-member' suggests both memory, which is prevented, and the putting together of body parts into a whole person. Language control is power, and disablement. Language controls expression, hides brutalities such as rape and murder at the hands of the 'tall, blond, blue-eyed, white-skinned man shooting', a figure who appears in many of the poems in the sequence.

'Adoption Bureau' (1993) utilises the Western myth of Prosperpine and Ceres to investigate contemporary Caribbean locations and claim kinship: 'she whom they call mother, I seek'. Ceres, searching the lands for her daughter, covers the many countries to which Caribbean people have emigrated. She gradually sees signs of her lost daughter, her girdle, and sings a birth song of the surf to her. In the series 'Cyclamen Girls' Philip explores truths and pains behind a photograph, 'circa 1960', of a Black girl in a white wedding dress, typically flowering young, pregnant too early, confirming contradictions in performing the roles that Black womanhood has assigned her:

> with the lurking smell of early pregnancy
> So there, circa 1960, she stands –

black and white in frozen fluidity
                    ageing

photograph of the cyclamen girl
                    caught between
blurred images of
                    massa and master

ORAL PERFORMANCE AND DELIVERY

What Brathwaite terms an 'explosion of grassroots artistic/intellec-tual activity' (1977, p.

58) took over in the late 1960s and 1970s, pro-ducing a vibrant, politically engaged oral poetry called dub poetry, whose Jamaican exponents were Mutabaruka, Oku Onuora and Michael (Mikey) Smith, and in the UK, Linton Kwesi Johnson. John-son wrote/spoke out against racism and charted violent responses from the Black community. His 'Five Nights of Bleeding' (1975) brings the Brixton riots (a reaction against institutionalised and everyday racism) to life. The Caribbean has both the scribal and the oral traditions and most poets move easily between them, but some, like the dub poets, and Louise Bennett the foremother of women's oral poetry, deliberately develop an oral tradition. Oral poetry is most often very accessible in tone, content, theme, rhyme and rhythm. It speaks about everyday things, hopes, fears, dreams, desires, fantas-ies and nightmares, popular cultural figures – writers, comic-book heroes and everyone's emotions – love, death etc. And it uses a speak-ing voice to do so.

Conventionally, there have been difficulties in finding critically analytical approaches to oral poetry. It is important to note that oral-ity has been central in the development of Black writing in many different contexts, and issues of the translation of the oral into the written remain of concern wherever we read Black writing (South Africa, Chapter 7; Africa, Chapter 6; Australia, Chapter 9). A chief element among African, Aboriginal and Caribbean Black oral liter-ature is the importance of the evocation of the particular lilt and linguistic everyday usage of the speech community, which has adapted English for its own expression in its own context. Poets who choose the oral tradition very often also publish in the written tradi-tion, especially in the Caribbean context. To decide to write poetry out of the use of this spoken language using neither the possibly more formal language of books, nor the high-flown content of English literature, enables people to recognise the importance of their own worlds and language, their own identity and values. Oral literature in both novels or storytelling and, in this discussion, in poetry of performance, concentrates on the importance of the speaking voice, idiomatic expressions, the particular local brand of expression and interest, contextual setting and particular interests and problems. This writing is a close expression of the feelings and everyday speech of the people themselves rather than a literature distanced from them (possibly, especially in the Caribbean context, a literature of the colonisers which misses out their presence and context entirely), and it trusts the energy of what is written to communicate to the inner ear. Some types of oral poetry include voice portraits or monologues, political manifestos, satire, folk tale and calypso.

Brathwaite's *The History of the Voice* (1984) makes many useful critical comments about oral literature, and particularly oral poetry, as a way of exploring the personal local experiences of one's own culture in the Caribbean, and of finding the right words, rhythms and sounds to express these experiences. In his view, the development of oral literature into published and performed forms goes along with developing a voice and celebrating the Caribbean landscape and peoples:

> What is even more important, as we develop this business of emergent language in the Caribbean, is the actual rhythm and the syllables, the very software, in a way, of the language. What English has given us as a model for poetry, and to a lesser extent prose...is the pentameter.   (Brathwaite, 1984, p. 9)

In the USA Walt Whitman tried to break or bridge the pentameter, Cummings to fragment it, and Marianne Moore attacked it with syllabics but it remained. The pentameter, an essentially traditional form, cannot capture the rhythms and energy of the Caribbean:

> the hurricane does not roar in pentameters.   (Brathwaite, 1984, p. 10)

> How do you get a rhythm which approximates the *natural* experience, *the environmental* experience?   (Anthony Hinkson, in Brathwaite, 1984, pp. 10/11)

Nation language, African influenced, informs Caribbean poetry:

> It is national language in the Caribbean that, in fact, largely
> ignores the pentameter. Nation language is the language which is
> influenced very strongly by the African model... (Brathwaite,
> 1984, p. 13)

It is an English not of the imported Standard but 'of the submerged,
surrealist experience and sensibility' (Brathwaite, 1984, p. 13). It

> can produce the sound of the wind or wave or machine gun or
> howl. [There is a] necessary connection to the understanding of
> nation language as between native musical structures and the
> native language. (Brathwaite, 1984, p. 16)

It is a musical, oral form. Performance of the sound of the language
enables a conveying of emotion and strength:

> The poetry, the culture itself exists, not in a dictionary but in the
> tradition of the spoken word. It is based as much on sound as it is
> on song. The noise that it makes is part of the meaning, and if you
> ignore the noise (or what you would think of as noise...) then
> you lose part of the meaning. When it is written, you lose the
> sound or the noise, and therefore you lose part of the meaning.
> (Brathwaite, 1984, p. 17)

To break down the pentameter, poets working in the oral tradition discovered the old form – the calypso. Calypso uses dactyls
instead of iambic pentameter, making the tongue sound different
syllabic and stress patterns. Other forms are the 'Kaiso' which has
dips and interval patterns, and the 'Kumina' and other more religious or ritual forms. Music connections are important here, as is the
theatre, for oral performance itself (several poets, including Mikey
Smith and Jean 'Binta' Breeze, have drama training).

Sonia Sanchez, Miles Davies and Langston Hughes influence
Afro-Caribbean performance poetry, Davies linking in with jazz
rhythms. One early performance poet was Miss Queenie. Brathwaite talks of seeing her perform – using her whole face and encirc-
ling arms, gesturing to become water or spear, enacting events or
elements. This poetry is both particular to the individual, and political in its intent and context. Brathwaite describes it as 'organic, it is

person centred, fluid/tidal rather than ideal/structured nature' ('Caribbean Peach', p. 49):

> the word becomes a pebble stone or a bomb and dub makes sense (or nonsense) of politics demanding of it life not death, community not aardvark, new world to make new words and we to 'overstand' how modern ancient is.   (Brathwaite, 1984, p. 50)

Coming from a political matrix, much performance poetry is a political or social statement. However, while poetry by many of the male poets, such as Mikey Smith and Linton Kwesi Johnson, concentrates on making political statements about inequality, racism and hypocrisy, women's poetry is more likely to be concerned with the social, with presenting relationships and individual personalities, and with reclaiming stereotypes. To do this they use 'women's talk':

> Women's talk, traditionally well known in the Caribbean, has become the basis of important Creole literary originality from the Jamaicans Louise Bennett (*Jamaica Labrish*, 1966) and the Sistren theatre group, with Honor Ford Smith as writer.   (Savory, 1989, in Butcher, p. 34)

Ford-Smith speaks of the use by the Sistren Women's Theatre Collective of testimony and 'labrish' or gossip, casual conversation, techniques in play-making:

> Oral elements woven into the texture of written work are so commonplace in Caribbean writing generally as to be a fundamental characteristic, born of the vitality and power of the speech and viewpoint of the ordinary folk, as against the colonially imposed and middle-class sustained conventions of elite language and behaviour. But in the case of Bennett, Sistren and Breeze we have a deliberate attempt to stay with the oral completely, and their work is in written form simply a transcription of something indeed for performance.   (Savory, 1989, in Butcher, pp. 34/5)

The work of Sistren, Louise Bennett and Jean 'Binta' Breeze needs to be perceived in relation to the cultural contexts and their work within women-orientated thoughts and practices. However, we might also wonder what other creative work is actually lost because such expression is seen as evidence of being disturbed. There 'are still parents who burn their daughters' writings out of fear that they denote serious neurosis and will prevent them from fitting into society' (Savory, 1989, in Butcher, p. 37).

Jean 'Binta' Breeze

Jean 'Binta' Breeze is often seen as having developed oral performance forms deriving from Louise Bennett. She lives and works in both the UK and the Caribbean and her roots are in the Rastafarian movement. She has appeared on television and sees her work politically, derived from her multiple experiences as a Black woman, single mother, in an extended family and wider community. Like Merle Collins, she uses music, song, mime and dance to produce electrifying performances. Her first collection was *Riddym Ravings and Other Poems* (1988). In 'The Mad Woman's Poem' women are oppressed by men, the landlord, the doctors. 'Hustler Skank' uses street talk, exposing arrogant male speakers. These are tightly controlled poems concentrating on recognising a woman's lot in life. Jean Breeze's poetry is powerful, vibrant, oral performance work capturing the rhythms of monologues and dialogues, the personal and the lived experiences of Caribbean people in the UK and back home.

Jean Breeze chooses to write and perform without the musical accompaniment of reggae or calypso etc., forms chosen by the male performance poets such as Linton Kwesi Johnson. Her choice is to re-create the lilt and rhythms, the individuality of the speech patterns and concerns of ordinary women faced with passing wisdom on to daughters, sharing lovers. Dramatising the lives of ordinary folk, Jean Breeze argues that her words are fluid, released from the mechanical rigidity of the beat and from the fixity of the page. She makes a distinction between the poet as maker and the poet as performer:

> For not only are the works in motion, unbroken by the beat, but the poet/performer, uncontained by the boundaries of the book, speaks face to face with an immediate audience. In the act of performatic transference, the speaker gets across the closure of the printed page. (Cooper, 1993, p. 82)

The performance is a privileged reading of the text. Breeze uses audio visual and kinetic power. You can't tell how wonderful it is going to be by just reading it on the page, 'somewhat like a musical score, the poem pressed to the page encodes performance' (Cooper, 1993, p. 82). Each performance is original, partly fired and inspired by audience engagement and response.

Jean Breeze's most famous poem is probably 'Riddym Ravings: the Mad Woman's poem' (*Spring Cleaning*, 1992). The persona, convincing and disturbing, is a pregnant country woman, psychotic, wandering the streets of Kingston Jamaica. In her distress she remembers rural Jamaica as positive and friendly, and meets only rejection in the city. This woman has been admitted to Bellevue Hospital many times, where she is operated on by the doctor, and she is oppressed in her house by the landlord, twin patriarchal tyrants. Her condition of madness is explicitly related to economic hardship throughout; not having enough to eat and sleeping on the streets. Breeze engenders the madwoman's despair with artistic control. She shows the proximity of madness and sanity, and the audience appreciate the dramatised suffering. The 'dissonant pain' (Morris, 1988, p. 69) of the madwoman's debased condition is dignified, undiminished by her fleeting moments of total lucidity. The radio DJ in her head keeps her 'sane', provides a sense of identity, comforting her in distress.

She tries to smile, but is ignored. She tries to eat even rejected rotten pork, but is shooed away, yelled at and finally hauled into the asylum again for electric shock 'therapy' to remove her 'voices' which she characterises as the 'radio in me head'. To her confused sight, tired, hungry and sleeping on the streets, the streets themselves seem to 'bubble and dally' but the language 'bubble and dally' is ironically taken from the exploits of young men for whom to bubble is to be having a good time and to dally is to weave and bob on a motorbike (Cooper, 1993, p. 84). She is more associated with rotten pork and back lots, her life is certainly not carefree like theirs. What she really cares about is DJ music, which provides her with some kind of inner control and some kind of identity. After each treatment she goes back on the streets and defiantly puts the earplugs back in, thus reclaiming her madness and her own identity, her own inner voices. Their actions against her are seen as sinister, oppressive and patriarchal.

Watching Jean Breeze perform is riveting. Parts of the poem are chanted and parts spoken. Parts, including especially the chorus, are sung:

> *Eh, Eh,*
> *no feel no way*
> *town is a place dat ah really kean stay*
> *dem kudda-ribbit me han*
> *eh-ribbit mi toe*
> *mi waan go country go look mango*
>   ('Riddym Ravings', 1992, p. 19)

The chorus rhymes (eh, way, stay, toe, mango), and the lilt of her voice takes listeners/readers through a series of sad reflections and attempts at declaring self worth, until an emphatic end. After another seemingly successful operation she almost loses her voice and cries 'pull up missa operator!' They have made their final attempt to shut out her voices and her inner self. On stage, Jean Breeze enacts the wandering, singing and the electrifying experience of the removal and replacement of the earplugs.

Like Mikey Smith, Breeze uses the words and rhythms of children's play, adoptions of persona and the tones and speech of ordinary folk, each performance original. Mervyn Morris notes of performance poetry:

> If the poem in print does, however minimally, alter with the specific context of its reception, the 'performance poem' is even more difficult to fix, dependent for its meanings on the variable interaction between text, performer, audience and occasion. (Morris, 1988, p. 19)

The community listening get to know the works but don't get bored by this; it is like Anansi storytelling time. (Anansi or Anancy is a trickster tale about a spider but the term refers to telling legends, myths, fairytales, proverbs.)

Less able performance poets become dominated by the dub beat, sound taking over from sense. Often poetry-reading performance is occasioned by commemorative events like South African Liberation Day or the International Radical Book Fair. Stewart Brown in his essay 'Dub poetry: Selling out?' (1987) warns:

> as dub poetry becomes a commercial product as its performers, like Benjamin Zephaniah or Mutabaruka or Ras Levi Tafari become media stars and strive to entertain a mass multicultural audience there seems to me to be real danger that the protest, the

anger, the fire becomes an act while the image, the dub/rant/ chant/dance become the real substance of the performance. (Brown, 1987, p. 53)

There is, he suggests, a problem with transforming rage into entertainment. Jean Breeze responds to this in an essay in *Marxism Today*:

> I'd rather we had only two or three artists in our community that represent what is finest and truest about ourselves than a host of poseurs who have been allowed to take on the title of artist simply because they are black. . . . I'm tired of people preaching to the converted and saying it's art. (Breeze, 1988, p. 45)

A broad thematic and tonal range characterises the work of the sophisticated performance poet whose work is not all protest and fire, concentrating on making individualised statements rather than merely being carried away by the beat or the moment.

There is a difference, Mervyn Morris notes, between dub poetry and the higher quality performance poetry where there is often a sense of chant, of different voices, of the accompaniment of body language and emphases to make the poem dramatic and varied. What characterises good performance poetry is the conjunction of word and beat, of a sense and sound of attitude, movement and atmosphere, using tags from ring games and chants, folklore and legend, myth and ironic wit. Like other Caribbean women poets, for example Lorna Goodison, Jean Breeze articulates different Jamaican and English voices, and embodies different persona in her poems, moving between the values of city and countryside Jamaica, and the lives of those who live in the UK communities. So she will dramatise the ageing immigrant looking back on her arrival, the young girl sent to the UK from Jamaica by her mum, long settled in London. In this she brings a community of individuals to life.

Some of her work, like that of Mikey Smith, interweaves oral and scribal characteristics and sources so we can read as well as hear it, although the written dialect is often quite difficult to follow unless read aloud, and it is decidedly better to get hold of one of her published tapes and listen along with the written word:

> as composed text, the performance poetry of Jean 'Binta' Breeze and Mikey Smith illustrates the sensitive deployment of a range of

rhetorical styles of both Jamaican and English provenance. The pure orality of Jamaican folk poetics (both rural and urban, folk song and reggae) engages in constructive dialogue with the scribal conventions of English metrics – in which both poets have been schooled . . . the meta-dub script of these skilled actors allows them to fully demonstrate their command of a broad repertoire of theatre idioms. In performance the word, unbroken by the beat, speaks volumes.   (Cooper, 'The Word Unbroken by the Beat', 1990, p. 84)

Looking at the representation of women in performance poetry, Mervyn Morris notes that there are negative views – presenting women as pathetic and powerless. There is also a *diablesse* character, a *femme fatale* who haunts some of the poems. Women authors often foreground gender and Jean Breeze certainly does so in her poems about relationships. Her poem 'Baby Madda' was provoked by living in the Clarendon hills with the Rastafarians – she became a Rasta after being at the Jamaican School of Drama. In an interview with Jean Small she has described her life as a woman in Rasta traditions – avoiding anything that is to do with 'Babylon' – money, consumerism, capitalism, entrepreneurism. The poem registers the pain and difficulties of being a woman – carrying and bearing children and then supporting them in growth, under patriarchy – and it registers that the baby's father has become an 'African' but also an oppressor because he has so little to do with the suffering and the support. In performance the satire is made more telling by the joyously affirmative rhythms of the Rastafarian drumming and the visual effect of a woman in open protest against her 'king'.

The everyday experiential roots to Breeze's poetry are expressed through her conversational language and tone, the repetition of speech rhythms, and of 'ah' or I. When she reads and experiences she uses the more colloquial 'ah', and when she takes on a poet's voice, finding her voice in her writing she uses 'I', so indicating a slightly more distanced and formal stance.

Many other of her poems are about people meeting in the street, chatting to each other in the market, women giving each other advice, mother to daughter, friend to friend, bewailing the behaviour of men and advising cunning. Woman's lot is a constant theme and often she interweaves the biblical with the everyday, so that in 'Spring Cleaning', the title poem to the collection *Spring Cleaning*

(1992), she interweaves parts of the 23rd psalm with housework, the two intertwining, showing the woman as a godlike figure but humble, coping, cleaning, one thought and action following on from the next:

> surely goodness an mercy
>
> shall follow me
>
> she pick up de broom
>
> an she sweeping
>
> all de days of my life
>
> an she sweeping
>
> an I will dwell
>
> in de house of de Lord
>
> she sweeping out
>
> sweeping
>
> out

The poem does not end with 'amen' because the work keeps going, but the woman has a caring control.

'Red Rebel Song' (1992) is a powerful performance piece and also highly literary in its references. Jean Breeze engages loudly and violently with the negative representations of Black women through history and through contemporary media, speaking out for her own identity and the individuality and power of herself and other Black women. 'Is lang time' repeats – and emphasises – how there have been centuries of abuse and silencing, of mythologising and of marginalising. She principally wants to escape from and deny the abuse resulting from racial oppression based on difference:

> is lang time I waan
> free Iself
> from de white black question
> (Breeze, 'Red Rebel Song', 1992, p. 2)

Sexual abuse is criticised – that meted out both to women slaves, who were felt to be the property of their Black masters, and to those who are taken to represent Otherness, sexuality. Traditionally, under colonialism and slavery, Western men transferred their lusts and hang-ups about sex onto Black women, otherising, iconising, then abusing them so that Black women are seen as objects of lust, not individuals. This patriarchal transfer of libidinous energy onto another means that the Other is both viewed by a voyeur positioning her as an object for a male gaze, and then criticised for causing the lustful response in the first place. In this poem, referencing Jean Rhys's novel, she crosses 'a Sargasso sea' to get rid of and deny lust, and the reification:

> is years
> of ungluing Iself
> from de fabric of lust
> dat have I
> in a pin-up glare
> > (Breeze, 'Red Rebel Song', 1992, p. 2)

She considers the role of the slave woman, whose blues song is forced to stay in her head unheard while the talentless white woman, her mistress, practises the piano. Her position is 'in-between'. She sees herself as neither historical figure, the white mistress or the black cook:

> my song lock up tight
> eena mi troat

If she ever voiced her own song, she says, mountains would split open:

> sitting on a timb bomb
> an I kyan get angry
> fah yuh would see
> mountain quake

She runs through complex political problems which still keep Black people in poverty, and which politicians seem unable to solve:

> delegation after delegation
> an still kyan solve
> a likkle irrigation

She calls to others to join her, to cross and straddle the space between, to be strong in their straddling of at least two cultures, although critically defined as a 'painted halfbreed centrespread'. This diasporan position – in two cultures at least – can give broad insights and strength, because being part of both cultures:

> I nah
>
> tek no abuse fram eida direction

For a grand overall mother figure, compromise is not possible. She seizes her own sexuality and calls others to join her in organising change based on their common position. Belonging to two worlds at least is a strength not a weakness. This she bases on historical and literary as well as personal political awareness.

The 'Sargasso Sea' to which she refers, separating the Caribbean from the UK, reminds us of Jean Rhys's novel, which exposes the historical treatment of Black or mixed-race women as sexualised Other, and as mad. Jean Breeze's poem might be in dialect – nation language in fact, a mixture of Dread Talk and Jamaican English, in order to express the feelings of a Caribbean woman, but it also has complex subtle literary echoes. She mixes the referencing and intertextuality common in post-modern works with a poem in nation language, rejecting the role of madwoman in the attic, happy in her own madness in rebellion, rejecting the derogatory element of that label, seizing the madness as celebratory, aiding identity. She says:

> I is de red rebel
> woman
> accepting I madness
> declaring I song
> nah siddung eena attic
> tek no fire bun

Bertha Mason jumps to her death in *Jane Eyre* amid a conflagration, Annette/Bertha, in Jean Rhys's novel, also jumps into the fire. The Rhys novel gives the Creole woman a voice. Breeze's poem takes up where Rhys's novel leaves off, seizing voice and power for the Black woman, the red rebel.

In terms of the strength and sound of the poem, she sings her own song, taking the 'song it loud / sing it long' from popular song writing, *Bridge Over Troubled Water*, from the Bible and Simon and

Garfunkel's song of the 1960s. There is a repetition and an emphasis on 'I', asserting identity so that she is the beginning and end of her own rainbow and song at the close of the poem. This is a powerful, engaged, repetitive poem. It takes from historical, literary, mythical and contemporary culture, placed in the voice of an ordinary woman, who is a red rebel – who has had enough and calls for action. Jean Breeze's oral performance poetry can be read, for example, noting the intertextual references and the arguments, as well as responded to in terms of the dramatisation of the character, the movement of the body in anger and love, and the rhythm of language in word and song. Hers is a poetry which explores individuals' lives, feelings and loves, on sexual politics, rather than concentrating on the more public politics found in Johnson and Smith.

Through their oral and written poetry and novels the women of the Caribbean critique both sexism and the racist legacies of colonialism, representing powerful, lively individualistic women, in their own varied language.

6

Women's Writing from Africa

Where are those songs?
Where are those songs
my mother and yours
always sang
fitting rhythms
to the whole
vast span of life?

(Micere Githae Mugo, 1990 [1972])

This chapter looks at the context and recent history of women's writing in Africa, concentrating largely on Nigeria, considering the effects of a history of pre-literate oral storytelling, examining the cultural context of African women writers in Nigeria and elsewhere, and focusing on their literary production. Issues which are popular in the work of those women discussed, are those of rural village life versus city life, motherhood, gender relations and relations of power, colonialism and the post-colonial response and legacy. They are also concerned with scrutinising 'Mother Africa', which is a national and political image valuing the land and its peoples. The image also tends to indicate a close connection between women and the land, women and the maintenance of certain social behaviours; an identification which limits women's own development.

Writers considered include Nigerians Flora Nwapa and Buchi Emecheta, Ama Ata Aidoo from Ghana, and oral storytellers and poets, especially Hausa women.

INTRODUCTION – CONTEXT OF AFRICAN WOMEN WRITERS
IN THE DEVELOPMENT OF BLACK WOMEN'S WRITING:
NEGOTIATING FEMINIST POSITIONS

Gay Wilentz and Lorraine Bethel remark on the roots of and the repression of African and African American women's writing:

> The history of Black women's literature started long before Black women were finally allowed their right to literacy. Their literature and other creative art were oral, rooted in storytelling and the African/African-American folk tradition. (Wilentz, 1992, p. xi)

> Because Black women rarely gained access to literary expression, Black women identified bonding and folk culture have often gone unrecorded except through our individual lives and memories. (Bethel, 1982, p. 179)

African women writers from a variety of very different contexts and countries have only published relatively recently, and Nigerian women are some of them more available to a wider, English-speaking readership, because of their education in English. When using the term 'African women', this chapter will largely be alluding to women writers from Nigeria, with some other specifically mentioned references, for example, to Ghana. This ostensibly, unintentionally, homogenising term is *not* meant to indicate that all African women's lives are identical. Rather, the vastness of the continent, the geographical, linguistic, political and economic differences under which different women live, cannot be each dealt with in a short chapter of this kind. The term merely suggests some similarities in the roles of motherhood in particular, and concentrates on Nigeria specifically.

In 1966 Flora Nwapa produced the first novel by an African Woman, *Efuru*, although there was a wealth of African women's involvement in oral storytelling which preceded literacy and publishing.

As we discussed earlier (Chapter 2, 'African American Women's Writing'), many women whose roots are in Africa, when starting to write, look back to their African foremothers. Zora Neale Hurston did this during the Harlem Renaissance, establishing a mode for the modern renaissance of African American women's writing. Alice Walker, Toni Morrison and others imagine versions of Africa and their African foremothers (Chapters 2, 3, 4). Alice Walker produces an Afro-Utopian community in *The Color Purple* (1983) among the Olinka, whilst Toni Morrison's *Song of Solomon* (1977) sees Solomon join the 'flying Africans'; an 'escape and achievement' myth. For many women writers, both those of (African) slave origins and those whose (non-African) indigenous foremothers suffered enslavement and abuse at the hands of invading Europeans, Africa is a symbolic home (representing roots, history) to which they turn for inspiration.

In Africa itself, and in Nigeria, on which this chapter concentrates, women's published writing is relatively new, although oral story-telling and poetry are timelessly established. Like their oral work, much writing by some African women concentrates on imparting cultural values and considers the kinds of roles women traditionally perform. One contemporary central issue is the negotiation of different responses to tradition and change. Maintenance of tradition can enable women writers to establish their centrality in some African cultures after the changes brought about by colonialism. However, buying into a very traditional culture can also be seen as reinforcing gender inequalities and preventing women's entry into a post-colonial, feminist world which asserts the importance of gender and economic equality. (By traditional I mean historically established and often limiting to women because of the emphasis on relations in which women have been restricted to conventional roles – passive, hard-working, largely silenced – considered valuable in relation to playing the roles of wife and mother, both before, during, and post colonialism): 'African women see their culture and traditions in both a positive and a negative light – as a life giving force as well as a restriction of women's rights' (Wilentz, 1992, p. xvii).

There is, however, no simple conflation of the post-colonial and progressive, or of feminism and the African women's movement towards gender equality. Indeed, many of the tensions in writing by contemporary African women novelists are located in the relations between colonialism, post-colonialism and feminism. Post-colonialism and feminism are themselves seen to constrict and inform re-descriptions of the world, overlooking or not cohering with African women's lives and their negotiations between equality and self-development. Feminist criticism provides a skewed reading of African writing as it:

> privileges the concerns and modalities of western feminism, as well as the African texts that conform to those modalities, and which implicitly if not explicitly present feminism as a western

phenomenon...white western feminist research is generally marked by Eurocentrism.

It may... represent itself as universal...but in so doing over-looks it's own cultural and historical specificity, including, as Andrade reminds us, its 'inscriptions within a European system of thought which is saturated by imperialism'. (Andrade, 1990, p. 92; see also Smith, 1982)

The problem is a new version of (feminist) cultural imperialism which fails to appreciate *dialogues* between world views and values in African women's writing: 'the prevailing trend in feminist criticism has been for African women's texts to be assimilated into a white feminist problematic' (Stratton, 1994, p. 12). Improved know-ledge of the cultural context from which African women writers write is crucial.

In considering African women's writing, Western feminist criticism tends to overlook the impact and legacy of colonialism. It also finds it difficult to negotiate different dialogues: between African tradition and its rejection, principally a rejection of conformity to male primacy and the valorising of mothering above all else; between the values and behaviours of village and town, the latter representing independence but loss of family links, increased freedom but alignment with Westernised materialism (a dialogue affected by colonialism). Escaping from husbands and patriarchy is not African women's only remedy: rejecting or questioning colonial power and the subordination of women arising from West-ern influences is another. Several African writers including Flora Nwapa and Buchi Emecheta have refused or qualified the word 'feminist', and argued that, while for European women, feminism suggests a rejection of various constraints of patriarchy and the development of certain attributes which empower women, these constraints and attributes have been a common and necessary fea-ture of the African woman's life.

True feminism is an abnegation of male protection and a deter-mination to be resourceful and self reliant. The majority of the black women in Africa and in the diaspora have developed these characteristics, though not always by choice. (Steady, 1985, p. 35)

Some form of (some African women's) feminism, even militant feminism, has been an everyday reality (Amadiume, 1987, p. 36).

Nana Wilson-Tagoe (1997, in Newell) uses gynocriticism to avoid the universalising monolithic concepts of feminism and relates women's experiences to their culture and gender, highlighting an interweaving of body, culture and language affecting women. However:

> African feminist critics, while acknowledging biology as a sphere of difference recognise the possible limitations and stereotyping that it can generate in an African context.   (Ogundipe-Leslie, 1987a, p. 5)

Historical, cultural and gender awareness is inevitable for women:

> Being aware of oneself as a Third World person implies being politically conscious, offering readers perspectives on and perceptions of colonialism and neo-colonialism as they affect and shape our lives and historical destinies.   (Ogundipe-Leslie, 1987a, p. 11)

WOMEN'S WRITING IN SOME AFRICAN CONTEXTS: CONCERNS

What do some women writers in Africa do to change the norms of African writing? Some, including Grace Ogot, Flora Nwapa and Buchi Emecheta, give women centralist positions, valorising women's experiences. They enable revisionist subversions of women's roles which are represented in conventional fictions as unproblematic, dramatising conflicts and illustrating how women simultaneously fulfil, question and move beyond their roles. Grace Ogot's protagonist in *The Promised Land* (1966) is one such example, as is Flora Nwapa's Efuru (*Efuru*, 1966). Ogot's character considers both migration and her life, in the colonial 1930s:

> in contemplating her opposition to migration and her impotence in preventing an action that may yet change her life, Ogot's female subject recognises that the claims of marriage as defined by her community are themselves forms of displacement and imprisonment and an abnegation of choice and will.   (Wilson-Tagoe, 1997, in Newell, p. 15)

Nwapa's is a woman-centred world concentrating on feelings of sisterhood between women who both demonstrate their strengths and bewail social impotence.

Women and Cultural Contexts

Western culture's materialistic, individualistic values are in opposition to the emphasis on the responsibility of the individual to the group common among many African cultures. Historically, in some African communities, women and men had strictly defined roles in both public and private life and this kind of social organisation actually produced some independence for women. In some parts of pre-colonial Africa, women had their own courts and were often in charge of the domestic affairs of both male and female villagers. Responsibilities and rules were divided. Ezeigbo notes that: 'gender interaction is regarded as being complementary and balanced... rather than being conflictual or competing for the same positions of social and political power' (Ezeigbo, 1997, in Newell, p. 95). However, both pre-colonial and colonial cultures valorised attitudes and behaviours of male superiority:

> African women... are weighed down by superstructural norms deriving from the pre-colonial past... gender hierarchy or male supremacy... was known or taken for granted. (Ogundipe-Leslie, 1987b, p. 133)

This was hardened further by colonial incursions. The exclusion and subordination of women is 'naturalised' within culture, described and enacted as if obvious and biologically determined. This, of course, she questions:

> Women are 'naturally' excluded from public affairs; they are viewed as unable to hold positions of responsibility, rule men or even be visible when serious matters of state and society are being discussed. Women are viewed to need tutelage before they can be politically active; politics is considered the absolute realm of men; women are not considered fit for political positions in modern African nation-states, though their enthusiasm and campaign work are exploited by their various political parties. (Ogundipe-Leslie, 1987b, p. 133)

Various rules made to protect female morality contributed to the continuation of women's economic marginality. African men in some countries are frequently migrant workers employed in the towns, sending money home to the women in the villages, left in a rural economy. Moving to the cities was not a preferred option for many women. Patricia Ruddy tells of mass arrests of single unaccompanied women in cities in post-colonial African nations, charged with being intent on prostitution. Women have few choices and many limitations:

> If in order to improve her economic status, she chooses to migrate to the city or seek employment, she is labelled a 'prostitute' or singled out as the cause of national 'indiscipline'. If, on the other hand, she elects to stay in the village or be a housewife, she is economically marginalised.   (Ruddy, 1994, in Stratton, p. 17)

Women writers such as Nwapa, Emecheta and Aidoo strive to destabilise the socially fixed positions of some African women from within, and not by providing polar opposites to men's version of women. Instead they produce a 'multi-dimensional discourse embedded in both male and female traditions, a complex discourse with several intersecting points, criss-crossing and interrogating each other continuously' (Wilson-Tagoe, 1997, in Newell, p. 27). They explore characters and stories which problematise the socially fixed positions designated for women, employing discourse deriving from a mixture of male and female traditions. What seem to be, on the surface, straightforward stories actually critique and provide comment on social roles and beliefs, often using comments of the local community to debate women's actions and choices.

Forms of Expression – Writing and Oral Literature

The economic situations and freedoms of women in some African contexts affect what they can write and whether they *can* write and publish. There is, however, in many instances, a long tradition of oral literature, as is also the case with many other women from different cultures (Aboriginal, Chapter 9; South African, Chapter 7; Caribbean, Chapter 5). Orature, the skill of oral storytelling, includes history, folk tales, songs, proverbs and other ways of passing on elements of culture. Importantly, oral cultures tend to revere their elders as well as forebears, and women here play an important part. Africa's traditional cultures often hold different world views from those of post-colonial cultures:

> a traditional world view is based on assumptions of a collective nature, that there is a body of expressive knowledge that each community is aware of and, to some extent, abides by. These values

are encapsulated in the oral traditions of the culture, and women play a large part by communicating this body of knowledge to their children. (Ong, in Wilentz, 1992, p. xxiii)

Individuals develop a version of reality which is a collectively shared view assured by custom:

> The folk tale is used in a more dramatic manner to initiate children and adolescents into their cultural heritage ... the Leader of the performance may be a man or a woman. But it is often the woman who plays the part because she is not as tired after the day's work as the man. The content of the tale is moralistic and the purpose of the presentation is didactic. (Taiwo, 1984, p. 8)

Women might traditionally be the 'griottes' or storytellers, but still their creativity is not necessarily recognised. Often the women's version of a traditional story was neither collected, passed on nor written down. The collector, frequently a colonialist, selected men's versions and ignored women's versions, names and the manner of the telling, so storytelling foremothers are anonymous, their versions lost. Buchi Emecheta recalls learning storytelling skills from her grandmother and other community women 'in moonlight sessions when she was young' (Taiwo, 1984, p. 100). Abena Busia, the poet and critic, sees Black women's 'herstories' as collective self-definition, as 'the incorporation of the folk culture, oral tradition in particular, into written texts' (Taiwo, 1984, p. 100).

Many African women writers from different contexts utilise some of the moral tale-telling and circular, repetitive shapes of oral storytelling. They often also suggest a community conscience and consciousness, commenting on the actions of fictional characters, much as a community would share a story and comment on the actions of others through gossip and news telling.

MOTHER AFRICA

Much writing by male authors figures Africa as a woman, 'Mother Africa', in a celebratory, essentialist, mythic way. But colonisers, Europeans in the nineteenth century in particular, also figured Africa as a woman and thought of Africa as the Other, the female, deceptive, fertile, to be owned and taken. It is difficult (but probably necessary) for women to write against the myth of Mother Africa.

It is especially difficult when it is, in the hand of Black writers, aligned with recognising national Black identity. The trouble is, whoever uses the myth and identifies women with it, ends up mythologising and subordinating women as merely natural, merely of the earth, merely procreative. The 'trope' or regular features and formulae of 'Mother Africa' position woman as subordinate:

> She is pure physicality, always beautiful and often naked. He is constructed as a writing subject, a producer of art and of socio-political visions; her status is that of an aesthetic/sexual object. She takes the form either of a young girl, nubile and erotic, or as a fecund, nurturing mother. The poetry celebrates his intellect at the same time as it pays tribute to her body which is frequently associated with the African landscape that is his to explore and discover. As embodying mother she gives the trope a name: the Mother Africa trope.　　(Stratton, 1994, p. 41)

The trope, when not attached to Africa, is recognisable in many other literatures, where woman is equated with the natural and the fecund, the mythic and procreative, but certainly not the artistic, intellectual or sociopolitical. This kind of simplifying myth is power-ful and entrapping. In the work of male post-colonial writers such as Chinua Achebe (*Things Fall Apart*), Ngugi wa Thiong'o and Soyinka, among others, the Mother Africa trope is used as a way of express-ing redemption, salvation, a new future, a rejection of the cultural destruction and paralysis which resulted from the end of colonialism. Women are used in many texts by great African male writers as metaphors for both ills and potential cures and resolutions. They are either a source of salvation: rich, fertile, dependable, returned to the village; or representing the evil debilitating corruption of the cities and the legacy of colonialism, and so figured as prostitutes. This does not actually enable women in fiction to have their own voice, and constantly places them in a sexually, politically and economically subordinated position as objects of the male gaze. Not surprisingly, engaged African women writers often reject the trope.

The Task for African Women Writers

In an interview, Mariama Ba spoke out against such cultural and lit-erary wrongs, so giving a manifesto to contemporary African women writers:

The woman writer in Africa has a special task. She has to present the position of women in Africa in all its aspects. There is still so much injustice.... In the family, in the institutions, in society, in the street, in political organisations, discrimination reigns supreme.... As women, we must work for our own future, we must overthrow the status quo which harms us and we must no longer submit to it. Like men, we must use literature as a non-violent but effective weapon. We no longer accept the nostalgic praise to the African Mother, who, in his anxiety, man confuses with Mother Africa. Within African literature, room must be made for women ... room we will fight for with all our might.

(Cited in Schipper, 1984, pp. 46–7)

There are women writers in the different regions of Africa, but we will be concentrating largely on Nigeria where there is the largest number whose merit has been recognised. We will also look a little at East Africa. On the representation of women's oppression and equality, Nigerian critic Molara Ogundipe-Leslie comments:

The effect of world wide concern about the woman's position in Nigeria has been varied.... It is ... multi-faceted and contradictory when it is not totally false and misleading. The male dominated society reacts in the usual fashion by denying that there is any oppression of women in Africa, glorifying an unknown pre-colonial past where our African mothers were totally happy; accusing conscious women activists of being victims of western ideas and copycats of white women; claiming that 'the family' is more important than the fate of individual women; brushing aside women's concern with hypocrisy that national development is a greater priority now than women's liberation; asserting that women anyhow do not need to be liberated because they have never been in bondage. So you have a compounding of historical and sociological falsification, all to the end of frightening women into quietude. The most vocal and courageous who continue to talk and act socially and politically are stigmatised.   (Ogundipe-Leslie, 1987b, p. 133)

Nigeria has a population of over 15 million and prosperity from oil – which has caused problems with pollution and political unrest. To date, it has a more favourable climate for women writers than elsewhere in Africa, with several regional universities and publishing houses publishing women as well as men. Nwapa (*Efuru*, 1966), who was the first African woman to be published by the Heinemann African Writers series (Achebe's *Things Fall Apart* was the first novel), started writing in the 1950s and eventually established a publishing house for women's and children's literature. Buchi Emecheta, who now lives in London, has won several prizes for her fiction and considerable international recognition. Nigerian writers include: Rebeka Njau, writing plays and a novel; Mabel Segun – satire and children's literature; Adoare Ulasi – novels; Zulu Sofola – plays; Eno Oblong, whose first novel *Garden House* won an NOMA award mention, 1988.

There are also new writers from Nigerian ethnic groups and areas previously unheard of, for example, the Hausa who have produced poetry, and also some francophone literature, since Mariama Ba won the NOMA award in 1980. Other West African women writers come from Senegal and Cameroon, often writing in French or even in Portuguese. (Writing was repressed because Portugal permitted very little formal education.) Women are changing the direction of West African literature through study, work and travel and they do not write only about domestic issues. Their female protagonists are often educated and urban, themselves examples of the rural/urban value conflicts common in the twentieth century for African women.

Mothering and Motherhood

Motherhood is central to the lives of many women in African states, their position and self-image within the community. As such, then, it is not surprising that the issue of mothering and motherhood is pivotal in much writing by many African women writers. While some Western feminists might view the role of mother as problematic, preventing economic freedom and self-realisation, many African women writers generally reject that view, whilst still critiquing a society which denigrates and marginalises childless women. Buchi Emecheta, for example, writes of enjoying the sound of children's voices while writing.

Women writers are seen as 'custodians of traditions' (Taiwo, 1984). They are a central part of the community with 'mothers' being the root of culture and values. In many African societies the term 'mother' is a broader one than in the nuclear families of the West, and usually means grandmother, the oldest wife of the family, and the community of women generally, who have a balanced relationship to other women and the compound. The community was disrupted during slavery, and then during colonialisation where Western values, such as the naturalising of gender inequality, caused gender hierarchising, and the demoting of women's roles as secondary. There has been a similar misvaluing and misrepresentation of both Aboriginal (Chapter 9) and Maori (Chapter 10) women's roles. Since slavery and colonialism, women have become less enfranchised and less powerful in many instances. Much of the work of African women writers aims to redress this imbalance, using perceptions of the importance of women and the voice of women to do so.

In her essay on Nwapa, Jane Bryce-Okunlola concentrates on the issues and treatment of motherhood. For many women in different African states, the pressure to have children is overwhelming and relates to a sense of self and social worth. Nwapa correlates the creativity of writing with that of motherhood:

> The privileges accorded motherhood within traditional society are counterbalanced by the penalties for childlessness, the failure to marry or simply to conform to social expectations. For a writer who by the very act of writing challenges the patriarchal appropriation of power over the Word, motherhood becomes a site for struggle. Its literary representations, explicitly or implicitly, and exploration by women of the last uncolonised territory, an integral part of a woman's identity as a writer. (Bryce-Okunlola, 1991, in Nasta, p. 201)

Flora Nwapa's *Efuru* (1966), *Idu* (1970) and *One is Enough* (1981) demonstrate the ability of women to transform childlessness into something positive in order to change their roles. Kenyan Rebekah Njau's *Ripples in the Pool* (1975) highlights the distortion of relationships within Kenyan society as a result of colonialism and studies the destructive effects of social expectations on women. Njau's protagonist breaks with convention and, childless, projects her needs onto a younger relative of her husband. Text and child are conflated in both Njau and Nwapa. They re-examine roles through the very images, strategies and behaviour which socially constrict them, that is to say, motherhood, and the position of women. In Nwapa's *One is Enough* the main character, Amaka, eventually leaves her useless husband who cannot make her pregnant, succeeds in business, takes a lover who leaves the priesthood for her, and becomes important in the federal commission as commissioner. When her mother tries to persuade her to marry, she sees that this along with the competitiveness of other women to get their daughters to marry, is all part of the same vicious circle of women's lives. 'Wife' is not a word connoting freedom but of belonging to someone:

> As a wife, I am never free. I am a shadow of myself. As a wife I am almost impotent. I am in prison, unable to advance in body and soul. (Nwapa, 1981, p. 127)

She de-centres the role of woman as wife but supports that of woman as mother.

For many African women motherhood is a site for debates about power, pain, social links, reproductive issues and identity, and writing about it is seizing power, redefining and valuing it their own way. Language becomes a country, a 'motherland', something with which, and against which, to define themselves and it is important to recognise the established traditions which have 'mothered' them. It is also interesting to think of these writers in relation to their treatment of their own mothers, the need to define oneself in relation to one's mother, not overwhelmed, but enabled to seek individual identity. Buchi Emecheta felt that her mother, moved from country to city, had not understood her.

In psychoanalytic terms, the French feminist Julia Kristeva (1981) writes about the relation with the mother as very strong, a partnership in the semiotic, the pre-symbolic, that big first relationship before we enter language (see Chapter 1). But it can be smothering for women, unlike boys, who enter into and relate to the world of the father, the symbolic order, more easily. There is a strength in recognising the link with the mother tongue, the pre-symbolic, but also an oppression. It is a delicate relationship between mother and daughter, one of sameness and of powerful, fruitful continuity on the one hand (see Lorna Goodison's 'I am Becoming my Mother' in Chapter 5), or of potential smothering, especially of daughters' desire and need for change and growth, at odds with traditional culture (see Kincaid's *Annie John* in Chapter 5). There are often links between women's loss of home and mother with their loss of identity. Motherless, they can be exploited by men (see the example of Soha in Flora Nwapa's story 'This is Lagos').

The whole relationship between women and their mothers, the motherland, mother tongues and the mothering they do themselves, is necessarily complex. The idea of 'Motherlands' involves both a seeking for roots and identity and a need to define oneself against the Motherland as constricting. 'Mother tongue' is a mode in which to speak of one's own life, yet also potentially restrictive in how much and to whom it can communicate (for further discussion see Chapter 5). However, with the role of mother, woman is equated with the 'Mother Africa' trope and lauded but mistreated. To reject the role completely, though, is to lose much, including the nurturing continuity role. A new kind of mothering, the act of producing writing, allows women to seek a voice, neither that of patriarchy and the father, nor completely the pre-symbolic of the mother, but their own, exploring the minutiae of the difficulties of being women, and mothers. Looking at motherhood as self-image in relation to power or powerlessness is of central importance.

Forms and Styles

Much women's writing in many African states is largely in the realist mode, concentrating on the historical day-to-day world of women's lives either in the villages or in the city. Women in many African communities have always played powerful, matriarchal roles as midwives, herbalists, wise women as well as mothers, wives and sisters in extended families. With the complexities of families comprising several wives, there is much to describe and discuss about inter-wife relations, while the move, in Nigeria particularly, from the village to the city, brings with it challenges to traditional ways. Their fictions are realistic, with local catch phrases, parables rather than fantasy and metaphor and often using many of the characteristics of oral literature such as repetition, circling of story line, and a sense of reporting community responses, articulated through phrases such as 'they said that' and 'it is said that'.

INDIVIDUAL WOMEN WRITERS: THE NOVELISTS

Flora Nwapa

Flora Nwapa has written poetry and much prose fiction: *Efuru* (1966), *Idu* (1970), *Never Again* (1975), *One is Enough* (1981), *Women are Different* (1986), and short stories: *This is Lagos and Other Stories* (1971); *Wives at War and Other Stories* (1980). When *Efuru* appeared it was well received by Grace Ogot and badly by male critics, for the same reason: its concentration on 'the women's world'. Nwapa's depiction of women's lives from a fresh perspective exposes a society close to pre-colonial roots. She has adapted English to reproduce the flavour of the Igbo language, and her use of this orature and folk tales enables her to capture the sense of passing on ideas and culture from generations of women. Flora Nwapa looks at the place of women in community life and uses their eyes and voices, showing that women are powerful, economically secure and socially important, but also limited in their choices in a restrictive culture. By using oral literary techniques, Nwapa evokes the indigenous traditions and society from which they spring. Her writing style is unique, understated and not very descriptive.

Efuru is based on a popular folk tale and concerns a remarkable woman who marries two worthless men of her choice. She has no children and worships a strong female lake deity Umahiri, whose influence empowers her as a woman. Nwapa exposes the pervasiveness of discourses of power as they control women's lives and health. Speakers use 'our fathers say' and 'people say' to back up traditional activities such as female circumcision, and their dialogue, full of anecdote and proverb, convinces even the frightened (see Walker's *Possessing the Secret of Joy*, Chapter 4).

The novel's tension lies in the conflict between a Western-style approach to women's marital and family relations and the security and stability of the African traditional system. The formal structure of the language based on choric repetition matches traditional beliefs about women's childbearing role, against which the childless but still socially valued Efuru is positioned. Utilising the folk tale, Nwapa radically questions the traditional valuation of women. Efuru's embracing of the symbol of the water goddess, who does not embody fertility, questions community beliefs and values of motherhood and fertility. Emecheta's *The Joys of Motherhood* (1979) grows from Nwapa's novel:

> the slave woman linked to the goddess destabilises not only traditional assumptions about fecundity and motherhood, but also old notions of slavery and elitism in a changing world. (Wilson-Tagoe, in Newell, 1997, p. 17)

Efuru spans 1900–1930, a colonial period during which questions are raised about how power relations are constituted between men and women when men have lost their power to new, colonial masters. Efuru still internalises rural values and idealises the rural men, but under colonialism their powerlessness is equal to that of barren women. She seeks her own new identity, and in this way provides a cultural challenge to both established forms of gender and colonial power.

A large-scale critical attack on Nwapa by Jones and Palmer is actually based on a male rejection of both the subject matter and the forms of women's writing (Virginia Woolf would have recognised this). The novel *Efuru*, they say, is 'full of small talk' (Jones and Palmer, 1967). In conventional criticism men are heard to use proverbs and their talk is considered important. Alice Walker critiques assumption of the superiority of one form of talk over another when, in *Possessing the Secret of Joy* (Chapter 4), she records the sexually oppressive proverbs and small talk of male elders. This talk is filled with myths underwriting women's powerlessness and silence. Nwapa deliberately uses women's voices and women's proverbs, developed from roots in orature, to enable the silent to be heard. It is not surprising that this radical move was both criticised and denigrated (Jones and Palmer, 1967, pp. 127–31).

Efuru focuses on many issues and practices of women's lives, illustrating the collusion, and the parallels between patriarchy and colonialism. Nwapa writes about women's production of local gin, an activity banned by colonialists, who made money from its importation. The women are resisting colonialism while the men collude. In her invented Igbo town, Ugwuta, girls' education is secondary to that of boys. There are discussions between women in the novel which show that educated women are considered lazy and collusive with the values of white women, not so industrious as their less educated women friends. Through the agency of the water deity, Uhamiri, with whom Efuru identifies, Nwapa challenges these beliefs that women might be lazy since those worshipping Uhamiri have constructed buildings. A goddess who has not experienced motherhood but is still powerful, satisfied, happy and successful, Uhamiri and her followers challenge Nigerian myths and social expectations.

Andrade (1990, pp. 91–110) explores Nwapa's privileging of women's world views. There is a dialogic tension or argument between the values of 'the discourse of tradition' and that 'of modernity'. Andrade argues that Nwapa cannot entirely escape the values and demands of African culture and 'Efuru's insistence on the virtue of its protagonist and on the importance of Igbo custom indicates Nwapa's privileging of the discourse of tradition over that of modernity' (Andrade, 1990, p. 97). However, perhaps the dialogue ends up as a more balanced response than Andrade suggests. Efuru internalised low self worth through village gossip, but in allying herself with the water spirit, and continuing her work as a teacher even after childbirth (Adizua's child, who dies in infancy), she regains that self worth. Without overthrowing village life and customs, Nwapa repositions women's value as more than mothers alone. As Florence Stratton puts it: 'female infertility is reconceptualized as a feminist strategy' (Stratton, 1994, p. 97).

Stratton identifies a tradition in alignment with the dialogic structure, that of paired women, initiated by Nwapa, continued by Buchi Emecheta, Mariama Ba and Tsitsi Dangarembga. One woman conforms, the other resists in relation to male power. In *Efuru* the sisters, Ossai and Ajanapu, represent alternatives to Efuru. Ossai is Adizua's mother – a submissive, substitute mother for Efuru. Ajanapu, on the other hand, is not submissive but successful in both business and motherhood. *Efuru* provides a model for Nwapa and other African women's fictions, legitimising women's power, crediting their role as subjects, in the face of post-colonial male supremacy.

The role of women in relation to the split between town and village is explored in Nwapa's short story 'This is Lagos' (1971). Soha, a village girl, initially comes to Lagos to look after her aunt's, Mama Eze's, children (women are called 'the mother of' their boy children or firstborn). Mama Eze warns Soha about Lagos men and Lagos values. Lagos is a paradigm for the wicked modern Westernised city, a place of potential downfall and moral danger, especially for women. Soha herself teases the man she meets with the possibility that he may have a wife, becomes embroiled in relationships, cars, money, clothes, shopping – a much faster life – and plans to move away from the yard or home area, gets pregnant, and marries the man. The underlying tone of the story indicates that she is considered in moral danger (village and family views) but that she is not, in terms of the modern city, actually leading an immoral life. Mr Ikenbule, example of the moral danger, is quite mild and malleable, never seen in the story as doing any overt harm. However, the dialogic nature of the story enables us to accept Soha's choices but also to recognise the problems they cause to traditional ways, and thus to Soha. Secret marriage and pregnancy are considered shameful and provoke confrontation. The story ends with the young couple failing to visit Soha's home to tell her parents. Their infringement of pre-nuptial rules ostracises them, which is a loss for all concerned.

It is a cautionary tale of growing up for a woman in the changing times, places and values of Lagos. This moral tale contrasting town and village life portrays different community responses without itself casting blame. There is a debate among many women critics about who or what oppresses women in writing by many African women, and how liberating or otherwise the depiction of the possibly educated, certainly more self-reliant, probably town-based women are. In *One is Enough* (1981), Amaka's eventual decision to divorce her husband and set up business in the city is aided by her 'bottom power' and relationships with men (who she will not marry even when one, a Catholic priest, fathers her male twins). However, Amaka chooses to buy economic freedom, individuality and self-reliance, as well as motherhood. Depending on the critic's stance this can seem 'loose' (which is a patriarchal concept and a way of denigrating women), or a real achievement (but the woman uses her body, so maybe this too colludes with male sexual power, or maybe it does not; she uses her own body as she wishes). Nwapa's novels engage in a debate about women's ability to refuse beliefs and behaviours embedded in patriarchal society and to achieve an alternative for themselves, rather than forcing a complete change of direction.

Women are Different (1986) is an indictment of Western ideologies of women's roles and the perpetuation of gender inequalities through the reading of 'true romances' such as those of Marie Corelli, who sold well in the 1940s and 1950s. In this novel four girls – Rose, Dora, Agnes and Comfort – deal with choices of love and marriage, marriages for money (a more traditional way) or Westernised true love romances (conformist choice). The three who pick love and marriage face the loss of their homes and savings, isolation and desertion and, worst of all, a constant internalised sense of disillusionment, of lack based on the promises of true romance. Comfort, on the other hand, listens to her own mother (two of the other girls have lost theirs) and lives happily, warning the others. Doris's daughter, Chinwe, makes similar financial choices. She decides not to marry but to remain single, a city businesswoman, with her own Mercedes. For this choice she receives criticism from the other women, who treat her life as a scandal, but Nwapa obviously supports her independence:

Chinwe had done the right thing. Her generation was doing better than her mother's own. Her generation was telling men that there are different ways of living one's life fully and fruitfully. They are saying that women have options. . . . Marriage is not THE only way. (Nwapa, 1986, pp. 118–19)

Nwapa's and Emecheta's novels establish a new form for much African women's writing in which women are not Other but self-defining. She also writes poetry using 'feminine' alternative voices, and deconstructs the use of images which represent women.

Buchi Emecheta

What Flora Nwapa starts, Buchi Emecheta takes more than a step further, acknowledging her literary female forebears and allying herself as 'their new sister' (Umeh, 1980, p. 25). She mentions Nwapa's success when Adah, her heroine in *Second Class Citizen* (1974), has her book thrown in the fire by her husband. Buchi Emecheta has written to date twelve novels and an autobiography, short stories, children's stories and television plays. She has been able to support herself by her writing since the late 1970s, stating: 'If I am now a feminist then I am an African feminist' ('Feminism' p. 175). Her work clearly rejects women's subordinated status, asserting the power and stoicism of many African women from different social contexts, their many abilities and skills and, in the earlier novels, rejection of the violence of some men. She questions traditional female roles within many African societies and the 'joys of motherhood' ideal. This, the title of her most famous novel, taken from the last words of Nwapa's *Efuru*, recognises through intertextuality a female literary tradition beginning with Nwapa. Escape to a new life in England, however, while sometimes bringing economic independence, is neither totally ideal (no real escape to a feminist dreamland because of the racism inherent in the daily life of the UK), nor is there a rejection of relationships with men. Emecheta enquires:

God, when will you create a woman who will be fulfilled in herself, a full human being, not anybody's appendage? . . . What have I gained for all this? Yes I have my children, but what do I have to feed them on? On my life . . . who made the law that we should not hope in our daughters? We women subscribe to that law more than anyone. Until we change all this, it is still a man's world, which women will always help to build. (Emecheta, 1980, pp. 196–7)

The Joys of Motherhood (1980) is an ironic tale illustrating not joys but externally enforced, internalised social and cultural pressures. Nnu Ego is the love-child of her father and his concubine. Her first marriage is for life but its childlessness is a source of torment. In Africa women's ability to bear children is thought to be directly related to their presumed morality and goodness: 'when a woman is virtuous, it is easy for her to conceive' (p. 52). She asks why women were not created in their own right but always in terms of how they relate to men. The marriage ends, she is subsequently married off to the revolting, brutal Naife, and although she conceives a child it dies. She escapes only to return to bear him children, buckling down, for a while.

We might imagine that sisterhood results in households with many wives but *The Joys of Motherhood* illustrates Emecheta's wry, sensitive response to the complexities of living in a such a household, coping with rivalries and hoping for solidarity. Nnu Ego and her sailor husband, Naife, have a working relationship when he is away at sea, and she enjoys spending the money he brings back, but the kind of independence she has been able to enjoy starts to disappear when he remains at home for a long time. He becomes 'the lord and master'. When the old customs prevail and her husband's brother dies, she has to learn to take into her household the husband's brother's wives, as her husband's wives: '"Oh Naife, how are you going to cope? All those children, and all those wives." Here she stopped, and the truth hit her like a heavy blow' (p. 54). Naife has to pay for Owulum's wives, two of whom are coming to live with them, and so he gets a job as a grass cutter. A battle of dominance and ownership ensues between the new wife Adaku, and Nnu Ego, each trying to ensure they are in favour, each speaking up, or biding their time.

The intertextual relationship with Nwapa's novels goes beyond the novel's title. Nnu Ego's mother was buried with a live slave woman – now Nnu Ego's 'chi', or spirit, who taunts her, holding a beautiful then a dirty baby before her and promising her several dirty babies. The same river deity Uhamiri is involved, which suggests transcendence over the slave woman as chi, defeat. Nnu Ego overcomes the social forces working against her but, mother of seven children, she dies by a roadside. Florence Stratton comments, 'critics generally view Emecheta's novels as providing an authentic representation of African women':

> *The Joys of Motherhood* stands as a model for other African women writers who wish to portray the actual condition of women and their response to their condition. (Stratton, 1994, p. 113)

In fact, Emecheta constantly shows how her protagonists' lives and successes, or otherwise, are related to their economic, historical and social, not merely their gendered, contexts. Nnu Ego's life is conditioned by her poverty as much as by her traditional sense of the need for children and obedience to her men. When her sons grow up they reject the values that she has tried to instil in them, adopting, instead, the Westernised city values of Lagos following their university educations, and so she is left alone. The second wife, Adaku, refuses to conform. She is not punished for this but retains ties with Nnu Ego when she leaves.

In this instance we see the difficulties of women in shared households and the kind of mastery men might develop when there is competition: issues of heredity and of sexual politics predominate. In everyday life there is little opportunity in such a competitive situation for women to develop genuine sisterhood.

Buchi Emecheta shows that there is little opportunity for many African women from different social contexts to change their lives because there are no options, only motherhood and work, no professional opportunities. The lone woman is totally displaced.

Emecheta's *Destination Biafra* (1982) has been seen as an intervention in the masculine tradition of records of the Nigerian civil war (1967–1970). Her African feminist intervention concentrates on recording the women's war, rescuing such experience from oblivion. It is a harrowing tale of long difficult treks through the bush, and of the inability of women to preserve their children in the face of a dehumanising response from young male soldiers. Emecheta exposes hidden histories: rape, disembowelling and the murdering of unborn infants. Debbie Ogedemgbe journeys across the warring country after the death of her (corrupt) wealthy father. For the reader she comes to represent the stoicism and determination to survive prevalent in writing by women from many African contexts. Escaping the war with her mother and servant, dressed in army uniform, Debbie and her party are attacked by soldiers. The moment is terrible, but Emecheta deals very clearly and delicately with the turning of the soldiers from bravado, to joking, to threats and ultimately to torture, rape and murder. Their own soldiers' response to the gang rape which Debbie and her mother survive but which results in the murder of the young woman and her infants (one unborn) is an apology of sorts:

'It's war, madam, I'm sure those boys were only provincial militia'

. . .

'Madam, the dead woman was an Ibo, you said so yourself.'
'What of my daughter?'
'Give her hot water to wash herself. Hundreds of women have been raped – so what? it's war. She's lucky to be even alive. She'll be all right.'

(Emecheta, 1982, p. 135)

Ethnic conflict seems to be taken as a perfectly legitimate excuse for dehumanising brutality; something we have seen more recently in the former Yugoslavia. Emecheta's is one of very few novels recording women's sufferings in war, within or without Africa. Debbie's rejection of the horrors of a war produced by conflicting men of power, which slaughters the innocents, is that of a woman who is also a colonial subject. Near the book's close, her rejection of marriage to her journalist lover, Alan Grey, is in response to insights resulting from suffering in the war, and her awareness of the role that imperialism and its power games have played and could continue to play in her life:

Why, why should you want to take me along with you? To start patronising me with your charity all over again? . . . I see now that Abosi and his like are still colonised. They need to be decolonised. I am not like him, a black white man; I am a woman and a woman of Africa. I am a daughter of Nigeria and if she is in shame, I shall stay and mourn with her in shame. No, I am not ready yet to become the wife of an exploiter of my nation. (Emecheta, 1982, p. 258)

Alan Grey's 'thoughtful' internal response is that Debbie is foolish. His tone is the coloniser's familiar one: 'That was the trouble with these Blacks. Give them some education and they quoted it all back at you, as if the education was made for them in the first place' (Emecheta, 1982, p. 259). Emecheta is not rabidly anti-male, she is exploring the complex relationships between gender, power and race throughout her work, whether it be set in Nigeria as this novel is (albeit at a distance – she wrote it in London and was protesting in Trafalgar Square while the Biafran war raged in Nigeria, so her objectivity is a useful perspective), London or South Africa (*Kehinde*, 1994), or London (*Gwendolen*, 1989).

In *Gwendolen*, Emecheta moves from her own surroundings in Nigeria and the UK and concentrates on the life of another diasporan woman, a Caribbean adolescent who comes to settle in London and tries hard to fit in but finds the culture and traditions set against her, her life and beliefs devalued.

Meeting her parents in the UK is exciting, and racism is not so overt (the white cab driver thanks her Black father for his tip), but Gwendolen none the less recognises a kind of invisibility as a covert racism:

> many white people did not actually insult her parents, but they treated them as if they were not there. And whenever her mother tried to communicate with them they made her repeat herself several times.   (Emecheta, 1989, p. 72)

She is regarded as a 'free dinner' because of prejudicial assumptions (despite her parents' good wages) that all Black children are on welfare. Emecheta steps out from the story to point out the cruel absurdities of everyday racism:

> Those who made society's laws are still a long way from knowing that Gwendolen's inability to speak or understand one brand of the English language does not automatically mean that she need be considered an imbecile. But to keep a school like hers running smoothly and with less friction for all concerned, it was easier for her to be regarded as one.   (Emecheta, 1989, p. 74)

Gwendolen's family is not idealised. She has suffered incest and abuse, and it recurs, this time from her own father, who beats his wife as well as raping Gwendolen. Pregnant, she fears her boyfriend will reject her when he discovers the child is not his. However, actually having the child, Iyamide, gives Gwendolen a full sense of purpose and identity. She can rise above her mother's referring to her as bad luck and establish her own life. In this case, childbearing brings a sense of identity, a new reading of the joys of motherhood in the UK.

There is a dialogue in Emecheta's novels between women's search for self-identity and self-affirmation, against colonialism and racism, and the possible relations with men in all their conventional and not so conventional forms. In her latest novel *Kehinde* (1994) this is developed to interesting cross-cultural effect. There is a fascinating exploration of an educated Nigerian woman in the UK whose life of relatively equal opportunities is threatened by the reclaiming of her husband into traditional Nigerian ways. Kehinde's husband Albert returns to Nigeria, as if that were a necessary next step (as his sisters insist) in order to become 'someone' and parade his wealth. Her friend Mariammo insists that she will have a life of power and leisure, advising her: 'be a been-to Madam. Put your feet up. Be a white woman' (Emecheta, 1994, p. 52). Ignored by some of her more pretentious friends because suddenly without a husband, she eventually moves to join him, but finds the traditional ways unbearable. In the Nigerian house Kehinde suddenly discovers she is supposed to be head wife: Albert has taken a second, younger wife, a teacher who has a baby by him. The sisters find this normal, and are pleased that Kehinde will have no other role. Rike, the second wife, is interestingly described, her education (as in Nwapa's novels) is a route to earning, but often a hindrance to wifely success. However: 'Rike is a clever African woman, in spite of her book knowledge' (Emecheta, 1994, p. 74). She won lonely Albert over, and her second child is on the way. Kehinde is not even expected or invited to Albert's bed when she arrives, so when he does come to her bedroom she decides to assert her independence and shows him the door. She cannot find economic independence because she cannot work, and in her idleness she is deemed lazy even by the second wife's servants. There is no glory or peace in this once revered role. Even her children, now at boarding school, provide no role for her day-to-day existence. Kehinde rejects the oppressions of the vacuously urbane version of traditional Nigerian ways; Albert is still boastful and wasteful; the new wife has debts and there is the threat of a third woman whom he meets on his working trips. Borrowing money from her friend in the UK, she returns to her own London home and relative economic security.

Emecheta negotiates a dialogue between traditional and modern ways, African and Western feminism. Kehinde's return could be seen as a triumph for Western feminism, but it is not so simple. Despite her qualifications and previous role in a bank she finds the only work an African woman is thought capable of in London is cleaning, as 'an educated black person in a responsible job is too much of a threat' (Emecheta, 1994, p. 125). Emecheta shows the difficulties of different kinds of existence, the common factor being that women alone, with ability, can rely on their own stoicism but not much on justice in the UK, while in Africa, independence would be impossible. There are problems in each situation. Kehinde, however, is strong of spirit and does not despair. Her son, returning with African patriarchal beliefs, is shocked at her lifestyle and expects to own the house. Property rights are not his in the UK, however. She points out: 'How could you deal with a rebel who happened to be your mother?' (Emecheta, 1994, p. 141). Kehinde develops an undemanding relationship with her Caribbean lodger. They live happily together without having to marry or conform to the structures of either society in terms of their relationships. Kehinde has found a way of managing, enabling her to locate her own values.

Like Nwapa, Buchi Emecheta often uses paired women who make different choices. While her men are shadowy or stereotypical, her women are socially, culturally, economically, and historically contextualised, and her novels develop a finely tuned social dialogue between economic, gendered and racial values and behaviours.

Grace Akinyi Ogot

Born in Kenya in 1930, Grace Ogot trained as a nurse in St Thomas's Hospital, London, married in 1959, studied at Makeree University in 1963–4 and became an announcer for BBC radio and principal of the women's training centre, Kisumu Kenyashe. Ogot has been a UN delegate, a member of UNESCO, a Member of Parliament and founding chairperson of the Writers' Association of Kenya. Her first novel, *The Promised Land* (1966), was the first imaginative book in English by a Luo writer. It highlights her concern for women's roles and fascination with the supernatural and mystery. A young couple moving to farm in Tanzania, despite the wife's misgivings, discover that witchcraft is causing the husband's illness, which can only be relieved by leaving. Ogot's short stories (*Land Without Thunder*, 1968) are folk tales of fantasy and magic. They mix travel stories and conflicts between Western and African tribal healing practices, querying women's traditional roles. In 'The Rain Came' Oganda, the chief's daughter, due for traditional sacrifice to the lake monster to provoke much needed rain, is rescued by the love and cunning of her betrothed, Osinda. The rain falls anyway, so questioning traditional beliefs in myths. *The Other Woman* (1976) mixes magic and realism. Later work, *The Island of Tears* (1980) and *The Graduate*, a novelette (1980), focus on tensions and benefits created when women travel, become educated, return as an educated elite and participate in social change. Ogot negotiates a gendered political-change agenda, and a questioning of the powers of traditional myth and magic, which frequently oppress women.

Ama Ata Aidoo

Ama Ata Aidoo of Ghana has written several plays and novels and is extremely innovative, writing of issues of political concern with a sense of humour. She maintains that women are sensitive, traditional victims of a male power and abuse, developed in response to social pressures and powerlessness. *Our Sister Killjoy* (1977) represents relationships between men and women in a wider social and cultural context:

> By placing love and sexual relations solidly within the domain of politics, Aidoo widens the woman's sphere and makes it the site of interrogation and debate. Love, she insists, cannot be meaningful for an African man or woman unless it can also acknowledge and contend with that monumental power and lure of Europe, which continually threatens the very survival of African Identity. (Wilson-Tagoe, 1997, in Newell, p. 24)

Keeping a grip on reality and community are very important to her. As in novels by many African women more generally, Sissie herself challenges versions of women as meek. The novel, dynamic and aware, invites us to witness artistic creation. Africa's place in history is central, both to the first few chapters of the novel and to Sissie's claim for equality alongside African men. Using the novel-within-a-novel structure, the novel can be seen as 'written by Sissie', bold and courageous, readier to accept her lover abandoning her than compromise over a new view of love and identity. It concentrates on critiquing the bad dream of Africa's relationship with the

West through Sissie's uniting old values and new possibilities of male–female relationships in post-colonial Africa:

> Aidoo's works privilege a woman's sphere of existence instead of representing it as something given. Aidoo's privileging process extends beyond revision and polemic to encompass the domain not only of men but of the entire social world.   (Wilson-Tagoe, 1997, in Newell, p. 22)

ORAL STORYTELLING

Many of the novels by Nwapa, Emecheta and others utilise oral storytelling forms, which flourish, especially in Northern Nigeria, among the Hausa-speaking people: 'Women's art of oral storytelling is as ancient as the people themselves in Hausa-speaking areas of northern Nigeria' (Abba Aliyu, 1997, p. 149). Hausa has had alphabetisation and an Arabic-based script for many years. There has also been some development of literacy among married women, who, under Islam, are likely to be married to polygamous husbands. Traditionally, women were left behind when the men went off to work, and in the dark and the time of the rains they would gather extended families together and weave stories where:

> the art of narration was sub-divided, with different genres distributed along gender lines. It appears that storytelling was consigned to women while other forms of narratives such as the hikaya and labari, perceived by male-dominated societies to be more serious, were the verbal province of the males.   (Abba Aliyu, 1997, p. 150)

In this largely non-literate community, women express their intellect and creativity in the imaginative re-retelling of stories, usually to adolescents and children. Hausa women are versatile and good at using linguistic resources, and they are socially involved because of families, child-rearing and trading. When marriages take place the bride leads marathon sessions aided by friends' contributions and applauded by the many children who will congregate to listen after the ceremonies. 'Hausa women, children and the marriage institution are therefore vital to the survival of oral storytelling' (Abba Aliyu, 1997, p. 151). Often they start with riddles and answers sharpening wits, and there are opening and closing conventions, including moral tags and symbolism. As the Hausas were dragged into the economic system, social attitudes to, and the contents of storytelling have been affected. After Independence in 1960 indigenous radio broadcasts were boosted, women took their storytelling onto the air, and 'Shafa Labari Shuni' ('Making Stories Sweeter') began. In the 1980s Hausa narratives turned to pulp fiction and to younger writers, but the programme has continued: 'fluent, persuasive and skilled women narrate each broadcast' (Abba Aliyu, 1997, p. 155). 'What has emerged in contemporary broadcasts is therefore a coalescence of storytelling traditions, the women's narrative expertise, and the historical exigencies of Hausa broadcasting' (Abba Aliyu, 1997, p. 155).

The most popular narrators are Mairiga Aliyu, replaced recently by Habiba Rabiu Bako, both with only elementary Western education. They appeal to mothers and grandmothers and have not been exposed to popular fiction. The programmes are listened to by 35 million to 50 million listeners and recently people were requested to send in reading materials – their own work. However, this storytelling broadcasting is very traditional:

> In the traditional oral storytelling milieu, female narrators were confined to the home, exercising their skills on children: in contrast the male narrators on the radio have achieved almost limitless patronage. This prominence of female storytellers does not extend, however, to decision-making in male-dominated Hausa society. All of the key decisions in Shafa Labari Shuni are taken by men, and the women simply carry out instructions from above. Furthermore, the content of the scripts they read is frequently *yani* – women. Whether classical works of Hausa literature or 'pulp' fiction from Kano, their stories regularly depict women in subordinate roles, totally dependent on men for their survival in society. (Abba Aliyu, 1997, p. 156)

It will take more than women storytellers to challenge negative stereotyping of women in Nigeria, particularly among the Muslim women.

In pre-colonial times, Muslim Hausa women, secluded in their homes, were praise singers. There are two terms, *waka* – appropriate to praise songs for important individuals – and *wakoki* – which are extemporaneous. The written works are more private, the *wakoki* often appear in newspapers. The praise singer is considered to be of a special class with which Hausa people do not wish to be associated:

> The northern Nigerian women who perform extemporaneously forfeit for their profession even more respectability than do their male counterparts because they are neither secluded nor subject to a husband's demands.   (Mack, 1986, p. 183)

Some of the verse is bawdy, which is controversial. However, the poets are not necessarily lone, rebellious women. Some travel, leaving husbands at home. Some women perform extemporaneously, others with an accompanying chorus of women beating on calabashes. Others perform more established verse of greetings, thanks and praise. One woman, Binta Katsina, has become known for her song advocating women's participation in the Nigerian workforce (Mack, 1986, p. 185):

> You should do every kind of work,
> You should know every kind of work,
> You can write papers, you can pound the typewriter,
> You can fly aeroplanes,
> You know how to be in the office,
> You could do the government work,
> And you could be the police workers,
> You could do the customs work.
> Lets give you the chance
> Women of Nigeria.
> Women of Nigeria, you know every kind of work.
>   (Katsina, 1980, 'Wakar Matan Nigeria' – [Song for the
>   women of Nigeria], in Mack, 1983, pp. 70–9)

Much poetry by Hausa women is irreverent and revolutionary. Two women, Hauwa Gwaram and Hajiya 'Yar Shelu, reinforce established views about hygiene, childcare and women's roles. They put 'Alkalami A Hannun Mata' [a pen in the hand of women] (Katsina, in Mack, 1986).

Whether writing poetry or prose fiction, many women writers challenge established traditional versions of women's roles, celebrating women as individual subjects who are able to take on a variety of roles, without either losing or being overwhelmed and entirely defined by their roles as mothers.

7

South African Women's Writing

Sometimes when it rains
Rains for days without break
I think of mothers
who give birth in squatter camps
Under plastic shelters
At the mercy of cold angry winds ...

(Mhlope, 'Sometimes When it Rains', 1987, p. 205)

INTRODUCTION – CULTURAL CONTEXTS

This chapter concentrates on women's writing from South Africa, looking initially at the historical and political context in which women have written since the beginning of the century. It briefly considers writing by Olive Schreiner, the first South African woman writer to really achieve prominence, and the foremother of contemporary South African women's writing, looking briefly at *The Story of an African Farm* (1883), then moving on to the mid-twentieth-century work of Doris Lessing. Most of the chapter will concentrate on Black South African women's writing, with particular interest in Bessie Head and Zoe Wicomb, both bi-racial Black South Africans who, among many others of their generations, left the country in order to write about it. During and post-Apartheid, other writers have also published, such as Miriam Tlali, and the Afrikaner writer Ingrid de Kok. Many women write about living in exile and explore sufferings and isolation caused by sexism and racism, either reporting these in factually based stories (Miriam Tlali) or in semi-fictionalised autobiographical writing (Bessie Head and Zoe Wicomb). Others, like Gcina Mhlope (above), document the hardships and horrors of daily life under apartheid, concentrating on how ordinary

159

people try to live their lives in conditions of poverty and under threat.

Racism is a key issue in South African writing, as Olive Schreiner put it:

> Irrespective of nationality and time, the line at which light race meets dark is the line at which human society is found at the lowest ebb; and wherever that line comes into existence, there are found the darkest shadows which we humans have cast by our injustice and egoism across the earth. (Schreiner, 'Thoughts on South Africa', 1923)

Henrik Vervoerd, Prime Minister in 1953, limited educational opportunity and opportunity for life:

> if the native in South Africa today, in any kind of school in existence is being taught to expect that he will live his adult life under a policy of equal rights, he is making a big mistake. There is no place for him in any European community above the level of certain forms of labour. (Vervoerd, 1953, in Pomeroy, 1971, p. 22)

Apartheid's deliberate repression of the hopes, quality of human life, and ability to read and express experiences of, and feelings about, those lives restricted the opportunity of writers for many years. T. T. Moyana argues that its totalitarian laws were 'legislating literature out of existence': 'An additional difficulty for the creative artist in South Africa, especially the black writer, is that life itself is too fantastic to be outstripped by the creative imagination' (Moyana, 1976, p. 95). The Publications Control Board, founded in 1963 amid protest, decided on what was to be published. There were around 15,000 books banned by March 1971.

Despite these difficulties, the people of the Republic of South Africa have actually produced fine writing against a backdrop of oppression and with little leisure time to write, particularly women. There is also little education, and much poverty. Manoko Nchwe, an unpublished woman writer, told interviewer Bottumelo:

> Women reside outside of the networks which facilitate the production of literature.... They must be given the opportunity to express or present their works without feeling that there are few women writers around. (Manoko Nchwe, with Bottumelo, 1986)

If the writers wished to write, inevitably, about racism, they were banned, or had to do so from a position of exile, like Noni Jabavu, the first modern writer of South African women's novels. Amelia House left South Africa for England and Bessie Head was a stateless person for years in Botswana. Others remained behind but had their work curtailed. Ellen Kuzwayo, a middle-class woman, wrote *Call Me Woman* (1985), an autobiography illustrating how Black people have survived with fortitude. Winnie Mandela lived under house-arrest, and phoned her autobiography, *Part of My Soul Went With Him*, in 1985, to her publisher abroad. Miriam Makeba related her story to James Hall; Nadine Gordimer wrote about the situation in essays, novels and short stories. Miriam Tlali, who remained in South Africa, published *Muriel at the Metropolitan* in 1975, *Amandla, a Novel* in 1980, and *Soweto Stories* in 1989. She was not allowed to enter the library because she was Black (her book was within). Lauretta Ngcobo left for London in 1966. Her 1981 novel *Cross of Gold* (banned in South Africa) portrays guerrilla struggles across South Africa. Farisa Karodia, now in Canada, writes of some Canadian settings and themes but in *Daughters of the Twilight* (1986) and *Coming Home and Other Stories* (1988), reflects the problems of ethnic groups in South Africa. Zoe Wicomb spent years in Britain, returned and now lives in Scotland, her fictionalised autobiographical short story sequence/novel is *You Can't Get Lost in Cape Town* (1987); Jayapraga Reddy produced *On the Fringe of Dream-Time and Other Stories* (1987), and has been working towards a novel; Sheila Fugard moves between New York and South Africa. Agnes Sam produced *Jesus is Indian and Other Stories* (1989).

Black creative writing in South Africa began in the middle of the nineteenth century, encouraged by the missionaries. Writers initially produced religious works, encouraged by the Rev. Shepherd, who eventually wanted to see a cultural revival and Black publishing houses. The first novel was *An African Tragedy* (undated) by Hie Dhlomo who contributed to journals, such as *Bantu World* and *The Sjambok*. In the 1950s Black writers began publishing in, for example, *The New Statesman*, where some of Bessie Head's stories appeared. Magazines such as *Transitions* encouraged young Black writers. Some exiled writers became established and published, but for women, publication was slower due to lack of money. There were few outlets for novels until recently, and no patronage.

Apartheid literally separated – divided to rule – the different racial groups which comprise South Africa, and separated from the world the experiences and the writing of these groups, denying their reading freedoms by making any South African writing, particularly that by women, an all-pervading absence in their own (and our own) classrooms. Betty Govinden writes of her apartheid education, that the journal *Drum* was read at home, but never appeared in official reading. Under colonialism, indigenous writing was unavailable and discredited for readers:

> Can it be true that black women writers were writing since the turn of the century, yet they never made their way into my classrooms in this town on the north coast of Kwazulu-Natal. Even Olive Schreiner's *The Story of an African Farm* (1883), though presented to me as an exemplary model of 'indigenous' writing, was not depicted for its singular South African perspective, nor for its place in feminist thinking at a time when the world was moving into the second wave of feminist thinking and writing. (Govinden, 1995, p. 174)

Reflections of her own experience were absent: 'this daily history was slighted by a politics of selection working invisibly on behalf of my colonised self' (Govinden, 1995, p. 175).

Olive Schreiner

Schreiner was active for women's rights in the early part of the twentieth century, spending some of her time in the UK. A polemical writer, her essays *Woman and Labour* (1911) explicitly linked the subordination of women to their economic position, their role within marriage, described as a kind of prostitution since women were dependent upon their husbands for financial support. Her novel *Story of an African Farm* (1883) depicts the experience of living in South Africa, highlighting difficult relations between people of British and of Afrikaner or Boer descent and the local people or 'Hottentots' and 'kaffirs', as they are called, concentrating on exploring the limited potential for women at that time. Schreiner focuses on a monstrous Boer woman, Tant Sannie. Her repressive regime, bolstered up by the transient Bonaparte Blenkins (his name suggests tyranny), dominates the lives of two young girls. One, Em, is the typical motherly wifely sort, never seeking any other kind of life; the other, Lyndall, is far in advance of her generation's opportunities (in that context) for free-thinking women. In the figure of Lyndall,

Schreiner explores the possibilities of the new woman. Lyndall rails gainst sex slavery in marriage and against the ways in which women are encouraged to appear vacuous and pretty. Her own light form constantly provokes others to admire and praise her, and this in itself somewhat limits her own possible development. Lyndall, becoming pregnant and refusing to marry, treks off, sees her baby die, and resides in our memories as a sad figure whose potential is thwarted because of her cultural and temporal context. In the novel some men operate in an alternative way; one, Waldo, is a philosopher and another, Gregory Rose, actually cross-dresses as a nurse to help nurse Lyndall. Schreiner, like Woolf her contemporary, investigates the crushing results of gendered roles in her society, a correlative to her polemic and her utopian writing (e.g. 'Three Dreams in a Desert'). During and after the Boer War (1902–4) Schreiner wrote articles against colonial and imperialist racism but to a contemporary readership she is a paradoxical figure because of her interests in eugenics (a theory of the improvement of the race, which underpinned Nazism and is itself a racist approach based on social Darwinism – the survival of the fittest, or rather, what one controlling racial group would define as fittest and best in humankind). The last few years of her life were spent initially in England, active in pacificist political work, then in South Africa.

Bessie Head

> Head's writing is not unpolitical; it is fiercely committed to a politics of localism: small scale, decentred, heterogeneous, agrarian and egalitarian; flexible and opportunistic. Such politics, though, stand opposed to the grand recit of national liberation struggle that constitutes the dominant narrative mode of political fiction in Africa. (Lazarus, 1990, p. 211)

Bessie Head was born in Petermaritzburg in 1937 in a mental hospital. Her wealthy white mother had a dead child and failed marriage behind her and Bessie was the product of her relationship with a Zulu stable boy. Her mother died six years later, her family having rejected her. Bessie was put into care first with a 'coloured' foster family ('coloured' in South Africa refers to people who are of mixed race, rather than of Black African descent. Hierarchically, under Apartheid, it was thought to be socially superior to be 'coloured' than to be of Black African – Xhosa, Hausa or Zulu most probably in

South Africa – descent). Then she was placed in an orphanage until she finished school at eighteen. She became a teacher and journalist, and in 1962 married Harold Head, a fellow reporter. Her son, Howard, was born in 1963. Although refused a passport, she left in 1964 with her son to live in Botswana: 'I desire above all else to be ordinary', she said. Bessie lived in the bleak arid Serowe for years writing of this rootlessness, 'restless in a distant land'.

She chose Botswana wisely, putting down roots. As Craig Mackenzie, the editor of her autobiographical writings, comments: 'The sense of Botswana's almost uninterrupted African history had an immediate and profound influence on her, a victim of almost total deracination in the land of her birth' (Head, 1990, p. xvii).

Her first novel, *When Rain Clouds Gather* (1969), was based on her time at the Bamangwato Development Farm, and shows the problems of development in a Third World agrarian society. Her work is filled with imaginative power and moral engagement. The description of the dryness of the area and the sense of death and suffering is very fine and detailed. The novel deals with an experiment to found an ideal 'new world' at Golema, where, although sexual equality is intended and much practised, there is still male leadership in the cooperative. This utopia provides a cutting comment on the non-utopian world outside the community. Her moral idealism is a response to the harsh realities around her. *When Rain Clouds Gather* promises rewards if the people work hard and invest in their future.

Head is practical and interested in both communal development and the inner self. 'In her concern for women and madness, Bessie Head has almost single-handedly brought about the inward turning of the African novel' (Larson, 1973). Her work is very thoughtful and self-conscious, much of it containing traces of autobiography. *A Question of Power* (1974) relates to her own breakdown and mental illness. After fifteen years she received citizenship and travelled internationally to writing conferences. She says she chose the novel because it was 'like a large bag into which one (could) stuff anything – all one's philosophical, social and romantic speculations' (Barnett, 1983, p. 119).

> I believe in the contents of the human heart, especially when that heart was a silent and secret conspiracy against all the insanity and hatred in mankind.   (*Makeba Muse*, Donga, February 1977, p. 6)

She is the only non white South African woman writing in English to deal at length and in any significant terms with sexual roles and racial identity as they are related to each other, and as they represent the author's view of the world at large. There is a special bleakness in Head's vision and world view, one that seems to have been stimulated by an intense sense of isolation. (Brown, 1981, p. 159)

A Question of Power is a very subjective novel. The narrative is filtered through the perception of Elizabeth, the protagonist, who is working in Motabeng in Botswana as a teacher. The dominant reality of the novel is Elizabeth's consciousness, which is filled with self-doubts, always partially in a breakdown, and removed from the events of her social environment. Elizabeth, like Head, is told her white mother died in a mental hospital. Her hallucinations revolve around Sello and Dan, two male figures who nightly operate a power game through her semi-waking dreams. Sello is the symbol of love and compassion, Dan of male, destructive egotism and power. Although they resemble men she knows, they are actually constructs of her imagination. They war in her perception, reflecting ways in which she perceives the men in her life, and more broadly, the oppressions of misplaced power. Dan is erotic and seductive, disgusting and powerful; Sello seems Dan's opposite – standing for love as a religious principle and harmony. However, Sello has developed this play between the two of them in order to test Elizabeth, so he turns out to be yet another manipulative male. Her dichotomous view of the world dominates her hallucinations: moral idealism versus power and evil, but Elizabeth moves gradually to a notion of being able to recognise these two images for what they are, ways of helping her to deal with her own conflicts and of analysing the insidiousness of power (racial and sexual) which she has experienced. She is hospitalised, then moves out of her breakdown into self-awareness and a sense of possibility for change. Like the work of Doris Lessing, Head's investigations into breakdown as a form of breakthrough are highly topical for women writers at that time. The process of Elizabeth's mental breakdown, her hallucinatory sessions, her restless nights of torture from the monsters that torment her can only be so accurately and so intensely created, as Arthur Ravenscroft says, by a novelist who had herself gone through a similar experience:

in assessing her particular achievement in this regard, the critic must marvel at such perfect fusion of subject and object, and the calibre and stature of a creative imagination which is capable of maintaining such a clear separation of identity between Elizabeth the fictive character and Bessie Head the novelist.   (Ravenscroft, 1976, p. 185)

In both *When Rain Clouds Gather* and *Serowe, Village of the Rain Wind*, Bessie Head concentrates on celebrating the stoicism, the working realism of the women who throw themselves into agricultural work and child-rearing, recognising that romance is an irrelevant Westernised pastime and not a foundation for marriage:

> This feminist representation rejects the usual dwelling on marriage and motherhood for an exploration of the more profound terms of power relationships where the key to a betterment of women's position, which she desires and advocates, lies in keeping the power-hungry system, personalities and aspects of one's character in check. Head understood their predicament. . . . Head highlights their adaptability in the face of physical and emotional deprivation, economic and sexual abuse: their survival strategy. (Ola, 1994, p. 71)

'Private growth as a prerequisite for social change' (Ravenscoft, 1976, p. 180) moves Head's work, like these other fictions, away from mere protest and towards suggestions for development and change. She finds separation of people an intolerable evil. In *Maru* (1971) she confronts the horrors of racism directly, concentrating on the life of missionary-educated teacher Margaret Cadmore, a Bushman (or San, considered the lowest form of humanity by Africans). Margaret experiences discrimination and abuse in her first job, but, loved by Maru, who is set to be chief, befriended by the powerful Dikeledi, and talented in her teaching and artwork, she rises against this destructive version of herself and achieves a sense of self worth. Discrimination based on race and colour is challenged by this novel, set against the beliefs that

> if the white man thought that Asians were a low, filthy nation, Asians could still smile with relief – at least they there not Africans. And if the white man thought Africans were a low filthy nation, Africans in Southern Africa could still smile – at least they were not Bushmen. They all have their monsters.   (*Maru*, 1971, p. 11)

Alice Walker recognised Bessie Head as one of her favourite uncelebrated foreign writers. Gillian Stead Eilersen's edition of some of Bessie's short narratives in *Tales of Tenderness and Power* (1989) and Craig Mackenzie's *Bessie Head: A Woman Alone – Autobiographical Writing* (1990) provide chronological samplings of her prose and large numbers of her works. Kolawele Ogungbesan comments:

> and herein lies the taproot of her other vision, for alienation is not everything in her, she also gives us a sense of a much wider commitment to the main ethical and social attitudes of the world at large than any contemporary South African writers. Here 'commitment' denotes a binding engagement of oneself to a course of action which transcends any purely personal advantage.... Miss Head's uniqueness derives from her combining an intense awareness of alienation with a commitment to issues larger than personal interest. The clue lies in her life, which made alienation not an endless discovery demanding expression, but merely the initial premise. (1994, p. 207)

Cherry Clayton, writing of Head in *A Bewitched Crossroad* (1984), considers her liberation from constricting protest paradigms, creating an 'artistic matrix, an imaginative equivalent of her moral and social ideal for Southern Africa' (p. 55). Historian and artist, she focuses less on the daily problems of apartheid and more on underlying cultural beliefs and formations.

Her treatment of women is realistic and emphasises the need for social and political recognition of equality. Dikeledi in *Maru*, although of noble birth, carries out domestic functions, also playing an important part as an intellectual and leader. The imaginative powers of women provide alternative world views to the popular imaginary in which women would be silenced and secondary or iconised as fertile mother nature (see Chapter 6 on 'Mother Africa'). Head's women are complex, emotional, talented and sensitive, and struggle with the real problems of marginalism and racism: in *A Question of Power*, with identity crises, and in *Maru*, with intense racism.

In her short stories *The Collector of Treasures* (1977) she is concerned with Botswana's history, myths and legends, exploring the meanings of traditional life and values. 'Life' uses the tones of village gossip to investigate an urban girl's inability to fit in with the constraints of village life, her promiscuity eventually leading to tragedy. Like the conflicts between urban and rural life in African women's writing (Chapter 6), this articulates the difficulties faced by women in a changing society. So too does 'Portrait of a Wedding', where the young man, choosing between the old-fashioned girl who bears him a child and Neo, smart, sharp, who earns a typist's wage, foregrounds the difficulties both these young women face in a changing society. She will use 'People say', gossip, myth, African proverbs, the tones of village gossip, making this a parable, a tale formed from oral storytelling modes.

In *When Rain Clouds Gather, Maru* and *A Question of Power*, Head problematises motherhood too, reflecting alienation and internal exile. Motherhood is the site where conflicting emotions of anger, frustration, guilt, caring, responsibility and ultimately joyful release coalesce (Bryce-Okunlola, 1991, p. 214). Though she lacks a mother country and mother tongue, her mothering role brings her back to her senses out of a nightmare world.

Zoe Wicomb, 'A Clearing in the Bush' (1987)

> When I have control over native education I will reform it so that the natives will be taught from childhood that equality with Europeans is not for them.   (H. F. Vervoerd, Minister of Native Affairs, on the creation of the Department of Bantu Education in 1958 following the Bantu Education Act 1953)

Zoe Wicomb's semi-fictionalised autobiographical story sequence *You Can't Get Lost in Cape Town* (1987) recalls the book sequence of African American Maya Angelou (Chapter 2) and work by Aboriginal women writers such as Sally Morgan and Ruby Langford (Chapter 9). It is an empowering mode which combines the personal testimony with the creativity and shape of fictional form in order to speak to, from and about a community from the life of an individual.

> Wessex spread like a well-used map before me, worn and dim along the fold-lines.... The scuffed greenstrop is the chase where God knows what happened. Seduced, my notes say. Can you be seduced by someone you hate? Can trees gnarled with age whisper ancient ecstasies and wave of darkness in dark lap until the flesh melts? I do, of course, not know of these matters, but shudder for Tess.   (Wicomb, 1987, p. 41)

The clearing in the bush betrayed Tess, the landscapes of the coloniser fill the imagination of the girls in contrast to her own surroundings of 'blue gum trees, and behind them the bush stretches for miles across the Cape flats. Bushes, I imagine, that send out wayward limbs to weave into the tangled undergrowth, for I have never left the concrete paths of the campus'. Retief's correspondence university notes refuse her reading (Tess was raped, not 'seduced'). Frieda's need is to explore her own reading and experience, denied by the concrete rigidity of the university campus paths and paths of reading she must trace to conform and pass. Her experience is denied as a bi-racial African woman in her own country. She is as restricted in experience as Tess, with whom she identifies.

When we look at Zoe Wicomb's 'A Clearing in the Bush' we are aware of alternative loci of enunciation in a colonial space. She engages with political dimensions, the collusion and rejection of the values of apartheid in an academic environment; political and social dimensions of class and origin, when Tamieta, the working-class African cook, is excluded (unnecessarily) from the student boycott of Vervoerd's memorial service; and gender/culture/political dimensions, i.e., the effective silencing of the student narrator in her response to the imperialist-originated text *Tess of the D'Urbervilles*. *Tess*, itself, ironically enables engagement with issues of readings and misreadings of events and values, in a gendered and class-related manner, both within the text and in its critical reception.

The 'clearing in the bush' is the university – an intellectual clearing for students – and the space in which the university holds Vervoerd's remembrance service. The party line of the university administration is that this great man has been assassinated and that this is a sad loss. However, the architect of apartheid can only be so treated ironically. The sadness is that Tamieta does not know of his evil actions and just feels herself confusedly in the wrong for having attended the service:

Tamieta had no idea that the ceremony was for white people only. Oh, what should she do, and the shame of it flames in her chest. Wait until she is told to leave? Or pick up the bag of working clothes she has just tucked under her chair and stagger off? (Wicomb, 1987, p. 57)

Underpaid and overworked, she is isolated from the intellectual community of the university because of class and economic position rather than colour. More subtle then is her awkward position. She is vulnerable in the clearing, a space used in other contexts for protests, suggestive of clearing away dead ways and beliefs, clearing out and moving on.

In another story the protagonist, Frieda, must seek an abortion as the union between her and her white lover has no place in South Africa. Other experiences of the intersection of race and gender abound. Wicomb's short stories interweave different perspectives and experiences. In this way there is a dialogic relation between the different versions of life in South Africa. So in 'Behind the Bougainvillea' (1987), a story Dorothy Driver examines at length (Driver, 1996), Freida returns from her education in the UK, then, ill, must wait in the yard at the white doctor's because of her colour, which relegates her to a secondary position. She undergoes experiences from a number of different subject positions because of colour and travel. Henry Henrikse, a Black South African freedom fighter, ANC member, once rejected in her past, rescues her from the yard and they have a brief sexual exchange, something of an atonement for her past rejection of him and what he stood for. Driver comments:

> It is a writing...fully worthy of the story of black women's resistance to racist and capitalist exploitation and suppression, and to the ongoing battle to bring gender into current political negotiations....Wicomb's particular combination of Black consciousness and feminism, where each mode of thinking contradicts and informs the other, permits her to trace in a South African context the ways subjectivities might be differently constructed through a recognition of the dynamic between specific experiences and desires, on the one hand, and political demands, decisions and discourses on the other. (Driver, 1996, p. 51)

She revalues women's roles, and reclaims her version of the language from the coloniser who would sanitise it of local references:

> Her writing bears witness to a history of deprivation, yet it also suggests ways which subvert this history: not through political or economic change but through a psychological change whose major route is in re-writing representation. (Driver, 1996, p. 45)

Ellen Kuzwayo

The autobiography of Ellen Kuzwayo 'puts aside the rhinoceros hide, to reveal a people with a delicate nervous balance like everyone else' (Head, 1990, p. 89). The documentation of human suffering is terrible she notes, but at its end:

> one feels as if a shadow history of South Africa has been written; there is a sense of triumph, of hope in this achievement and that one has read the true history of the land, a history that vibrates with human compassion and goodness. (Kuzwayo, in Head, 1990, p. 89)

Born into a family with land tenure, Ellen Kuzwayo was taught to be a Christian and to serve others. Her move from a rural background, as a child, to the slums of Johannesburg, is one familiar to many South African women, and charted elsewhere in Miriam Tlali's *Soweto Stories* (1989). The men move to the city for work to pay the poll taxes, and starving women follow, working in domestic service. Ellen Kuzwayo, looking most particularly at the difficulties faced by women in these dreadful conditions writes that 'it is not easy to live and bring up children in a community robbed of its traditional moral code and values; a community lost between its old heritage and culture and that of its colonists' (Kuzwayo, in Head, 1990, p. 90). She charts the violence and injustices of the 1976 Soweto unrests, including her own and her son's detention.

Gail Reagon, in 'Ellen Kuzwayo and Ways of Speaking Otherwise' (1994, pp. 34–5), positions Kuzwayo's texts as 'both oppositional and testimonial':

> The testimonial dimension in Kuzwayo's autobiography is not an unproblematic assumption of her typicality, that she is represent-ative enough to stand in for the black South African community or for all black women. Rather, it points to the trenchantly political or interventionist nature of the narration. For Kuzwayo, the personal 'I' is inescapably bound to the collective 'we'; her identity is consti-tuted as an extension of the community.

Motherhood in relation to motherlands empowers Kuzwayo in her autobiography. Homelessness and a sense of place paradoxically coexist, as does individual identity and the individual as community member. Through all of this the position of the Black South African mother is one of empowerment, which turns the conventionally disempowering and silencing around. Like Wicomb, Head and African American women writers such as Toni Morrison and Alice

Walker in particular, hers is a dialogic work: she speaks from these dual, previously oppositional or dichotomous positions, and this is in the face of the kinds of dominant discourses which would render black woman and autobiography absent, silenced and devalued. Of course, under patriarchy, racism and sexism, it is difficult to entirely escape the discourse which these have shared, and also to escape accusations at least of falling into the other various traps women have discovered in writing of their lives and the lives of others, such as essentialism, and suggestions of homogeneity. Tensions remain in the work, as they do in that of Wicomb and Head. How could the truly radical alternative autobiographical work refuse dominant discourses and constraints entirely – since the self and the representations of the self are themselves constructed from such dominant pressures and discourses? Gael Reagon finds Kuzwayo's project in revaluing motherhood and identity as ultimately unsuccessful, accusing her of homogenising Black womanhood into a universal earth mother figure.

The difficulites of self-recognition and expression are faced by many South African women under apartheid. This difficulty could easily lead to silence but, for the women considered here, it has led instead to exploration and expression of the individual's experiences both as individual and as part of the community:

> Telling our stories, using the 'self as subject', shows the intersection between the individual and the larger forces of our history. In telling our stories we attempt to understand both intellectually and emotionally.   (Govinden, 1995, p. 70)

In testimonies of the past and reclamations of the individual voice through semi-fictionalised autobiography, the women writers of South Africa give power and voice both to their personal lives and to the changing, shaping identity of South Africa itself.

The pain of enforced removals and enforced establishments of temporary living spaces is a very destructive influence on women's lives. Attempting to bring up families, with the dangers and deprivations of dispossession and transience, and the conflicts between the values of the town and the rural village are subjects explored and dramatised by Bessie Head, Miriam Tlali, Zoe Wicomb, Gcina Mhlope, Ingrid de Kok and others, including the writers of the COSAW (Congress of South African Writers) collective whose work appears in *Like a House on Fire: Contemporary Women's Writing from*

South Africa (1994). But even these transient living spaces have, through being inhabited by people, become communities whose existence enables a sense of identity to develop and, as was seen in the apartheid period, a community which engendered revolt and direct political action. The creative human spirit, under pressure, identifies with and occupies space unrecognised as nurturing by others.

Gcina Mhlope actually found space, in Johannesburg, to write in a toilet (a new take on 'a room of one's own'), recalling this in her short story 'The Toilet' (1987). The confining space gave warmth, dryness, privacy and security:

> I was really lucky to have found that toilet because the winter was very cold. Not that it was any warmer in there but once I'd closed the door it used to be a little less windy. Also the toilet was very small – the walls were wonderfully close to me – it felt like it was made to fit me. I enjoyed that kind of privacy.   (Mhlope, 1987, p. 3)

She occasionally sneaked in to stay with her domestic servant sister, but felt worried she would be caught in the white household. The toilet provided her own space. However, when she found the door locked one morning, she was still able to write, having now begun. Gcina Mhlope's poetry conjures up the pain of displacement and poverty. Children suffer, families are split up or moved on, employment and subsistence are denied. Here the bare necessities of life are denied, and with it, identity and the power to imagine a new future, are dangerously threatened:

> Sometimes when it rains
> I think of 'illegal' job seekers
> In big cities
> Dodging police vans in the rain
> Hoping for darkness to come
> So they can find some wet corner to hide in
> (Mhlope, 1987, p. 205)

Miriam Tlali

She writes from the heart of those turbulent cities.   (Ngcobo, Introduction to Tlali's *Soweto Stories*, 1989, p. xv)

Miriam Tlali's stories depict the dispossession, displacement and poverty suffered by South Africans. These people have little hope and no home. Women were and still are traditionally left behind in the townships or in impoverished rural areas while the men seek work in the cities. Living conditions are intolerable, child mortality high, and danger of rape or abuse constant for women. Tlali's work grows from a period of tolerance of protest writing in the grim days of the 1970s:

At the beginning of the 1970s a new spirit emerged with dramatic force. The youth of South Africa discovered a less vulnerable form of protest writing – a new form of power.   (Ngcobo, Introduction to *Soweto Stories*, 1989, p. xiv)

Miriam Tlali's characters tend to be homeless, transient, 'illegal' job seekers or people vulnerable just because they try to work, travel between lodgings and workplace, bear and bring up children. 'Vigil with the Flies and the Bed Bugs' features a traveller stranded late in a village and forced to sleep the night in an infested room, eventually sleeping on the table. 'Fud-u-u-a!' concerns women travelling for safety in pairs on congested Black-only trains, fearful of sexual threat. Everyday life is difficult and threatened in Doornfontein, a Johannesburg suburb, and Soweto, both of which have been home to Tlali, of whom it is said:

She dared hold and express opinion. She dared not only to speak out against the dominance of male writing which had attended black literature from the very beginning. She struck out bold and fearless. She could not help but be noticed for she was not only among the first women novelists to resurface, but she was also the first woman novelist inside South Africa to take her place among the national gallery of our black literary figures.... She is among the very few writers which have refused to be intimidated and 'smoked' out of South Africa, by the harsh treatment which is reserved for black writers.   (Ngcobo, 1989, p. xv)

Set in 1932 Sophiatown, 'Dimomona' concentrates on the difficult, impoverished lives of Dimomona and Boitumelo Kgope, together just to conceive a child. Dimomona normally lives back in the rural 'homelands' area. They 'were tenants occupying one of a chain of ten rooms, each housing an average family of eight people' (1989, p. 4).

Boitumelo happens to have left his passbook, testifying to his identity, on the table when the house is raided by brutal, bureaucratic police. Despite being a hard worker and supportive father, he is marched away and imprisoned.

Boitumelo loses his freedom, his reputation and, on finally returning, his job because, although he was rewarded with a bicycle for work, he is considered stupid to have not had his pass on him. Dimomona visits the boss's house immediately after her husband's arrest. The social and economic gap between the two families is glaringly obvious, the boss living in 'the big house with the towering palm trees and the blooming luscious garden'(1989, p. 53), with two big black dogs trained to attack: 'they were trained never to tolerate a strange black face, especially, Boitumelo had told her' (1989, p. 54). Children sicken, poverty grows, and the event ruins their lives, as they are forced to move back to the homelands.

Miriam Tlali's work highlights the difficulties for women, vulnerable to any abusive man, and vulnerable also to the harshness of apartheid which removes their husbands and husbands' jobs at a whim, reducing their struggle to one of subsistence alone.

ORAL POETRY

There is a long tradition of oral poetry in South Africa, including the lyric poems of the Khoi and Bushmen, praise poems (*izibongo*, *lithoko*) to recognise the importance and glory of individuals, songs to the clan, family songs, love lyrics, children's verse, work songs, lullabies, personal *izibongo*, religious songs, songs to animals, and songs of divination have all flourished. With the arrival of the missionaries, forms became influenced by 'the harmonies and poetics of the Christian hymn' (Brown, 1987, p. 123). Sothi women perform poetic narratives (*seoeleoele*) through songs and dance in shebeens and bars (Copland, 1987, pp. 13–24; in Brown, p. 123). There are similarities here with issues of the use of Creole and of a continuum of language registers including the vernacular and the language of English in schools and government documents (Standard English) found in the Caribbean (see Chapter 5). There are similarities with the Caribbean and with Aboriginal poetry in terms of the importance of orality and performance in representing versions of identity, passing on histories and myths, and so on.

Within these traditions lie the powerful political poems of male poets Mzwakhe Mbuli and Alfred Qabula, performed to large workers' groups. A gathering of workers at the Jabulani Stadium in July 1985 united workers and worker poets against oppression, expressing their desire to seize their own culture and cultural futures. They endeavour 'in Durban to build alongside our union organisations a cultural movement... over the last three years, choirs, dance-teams, plays, poems, written pieces are becoming important activities within the workers' struggle' (Qabula et al., 1986, p. 59). Performance poetry changes with the audience, and involves mood, repetition, coherence. It is usually performed in an energetic way, with facial gestures punctuating each line.

Nise Malange

Nise Malange's poetry is worker and performance poetry, concentrating on praising political colleagues who have fought for recognition of self worth and the economic, political cause.

In 'I, the Unemployed' she employs repetition, and a call to immediacy and visual unity. She dramatises, using the figure 'I', and testifies but in doing so she avoids the merely personal, and encompasses thousands of people's experiences in this:

> I am here dying of hunger
> And my country is also dying
> My children are dying too
> Look at them:
> How dull their eyes
> How slow their walk and the turning
> of their heads
> Nothing for them to eat
> Can you hear?
> They are crying.
>   (Malange, 1986, p. 51, in *Black Mamba Rising: South*
>   *African Worker Poets in Struggle*, ed. Ari Sitas)

Her poem concentrates on sound and vision, calling for the involvement of the audience, placing her experience as typical, one of many:

For reasons that are hard to explain, the poets and their writing enjoyed a form of official tolerance not accorded to any other kind of writer. This poetry became the only outlet for the increasingly grim experience of the 1960s and 1970s. For the first time literary expression in our writing took on a completely political perspective. (Ngcobo, 1989, p. xiv)

Ingrid de Kok

There are many white writers, teachers and others who spoke out against apartheid, some of whom were imprisoned for their views. Ingrid de Kok, an Afrikaner poet, trawls the racist deceptions of her own upbringing, explores childbirth and loss as it crosses cultures and race, and uses imagery of children, closed rooms and brutality to characterise the monstrous everyday destructiveness of life under apartheid:

> They took all that was child
> and in the dark closed room
> visions of a ripe split melon
> were at the tip of the knife
> they held to the child's dry tongue.
>
> ...
> And this torn light,
> this long torn light
> will repair itself
> out of the filaments of children.
> and all that is child will return to the house,
> will return to the house.
>   (De Kok, 'All Wat Kind Is', 1997, pp. 184–5)

This is a record of police brutality in Victoria West, but Ingrid de Kok, whose poetry consistently focuses on children as victims, expresses a glimmer of hope for change and return. 'Small Passing' recognises the pain of loss of a stillborn child whose white mother is brutally told to stop mourning 'for the trials and horror suffered daily by black women in this country are more significant than the loss of one white child'. Mothers losing childen, white or black, would understand her pain and sympathise. However privileged or unprivileged a mother, the loss of her child is beyond race and social politics, devastating. Children are mourned, lost, removed, their families split up and unable to support them. The destructive loss of this for mothers is devastating, a result of racism and economic pressure which removes hope and living standards from mothers trying to bring up their families. Results are isolated children, and a threat to the future:

> See
> The newspaper boy in the rain
> will sleep tonight in a doorway.
> The woman in the bus line
> may next month be on a train
> to a place not her own.
> The baby in the backyard now
> will be sent to a tired aunt,
> grow chubby, then lean,
> return a stranger
>   (De Kok, 'Small Passing', 1997, p. 195)

Stoical African women last on. De Kok's poetry transcends racial difference with an empathy born of gender alignment.

What validates the experience of an artist is knowing that somewhere out there someone will acknowledge and share your deepest thoughts, your joys, your pain, your muses. Yet in South Africa we have lived for a very long time in the stifling isolation of our separate worlds both as individuals and as groups. Only now do we, as South African writers and artists, self-consciously grope and reach out to find fellow South African kindred spirits. (Ngcobo, 1994, p. 1)

Creative isolation has been damaging to generations of South African readers and writers. Now their work is being written and read, and many women are recuperating versions of their past lives through the explorations and expressions of autobiography, producing oral or scripted poetry, publishing abroad and at home, and being studied on the syllabi of their own country, and across the world.

The poetry and fictionalised autobiographical works of Bessie Head, Zoe Wicomb, Lauretta Ngcobo, Ellen Kuzwayo and women of the COSAW collective (*Like a House on Fire*, 1994), Ingrid de Kok, Gcina Mhlope and Nise Malange testify to the daily difficulties of living under apartheid, the need to leave in order to write, to speak out politically and personally against injustices, economic hardships, the importance of maintaining a sense of identity and self worth against the indignities and dangers of their everyday lives.

8

Writing by Women from the Indian Sub-Continent

Around (the ideal woman) exists a huge body of mythology. She is called by several names – Sita, Draupadi, Parvati, Lakshmi and so on. In each myth, she plays the role of the loyal wife, unswerving in her devotion to her lord. She is meek, docile, trusting, faithful and forgiving.

(Desai, 1990, p. 14)

This chapter starts by sketching in details of the long-established and diverse culture of the Indian sub-continent. The overwhelming scale and range of this writing, both before Independence and Partition (1947) and afterwards, easily merits its own book. The choice of authors here reflects some of the diversity of women's writing within the boundaries of the issues with which this book is dealing; identity, language, women's roles and representations, mothering, history, magic, and so on. This chapter concentrates on work by individuals from both the sub-continent and the diaspora, writing in English, all of whom, by the nature of their critical engagement with language, identity, race can be recognised as post-colonial writers. While the main focus here, as in the rest of this book, is on writing which coincides historically with the end of British rule, it is not suggested that British colonial rule, in either its existence or its post-colonial disappearance, is the main factor in writing of issues of gender, and/or by women.

South Asia, or the Indian sub-continent, comprises India, Pakistan (a separate state since 1947), Bangladesh (East Pakistan until 1971), Sri Lanka, Nepal and Burma. It is culturally and linguistically diverse – with fourteen major languages and innumerable dialects. British influence began with trade in the seventeenth century and, although direct British rule ended with Independence in 1947, the linguistic and cultural legacy of Britain has lingered on. One of the key concerns for post-colonial writers is dealing with the cultural and linguistic effects of that lingering on, negotiating new writing practices, new concerns, and an integration of the inherited (South Asian, British, international) with the contemporary in the post-colonial space.

Women were oral storytellers throughout history and the regions; they were among the first writers; high caste and religious women wrote poetry in medieval times (and earlier) and women were the first novelists. After Independence (1947), women were involved in a movement for emancipation. Latterly, since the advent of feminism in the late 1960s and early 1970s many have been more outspoken as writers, often tackling the cultural constrictions upon women expressed in and emanating from those very myths with which Anita Desai's comments engage (above). Many concentrate on writing and re-writing these myths and recalling the past in relation to the representation of women, family roles, motherhood, wifehood, and daughterhood. There are tensions between tradition and emancipation in the work of many women writers. Freedom from tradition, discovering one's role, re-examining its constraints, establishing identity all relate to feminism but can conflict with national identity and even love of children and men. Many women write celebrating sexual freedoms within the constraints of family and society. Others, settled in the UK, US, Australia and all over the world, concern themselves with negotiations of identity, gender and equality in the diaspora. Their work often provides an acute analysis of racial difficulties inherent in imperialism, colonialism, the diasporan and the post-colonial existence.

In terms of form, many, like African American (Chapters 2, 3, 4) and Caribbean (Chapter 5) women writers, establish national identities by using their own language, rather than English, and by developing scripted versions of the mixed, spoken language Indo-Anglian/Anglo-Indian. Some of the new forms chosen by novelists and poets are less conventional; more conversational, ironic, streetwise, and/or influenced by the characteristics of post-modernism; likely to be fragmented, intertextual, interweaving Indian myth and experience with the international. Writers on whom this chapter concentrates are a small, but significant sample of those publishing today and include: Kamala Das, Ruth Prawer Jhabvala, Shashi Deshpande, Sunetra Gupta, Rukhsana Ahmad, Anita Desai, Bharati Mukherjee, Debjani Chatterjee, Eunice de Souza, Arundhati Roy and Meena Alexander. Women writers who originate from the Indian sub-continent will also appear elsewhere in this book, either on the grounds that they write from a diasporan perspective, that their work concentrates on moving between continents/countries, split between two existences, or that they have made their homes abroad. Suniti Namjoshi, for example, appears in Chapter 11 on Canada.

BACKGROUND

It is impossible to do more than suggest some of the writers of this enormous sub-continent, heavily populated, with people who speak diverse languages, have diverse customs, religious beliefs and practices and produce a diversity of literature. Much of this large, sophisticated literary output has been lost to us as Western readers because there has been no need, no drive to translate it, but we can thank the integration of Asian people into the UK and the rest of the English-speaking world for much of the interest in translation. Colonial and imperial rule did not actually generate such a response, more often producing an arrogant refusal to recognise the quality of the Other or of the Occident, a response traced neatly in E. M. Forster's *A Passage to India* (1924), Paul Scott's *The Raj Quartet* (1966; 1968; 1971; 1975), and Ruth Prawer Jhabvala's *Heat and Dust* (1975).

Women have traditionally been storytellers in the sub-continent, 'the chief upholders of and contributors to a powerful oral tradition which embraces myths, legends, fables, folklore and songs stretching back millennia' (Jaggi, 1993, in Buck, pp. 220–5). Oral literature predominated, and early writing was a transcription of this. Myth is central to our understanding of the restraints of representation against which many contemporary women writers rail. As Anita Desai points out: myths are 'the cornerstone on which the Indian family and therefore Indian society are built' [they keep women] 'bemused, bound hand and foot' (Desai, 1990, p. 14).

Literary production in Sanskrit dates back to the 'Vedas' or sacred hymns, 1500 BC, of which the most well known, the Hindu epic poems 'The Mahabharata' (400 BC–AD 400) and 'The Ramayana' (200 BC–AD 200), are filled with Hindu concepts and myths about caste and religion, dramatising the heroes Krishna and Rama and heroines who embody motherhood – Devi, Shakti, Ganga, or wifehood – Sita, Savitri, Draupadi, Radha, Lakshmi and Sati/Parvati. The ideals of womanhood they embodied were reinforced by the 'Code of Manu' (AD 1–200), which defined women in terms of their roles as wives, mothers, daughters, etc. These epics spread through local (mostly male) versions. Women writers from the Indian sub-continent are a prime example of feminist subversion and rescript-ing of such mythic and animal tales which consistently reproduce and enforce subordinate roles for women.

In the medieval period the Bhakti movement swept southern then northern India, giving rise to lyrical devotional poetry, a form embraced by many women poets (as it was in post-medieval Britain and Ireland). Women's poetry has been prolific throughout Indian history. One of the earliest recorded poets writing in Tamil was a woman, Uwaiyyar (second century AD). The earliest Bhakti poet, Karaikkal Ammaiyyar (a woman – seventh century AD), wrote poetry devoted to the god Shiva. In the northern region of Kashmir the most famous medieval poets are women – Lalla Didi (1335), Hubb Khatun (sixteenth century) and Arani-mal (eighteenth century). They wrote love lyrics. The most legendary of saint-poets is Mirabai, a princess in sixteenth-century Rajasthan, whose poetry celebrates her relationship with the god Krishna. Many of these female devotional poets, who use sexual longing as imagery of spiritual and devotional love, are now being re-read, recognised as expressing female rebel-lion and liberation. Women poets such as the late seventeenth-century Sufi poet Zeb-un-Nissar, daughter of Emperor Aurangzeb, wrote in the tradition of historical prose (see Jaggi, 1993, pp. 220–5).

Moves to reform women's position began in the nineteenth century, initially led by men seeking political change. The Bengal reformer Raja Rammohan Roy, who founded the Brahmo movement in 1828, campaigned for equal rights, while others agitated against child marriage and sanctions against remarriage of widows. In 1829 'sut-tee' (or *sati*) was outlawed although it persisted. Access to women's education improved, the first women's college being established in Madras in 1914, and autonomous women's organisations grew. In the 1910s and 1920s women campaigned for legal reforms over property and inheritance rights, marriage dowry and dowry deaths, the status of widowhood, polygamy, etc.

A nation's attitude to language is always an indicator of its sense of identity, and the language of publication, statute books etc., can be considered to demonstrate who has the power to name, speak and so understand and know, in a country or a nation. In 1835 Eng-lish was decreed as the medium of Indian higher education, English spread among the middle classes through the nineteenth century and Anglo-Indian literature resulted. Many early Anglo-Indian writers were women, including Bankim Chandra Chatterjee, the author of the first Anglo-Indian novel *Rajmohan's Wife* (1864), and Toru Dut, a gifted Bengali woman who wrote in and translated between both English and French, rendering Hindu myths and poetry into English in *Ancient Ballads and Legends of Hindustan* (1882). Dut died at 21, leaving a French novel and a fragment of an Anglo-Indian one, *Bianca; or The Young Spanish Maiden* (1878).

In the early days, most women's fiction was didactic and reformist, exploring individual women's struggles against repressive orthodoxies. Fiction then began developing in regional languages, notably Bengali and Urdu. Two writers concerned with reform were Sakhawat Hossain, and Begum Rokeya, a campaigner against purdah, writing in both Bengali and English. Other writers include Akbari Begum and Nazar Sajjad Haider, major Urdu fiction writers in the1910s. There is a great deal of writing in local dialects which critiques sexual repression, such as the poetry of Punjabi Amrit Pritam who writes of sexual freedoms. Although the remit of this book cannot stretch to work not published in English, it is interesting to note that, for example, as early as the late nineteenth century (and early twentieth century), bookshop raids were carried out and censorship attempted to entirely prevent the publication, sales and reading of Nagaratnamma's edition of Muddapalini's epic poem 'Radhika Santwanam' because of its alleged obscenity. The poem, an erotic, feminist interpretation of the tale of divine lovers Radha and Krishna, and Illadevi and Krishna, explored women's rather than men's sexual pleasure.

The women's movement, linked to nationalism against British colonial rule, focused also on equality and education for women. By the 1930s the social revolution harnessed progressive literary development, and the oppression of women was recognised as an obstacle to progress. Key women writers were Moslems, Ismat Chughati and Atia Hosain, both using Urdu storytelling traditions to write about restrictions on women in male-dominated society. Other women writers of the 1930s and 1940s included Hijab Imtiaz Ali, whose Urdu novel *My Unfulfilled Love* (1933) explored female sexuality. Women began writing in a more realist vein, with new experiences and new forms.

The Independence movement, under the non-violent, resistance-based leadership of Mahatma Gandhi (1869–1948), resulted (1947) in Indian Independence, and the creation of Pakistan as a separate Moslem State. English continued as the literary language after Independence remaining, with Hindi, as the Indian official language, crossing regional boundaries. Used mainly among the middle classes, it is mixed with Indian vocabulary and expressions. In order to recognise the great developments and differences which Indian life and expression have had on the novel, the term 'Indo-Anglian' writing was developed, drawing on regional literary traditions as well as regional languages and prioritising an Indian use of English. This development coheres with (among others) that in Caribbean, British and African American literary production (see Chapters 2, 3, 4, 5, 12) in two main ways: first, recognition of the legitimacy and richness of the many variants of English, and secondly, a desire to convey the texture of life and of the spoken word, expressible through writing in the vernacular. Collections in Indo-Anglian are, in the main, transcriptions from the vernacular form of many different Indian languages. These include *Truth Tales* (1986), *The Slate of Life*: (*Kali for Women*) (1990), *The Inner Courtyard* (ed. Lakshmi Holstrom, 1993) and *Right of Way* (1988, Asian Women Writers' Workshop). Two large volumes of translated extracts and poems by Indian women writers (eds, Susie Tharu and K. Lalita), *Women Writing in India. Vol. 1: The Nineteenth Century* (1992), *Women Writing in India. Vol. 11: The Twentieth Century* (1993), have also appeared, enabling new readers of English to become acquainted with some of the enormous range of women's writing.

Since Independence, women have written in a variety of different modes, notably travel writing (Santha Rama Rau) and novels, such as those by Kamal Markandaya and Anita Desai, whose reputation was established by *The Clear Light of Day* (1980) and *In Custody* (1984). Other well-known novelists include Shashi Deshpande, and Ruth Prawer Jhabvala (a Polish-German married to an Indian) who wrote *Heat and Dust* (1975). Nayantara Sahgal's work, particularly *Rich Like Us* (1983), is also highly acclaimed (for an extensive discussion of this last novel, see Walder, 1998). Many novelists recall and re-imagine history, focusing on issues of racial tensions and women's roles in a changing society.

Shashi Deshpande's work is overtly feminist. *That Long Silence* (1988) concentrates on a woman's growing awareness of the self she has repressed since marriage. Like Desai's *The Clear Light of Day*, it reconciles women's economic independence with more traditional family values, themes also considered in the work of Bharati Mukherjee, now a diasporan writer in the US (see below). Kamala Das, the best known Anglo-Indian poet, wrote confessional poetry in the 1960s challenging taboos around female sexuality. In their introduction (1993) Tharu and Lalita argue that their collection and translation of a vast range of writing by women is not merely to redress an obvious publishing imbalance and absence, but also to look at the contradictions, celebrations and struggles of feminist writers (specifically) from different castes and language groups:

> Not all literature written by women is feminist, or even about women. Neither is the scope of women's writing restricted to allegories of gender oppression. Besides, even when the writing is specifically feminist ... opposition to the dominant ideologies of gender can be discomfortingly class or caste bound and draw upon assumptions about race or religious persuasion that reinforce the hold of those ideologies and collaborate in extending their authority. Middle-class women, white women, upper-caste Hindu women might find that their claims to 'equality' or to the 'full authority' of liberal individualism are at the expense of the working classes, the non-white races, dalits or Muslims. For, as we shall see, given the specific practices and discourses through which individualism took historical shape in India, these groups had to be defined as Other in order that the Self might gain identity. (Tharu and Lalita, 1993, p. 38)

As Gayatri Spivak puts it, exploring such a variety of work fills the 'literary form with its connections to what is being read: history, political economy – the world' (Spivak, 1988, p. 95). This collection considers how women have turned established plots and forms to their own uses, how they had to concede to narratives of oppression, and at what costs they re-wrote and reinterpreted.

Women's Roles, Motherhood and Sexual Freedom

Ranjana Ash writes of 'The search for freedom in Indian women's writing' (1991). The concept of 'motherland' became highly charged before Independence (1947), images of Mother India bound in chains and waiting for her children to free her appearing in popular literature and art as the freedom struggle continued. Amrita Pritam, Anita Desai and Sahgal, living through the horrors of Partition in Pakistan and India, explored it in their work. Pritam writes both of the suffering inflicted upon women in communal riots and mass uprootings, and love poems linking the transcendental/spiritual with earthly love. Some interesting themes which Ash explores are the development

of women's self-awareness and identity; women's search for freedom in the family, and the question of the troubled relationship to
motherlands. She points out that many of women's problems relating to self-image, rights and position in society derive from the
'Code of Manu' which positions them, not as individuals in their
own right, but defined in relation to male members of their family:

> She can do nothing independently even in her own house. In
> childhood subject to her father, in youth to her husband, and
> when her husband is dead to her sons, she should never enjoy
> independence.   (Basham, 1971, p. 182)

Most young mothers in novels are seen as having a profound love
of children; child-bearing is not seen as an impediment to freedom
and the only writer who treats abortion (legalised in India) seriously
is Deshpande. The mother figure emerges in writing about Mother
India, used in linkages and allusions to help solve various problems
for the writers. There are three aspects of the notion of motherland
considered in Ash's essay: ideas of love; ideas of the ethical life; and
a positive awareness of the force of Indian civilisation. In the past,
men and women were represented as partners in love, and it is
Victorian England which insisted, under the Raj, on the separation
of the physical and the spiritual and women's secondary roles. Dance
and erotic sculpture abound in medieval times, celebrating the love
of Radha and Krishna, and mystically through the work of the Sufi
poets. Amrita Pritam's poetry reflects the variety of love found in
Indian writing ranging from fertility rites, devotional love and
ecstasy, to the easy, natural love of the classical Tamil poems. Indian
women are seen as finding pleasure in physical relationships within
marriage, but guilt and remorse outside it. Sexual liberation and the
role of mother is one issue, having a voice quite another. Spivak's
work (1988) problematises women's silenced position as historically
subordinated subjects (see Chapter 1). Discussing the paradigmatic
example of a Rani on the death of her husband, the Rajah, Spivak
indicates the silencing and absence, the disempowerment which
this woman suffers. She was caught between an imperialist and a
patriarchal discourse. If she chose *suttee* (that is, to burn as a widow)
she was seen as conforming to patriarchal discourse, but if she
refused it she was conforming to the discourse of the English rulers
who condemned the practice. There is no space for her, nothing she
can be or speak. Many post-colonial women writers (for example,

Desai and Jhabvala) try to find a language for such a subordinated subject. They react against both male-dominated and colonial languages and representations. As Susheila Nasta notes in her introduction to *Motherlands*:

> The post-colonial woman writer is not only involved in making herself heard, in changing the architecture of male centred ideologies and languages, or in discovering new forms and language to express her experience, she has also to subvert and demythologise indigenous male writing and traditions which seek to label her. An entrapping cycle begins to emerge. In countries with a history of colonialism, women's quest for emancipation, self identity and fulfilment can be seen to represent a traitorous act, a betrayal not simply of traditional codes of practice and belief but of the wider struggle for liberation and nationalism. Does to be 'feminist' therefore involve a further displacement onto another form of cultural imperialism?   (Nasta, 1991, p. xv)

The relationship between the development of a nation-state and that of women is interesting and problematic. The struggle between two adversaries – India and Britain – was played out and seemingly settled with Partition, a new Nation-State and the 1951 General Election based on universal suffrage. However, the ideal of establishing a new national unity meant that oppositional forces had to be contained. Elements of the controlling powers hitherto seen as repressive were redefined as supportive of the State, custodian of people's welfare, champion of economic development and industry. What was effected, however, was a translation of the popular imaginary in relation to the situation of women, and of different castes. Development action concentrated on the State rather than people, and in the face of this zealous unity, pleas for improvement and equality were sidelined. This situation is similar to the rise of national identity amongst African Americans and Caribbean peoples, where politically the nation or state are considered more crucial than the rights of women, sidelining women's efforts at equality.

WOMEN NOVELISTS

Anita Desai, Ruth Prawer Jhabvala and Arundhati Roy each deal with the condition of women in India, and with the complexity, diversity, confusion and richness of locations and life. They do so from differing cultural positions, and although all three write in the post-colonial period, they reflect the differing and changing responses to east/west relations during their times.

Ruth Prawer Jhabvala

Ruth Prawer Jhabvala's *Heat and Dust* (1975), made into a successful film, is best known as a cross-cultural romance. Her own position as a Polish woman married to an Indian man and now living in the USA, gives her a particular slant. As an outsider, inside, she treats the two periods of the latter years of British rule in India, 1923, and the 1970s, with insights into east/west relations. The novel is a romantic fiction in the realist mode and provides critiques of the idealisation involved in romantic fictions. The narrator is a 1970s girl seeking the history and reality of Olivia, the first wife of Douglas, a British administrator. Bored with the superficiality and trivia of everyday life for British women in the Civil stations in India, Olivia became fascinated with the local Nawab, a dashing ruler of rather dubious morality spending above his means, involved with the local bandit 'dacoit' group, intensely emotional, a social actor, playing his guests off, encouraging them in their worst prejudices and bad points. Olivia's *naïveté* is striking. Pregnant, without social status, she is a pawn between two male egos.

The modern girl looks after a young man, Chid, who has decided to be a sadipur, holy man, and to renounce all possessions. In the post-colonial period, several writers indict the nosiness, greed, and destructive selfishness, a new kind of imperialism, of Europeans travelling the East who abuse the natural generosity of poor people, and return home to middle-class comfort. In *Heat and Dust* several visitors lose possessions and suffer dysentery etc., in their pursuit of the eternal paradisal happiness of the East. Their choices are seen as rather hollow especially when Chid, first renouncing his own possessions, using her and her possessions as his own, then renounces his religious conversion, returning home to the UK on family money. Her relationship with Inder Lal parallels that of Olivia, but without fascination, restrictions or fantasies. She retraces Olivia's last days, climbing into the mountains, to give birth. The novel runs parallel stories in letters and journals, first- and third-person narrative, Olivia's tale told through the girl. Without the insights of symbolism or interior monologue it is difficult to fully engage with contradictions clear to the reader, commented on only in passing by the narrator. The parallel tales highlight the vacuity of British women's lives in imperial India where a small social group repeat historical anecdotes, retiring to the hills for the summer heat. Paradoxically, the book both clearly critiques and reinforces prejudices about Indian ways, for instance that all Eastern men have sexual designs upon Western women, and that Indian food always causes sickness.

Anita Desai

Was it not India's way of revealing the world that lay on the other side of the mirror? India flashed the mirror in your face, with a brightness and laughter as raucous as a street band. You could be blinded by it. Not if you refused to look into it, if you insisted on walking around to the back, then India stood aside, admitting you where you had not thought you could go. India was two worlds, or ten. She stood before him, hands on her hips, laughing that blood-stained laugh: Choose! Choose!   (Desai, 1998 [1988], pp. 85/6)

Baumgartner's Bombay (1988) re-creates the fascination, complexity and teeming life of India. On Baumgartner's apartment block pavement there lives a family of squatters bathing, drinking and cooking in the gutter. There are as many versions of India and the life you can make in it as there are millions of people. *Baumgartner's Bombay* concentrates on one of the twentieth century's perpetual Others. An only child of a Jewish family in the days leading up to the establishment of the Nazi regime, Baumgartner fits in neither with orthodox Jew nor with Germans. He is a victim who survives a lonely existence, first in Germany, briefly in Venice and then in India where he is interned as a POW during the war despite pointing out that, as a Jew, he is a victim not a Nazi supporter. He lives on the fringes of society. The novel operates through flashbacks to his childhood and life in the camp, his pre-war days in India with other Europeans, the rather flashy singer-dancer-drinker set – and then the contemporary world. As with Jhabvala's novel, European hippies in India are treated with both suspicion and a natural generosity shown all beggars. They track through with few possessions and many demands. One such, a blond, selfish, drugged giant, Aryan descendant of the Nazis who victimised Baumgartner's family, has to be adopted like a stray cat: a German sick hippie seems to be seen as his responsibility.

The boy murders the lonely man for his few silver racing trophies – all he has left of his past of material worth. It is a sad outsider tale but a very well observed and described set of scenes of east–west difference and cultural meeting points. The city supports strays on its margins, and not only Europeans suffer or cause suffering. The period after Partition is rendered vividly when we see terrorising of Muslims, the kind of ethnic cleansing/genocide observed with the Jews in Nazi Germany. People manage daily functions and a semblance of order, both Eastern and Western. Each is individualised and has their own prejudices.

Anita Desai deals with east–west relations, understandings and misunderstandings. In *The Clear Light of Day* (1980) she creates a lively, critical, liberated woman, Bimala Das (Bim), who argues that she will work, be independent, and also look after her family when she grows up, declaring that it is crucial to get an education before marriage claims you. Hers is a negotiation between the constraints of family and social responsibility and her desires for liberation set against the image of her aunt Miramasi who was married at 12, widowed at 15, and prematurely aged in domestic work, sidelined by her brothers, a telling example of women's subordinate position. Desai's works concentrate on the difficulties faced by urban women trying to balance achievement of identity, with family and caste demands. Women in Desai weave through the roles assigned in Anglo-India. Under the control of patriarchy they have to find new voices to speak of this developing freedom (see Shirley Chew, 1991, in Nasta).

Arundhati Roy

A production designer and screenplay writer, Arundhati Roy produced her first novel, *The God of Small Things* (1997), for which she won the Booker Prize. *The God of Small Things* is a novel of surprising range, epic in its development of a drama of passions involving a family and a whole culture with its caste system, Love Laws, and social rules about families, marriages and women's roles. It is a very sensitive novel concentrating on the slightest and most delicate of emotions of its characters, whose texture of life is conveyed to us through personal images and description. The novel traces the story of a family in Ayemenem (sounds like Amen – rather final) whose wealth has grown from pickles and preserves, their own fate tied up with the eventual inability to preserve old ways of life, pickle and prevent emotions, and the impossibility of moving beyond attempts at preservation and pickling in a society with such rigid caste systems, Love Laws and behavioural expectations for women in particular. The stories are essentially tragic – loves lost, deaths of passionate lovers and of small children – the end of hope for change. But the tone is most frequently wryly comic, ironic, aware of the paradoxes and contradictions of both Indian society and life in general which constantly refuses grandeur, offering the banal and comic instead of the great. This tone is partially a result of the consistent awareness that 'progress', as such, has merely been development. In losing some old, probably very bad ways, none of the pettinesses of the past have gone (the caste system, prejudice against mixed relationships, prejudices against women's seeking imaginative, independent lives, and so on), and the only real gift of the hurrying contemporary world has been development without progress – embodied in the comic image of Baby Kochamma munching on her sofa, too fat to move, wallowing in the excess of superficiality offered by the arrival of satellite television. Roy describes the airwaves as stuffed to over-flowing with an excess of Americanised images of wars, sport and soaps, and a local plethora of vacuous game shows where winnings provide supplies of unnecessary consumer items. Tourism trivialises the past and Westernisation brings cash but a destructive artifice. The hotel of the perverse white imperialist is now appropriately renamed the 'Heart of Darkness' (after Conrad's novel). As 'the History House', it resonates with dark secrets and past losses. Wealthy pool-side tourists pay for artificial renditions of bite-sized versions of ancient myths performed by the Kathakali dancers.

Roy concentrates on the twins Estha (Esthappen) and Rahel and their family life in Kerala. The tale mixes recall and the present, the past featuring a crucial moment when their uncle Chacko's estranged British wife Margaret arrives from England with Sophie Mol, a nine-year-old in yellow bell-bottoms. Sophie is drowned in a boating incident. We spend the novel flipping back and forth between Rahel's homecoming discoveries of an entirely mute twin, the family property in disarray, ruled by her spoiled, dominant, malicious aunt, and a gradual recall of the period around Sophie's arrival and death. Recorded in non-sensationalist terms as a momentary accident, Sophie's death is a crucial focus point for the narrative and everyone's lives. Storytelling modes reminiscent of complex oral forms interweave hints and parallels, revealing aspects of the tale from all points of view, as it affects all family members.

The climax is not merely Sophie's death, but the brutal victimisation and murder of Velutha, gentle, political, intelligent carpenter whose caste (Untouchable/Paravan) renders him both a permanent social victim, and a symbol of tragic love. Velutha and Rahel's divorced mother fall in love despite Love Laws, their secret trysts continuing alongside the boat-fixing visits the children make to Velutha. Passion isolates him, putting him in the frame as scapegoat for both the mother's transgressive acts (sex with an Untouchable) and the death of Sophie Mol. Culture and history catch up with gentle Velutha, and political change follows. It is a Romeo and Juliet/Tristan and Isolde story. Water is the medium of their coming together, first meeting and embracing on the river bank. Sophie Mol's accidental drowning is their undoing. The tale is epic, tragic, eternal, mythic, like the wild dance of the religious male dancers in the temple. It is also a product of trivial mistakes and ultimately of the maliciously petty mind of Aunt Baby Kochamma who needs victims and sufferers to redress her thwarted life, and who lies to the police to incriminate Velutha in a rape/abuse scenario, blackmailing and threatening the twins into corroborating her story. The god of small things is both Velutha and the small things of everyday lives governed by confusions and pettinesses, set in an epic frame, 'Edges, Borders, Boundaries, Brinks and Limits' (1997, p. 3). Their story could start with the death of Sophie Mol – a local event – but it is ancient:

> [I]t could be argued that it began long before Christianity arrived in a boat and seeped into Kerala like tea from a tea bag.
>   That it really began in the days when the Love Laws were made. The laws that lay down who should be loved, and how.
>   And how much.
>
> (Roy, 1997, p. 33)

Theirs is a tragedy of history. 'Estha and Rahel learned how history negotiates its terms and collects its dues from those that break its law' (1997, p. 54). Paravans, in the presence of Touchables, are expected to crawl backwards with a broom. Velutha and the story-telling mode of the tale actually carry this out, while also challenging and disrupting the convention. The story crawls backwards, sweeping out details, as Velutha appears to have to move backwards, caught by caste when intelligence and ability have removed him from its restraints. Rahel's mother, Ammu, socially rejected, sickens and dies:

The man standing in the shade of the rubber trees with coins of sunshine dancing on his body, holding her daughter in his arms, glanced up and caught Ammu's gaze. Centuries telescoped into one evanescent moment. History was wrong-footed, caught off guard. Sloughed off like an old snakeskin. Its marks, its scars, its wounds from old wars and the walking backwards days all fell away. In its absence it left an aura, a palpable shimmering that was as plain to see as the water in a river or the sun in the sky. As plain to feel as the heat on a hot day, or the tug of a fish on a taut line. So obvious that no one noticed.   (Roy, 1997, p. 176)

Divorced women have no place socially and are considered to be of the same social status as whores, although the double standards enable uncle Chacko to service his needs through his employees. Rahel's own role as a woman in America is briefly touched upon; she is taken up by her husband for her exotic difference, mostly indifferent silence on her part, but also accosted suggestively by almost any white male who feels like it – an appropriation of the Eastern woman as exotic sexual object commented on in work by, for example, Teresia Teaiwa (in Chapter 13), and by Bharati Mukherjee. Patriarchy operates – Pappachi regularly beats Mammachi with a brass vase so her head shows scars. The twins, in their doubleness with their private intuitions, break these kinds of boundaries. There is no cultural difference between them because of their gender and in fact Estha, mute, internalising guilt over Velutha's death, becomes more of a victim than Rahel. Their lives break gendered laws.

Roy's novel is intertextual and post-modern in its wealth of reference, its conscious alterations and jugglings of events, its layering of the everyday and the mythic/epic, and its use of the comic and carnivalesque amid the tragic. It also reveals a variety of inequalities suffered by women.

Each of these three novels creates a sense of teeming life, caste, hierarchies, rituals, vitality, structures and chaos, rich, complex human life. They highlight destructive, rigidly held differences where life is particularly restrictive for women.

DIASPORAN WRITERS

Many great Indian writers live in the diaspora, which extends throughout the world, from the Caribbean, South and East Africa through Britain to the USA and Canada, to South-east Asia, Fiji and Australia. Diasporan writers frequently concentrate on the differences between their adopted country and their original family home. They are torn between the cultures of both and, like Mukherjee, point out both the humorous and the tragic elements of clashes between behaviours, religious and family expectations, and between cultures. Writers of the diaspora use India for a setting, and look at issues related to their migration, marginalisation and cultural confusions. Debjani Chatterjee is UK-based, Bharati Mukherjee is based in the USA/Canada, Suniti Namjoshi in Canada.

Debjani Chatterjee

Debjani Chatterjee is articulate about the difficulties of recognition and publication by mainstream UK presses. The stereotypical Asian woman, she insists, is always in the background, clearing things away, serving the tea and chapattis, seemingly easily ignored because certain behaviours – not looking strangers in the face or smiling, keeping eyes down – seem to connote deference and obeisance. It is too easy to ignore one who effaces herself. Chatterjee re-writes both Eastern and Western myths which perpetuate images of women's subordinate position. Cinderella in 'I Remembered Cinderella' undercuts the fairytale of finding a shining prince:

> But, I say, no woman deserved the fate
> of prancing with that dunce in the first place!
> . . .
> I realise then
> that it is men
> who have fetishes
> about women
>
> (Chatterjee, 1989, p. 39)

and in the Eastern myth in 'Your Story Sita', Sita's consistent obedi-ence to her man causes a legacy of pained subordination among her daughters:

> Dutiful daughter, perfect wife,
> devoted mother, best of women,
> role model for all time –
> . . .

From the blaze where you lifted scorching eyes
to the crowd with shuffling feet and bowed heads,
did you foresee the dowry-deaths your daughters yet endure?

(Chatterjee, 1989, p. 23)

Debjani Chatterjee writes in 'Reflection' (1989, pp. 45–6) of grand-parents and the memories, many false, of powerful relationships within the family, in which she sees herself as posing, artificial, if dutiful. It is a re-memory questioning the roles she played and her position within a patriarchal situation. 'Voice and Vision' looks at the variety of tongues in which she speaks, a writer of the Indian diaspora, moving between cultures, claiming identification 'Moulded by the black experience' (1989, p. 34). 'Distance' takes a similar diasporan theme, while 'Animal Regalia', like Namjoshi's 'Among Tigers', focuses on the pigeonholing of the Indian Other within British society. Chatterjee's work interrogates ways in which British people treat Indians as stereotypes, re-examines Indian mythic women, and asserts diasporan identity.

Bharati Mukherjee

Born in 1938 in Calcutta, Bharati Mukherjee moved to the USA in 1961, graduated from the University of Iowa in 1969, has received writing grants and taught creative writing at Columbia University, City University (New York), and Berkeley in California. Hers is a wryly humorous, perceptive diasporan record of cultural awkwardnesses and Indian women's striving to find identity in the US. In *The Tiger's Daughter* (1972), a Westernised Indian returning to India sees anew the poverty and hunger. *Wife* (1979) articulates anger against cultural traditions oppressing a passive Bengali wife living in New York, the land of the American Dream. Moving from India to the promise of the USA, the wife, Dimple Dasgupta, is drawn tragically into both the liberation and the flexibility the US offers, and finally into a terrible cultural isolation. One highly intelligent friend wastes her life, conducting a destructive affair, finding no outlet for her need to develop. Dimple Dasgupta/Basu follows suit but as in a dream. Tempted at a party, Dimple thinks of the staidness her husband represents: 'But Amit would always be there beside her in his shiny, ill-fitting suits, acting as her conscience and common sense' (1979, p. 127), and her new experience renders her wordless:

There were no words she had ever learned to describe her daily
feelings. She would have to give up trying to write. She would
give up trying to preserve old friendships. Because there was
nothing to describe and nothing to preserve.   (Mukherjee, 1979,
p. 120)

Trivia dominate her life: she cannot fit into the clothes of the more
liberated USA offered by her friend; she lives in the apartments of
others, drifting into an affair with vacuous Milt Glasser, 'he was, to
her, America' (1979, p. 175). Neither an intellectual nor a radical, she
finds she has no activities or fulfilment in her everyday life, and is
increasingly haunted by destructive media and TV images invading
her mind until, living a daily murder/game show, she cannot distin-
guish truth from fiction, and murders her husband. This extreme
response singles her out as a victim of the cultural displacement of
diasporan living, and of the American Dream which promises so
much but provides only material comforts and artifice.

In *The Middleman and Other Stories* (1988 – National Book Critics'
Circle award), Mukherjee shows how immigrants, transformed by
living abroad in the USA, construct an uneasy version of American-
ness, at odds with their Asian origins. She writes about the difficulties of this incorporation, her diasporan experience. In 'The Wife's
Story', an Indian wife studying in the USA copes with her husband's
visit from home. Her life has offered loneliness, racism and a new
freedom: she has irrevocably found her own identity. Part of her alienation is presented in the inability to wear costly Indian jewellery
which would mark her off as a rich target. It also emerges in the
sensitive, humorous gaze she levels at him in his foreign suits with
his tourist/victim responses. Concentrating on her perception provides insights into her changing world view.

Meena Alexander

Meena Alexander studied for her Ph.D. at Nottingham University
and now lives and works in New York. Not surprisingly, her work,
like that of other British or US-educated Asian writers, intermixes
the wealth of India and South-east Asia with a modernist and post-
modernist background, a history steeped in Austen and the Brontës,
as well as Joyce and Woolf. Alexander's poetry records living in
many places. Her work shows influence of the American poets Walt
Whitman (on whom she worked for her Ph.D.), William Carlos

Williams and others. Her poetry and prose are descriptive, capturing subjectivity, nuances of mood, and individuality of people and places. In 'Sidi Syed's architecture' (1991, p. 20) she imagines Syed the architect and stonecutter's perceptions:

> Loitering by the river
> he watched infants with blackened eyes
> swinging in their cradles.
> Mothers with chapped hands loitering.

While in 'Hotel Alexandria', always a watcher who gets inside those she watches, New York people are her focus:

> Corner of Broadway and 103rd Street. I stand in the cold staring at Alexandria Hotel, a hospice the city kept its poor in. They're dismantling it now, tearing out pipes, bricks, even the tiles that lined the dingy basement. Two men carry out a sofa; it has black and blue stripes on its arms.... There's barely room for the old woman who approaches, three plastic bags bound to her thighs, a man's jacket slung over her breasts. A woollen blanket someone threw out years ago covering her head so that only a tangle of hair shows. Hair acrid as salt. Newspapers are tucked in under her jacket. I see their rims, wasted with cold, fluttering.   (1991, p. 25)

The details are acutely perceived: the woman's life and feelings indicated in her movement and clothes, the city's rejection of her paralleling the destruction of the hotel/hospice.

Alexander's critical work also concentrates on subjectivity, and the writing of the women Romantics. Her short story 'Grandmother's Letters' (*Slate of Life*, 1991) recalls the courtship of her grandparents: rich, alive, filled with dramatised memory, searching for identity through the reconstitution of these letters and their context. It is a semi-fictionalised biography interspersed with her own thoughts and responses.

Shashi Deshpande

Deshpande won the Sahitya Academy Award in 1991 for *That Long Silence* (1987). A central theme in her work is women's sexuality, and her outspokenness is an issue seized on by critics, but Deshpande recognises this as her theme and her voice, and feels few restraints:

But of course for an Indian woman writing, there are all sorts of inhibitions which you have to learn to get past, simply to acknowledge women's sexuality, leave alone foregrounding it. I don't wish to restrain myself from what should come from reasons which have nothing to do with the novel and what belongs there. Social reasons for example, worrying about what people will say. These don't count for me when I am writing – although I am told some women have to take these things into account....

...We relate a great deal of our personal lives, our daily lives, to the myths.   (Interview with Lakshmi Holstrom, 1993, pp. 23–4)

SOME INDIAN WOMEN POETS

Kamala Das

Das started writing as women's poetry moved on from outmoded themes of legends, and praise of peasants. Her work is contemporary, less artificial, moving away from earlier women's poetry which concentrated on platitudes of romantic love, into a highly personal voice, technically aware. She was brought up in a warm, tight-knit Kerala family, then uprooted to Calcutta. Many of her poems about her life, collected in *My Story* (1988), recall this warm time, memories, and the family house. There are mercurial mood changes in her poetry but a core of identity. She sees the soul as separate from the body, hides the loss of her grandparents, writes of freedoms her husband allows and of sexual disappointments, moving between conquests and a sense of void, *carpe diem* and unhappiness. She laments the loss of childhood wholeness and sexual innocence in her grandmother's great house, feeling that her new sexual licence has somehow betrayed her:

> That was long ago.
> Before the skin,
> intent on survival,
> learnt lessons of self-betrayal.
> Before the red house that had stood for innocence
> crumbled
> and the old woman died
>
> ...
> The tragedy of life

is not death but growth,
the child growing into adult.

(Das, 'Composition', 1988)

Her syntax, vocabulary, idioms and verb choices are an accomplishment of the Indianisation of English, an important development in a national literature blending various experiences:

In the poetry of Kamala Das and such younger women poets
as de Souza and Silgardo the directness of speech rhythms and
colloquial language is an expression of emotional involvement.
Their language reveals feelings in all their quirkiness and unpre-
dictability, whereas with previous women poets language stands
in the way of emotion, poeticising and generalising rather than
reflecting it. Das, de Souza and Silgardo offer a range of highly
volatile emotions with poems unexpectedly changing direction and
gaining effect from their inner contrasts, conflict, ironies and
extremes. (King, 1987, p. 155)

Das has enabled a climate for more honest, revelatory confessional
women's poetry but her style is sometimes much more stilted than
the forceful contemporary street style of other women, for example,
Mamta Kalia, Eunice de Souza and Melanie Silgardo.

Eunice de Souza

Eunice de Souza re-writes myths ('Remember Medusa', 1987), overturns the static self-loathing and repression of women's roles, and
reconsiders relationships. Wit, irony, reversal, colloquial language,
and popular culture predominate such as in the Indianised image of
an arrogant partner, 'Jamie Bond' ('He speaks', 1987). She incorporates the intermixed languages of her Anglo-Indian/Indo-Anglian
condition. 'Fix' offers a thinner, less rich world than Das in terms of
sounds, images, languages, phrasing, cadences and line lengths and
avoids Das's emotional excess, choosing economy and control. Most
of de Souza's poems are satires or confessionals, mining deep-seated
fears. She satirises the church, marriage, Catholic motherhood,
Goan vulgarity and the alienation felt by many Goan Catholics
towards Hindu India, utilising an offhand, controlled, cold, distanced, ironic voice. Her poems grow from social situations such as
Goan aunts discussing marriage, looking for insanity signs. Early

poems are nationalist, rebelling against stifling, crude, religious and family upbringing, identifying with the wider India and Hindus. In 'My Students', she satirises beliefs that only foreign men, not local women poets, can write poetry:

> my students think it funny
> that Daruwallas and de Souzas
> should write poetry.
> Poetry is faery lands forlorn.
> Women writers Miss Austen.
> Only foreign men air their crotches.

Many poems are psychological, concerned with conflicts with parents, for example, 'Forgive Me, Mother'. Her poems are spare, sometimes conversations with friends:

> It was kill or die
> and you got me anyway:
> The blood congeals at lover's touch
> The guts dissolve in shit.

She uses confessional, contemporary language, understated irony arising from alienation and rejection, feminist in its vision and affirmations.

Melanie Silgardo

Silgardo, also from Goa, learned from de Souza. She projects her anxieties onto disturbing emotional images, considering the inauthentic, female, artificial, cosmetic self and fear of decay. Love for her and de Souza is not the conventional poetic answer. Her one love poem, 'A Memory', rejects the ideal strong man 'at the waiting end / big and brave like a brother', substituting 'If I must meet you / it must be half way.' She does not want the intimacy of an earlier generation: 'No, there is no togetherness to us / I cannot merge.'

There is an aloneness in much contemporary women's poetry. Fathers often dominate memories, and assurance and crude ease are contrasted with insecurities. Language is an index of content. These poets had to reject the artificial, formal language of Deshpande, moving into new ways of writing about consciousness, emotions, experiences disassociated with conformity of attitudes.

Many contemporary women from the Indian sub-continent scrutinise and re-write the myths and stereotypes which restrict Indian women, finding, as they do, a new outspokenness and inflection in their use of the language and new ways in which to express liberated identity.

9

Writing by Women from Australia

Come and experience
The lifestyles and
Mystical spirituality
That is quintessential
To the life and existence
Of a Traditional Aborigine
We'll also have a real
Properly initiated Elder
Who will empower you
With Dreamtime secrets

(Lisa Bellear Noonuccal, 1996, 'Souled Out', p. 43)

The history of Australia is one of exploration, journeying, challenge, and settlement. Those who immigrated to Australia were often displaced from their homelands, and they in turn displaced indigenous peoples, carving the lands to fit their developing needs and ways of life. The establishment of settlements in challenging new circumstances featured people who were tough, dedicated survivalist 'battlers'. This chapter will concentrate on settler writing (European, Asian or originated elsewhere), writing by Australians, and Aboriginal writing by indigenous women writers, the latter being the group who have come to publication more recently. It begins by sketching in some background to the settlement of Australia and the development of women's writing, then moves on to look at Aboriginal women's writing, particularly the work of Oodgeroo Noonuccal (Kath Walker), the best known poet, Bobbi Sykes and other poets. It considers Sally Morgan, Glenyse Ward and Ruby Langford, well known writers of semi-fictionalised autobiographies, a popular Aboriginal form of contemporary writing developed from oral storytelling which enables a record of individual and community lives. Writing by Thea Astley and Elizabeth Jolley is discussed in the context of other white Australian women's writing including, briefly, that of Kate Grenville, Helen Garner, Eleanor Dark and Shirley Hazzard. There are numerous really good Australian writers for whom there is no space here and the selection has largely been based on a concern to look at establishing identity, reclaiming history, developing versions of a woman's voice to explore women's lives, and dealing with issues of race and culture.

Australia is a vast continent, considered empty of people (almost) by its original settlers, who set about dispossessing Aboriginal people of their homelands, their sense of identity and history. Aboriginals rightly see this as a history of invasion, conquest and genocide, sadly an all too often repeated experience in the history of colonialism, but particularly shocking and excessive in the context of Australia (see Chapter 10 on Aotearoa and Maori people, and Chapter 13 on Oceania where settlement did not lead to such brutality). The vastness of the continent and the harshness of the lives of migrants go some way towards explaining this:

> Australians not of Aboriginal descent, and relatives of many who are, are migrant or the descendants of relatively recent migration. Many migrants had experience of invasion, civil war or oppression in their home countries, or migrated to escape the dangers of minority status.   (Pettman, 1992, p. 1)

WOMEN'S WRITING – HISTORICAL BACKGROUND

> [T]he distinctive feature of women's writing in Australia is its energy, its resilience, and its determination to tell the truth, even when this contradicts the comfortable complacencies of Australian belief.   (Shirley Walker, 1993, p. 170)

Much twentieth-century Australian women's writing has worked against the representation of Australia as full of 'mateship', caring and sharing, community and pioneer spirit. Writing aims to dispel some of the established myths of rugged pioneer women, such as appear in the several versions of 'The Drover's Wife' (Henry Lawson and others, Murray Bail, Frank Moorhouse and Barbara Jefferis; see John Thieme, 1996), which represent a fearless, resilient, tough, motherly heroic type. Most often women's writing has challenged the rather optimistic mythic view of Australia and of the toughness of pioneering women at one with the country's drive. Much highly politicised writing emerging from Australia has developed in the latter part of the twentieth century a very strong, unique, complexly theorised and articulate feminist response. Speculatively, this toughly intellectualised, articulated and politically activist feminism might be said to have arisen in response to the interlocked pressures of women's economic and gendered positions in a society which, while maintaining its comradely, healthy open image, has many contradictory forces at work, not least a persistent racism against migrants (Asian migrants in particular) and a persistent sexism against women. Pauline Hanson's recent 'one nation' party activism has stirred up the former of these two.

Australian feminist writing has a different kind of pioneer spirit. There is also a history of autobiographical writing among Australian women, whether settlers, migrants or Aboriginals, a realist tradition of 'telling it as it is', or was, of hardships, resilience and a struggle for identity, individuality and family community. This strain unites the work of a very broad variety of women writers. There is also, recently, a rich development of both fantastic and erotic writing, the latter arising from lesbian feminists in the most part. Experimental in terms of both form and content, these are important contributions. Australian government grants and fellowships have aided twentieth-century women's writing.

Early women's writing by settlers is largely in the form of diaries, letters, memoirs and journals, recording the hardships of life in the bush. Feminist accounts of women's experiences, such as those by Kay Daniels and Mary Murnane (*Uphill all the Way*, 1980), also help build up a picture of women's lives. Historically, there was variety in the form of some fictionalised and autobiographical writing such as that by women convicts (for example, Margaret Catchpole – twice sentenced to death for horse stealing). Settlers, such as Eliza Brown, Georgiana Molloy and Rachel Henning, left their diaries, as did women pioneers, for example Elizabeth Macarthur who testified to the hardships in the wool colony. Similar accounts of hardships in early colonial life can be found in writing from Canada (Chapter 11) and Aotearoa (Chapter 10). A nineteenth-century romance tradition engaging issues of women's work and independence produced works such as Elizabeth Murray's *Ella Norman, or A Woman's Perils* (1864), one of many novels dealing with the perils of drunken men and women's vulnerability in the late nineteenth and early twentieth centuries.

The first Australian woman's novel was by Anna Maria Bun, *The Guardian* (1838), followed by Catherine Spence's *Clara Morrison* (1854). More 'vapid' romantic fiction rather than tough pioneering romantic fiction was later produced by, for example, 'Tasma' (Jessie Couvreur), Ada Cambridge and Rosa Praed whose *Affinities* (1885) has been read as a lesbian text.

A landmark work was Miles Franklin's ironic *My Brilliant Career* (1901). Using a realistic yarn, a male tradition, the defiant young Sybylla Melvyn moves through difficult jobs such as working on a dairy farm, and as governess to a bush family. Bush life is seen as dirty, relentless hard work. Barbara Baynton's *Bush Studies* (1902) followed, a series of short stories using realism to record abuse, racism, sexism, and callousness.

Drusilla Modjeska's *Exiles at Home: Australian Women Writers, 1925–45* (1981) and *A Time to Write* by Kay Ferrers (1984) give full details of, and place the work of, Miles Franklin, Flora Eldershaw, Marjorie Barnard, Eleanor Dark, Katherine Susannah Pritchard, Jean Devanny and the critic Nettie Palmer. Pritchard and Devanny were committed communists, Pritchard writing *Coonardoo* (1929), dealing with a relationship between an Aboriginal girl and a white station owner whose son she bears. Jean Devanny's *Sugar Heaven* (1926) focuses on terrible cane-cutting working conditions while *The Butcher Shop* (1926) looks at New Zealand country life. Also notable was Henry Handel Richardson (Ethel Robertson)'s realist epic *The Fortunes of Richard Marhoney* (1930). There are great poets who include Judith Wright, Rosemary Dobson, Gwen Harwood, Dorothy Hewett and, more recently, Fay Zwicky. There is also a strong tradition of writing for children.

Since the 1960s a real increase in women's writing, especially feminist writing, has occurred and notable writers here are Thea Astley, Shirley Hazzard, Elizabeth Harrower, Christina Stead, Jessica Anderson, Elizabeth Jolley, Glenda Adams, Marion Campbell, Helen Garner and Kate Grenville, the best internationally known of these being Christina Stead, whose *The Man who Loved Children* (1940) looks at her relationship with her difficult father, and a search for success in both artistic endeavours and love. Short stories have been written by most of these, but other short-story writers include Jean Bedford and Olga Masters. There has recently been an upsurge in fantasy and erotic writing such as we find in the collection *Moments of Desire,* edited by Susan Hawthorne and Jenny Pausacker (1994), and *She's Fantastical,* edited by Lucy Sussex and Judith Raphael Buckrich (1995). Vampire tales have been produced in profusion, notable amongst which is the work of poet and fiction-writer Tracey Ryan (*Vamp,* 1997), and in the collections *Screams* (1996) and *Scream Again* (1997), writers such as Darryle Caine. These latter are in reaction against the realist tradition of Australian women's writing, and buy into the international interest in using the figure of the vampire to investigate the experience of the Other, our other selves, the selves we fear and desire. The border-breaking nature of vampire fictions (based on transgressions of life/death, and male/female binary divisions) seems to offer an imaginative exploratory outlet for the Australians who write them. This perhaps aligns with the earlier exploratory, boundary-breaking works (geographical boundaries) of earlier Australian fictions. They offer a challenge to realism, and so too does experimental technical writing. *She's Fantastical* (1995) challenges the conventional term 'the Mother' and contains several Goddess tales.

Since the Second World War there has been an increasing number of immigrants, particularly from Asian countries, and women writers among them include Antigone Kafala, Ana Walwicz, Rosa Cappiello and latterly Beth Yahp.

Anna Couani and Sneja Gunew in *Telling Ways: Australian Women's Experimental Writing* (1988) note the increasing presence of women's writing in bookshops, but a preponderance of realist writing:

> we note the dominance of a mode, the realist, in this emerging continent, as it has dominated fiction generally since the nineteenth century. There appears to be a limitless appetite for narrative of women's lives: for narrative (a highly shaped, familiar system of representation predicated on cause and effect), for life (the constant affirmation of a unified female subject)... (Couani and Gunew, 1988, p. 5)

Popular fictional genres, for example detective fiction, science fiction and so on, have flourished, and feminists intervene on the genres. Gunew points out that, while experimental writing is dedicated to transforming the ways in which texts generate meanings, the involvement of irony and ambiguity in this is dangerously open to misinterpretation and so feminist criticism is often concentrated on analysis of surfaces, on images of women, representations 'women need to negotiate woman, the figurative tradition of femininity, within various systems of representation' (p. 6). They negotiate the difficult issue of how to write about and represent women without falling into the construction of an essentialist 'woman' figure, in response to Teresa de Lauretis's point that 'woman is inside the rectangle, women are outside; the female subject of feminism is in both places at once' (1987, p. 114). Couani and Gunew use arguments from Kristeva in relation to the critique of the notion of a unified subject, an essentialist version of 'woman' which seems to be constructed in realist writing. They argue for a sense of women as not fixed but changing subjects, a 'subject-in-process' (Kristeva, 1984, pp. 232–4; and see Couani and Gunew, 1988, p. 7):

> Experimental writing shows women in process, engages with critique, irony, ambiguity, rescues the work of this still new land from merely recording the life of representative woman. But the experimental writing of Australian women (and much other writing) is still largely with the journals and small presses. (Couani and Gunew, 1988, p. 7)

Anna Couani and Ana Walwicz's work, among others, is experimental, using 'stream of consciousness' and 'interior monologue' in continuous bursts to represent racism, sexism, and erotic experience (see Walwicz's 'Vampire' in *Telling Ways*, ed. Couani and Gunew, 1988).

ABORIGINAL WOMEN'S WRITING – ISSUES OF LOCATION AND RECOGNITION

Aboriginal women's writing is frequently in the realist, semi-fictionalised, autobiographical mode, or concentrates on re-telling myths. When we attempt to locate the critical value of this work we are in danger of falling into historical traps in relation to Aboriginal peoples. Some insight into the dangers of translation, appropriation, and misrepresentation is useful here. Misrecognition and mistranslation have always been a problem for Aboriginal women since the first 1788 landing record misunderstood friendship as sexual offering:

> If they ever deign to come near you to take a present they appear as coy, shy, timorous as a maid on her wedding night. But when

they are, as they think, out of your reach, they holler and chatter to you, and frisk and flirt and play a hundred wanton pranks, equally as significant as the solicitations of a Covent Garden strumpet.   (Bradley, 1788, cited in Jennings and Hollingsworth, 1987–88, pp. 113–33; p. 129)

Bradley's translation of friendly and inquisitive actions is fuelled by an alarming male imperialist response; an equation of the indigenous with the sexually available and (like the newly discovered lands) exploitable. This quotation reminds us, however, that in our reading of Aboriginal women's writing we need to avoid intentional or unintentional imperialism, colonialism and appropriation when (necessarily) trying to locate and describe writing within familiar critical frameworks of, for example, the novel. Much of our reading of the work of Aboriginal women can initially be aided by considering some of the critical issues with which we are familiar from reading writing by other post-colonial women. These include folk and oral traditions; the use of national language; oral literature and women's place in its dissemination; individual testimony; and a politically aware articulation of the need for recognition and identity. Reclamation of power, of racial and gender equality, of community are notable here, partly achieved through a rediscovery of roots. Technically this is enacted and expressed through a crucial stylistic mixture of recording and re-telling history in a way which recognises both lived experiences and the power of cultural myths, of the metaphorical, the spiritual and the magical as different dimensions of experience. Concerns are similar, but conditions and forms of production are different from those of, for example, African American women writers.

Aboriginal women writers themselves are well aware of the dangers of forcing their works into forms which do not reflect their experiences, their traditional forms of expression, or their voices. They are aware both of the disempowerment of remaining absent and silent (available in oral literature forms to only a few in the close community), and of the reality of appropriation, of being mispresented in any transaction which offers them and their works some wider dissemination. Scripting and publishing the work of Aboriginal women writers is and has been a sensitive issue. There are other sensitivities for us as readers, students, teachers, and critics. Locating their works, 'labelling' them, and finding critical frameworks with which to describe them must therefore be a tentative step, set, as much as is possible for the reader and critic, against a context and background of understanding of traditional Aboriginal forms of expression and the history of repression and abuse from which these women speak.

Fictionalised autobiographies are popular Aboriginal women's writing forms. Similar to African American slave narratives, to women's diaries, and to oral literatures, fictionalised autobiographies bring the issues of who writes, of the politics of co-authorship, of claims of identity, and of how we read such works, to the fore.

Aboriginal women writers such as Sally Morgan, Kath Walker (Oodgeroo Noonuccal), Glenyse Ward, Bobbi Sykes and Ruby Langford write an emerging literature which has faced immense barriers in relation to publication and dissemination.

Ignorance and silence are destructive. Many white people in Australia, let alone Europe, have no idea about the abuse suffered by Aboriginal peoples, for theirs is a history only just being written, and their writing of their own history and own lives returns at last the power of naming and owning, of identification and identity. Maureen Walker, in conversation with Bronwen Levy, charts a history of genocide, of gold sovereigns offered for Aboriginal scalps, of slaughter, rape, and the younger generation's guilt about racism, alongside their ignorance. She says:

> I just don't think white people have come to terms with themselves, and their history here in this land yet. And so it's very difficult for them to come to terms with Aboriginal people, and its very difficult for them then to try and pass onto their children, or teach them anything about Aboriginal culture, or Aboriginal history. And so, they choose not to do it. Or, they'll present only the traditional culture.   (Maureen Walker, in conversation with Levy, 1991, p. 189)

And younger generations of Aboriginal writers are also aware of the often liberalised ignorance of even other Australians, as Lisa Bellear (Noonuccal) comments, adopting the voice of a white Australian feminist, fairly well-meaning but misguided, and selfish in her assumptions of homogeneity and shared struggle:

> I don't even know if I'm capable
> of understanding
> Aborigines, in Victoria?
> Aboriginal women here, I've never seen one,

and if I did, what would I say,
damned me if I'm going to feel guilty
(Lisa Bellear Noonuccal, 'Women's Liberation',
1991, pp. 204–5)

Sharing a feminist position is not enough when reading the work of women from different cultural contexts. Middle-class white feminism has had a rather poor history in its ability to recognise the difference that race and class add to a Black woman's experiences of sexism and abuse.

HISTORICAL AND CULTURAL CONTEXT

Australia is a vast continent and while white settlers tend to live in urban or farming areas, many Aboriginal people live in remote communities hundreds of miles apart. There are high illiteracy rates particularly among women. Aboriginal people live with a constant struggle for land rights, their family and community groups decimated initially by genocide, then latterly by policies of the removal and adoption of Aboriginal children. They have suffered a history of racism. Wiped out, disenfranchised, their values and beliefs and rights denied, they have been treated like animals, uneducated, unfed, with no-one in power to speak for their rights. Women in particular have suffered from misrepresentation, and the destruction of their families:

> With the onset of white colonization women's traditional functions were either severely truncated and rendered marginal in a reconstituted social environment or utterly destroyed as their populations were decimated and their society and culture dismembered and fragmented. During this process the position of black women plummeted from being co-workers of equal importance to men in the balanced use of the environment to that of thoroughly exploited beasts of burden. It fell from being valuable human resources and partners within traditional sexual relationships to that of degraded and diseased sex objects and from being people of recognized spiritual worth to that of beings of virtual animal status in the eyes and belief systems of their exploiters.　(Evans, 1982, p. 9)

Powerful within their own dwindling communities, Aboriginal women have fought genocide and dispossession. Many were creative but, like Alice Walker's examples in *In Search of Our Mothers' Gardens* (1983), this was transient, consumed. Much Aboriginal women's creativity, whether based on the visual or the oral storytelling modes, was and is purely community oriented. Since the 1970s however, Black female activism has paralleled the emergence of feminism and a voice has developed in film making with both *Sister If Only You Knew* (produced by Film Australia in 1975 and featuring Aboriginal women describing their work in community activities, and white controls), and Tracey Moffat's film *Nice Coloured Girls*, in the late 1980s, which, by cutting between voice-overs of Aboriginal girls taking a white man for a ride in the Kings Cross area and scenes of the boarding of the fleet in 1788 by young Aboriginal women (see Bradley, above), makes the point about reclamation of power for Black women. Reclaiming a voice and telling the truth is of prime importance.

Women were oral storytellers, like the griottes of Africa, and also the repositories of ritual and ceremony, the custodians of the stories of the Dreamtime in which the essential beliefs of the Aboriginal peoples reside. This is understood as: 'to be saturated with the primordial Power of Nature which seemed to pulsate through all creation' (Martin, 1979, p. 155); and according to Evans:

> Hence the Dreaming, the legendary cycles, the sacredness of land, the magical songs, the mesmeric rhythms of music and chant and dance, and the primacy of religion as the core and defining characteristic of that society.   (Evans, 1982, p. 8)

Women have secret ceremonies performed at important life moments such as puberty, pregnancy, childbirth and sickness, and as love magic, which have important social and psychological functions. White male anthropologists mistakenly rendered the women who held the secrets of these myths and beliefs secondary, wrongly evaluating their gathering roles as subordinate to the hunting roles of their menfolk. Ruby Langford and others have reasserted the importance of women's storytelling, emphasising the ways in which Aboriginal writing functions:

> Our ancient tribal people sat down and sang the spirits into this land giving it its physical form. Whiteman called our dreamtime a myth. Our people know it is a fact, it was before creationtime! They sang the trees, they sang the mountains, they sang the valleys,

they sang the rivers and streams, all round, all round.... They
sang life in its vastness, into this brown land; and the spirit lives
still, never has it been silenced, by whiteman or his restrictive
ways, and the song had a beginning, and there will never be an
ending until justice is returned to the singers of songs, our ancient
tribal people!   (Langford, 1991, p. 36)

Many Aboriginal women do not seek publication, but prefer to
create within their own communities. Others do, and to achieve an
engaged, wide public recognition, many have had to work initially
with white co-authors, who have necessarily become something like
cultural translators, altering the women's work and somewhat mis-
understanding the circling, repetitive patterning of the established
forms of storytelling. Aboriginal women writers contribute to an
established oral literature by enabling their works to be scripted, but
something is changed in the process.

Latterly these have often been succeeded by works by Aboriginal
women writing without a translator, such as Sally Morgan's *My
Place* (1987), an autobiographical record of the lives of her family and
her people, or Glenyse Ward's *Wandering Girl* (1988). The style of the
latter is realistic, wryly humorous, a testimony to the ability to survive bigotry and racism. It shows that this lively, outspoken, self-
aware Black woman is able to speak out for others like herself,
brought up in a Mission away from her family then employed for
basic wages in domestic labour.

Tracing the experiences of Aboriginal women in Queensland
history, we discover systematic racist abuse:

On all Australian colonial frontiers, from Bruni Island to the Rum
Jungle, from Fraser Island to the North West Cape, Aboriginal
women were progressively reduced to a position of extreme
dehumanization in white eyes and into the lowest ranking position in the white social hierarchy.... From this time, Aboriginal
women, being both female and black, were subjected to dual patterns of oppression and to the intense, derogatory stereotyping
which accompanies the interplay of racist and sexist ideologies
and practices.   (Evans, 1982, p. 7)

The Aboriginal population was reduced in Queensland from 120,000
in the 1820s to less than 20,000 by the 1920s. White male settlers misunderstood established modes of relationships and sharing, treating
Black women with the mixture of desire and guilt which bell hooks

writes of in the USA (1982), transferring their own repressive guilt and self-loathing, blaming the women for the sexual activity into which they forced them: 'Black women were viewed by white males as being founts of insatiable libidinal desire' (hooks, in Evans, 1982, p. 11). Raped and devalued like the land, women were dehumanised with animal terminology, brutality cloaked with labels. There are numerous tales of running down or 'mustering' Black girls, who were called 'gins', and keeping them with shearing teams, to be repeatedly raped, then releasing them at the end of the season. On farms women were used both to provide sexual services and to carry out domestic chores. Raping was called 'gin busting' and keepers of Aboriginal women 'gin shepherds' and 'combos', while the women themselves were 'stud gins', 'black velvet', etc. These station and homestead girls were misused, then discarded at the end of the season. The results were catastrophic for families and communities as venereal disease, starvation, exposure and a rise in infant mortality followed. Removed from their families into service, and later into forced adoption, Aboriginal children lost touch, families dissolved and bloodlines were confused both by separation and by intermixing. Difficulties over the maintaining of family relationships have continued late into the twentieth century. Political decisions to remove Aboriginal children from their families split them permanently, creating a stolen generation who are still trying to find their relatives, rootless in foster care and Missionary upbringing:

> The state has interfered constantly in Aboriginal families through its forced movement, control and surveillance of Aboriginal people, and most brutally through the seizing of Aboriginal children.

> One out of every six or seven Aboriginal children in New South Wales were 'taken into care' compared to one in every 200 non-Aboriginal children. Aboriginal children are still being taken into care in overwhelmingly disproportionate numbers. (Pettman, 1992, p. 30)

REPRESENTATION AND WRITING

Mistranslation, misappropriation, and disempowerment are the background against which Aboriginal women write of their lives, of their family and community. They create a cultural identity and history through this testimony, both explaining the causes of and dispelling the consistent image of drunkenness and idleness among Aboriginals. The history of this literary production is short. Only recently has there been funding to help those willing to tell their stories, and some monetary and political recognition of the import-ance of maintaining cultural rituals, behaviours, values and beliefs.

Jan Larbalestier comments on the difficulties of being Black in Australia and the engagement involved in writing about it:

> The very act of writing their lives is a challenge to the ways in which Aboriginality has been constructed in dominant 'white' discourses. In contemporary Australian society, 'living black' and writing about it can be seen as a process of political confrontation. (Larbalestier, 1991, p. 90)

Writing is to some extent a collusion with established white man-aged forms, but also an empowerment, all the more so when Abori-ginal writers start to write on their own without co-authors. Mudrooroo Narogin (Colin Johnson), author of the first Aboriginal novel by a man, *Wild Cat Falling* (1965), comments:

> It is only in the last few years that black literary texts have been allowed to speak for themselves: that is, the Aboriginal allowed to say what she or he wants to say and in the language she or he wishes it to be said.   (Narogin, 1990, p. 158)

Dual authoring and editing of Black women's writing by white col-laborators – male or female – must affect the writing and treatment of issues and Narogin argues that it seriously affects the themes and forms used in *Karobran* (1978) by Monica Clare, as it also does in *An Aboriginal Mother* (1984) by Labumore (Elsie Roughsey), of which the two male non-Aboriginal white editors said at the time:

> it became apparent that some editing would be required in order for it to be acceptable for commercial publication and accessible to the average white Australian reader.... Despite the changes to the text, we feel that we have preserved the flavour and flow of Elsie's work. It remains comprehensible to her fellow Mornington Islanders, and will be of interest, no doubt, to many Aboriginal readers, as well as to the white audience.   (Memnott and Hors-man, Preface to *An Aboriginal Mother*, 1984)

Margaret Somerville, who worked with Patsy Cohens on *Ingelba and the Five Black Matriarchs* (1990), recalls Patsy's resistance to scripting the oral literature form. She wished to retain her 'wandering around and around' (1991):

> If this story about my life is jumping from one thing and place to another, that is because that's how memories are. It is as if life is a big puzzle and we live through bits of it, and then later, from another spot in our years, we look back and that piece fits in. But while we are living it, can't really answer all the whys and wherefores of it.   (Somerville, 1991, p. 95)

Any co-authoring or scripting of oral literature involves the unavoidable bias of the researcher. As Paul Hamilton acknowledges, researchers' intentions shape and select so that, even with the most sensitive researcher, Aboriginal women will not quite be telling their own tales (1990).

Gradually women are writing their own tales their own way. Carole Ferrier notes the differences in Aboriginal forms of writing which enable cultural resistance. Carole Ferrier (1985) highlights the use of wry humour and irony, the Aboriginal form of resistance through withholding information, or through deliberately telling, and the use of a spiral, non-linear narrative form. In Sally Morgan's *My Place* (1987 – see below) we are aware of a layering and repetition, a build-up and patterning as family members Nan and Uncle Arthur Corunna join in with their own stories, and certain incidents are re-recalled, as with an oral form. While this form appears straightforwardly realistic, the layering, patterning and use of certain repeated items and oppositions provide an underlying abstract text, a symbolic or a formal comment and reading which runs with the tale-telling and testimony. Bob Hodge and Vijay Mishra say of the ostensibly simply realist elements of Aboriginal narratives:

> Aboriginal realist texts are always structured by an underlying abstract text which is a primary means of encoding Aboriginal meanings and the metameaning of Aboriginality itself.   (Hodge and Mishra, 1991)

There is a 'dialectic between speech and silence in working simultaneously with and against history' (Ferrier, 1985, p. 215).

Glenyse Ward and Ruby Langford also circle round events, repeat and recall different elements, withhold or reveal information with a witty *naïveté*. Incidents recalled are likely to be typical, not necessarily individual.

STARTING TO READ – LOCATION AND INTRODUCTIONS

Growing out of the oral tradition, many of the works we might discover are life stories, some co-authored, some semi-fictionalised. The first published work by an Aboriginal woman was Ursula McConnel's *Myths of the Munkan* (1957). Autobiographies include Evonne Goolagong's *Evonne! On the Move* (1973) and work by Margaret Tucker, Theresa Clemens and Shirley C. Smith, who, with the assistance of Bobbi Sykes, wrote *Mumshirl: An Autobiography* (1981). Marnie Kennedy's *Born a Half Caste* (1985) and Sally Morgan's *My Place* (1987), Glenyse Ward's *Wandering Girl* (1988), and Ruby Langford's *Don't Take Your Love to Town* (1988) followed. The very first women's novels have a great deal of autobiographical content. These are Faith Bandler's *Wacvie* (1977) and Monica Clare's *Karobran* (1978). (Fuller lists are available in Claire Buck (ed.), *Bloomsbury Guide to Women's Literature*, 1992, and Jack Davis et al. (eds), *Paperbark: An Anthology of Black Australian Writing*, 1990.)

Autobiographical and semi-autobiographical works are in a long tradition of Aboriginal creative response:

> The widespread use of biography and autobiography by Aboriginal writers can be linked to a cultural tradition in which verse or song would detail the lives of dreaming ancestors.... It remains to be seen if this tradition was used to detail the lives of ordinary people.... It may have been so. (Narogin, 1985, p. 2)

But the scripting of oral storytelling and oral histories has its losses as well as its gains, and only the sensitive Aboriginal *author* can retain and build upon the cadences and the spiralling forms of the traditional modes of story and life tales. What can be lost in the written recording of oral history or oral literature is a 'different voice':

> Its rhythms, its spiral not linear chronology, its modes of non-verbal communication, its humour, and its withholding of information.

Many of these things will be untranslatable to the printed page.
(Ferrier, 1985, p. 135)

FICTIONALISED AUTOBIOGRAPHIES – SALLY MORGAN, GLENYSE WARD, FAITH BANDLER AND RUBY LANGFORD

Jackie Huggins notes the importance of the development of Aboriginal women's writing without partnership and cultural translation:

A new phenomenon of contemporary Aboriginal writing is emerging whereby women writers have the double advantage of relating their history in literally black and white terms, and simultaneously transcending and cutting across cultural boundaries. (Huggins, 1987/8, p. 22)

Sometimes women write the life stories of their relatives, whose specific situation and often representative sufferings have been hidden from history. One such was Faith Bandler, an Aboriginal rights activist and writer from Murwimballah, New South Wales, discovering the history of her father who was brought from the beautiful Pacific Islands into slavery in Queensland. She decided to retrace his footsteps and to write his tale in order to claim his and her own history, and to record the lost histories of the slaves. It was a well kept secret that plantations and stations developed through slave labour.

I came home determined that my father's story should be told. There were other reasons why the book had to be written. The slave trade of Australia had never been included in school curricula. I found that most Australians do not believe that slave labour was used to develop the sugar cane industry. Those who were enslaved did not have the opportunity to tell their story. The story has only been told by historians with a detachment from the thoughts and feelings of the people concerned.   (Bandler and Fox, 1980, Introduction)

Wacvie (1977), Faith Bandler's first novel, was followed by *Marani in Australia* (1980, with Len Fox) in which she traces her father's capture from his home island, Ambrym in the New Hebrides, to work in Queensland. He escaped in 1897, settling in Tumbulgum in

New South Wales. Returning to her father's island she is greeted as family and everyone attempts to trace her ancestry.

Sally Morgan and Glenyse Ward from Western Australia, the other side of the continent from Faith Bandler, have written of their own life stories. Sally Morgan's personal, powerful tale *My Place* (1987) locates her and her family as Aboriginal people with their own history and lifestyles in a racist white society which devalues indigenous people. Her search for identity develops as school-mates question her origins. Ironically not only has she never realised she has a Black Aboriginal grandmother, but her knowledge of her own cultural identity has been hidden and unspoken because of her family's awareness of the ostracism and denigration which would follow upon its discovery. Sally is told to say she is Indian, which is both exotic and devoid of the stigma of being an original Australian: an ironic situation indeed.

> The kids at school had also begun asking us what country we came from. This puzzled me because, up until then I'd thought we were the same as them. If we insisted that we came from Australia, they'd reply, 'Yeah, but what about ya parents, bet they didn't come from Australia.'
> One day I tackled mum about it as she washed the dishes.
> 'What do you mean, where do we come from?'
> 'I mean, what country, the kids at school want to know what country we come from. They reckon we're not Aussies. Are we Aussies, Mum?'   (Morgan, 1987, p. 38)

Poignant and powerful, the relationship between Sally and her family, particularly her grandmother, develops as Sally grows to realise that her Nan is Black and to glean from her her story and that of her brother. Nan's hoarding of Australian coins about to be devalued symbolises her treasuring her Aborginality which contemporary culture devalues. Nan's artwork and values unknowingly inherited by Sally enrich and unite the family but are denied and devalued at school. When Sally ingests a set of cultural values which deny her artistic heritage and burns her artwork in shame, Nan is furious, exclaiming against their cultural *naïveté*:

> Nan punched. She lifted up her arm and thumped her clenched fist hard on the kitchen table.

'You bloody kids don't want me, you want a bloody white grandmother, I'm black. Do you hear, I'm black, black, black!'   (p. 97)

Sally, beginning to acknowledge her Aboriginality, is confused by
stereotyping and racial prejudices:

> 'Don't Abos feel close to the earth and all that stuff?'
> 'God, I don't know. All I know is none of my friends like them.'
> (p. 98)

Ostensible friends distance themselves.

The book is personal, funny, a lively, inquisitive revivifying of a
lost past hidden because of the fear of prejudice. Fuelled by the need
to establish identity, it reclaims Aboriginal legacy, with joy and
pride.

Glenyse Ward's *Wandering Girl* (1988) and *Unna You Fullas* (1991)
deliberately set out to speak for Aboriginal women in the community. This is an important political statement as Bruce McGuiness
comments, emphasising the importance of authenticity:

> If it's going to be legitimate Aboriginal literature, then it must
> come from Aboriginal people and their communities without any
> restrictions placed upon them.   (McGuiness in Davis and Hodge,
> 1985, p. 49)

Glenyse Ward's experience is one of removal from her family
and upbringing in a Mission, followed by employment in domestic
service. This was a common pattern in the (unrecorded) lives of
many Aboriginal women, who suffered racist abuse and a dehuman-
ised, subordinate role within the households. Here Glenyse's experiences are recorded using binary oppositions; lively friendship at the
Mission contrasted with the strict regime and the wearing of flour-
sack clothes; the eating of beans and drinking from a tin mug used
normally by pets, contrasted with the lavish food of her employer
Mrs Bigelow, and contrasted again with the feast of wholesome food
which she prepared for herself and ate from bone china in
Mrs Bigelow's absence. Glenyse's story testifies to her own lively
humour and survival spirit against the bigoted ignorance of those
around her who treated her as subhuman. 'No washing up other
people's dishes' is the aim she emerges with for her own family in
her epilogue to *Wandering Girl*, set against her own lack and servitude.

Her authentic voice is not translated by a co-author: it emerges clearly, in colloquial phrases – the carpet is 'stained terrible' (1988, p. 26), 'I felt shame' (1985, p. 27) and the cream cake 'went down real well' (1985, p. 56). Kathy Willetts comments:

> The author's use of understatement, ironic humour and simple language make the narrative both credible and moving....
> The authentic voice of the author has not been suppressed by editorial influence. Ward sets up a series of binary opposites whereby white bigotry and oppression are contrasted with Black consciousness, and responses to an imposed subservience. These binary opposites enable the Aboriginal reader, in the active process of decoding, to identify with the author's Aboriginality, dignity, intelligence and final decision to take control of her own destiny. White readers, too, are invited by the careful structuring of signs in the text, to disassociate themselves from the insensitivity and domination of the callously 'charitable' Mrs Bigelow. (Willetts, 1990, p. 167)

Glenyse Ward's tale draws from a history of the removal of girls for work on sheep-shearing stations, stock work, and domestic service, graded in relation to their colour. Here, historically, they received systematic racist abuse. From earlier times, Archibald Meston wrote of the sexual harassment of Aboriginal women:

> The Aboriginal women are usually at the mercy of anybody, from the proprietor or manager to the stockman, cook, roustabout and jackaroo. Frequently the women do all the housework and are locked up at night.   (Meston, 1897, p. 14)

Glenyse Ward's books are episodic memoirs, livened up by wry humour, personal tone, and a consistently sound self image. Like Maya Angelou in *I Know Why the Caged Bird Sings* (1970, see Chapter 2), who drops a tray to emphasise the importance of using her real name, Glenyse's mixed record of her original naivety and her latter ironic awareness shows up the bigotry and racism of a roomful of Mrs Bigelow's snobbish friends when she decides to join them and make herself known:

> Soon as I opened the door all the chatter and laughter stopped. You could hear a pin drop as all eyes were on me. All of a sudden

some poshed-up voice, with a plum in her mouth came out of a crowd, 'Tracy dear, is this your little dark servant?'
  I just stood there smiling. I thought it was wonderful that at last people were taking notice of me. There were sniggers and jeers from everywhere. I turned to the lady who did all the talking and said 'My name is Glenyse'. She was quite startled and said, 'Oh dear, I didn't think you had a name'. (Ward, 1988, p. 24)

Ruby Langford's *Don't Take Your Love to Town* (1988) tells her battling tale of bringing up children, working and living in the bush erecting posts. Latterly she lived in the town, campaigning for decent living standards, gradually becoming a political activist for Aboriginal people. Her writing also testifies to the difficulties and pleasures of transposing literary reading from Britain into the Australian landscape, a difficulty noted also by Caribbean writers. Reading a poem about a dingo and looking out of the window the children intermix local poets (Banjo Patterson) and Victorian British poets:

and when we looked out the windows we saw Clancy with her thumbnail dipped in tar, and Andy crossing for the cattle and the Man from Snowy River galloping up the rise. Through the same windows we saw the Lady of Shalott, we saw the solitary reaper, the deserted villages, the swains and bowers and the golden sheaves and behind that the boys' toilets and the woodwork room. (Langford, 1988, p. 30)

Hers is a cleverly recalled, circling oral literature-based narrative. She foretells incidents of the future, later in the narrative, and recalls parallels and hints from the past, proceeding through events in time and then returning to remind us, to repeat, fill in gaps, reinterpret. The dispossession of Aboriginal families and communities is summed up:

I felt like I was living tribal but with no tribe around me, no close-knit family. The food-gathering, the laws and songs were broken up, and my generation at this time wandered around as if we were tribal but in fact living worse than the poorest of poor whites and in the case of women living hard because it seemed like the men loved you for a while, and then more kids came along and the men drank and gambled and just disappeared. One day they'd had enough and they just didn't come back. (Langford, 1988, p. 96)

She does not seem resentful and depressed at this; it causes her to develop more strength and to concentrate on her kids, one of whom, like so many young Aboriginal men, is imprisoned several times and destroyed by this incarceration. Through her life we see the everyday hardships and valiant spirit of a tough Black woman, individual community representative, speaking for the lives of others and herself, and doing this through telling her own tale, and through political activism.

Assimilation through absorption policies enabled Aboriginal families to live in the homes allocated to them but separated them from other Aboriginal families, stranding them in lone areas where they experienced daily discrimination and had to live extremely restricted and restrained lives, their living and habits constantly frowned on as wrong because different. In her work, she deliberately overcomes the difficulty of speaking out as an individual subject, claiming identity and a voice, and also speaking for the community. When she and her friends and family make an important journey to their cultural centre near Ayers Rock, at Uluru, their trip is to get back in contact with their tribal roots in a way which their urban-fringe and assimilated experience had denied them. Her book helped her not only to articulate and form a shape to her own life but to speak for the people of Australia:

> I knew when I finished this book a weight would be lifted from my mind, not only because I could examine my own life from it and know who I was, but because it may help better the relationship between the Aboriginal and white people, that it might give some idea of the difficulty we have surviving between two cultures, that we are here and will always be here.   (Langford, 1988, p. 269)

As more generally with the identity 'Black', often Aboriginality is a chosen category, though more often it is imposed and has attached to it the history of denial of rights, genocide. There are some ironies in all of this. Denial of Aboriginal land rights is sometimes a product of refusal to recognise bi-racial Aboriginals' rights, the ironic result of assimilation policies. Forms of Aboriginal identity are often imposed, Pettman tells us, from the outside, in response to 'the Europeans' spiritualizing gaze' (Rowse, 1988, p. 271), in which representation is 'racialised through its association with colour or blood. It is popularised through notions of Aboriginal art in the galleries and tourist uses' (Pettman, 1992, p. 108). Keesing comments: 'The ironies and contradictions of Aboriginal peoples being denied land rights they believe are culturally illegitimate on the grounds that they do not fit an anthropological model have chilling implications' (Keesing, 1989, p. 34). On the part of the Aboriginal identified and originated peoples however, identity is embraced positively and asserted in relation to economic rights, land rights and family histories. As Keeffe puts it (1988, p. 67), 'the construction and use of an ideology of Aboriginality is a specific attempt by Aborigines to regain and retain control over both things and ideas'.

ABORIGINAL POETS

The work of poets Kath Walker, Lisa Bellear (see pp. 202 and 209–10) and Bobbi Sykes has an oral base in performance poetry and deals with race and gender.

Oodgeroo Noonuccal – Kath Walker

Born on Stradbroke island, where she eventually settled in a cara-van, Oodgeroo Noonuccal, the best known Aboriginal woman poet, has spoken internationally and locally for land rights, cast a quiz-zical eye over European notions and practices of 'civilisation', and celebrated the lives of individual community members. Her work includes *We Are Going* (1964), *The Dawn is at Hand* (1966), *My People* (1970), *Father Sky and Mother Earth* (1985), and a myth-tale based on the Dreaming, *Stradbroke Dreamtime* (1972). Sadly testifying to the loss of community, land and spiritual connections, the remnants of an Aboriginal group enter the town:

> They came in to the little town
> A semi-naked band subdued and silent,
> All that remained of their tribe.
> They came here to the place of their old bora ground
> Where now the many white men hurry about like ants.
> Notice of estate agent reads: 'Rubbish may be tipped here'.
>   (Walker, *'We Are Going'*, 1992, p. 107)

In 'Cookalingee' (1992 [1966]) the Aboriginal cook on the white man's station feeds her hungry people at the door, retaining links but needing to live the white man's ways in order to survive.

She writes also of the plight of Aboriginal women raped and abused by station owners and workers. In 'Dark Unmarried Mothers' (1992 [1966]) they are:

> fair game for lechers –
> Bosses and station hands,
> And in town and city
> Low-grade animals
> prowl for safe prey.
>
> (Walker, 1992 [1966], p. 27)

No-one is accused as they would be if the girls were white. Instead it is condoned, the victims advised to 'Shrug away the problem' (Walker, 1992 [1966], pp. 27, 28). In 'The Child Wife' (Walker, 1992 [1966], p. 32) a young woman, married now joyless to an old man, mourns the loss of her lover. More celebratory poems record the tough organiser Daisy Bindi:

> But Daisy the militant no man subdued,
> Who championed her people out of servitude.
>
> (Walker, 1992 [1966], p. 128)

and the girl who celebrates life:

> I love joy of life,
> I love arms around me
> . . .
> High eagles, the light in the eyes we love,
> The camp crying for joy when one returns
> (Walker, 1992 [1966], p. 34, 'The Young Girl Wanda')

She looks at racial equality and difference as opposed to division. Kath Walker's poems use oral poetry rhythms with regular metre and rhyme, circularity and repetition, often giving Aboriginal people their own voice.

Bobbi Sykes

Bobbi Sykes, from Townsville in Queensland, who completed her education at Harvard, is of a younger generation. Her work is influenced in its rhythms by the American Beat poets, and in its tones

and outright political comment, by US-originated Black Consciousness, an awareness helping many Aboriginal people to recognise an
international community consciousness. Some poems deal with the
inequality of life for Aboriginal women in relationships. Others concentrate on a time of change, when it is politically popular to be
Black but when the embracing of a Black cause overlooks the triple
inequality of gender, as well as race, and class/economic position
(see Zora Neale Hurston's 'triple burden' in Chapter 2):

> black women are on the way '*up*'
> you now must wonder who will babysit the kids
> while you make your (unpaid) t.v. appearance
> you must try not to let your bitterness
> be construed as 'black racism'
> as you recall the abuses
> heaped upon you all your life
> and you view your 'liberation'
> with a scepticism born of poverty,
> corrugated iron shacks, no water.
> four children from six live births
> and the accumulated pain of two centuries
> (Sykes, 'Black Woman', 1979, p. 53)

THEA ASTLEY, SHIRLEY HAZZARD, ELIZABETH JOLLEY AND OTHER NOVELISTS

The history of Australia is one of migrants escaping the kind of
oppression which ironically many then transposed to the indigenous
peoples of Australia. Many later twentieth-century women writers
have themselves engaged with re-imagining and writing the cultural history of the settlement of Australia. Several narratives either
offer a long-range family history, such as Thea Astley's *It's Raining in
Mango* (1987), or imaginatively place a central character in significant
historical scenes and moments. Both forms recall and reshape the
memories of families to record their experience of settling a rich,
wild land. The pioneering spirit of many early women writers has
grown latterly into a measured recognition of the pleasures and
problems that that spirit produced. So with the work of Thea Astley,
Elizabeth Jolley, Kate Grenville, Eleanor Dark, and others, there is a
sensitive record of historical confrontations and boundary crossing.

Eleanor Dark

Eleanor Dark's largely social realist writing also uses some symbolism such as that of the thickly, quickly spreading and all-covering lantana in the novel *Lantana Lane* (1986 [1959]). This novel looks at a small, tightly knit community and the relations between men and women within it before women's liberation, pointing out with neat ironies how the men enjoy bulldozing and flattening while the women are involved in domestic work – everyone tested by the contradictions forced on them in their lives. It is reminiscent of *Lark Rise to Candleford* or Thomas Hardy in its rich evocation of local folk, who prefer cyclones, which give them a sporting chance, to the men who do not.

Kate Grenville

Joan Makes History (1989 [1988]) grows out of books, including *Tristram Shandy*, which chart the lives of people through time, using interior monologue and first-person narrative – though in this case experimentally in so far as the book charts the life of the very long-lived Joan, who is present, like Forest Gump, at all the major happenings throughout Australia's history and so can be said to accrue a kind of national history around her. First she lands with her husband Captain Cook in 1770 on *The Endeavour*:

> That land lay somewhere ahead of us, if it lay at all steaming and swelling, growing humid and huge in our imaginings with its jungles and waterfalls, waiting nuggets and tigers. (Grenville, 1989 [1988], p. 20)

This is an early thought, prior to Joan deciding to make many histories for herself. The different stories are told of different kinds of people who have landed and lived in Australia. She walks amongst the streets of the Chinese immigrants, constructs furniture from trees, notes the difficulties of settlers' lives in the bush, and tells of knowing Ned Kelly. Finally, giving us a cumulative sense of history moving through the land and absorbing people and their lives, she says:

> what a big thing this business of history is, and what absurd bits and pieces make it up! ... That handful of dirt rejected nothing: it soaked up the steaming urine of babies as they crawled across it

laughing, and the tears of twig-like grandmothers slipping a hand under a cheekbone and waiting for the last sleep. Men and women lay down and melted into the dirt, or were put into holes and buried... (Grenville, 1989 [1988], p. 283)

It is an individual story, and also one of Everywoman; the style changing to reflect the ages of which she writes.

Elizabeth Jolley

Born in the industrial Midlands of the UK in 1923, Jolley moved to Western Australia in 1959 and is acclaimed as one of Australia's leading writers, publishing several collections of short fiction and essays and ten novels, of which *Mr Scobie's Riddle* and *My Father's Moon* won the Age Book of the Year award. Other novels won other awards.

The George's Wife (Age Award) (1993) concerns a migrant woman from the Midlands whose strange life leads her into a variety of relationships, none of which fully sustain her nor bring her into 'respectable' life, but from all of which she derives enjoyment and strength. She is a naïve narrator whose *naïveté* forces the reader to fill in gaps in what she tells us partly from her record of others' responses. The key relationship is with Mr George into whose house she arrives with her small child looking for domestic work. She ends up not only working but also in his bed, and bearing him a child – her second daughter. This is her second or third triangular relationship. His spinster sister loves the children. Previous relationships were with a doctor, and a woman called Gertrude. Each group use her, particularly the consumptive artistic couple Noel and Felicity who remind us of the Lawrences (D. H. and Frieda) in their bohemian existence. She is never truly critical and always notes the benefits although readers and her old fashioned, traditional yet supportive family see the problems. Through it all she rises, self-educated, to being a doctor. The story is circular, parts of it recalling the beginning. The whole frame of her life is set out retrospectively when she notes:

The strange thing about living, I often nearly speak of during a consultation, is the repetition. It is as though the individual enters the same experience again and again. The same kinds of people make the same demands, and the giver blessed with giving, gives yet again in what turns out to be the wrong direction. (Jolley, 1993, p. 3)

There are moments of high comedy such as the visit of her mother and the prim widow neighbour to Noel and Felicity who can be heard screeching and playing in the bath, from which they then emerge naked. Afterwards a rather neat tea is set in contrast to this strange wild behaviour. Her life is alternative and unusual. It is not surprising that this is the background of a migrant, an outsider in her own country. She leaves for Australia and a new set of opportunities, travelling on the same ship but a different class of cabin to Mr George, irritating him by befriending a rice widow, against whose part she plays that of the migrant. Finally they settle in Australia. Pushing Mr George in his wheelchair and reminiscing (the events of the novel), the radicalism of the novel's relationships and Vera's opportunities as a new woman are summed up in their final conversation about the word 'couple': ' "Why do you bother, Vera," Mr George replies, "with such an ugly word?" ' (p. 225). The novel explores the life of an unusual woman, whose alternative lifestyle is too constrained in the UK, but can blossom in the opportunities offered by Australia.

Shirley Hazzard

Shirley Hazzard's work has been acclaimed as written with an elegant, established style. Particularly well known is her *Transit of Venus* (1980), which interweaves a tale of death and intrigue with that of the love and losses of two Australian sisters living in Britain. This is a tale of Australians abroad. Caro and Grace Bell live freer, more adventurous lives in Britain than they could at home, but their employment possibilities are stifled by their gender and position. It is a beautifully written story of love, losses, lies and limitations as well as of fictionalising and art itself.

Thea Astley

Astley's novel *It's Raining in Mango* (1987) traces one family throughout its history in Australia and in so doing reveals the attractions of movement, boundary-breaking change, the beauties of the tropical land, and the contradictions, gendered, economic and racial, which Australia throws up. Each opportunity and contradiction is lived through in an almost representative but brilliantly imagined way. It is a beautiful, descriptive, sensitive, historically resonant novel which captures the range of migrant settler experiences: settling in a new land, pushing forward the boundaries, and reacting against the inequalities and daily brutalities meted out to the indigenous Aboriginal population. The novel concentrates on a white Australian family with liberal and activist responses to racism.

Thea Astley's novels are experimental in form, showing her to be a subtle social critic, looking at the darker side of Australian life, its racism, sexism, small town mentality and oppression, drunkenness, prostitution. Like most of her works, *It's Raining in Mango* is set in tropical Queensland. The novel begins in the near present, told by Connie, the descendant of Cornelius Laffey, a Canadian Celt. Connie's son Reever takes part in a contemporary protest against road development and tree felling, an event aligned with the family history of liberal revolt. With few lapses into the present, Connie recalls the full history of her family from the landing in 1861 of Cornelius, teller of yarns and honest journalist. Cornelius evokes the newness of Australia: 'the nothingness appalled him, quite apart from the heat, the mangroves the flies' (p. 19). He has sympathy for the dispossessed Aboriginals whose horrific deaths accompany the pushing forward of the diggers into the landscape of Queensland, claiming Australia for Europeans even as they renamed Aboriginal lands, removed Aboriginal food sources and decimated Aboriginal peoples, leaving the dead and dying hidden in stinking mounds behind bushes. Diggers re-described the people they murdered as not quite human, to excuse their actions.

> 'They're not human, missus,' one of the diggers explained patiently. He was flushed with killing and excited. 'Can't talk with them. They got to learn to leave our horses be, missus. These horses could mean the difference between life and death, eh?'...
> 'They looked human', she persisted, 'They had all your features.'
> (p. 27)

'The repository of the by-products of our Christian greed' (p. 30) is Cornelius's description of the sad heap of bodies George finds. Cornelius writes (but cannot have published) 'Now attempt to understand the feelings or even the natural rights of the indigenous peoples along the rivers. Their fishing grounds have been disturbed. Their hunting areas are invaded' (p. 31).

The brutality of the pioneers' racism is set against the disgust articulated by Cornelius and other white Australians who show a humane response. This enlightens what has often been painted as clear-cut oppositional sides in the genocide. For writing a striking journalistic piece decrying the unnecessary slaughter and insisting on Aboriginal land rights, Cornelius is effectively silenced as a journalist. Soon after, he takes a ship and disappears from his long-suffering family whom he has dragged with him through the bush into more and more remote pioneering areas to capture the spirit of the new land, seen by some as 'mainly scenery' (p. 27).

Linguistic trickeries such as 'dispersal' (murder) are ironised within the novel. Moving into the thought processes of Bidiggi (later Anglicised to Bidgy Mumbler), a young Aboriginal, we can see the strangeness of this invasion from another point of view. Bidiggi's viewpoint is often explored and explained. The family meet and welcome the Black youth, and George befriends him, but in later life he suffers abuse from the less enlightened settlers. They are all victims in some way of the development of the country. George's stunningly beautiful sister Nadine has no place there, takes up with a drover, becomes pregnant and, when criticised, flees in a fit of independence and pique to a brothel further up north in wilder lands. A terrifying storm dislodges, uproots and washes away the town and Nadine with it. The language is ironic, mixing wildness with an absurd celebration: 'the river, lusting for the sea, gave a final rabid thrust, and she felt the house surge, and lift like a boat and then begin its slow-turning waltz out to the waters of the bay' (p. 64).

One of the most terrifying moments in the novel, equal in tone and content to the arrival of the slave-catcher in Toni Morrison's *Beloved* (published the same year, 1987), is the deceptive arrival of the police to capture Aboriginal children and take them from their families. They promise an event, and everyone comes, hoping for a 'feed'. However:

> the morning the men came, policemen, someone from the government to take the children away from the clack camp up along the river, first there was the wordless terror of heart-jump, then the wailing, the women scattering and trying to run dragging their kids, the men sullen, powerless before this new white law they'd never heard of. Even the coppers felt lousy at seeing all those yowling gins. They'd have liked the boongs to show a bit of fight, really, then they could have laid about feeling justified.   (p. 83)

Using the abusive terms 'boongs' and 'gins', Astley's novel positions the white police in their roles as thieves and violators. The stunned Aboriginal mothers screaming at the loss of their children and Bidiggi's daughter-in-law's terrifying race into the bush with her son, are testimonies of a racist confrontation redolent with all the arrogance and power imbalances of Aboriginal history under white rule. The woman and child are taken in and hidden in George's home, but the offer of permanent safety after the police have departed, suspicious and threatening but unable to find the child, is one which touches the chord of the endless inarticulate loss Nelly feels for her lifestyle and community. Even cross-race kindness cannot replace the importance of valuing and enabling different ways of life to continue without the insistence of one, that theirs is somehow better and privileged, and in a position to destroy the other. Nelly thinks:

'He still hadn't understood.'
The old men old women uncles aunts cousins brothers sisters tin humpies bottles dogs dirty blankets tobacco handouts fights river trees all the tribes remnants and wretchedness, destruction and misery; her second skin now.
    'Not same,' she whispered. And she cried the centuries of tribal dream in those two words, 'not same'.

(p. 90)

Attempting to control the land he owns with rolling lawns and beautiful gardens, Will, George's son, allows a group of hippies to stay on his land to help him garden it and the stunning beauty of this strange, semi-settled land explains clearly why the settlers stay:

God, it's so beautiful he thought. So beautiful. The house shone white against the drooping swags of bougainvillaea. A deeper green shade lay under the canopies of cascara trees and flamboyants. His greatest pleasure came after each fresh mowing when the razored lawns swung richly away towards his eastern and western fences under the overpowering fragrance of cut grass, under the sociable groupings of shrub and tree, leading the greedy eye on to further groves.   (p. 171)

The appreciation of local beauty and need to manage and improve it is celebrated, although there is criticism for the control and greed it also represents. This is an even-handed book which recognises the different needs and dreams of different peoples but also indicts those whose inability to recognise difference leads to inhumanity and violence. As in Anita Desai's *Baumgartner's Bombay* (see Chapter 8), the careless, selfish cruelty of some hippies comes in for criticism. They invade others' lands and, pretending to be ergonomically and racially friendly, merely steal.

The journeying, pioneering spirit is treated with tender under-standing and some sad irony. There are several men who walk through the book, moving on into the wilder lands, looking still for something, sometimes walking really quite off the map. Will does this when freed from his garden at the novel's end. Even despite the appalling hardships of wild landscape and deprivation, shanty-towns of tents and lack of provisions, extreme weather and rough relations, the need to follow a nameless dream into newness and beauty which must have inspired pioneer Australians (and other settlers, Canadians, New Zealanders, South Africans) is dramatised with sympathy.

MIGRANT WOMEN WRITERS

The term 'migrant women' cannot be simply applied to all women who migrated to Australia. Their position is complicated not merely by their migration, from countries where work or food was scarce, from political turmoil to seek a new and interesting life – or for whatever reason – but also by their ethnic origin and class or eco-nomic position. When Australia's original 'white Australia' policy was relaxed to enable Asian and other ethnic groups to emigrate to Australia or even to live there for a while, for example as students or workers, many women met racist responses, especially as the wave of racism started to grow from 1984 onwards (Jan Pettman, 1992, p. 45). Class relations, a labour market segmented in relation to country of origin, and gender differences all confuse the picture when we wish to find out about the lives of Australian women.

Beth Yahp

Malaysian-born Beth Yahp's *The Crocodile Fury* (1992) has much in common with the work of Singaporean Catherine Lim (see Chapter 12) in its use of the magical, and oral storytelling characteristics.

The story weaves and repeats, hiding the central relationship between the crocodile which roams the jungle, and the girl student's thoughts of escape and adventure, set against the history of a relationship between a rich man and his mysterious lover. Three generations of Chinese women's stories interweave their histories and parallels, including the girl's mother and her grandmother, an ex-bonded servant. It is witty, mixing the realistic record with the magical and spiritual to comment on women's lives and the attractions of the mysterious. We follow the girl student's growth through adolescence until she inherits the magic, the love, violence and myth of the crocodile in the wild mountain forest and escapes colonial and convent rule, hand in hand with the legendary lover. The wild, bad-tempered, spell-wielding grandmother is unforgettable:

> My grandmother knows about ghosts. She is an expert on ghostly sightings, on the habits and hungers of spirits and demons, on ghostly vengeance or favour reaching to spook humans from the other side. Grandmother has creaked down many a steep and gloomy stairway.... She has gripped her never-fail matches and shortburning candles, stabbed her special ghostslashing knife at shadows daring to come too close. (Yahp, 1992, p. 28)

Australian women's writing is fast growing and changing, the influences of Aboriginal and migrant writing contributing to the debates both about the tension between realist and more mythical, fantastic or magical writing, and about ways of representing the very diverse experiences of the very diverse women living in Australia. For a consistently sound and comprehensive response to such issues, the Australian multi-disciplinary feminist journal *Hecate* is an excellent reference source.

10

Aotearoa – New Zealand

For Maori women in a colonial setting (we avoid using the term post-colonial since we believe that this country remains very much colonial), much of ourselves has been denied, and hence, for many Maori women there is an ongoing struggle to centre ourselves, to deconstruct colonial representations and to reconstruct and reclaim knowledge about ourselves. Maori women have been struggling with such a process from the margins, and many have said that in order to fully release such a process we must locate ourselves at the centre. This includes an inverting of dominant discourses that define Maori women as 'Other', seeking to make ourselves visible and to create space for Maori women's stories, opinions and voices to be heard, we must provide forms of analysis that ensure that issues of race and gender are incorporated and their intersection engaged with.

(Johnston and Pihama, 1994, p. 95)

This chapter focuses initially on the background and historical context of writing by Pakeha (white settler) and Maori women. Early settler writing was pioneering, like that of Canadian and Australian women (Chapters 11 and 9). This led to rather refined romance, and genre writing. Notable among early white New Zealand authors is Katherine Mansfield, and among contemporary writers the internationally acclaimed Janet Frame. Writing by Maori women only came into prominence in the 1970s and 1980s, particularly after the Booker Prize success of Keri Hulme's *The Bone People* (1984). Work by Mansfield, Frame, Hulme, Patricia Grace and other contemporary women writers is considered here, largely concentrating on their treatment of women's roles and constraints, on issues of establishing and maintaining gendered and ethnic identity.

234

WRITING – HISTORICAL LEGACY

New Zealand women's writing was largely categorised as either kitchen sink realism or romance, marginalising it as of secondary importance. Historically there were novels and memoirs which had gentility as their background, or that charted life in the farming industry, and a writer central to this was Lady Mary Anne Barker who wrote *Station Life in New Zealand* in 1870, while the novelist Mrs Evans wrote for an English audience about English gentry in a New Zealand landscape, producing *Over the Hills and Far Away* (1874) and *A Strange Friendship* (1874), but her record of gentility was at odds with the actual trials and hardships experienced by missionaries' wives and recorded in their journals, noted in Alison Drummond's *Married and Gone to New Zealand* (1960), which contains extracts from missionaries' wives' writings. The main production of women's writing was either popular fiction, romance, etc. – or recording experiences of living in the new country. Courtship romances gave way to social records in the late 1890s. More engaged writing which dealt with gender politics emerged with the work of the communist writer Jean Devanny in the 1920s and 1930s, the 1890s writer Edith Searke Grossman, and Jeane Mander of the early twentieth century (see Lydia Wever, 1992). Devanny in particular writes about gender and class politics, inheriting interests from the temperance movement. The first writer to tackle issues of race and racism was Robin Hyde/Iris Wilkinson, who wrote largely poetry and journalism, commenting on the dispossession of the Maori peoples, and women's social roles.

Two traditions emerge in New Zealand women's writing: one is socially and racially aware and politically engaged, the other highly conventional, concentrating on romantic fictions, kitchen sink stories, and poetry of the landscape and locale. It is the latter tradition which gained the most recognition in New Zealand, and many who wrote in the former have only recently been rediscovered both at home and abroad, often because of the work of contemporary scholars such as Carole Ferrier at the University of Queensland, who has researched the work of Jean Devanny. One poet of the conventional school is Robin Hyde's contemporary, Mary Ursula Bethell, who wrote poetry mainly about gardening and landscapes, as did Eileen Duggan who wrote on regional landscape and Catholicism. As Lydia Wever points out, many New Zealand women concentrated on 'refinement and culture' to the detriment of their literary reputations (1992, p. 178).

A large number of women wrote for children, including Edith Howes and Margaret May, and there were many popular writers whose work was read internationally, among them Mary Scott, Essie Summers and Ngaio Marsh, the crime writer.

In the 1970s there was an increase in the publication of work by women writers including Sue McCauley, Lauris Edmond, Fiona Kidman, Rachel McAlpine, Cilla McQueen, and Elizabeth Smither who concentrated on issues to do with women's lives and social and political issues. Sue McCauley says of her reading:

> When I was young there was a terrible dearth of books about women – or about new Zealand for that matter. Most of the stuff I read wasn't relevant to me. It wasn't about New Zealand; it wasn't written by women and the men that were writing it weren't covering territory that related to my ordinary, everyday experiences.   (McCauley, 1989, quoted in *The Bloomsbury Guide to Women's Literature*, 1992, p. 179)

Poetry affected by feminism has been written by Cilla McQueen, Rachel McAlpine, Dinah Hawken, Michele Leggot, Jenny Borhnholdt and Elizabeth Nannestad. Work by Maori women writers began appearing from the late 1950s and 1960s onwards, sometimes, as with work by J. C. Sturn, appearing in magazines such as *Te Ao Hou*, along with Rora Pahi, Arapera Blank (Hineira) and others.

The 1970s saw an upsurge in feminist writing, with the publications *Up from Under* and *Broadsheet* appearing regularly from 1972, and *Circle* from 1973, the first lesbian magazine, published by Herstory Press; and *Herstory Press diaries*, which began in 1977, combined the diary function with responses from many women's groups. The Women's Studies Association was founded in 1977 with conferences etc. New Zealand was actually the first country in which women gained suffrage on a national basis, in 1893, and in the centenary year, 1993, there was a flurry of publication charting the history before and since, giving social and economic information about women's positions and the family:

> The ignoring of differences between women . . . is now recognised by most feminists in New Zealand and elsewhere as having been a mistake made by early white middle-class heterosexual

feminists universalising their own experience. (Hyman, 1994, p. 27)

Fergus Barrowman (1996) characterises writing as the product of the complacent 'Provincial Period' and, latterly, recent developments in fiction as growing from the first and second 'Post-Provincial Periods'. Janet Frame writes out against the insulation of New Zealand during the Provincial Period, a period which congratulated itself on its excellent race relations, ignoring cultural marginalisation. Margaret Mehy, Fiona Kidman, Sue McCauley and Maori writers Patricia Grace, Keri Hulme and Apirana Taylor, represent the first Post-Provincial Period, its 'signature' book being Keri Hulme's *The Bone People* (1984), its characteristics a recognition of the isolation of the country; the need for internationalism, and the importance of identity and status for Maori people as 'tangata whenua', people of the land. The destructive polarities of the colonial gaze left a permanent scar.

The writer whose work first introduced new Zealand to a European reading public was Katherine Mansfield. However, we cannot read Mansfield's work as representative of New Zealand because of her choice to write from Europe and her direct influences from the modernists and the 'Bloomsbury Group' such as Woolf, John Middleton Murray, and others.

Katherine Mansfield

Katherine Mansfield's aim to make her 'undiscovered country leap into the eyes of the Old World' marks one of the difficulties faced by women writers from New Zealand: recognition when confronted with varieties of marginalisation. The weight of writing by European-originated men overwhelmed recognition of women's writing for many years with few exceptions, and Mansfield was unusual in that she escaped the parochialism of New Zealand's writing scene when she left for Europe and particularly the UK in the early years of the twentieth century. Mansfield is probably the first and best-known New Zealand-originated woman writer. Her merging with the modernist movement and the tendency of those modernists for a kind of rootlessness somewhat detract from our reading her work as representative of New Zealand, for much of it reflects her own rootlessness as she moved through Germany and then Italy as well as the UK, living a Bohemian life, then one of exile because of her declining health. The short stories, 'The Aloe', 'At the Bay' (1922) and 'Prelude' (1921) (into which 'The Aloe' developed), are bright with the sunshine and difference of a world far from the dullness of damp London: strange plants, sea, heat.

But the women suffer the patriarchal controls of various men, particularly Stanley Burnett, the father figure in this series of short stories. Mansfield explored inner thoughts in a stream-of-consciousness variant, infused her short stories with symbolism and imagery, and wrote consistently of the constraints of established roles for women: Betty, the adolescent yearning for romantic fulfilment but finding her dreams rather punctured by local lechery; a mother dubious about mother love; couples behaving like children in their refusal to face reality ('Mr and Mrs Dove'), and the overwhelming insistence on the importance of a woman bearing and raising children as her only real role in life. These themes emerge throughout her short story collections *The Garden Party* (1922), *Bliss* (1921) and *In a German Pension* (1911), and also in her diaries, journals and letters where she tells of recognising that, were she to have children, she could and would soon lose herself vicariously in their lives. The 'strange high voices' irritate her – as does the expectation, while Middleton Murray talks intellectually with his friends after dinner, that she, an equal intellectually, should spend her time with her arms in the sink washing up.

Perhaps it was necessary to leave New Zealand's parochialism in order to speak out against women's roles in this way and also to join with the technical revolution that was European and American modernism. Her interests in mothering and motherhood are very different from those found in the world of, for instance, African women. Mansfield is first disgusted at the treatment of women and children. *In a German Pension* (1911) expresses fear at childbirth and distaste at the German habits of equating production of children with consumption and success, while women are marginalised in 'Frau Bechenmecker attends a wedding', and 'Germans at Meat'. In later life, her journals testify to an interest in having a child but also to her further fear of deferring all her own interests and energies into such a child. Her short stories interrogate childlike relationships ('Mr and Mrs Dove') and social artifice ('The Garden Party'), investigating ways in which women are fitted into social roles within the family, and using her acute irony to represent the petty domestic tyranny of family men ('At the Bay'). Mansfield cannot, however, be said to represent New Zealand women's lives, and her audience was constructed elsewhere in Europe, but to a European readership the glimpses of her outsider attitude and her 'undiscovered country' provide an interesting entrance into the landscapes and lifestyles of middle-class New Zealanders. Certainly other writers of New Zealand, because of their marginalisation, from which Mansfield escaped, have remained much of a mystery to international readers until the arrival of Janet Frame and then the Maori writer Keri Hulme.

Janet Frame

> A contemporary ingredient in the cauldron world of the witch-novelist is a pilot's thumb. (Frame, 1965, p. 3)

> I must not dream this. I dread going to Waimaru. The world of childhood widens with every wish of the child that it may be worn like a magic cloak about the shoulder. I shall return to Waimaru and find it, like the skin of the old ass, shrivelling at my every desire, a shrunken scrap of wrinkle between enemy thumb and forefinger. (From *Owls Do Cry*, p. 135, in Ferrier, 1995, p. 23)

Janet Frame is a writer of international acclaim whose full power is still being recognised. She writes of identity, memory, the interior world of the creative and those deemed mentally ill somewhat in proportion to their dammed up radical and rejected female creativity. She is able to adopt simple, childlike or mentally disturbed, and highly sophisticated, ironic narrative voices, immersing the reader in the internal world of her characters and narrators, and always providing a sharply acute ironic eye on the false promises, deceptions, rough authoritarian readings and impositions on children and adults alike. She writes also, throughout, of the fictionalising process itself, making us aware of her deft control of metafiction, the imagination and linguistic skills of the artist who transmutes what she sees. Her descriptions of her surroundings are brilliantly and hauntingly drawn. The language is sensual and suffused with feeling and meaning. So, of the lagoon, which features in both short stories and novels, she writes:

> At low tide the water is sucked back into the harbour and there is no lagoon, only a stretch of dirty grey sand shaded with dark pools of sea water where you may find a baby octopus if you are lucky, or the spotted brown old house of a crab or the drowned

wreckage of a child's toy boat. There is a bridge over the lagoon where you may look down into the little pool and see your image tangled up with sea-water and rushes and bits of cloud. And sometimes at night there is an under-water moon, dim and secret. (Frame, 1951, p. 7)

And Frame is aware too of her role as a 'witch-novelist', one who uses an outcast, an outsider, but has intense insights, intuition, a radial world view, and who speaks out, inspiring others, women in particular, to do so too, validating alternative visions. Frame was like a witch, ostracised for her different vision and powers, and was and is inspirational for these same reasons. In *The Adaptable Man* (1965) she notes:

> Witches still have tough constitutions; there's a kind of unselfishness, detachment in their devilish cooking. They can't eat it themselves. What do they eat? Maybe they feed on each other. Life on a heath with thunder and lightning, mixing a cauldron of uneatables for others to observe, admire, shrink from, is not much fun. But who wants fun? (Frame, 1965, p. 3)

She uses both verbal and dramatic irony, ranging from the teasing to the tragic. It is the source of both humour and her social critique, becoming almost the structuring element in *The Carpathians* (1988).

> Many works of the period are marked by this sense of tortured good seeking after tainted food. Frequently in semi-gothic mode, these novels feature an atmosphere of contamination threatening the naive protagonist. (Bergmann, 1994, p. 221)

This often concentrates on children losing innocence, affecting Frame's work of the sixties and seventies. Carole Ferrier notes of Janet Frame's work that:

> in its central preocccupations, its philosophical and political complicity, and its innovative narrative strategies it is both separate from the currents of literature of this period and centrally of them. (Frame, 1995, p. 11)

Her works have been described as ahead of their time, challenging, beyond post-modern: 'they were states of consciousness, interior landscape and the prose seemed to catch light, like mirrors' (Alley, 1995, p. 164, in Ferrier, p. 12). Indeed, Frame herself uses the image of a 'Mirror City' (*The Envoy from Mirror City*, 1985, p. 175) and 'repeated journeys to Mirror City feed the creative imagination that can invent, even if only in words at first, alternative futures' (Ferrier, 1995, p. 222). Finding the language to articulate the visions is the artist's creative role for Frame, and her visions are often too sensitive and complex, too insightful a comment, and imaginative an alternative or visionary insight to find the words easily. Of a visit to Mirror City, Frame says:

> it affords the transformation of ordinary facts and ideas into a shining palace of mirrors. What does it matter that often as you have departed from Mirror City bearing your new, imagined treasures, they have faded in the light of this world. In their medium of language they have acquired imperfections you never intended for them. They have lost the meaning that seemed, once, to shine from them and make your heart beat faster with the joy of discovery of the matched phrase, or cadence the clear insight. (*The Envoy from Mirror City*, 1985, pp. 175–6)

Like Katherine Mansfield's, hers is an international vision and talent. Her settings and the worlds she explores are of her home, New Zealand, and Britain and elsewhere. Frame provides alternative cultural visions and explorations most liberating to readers and writers, including the Canadian Alice Munro who saw 'risk and abandonment' (Munro, 1987, p. 86, in Ferrier, 1995, p. 223), and an un-English liberating quality in her work. Anna Grazia Mattei said of her work that it was crucial in 'decolonizing our European metropolitan minds but opening them up to dynamic cross cultural encounters' (in Ferrier, 1995, p. 12). It is often focused, as is Lessing's work, on the mental traveller, interior dreamscapes, the unreality of the exterior world, and on the fictionalising experiences themselves. Since much of her work does deal with the creative imagination, which has a particular perspective on the world, it highlights the writer as outsider, as different, as wrestling most creatively with the limits of language's ability to evoke imaginative and shared real experience. Gina Mercer comments:

> She is in love with language but, realising its power, sees the necessity to make war on it. To bring about change she feels there

must be an effort to split the alphabetical atom, to re-explode the current construction of language to create something new. (Mercer, in Ferrier, 1995, p. 167)

Born in Dunedin in 1924, she grew up in Oamaruk, attended teacher training college in Dunedin and Otego University, moved out of teaching, then took odd service jobs, spending several long periods in mental hospitals, as is recorded in her second novel, *Faces in the Water* (1961), where she explores the horrors of facing electric shock treatment. But while she was in and out of hospital she won a prize for her first book, *The Lagoon and Other Stories* (1951), and the doctor rescued her from a possible Leucotomy as a result; an incident recorded in the autobiographical *An Angel at My Table* (1984) (made into a powerful film by Jane Campion). Her acute sensitivity to the experience of consciousness, sounds and senses recalls the work of Virginia Woolf, as well as that of Doris Lessing and Sylvia Plath, particularly in *The Bell Jar* (1963). Woolf's own experiences of mental breakdown after major novels and the strain of creativity and expression, echo the fictionalised versions of breakdown and breakthrough in Lessing's work, for example *Briefing for a Descent Into Hell*, *The Summer Before the Dark*, and find parallels in Frame's own experiences as recorded in *An Angel at My Table*, in particular. It is, as Carole Ferrier notes, not uncommon for the creative outsider, and particularly a woman, to be pushed either into mental breakdown or into a designation of madness – almost as if her sensitivity and creativity are themselves seen as too insurgent and radical: 'Frame's sense of alienation both personal and literary within New Zealand society, was undoubtedly compounded by being female' (Ferrier, 1995, p. 15).

We find in her work such insights and ironies, a spiritual, philosophical, social and sexual awareness, and a striving after perfect evocative expression that make her talent a major one. She herself acknowledges the impression of feminism, although much of her work clearly pre-dates the flowering of feminism in the 1960s and beyond. It enabled her to focus her sense of critique of the incarceration and limitation of women's roles especially within the family, which she saw as preventing the difference of her felt experience and the valuing of her expression. Carole Ferrier's selection of Frame's work captures this variety of prose poetry, autobiography, prose fiction, poetry, essays and interviews. But Frame herself argues that hers is fiction rather than autobiography. Even Jane Campion's film of *An Angel at My Table*, which has been seen as autobiographical of Frame's life, while bringing new readers to her work, could mislead because it is an *interpretation* of a fiction, similar though some of the events of the fiction, film and Frame's life might actually be. Ferrier talks of 'Frame's own complex methods of linguistic play, that mobilise allegory, metaphor, and metonymy, and a kaleidoscopic pattern of symbolic meanings' (1995, p. 22).

There are some marvellous short stories. 'Miss Gibson and the Lumber Room' is an admission by a 21-year-old to her old teacher that she fictionalised when records were demanded. Faced with the rigid demand of 'intermediate composition' she had listened as Miss Gibson had, with emotion, told a tale of a man entering an old lumber room and finding remnants of his past. Making up tales of the house, dolls, copies of Shakespeare in the lumber room, and her own delicate imaginative sense of her past relived through this revisit, she conned the teacher with what she had wanted to hear (even though 14/20 was written, improbably, beneath the composition). It is an amusing record of the fictionalising talents of one aware of her audience. Another delicate and amusing tale, 'Spirit', dramatises an interaction between a newly dead spirit, no. 350, and a heavenly presence trying to decide on his new spirit form. 'There's nothing much to say' is his comment on his life (p. 60 in *The Lagoon*), 'we are creatures of habit' (p. 61). So dull and unimaginative and basic was his life that the heavenly regulator decides there is little change needed to enable him to live as a slug on a juicy leaf – a rich comment on the boredom of a bare existence! Some of the tales are disarmingly and ostensibly simple, adopting a child's-eye view, a narrative tone of deceptive simplicity, of a frightening but liberating day at the beach which turns out not to be as idyllic as expected, of a child who wishes for and receives a tiger for Christmas, of mental breakdown and a simple world view, of family interactions and sensitivities. In 'The Secret' a young girl is told her sister Myrtle, who is lively, bright and wishes to be an actress, is going to die with a weak heart. She thinks about:

> the poor little bright-green frog that died down by the stream and poor Pinny, the poisoned cat with bright eyes and not dry nose. Myrtle could die. But that night, in the middle of the night, I woke up. The shadow of the plum tree outside was waving up and down on the bedroom wall, and the dark mass of coats at the back of the door made fantastic shapes of troll and dwarf. It was cold

too, because all my blankets were gone off me. Myrtle, I said, Myrtle. Myrtle didn't answer. She was lying still.   (pp. 16–17)

At her heartbeat, the girl feels reassured (temporarily). Evocations of a child's view and language are rich and realistic. Janet Frame's ironic, sensitive vision and voice are international in appeal.

MAORI WOMEN – HISTORY AND WRITING

More notice is now paid to Maori and Pacific Islander voices and differences, but there is in Aotearoa, as elsewhere, a definite contradiction between the problems over identity politics, of which feminism has been highly critical (the issue of 'I' in writing, etc.), and the need to actually establish difference: 'recognising the importance of different facets of identity does not necessarily involve a hierarchy of oppressions' (*Hecate*, 1994, p. 27).

Maori women's feminism is a way forward:

Maori women are building a feminism which combines the perspectives of the experience of colonisation, respect for past and future generations and their relationship to land and other natural resources, sovereignty issues and feminist concerns. (*Hecate*, 1994, p. 28)

They are arguing for a recognition of the importance of women as signatories of the land rights treaty of Waitangi which grants sovereignty (*rangatiratanga*). Some Maori feminists also argue for a decreased state role. There is much space devoted to reclaiming past histories, lives and stories of New Zealand women, and there is similar recognition that cultural isolation continues: it is difficult for southern-hemisphere feminists to be published elsewhere because their views are frequently so different. Reclaiming the historical power of Maori women, Maori feminists remind us that three women signed the treaty of Waitangi, but that men and Pakeha (white settler) people all marginalise and silence them, recognising only certain ritual responses and encounters as valid and so restricting what and how they can comment and respond. Men are allowed certain forms of expression in the *maraeatea*, rather than women, and 'female oratory should be restricted to rituals of encounter' (Evans, 1994, p. 58), only:

it is not just the debate about speaking rights on the marae which is the issue but more the fuel which this powerful metaphor of restricted rights adds to Maori male hegemony – how it doubly oppresses and entrenches, how it silences and vaporises, how it extinguishes the collective voice of women.   (Evans, 1994, p. 59)

Since 1988, Maori broadcasting has grown, based on a struggle for the retention of the language, although, as a minority language, it still faces majority restrictions and, overwhelmed by American and Eurocentric broadcasting, Maori is not defined as a populist culture.

Throughout new Zealand history, women were treated differently from men because the colonists brought with them specific ideas about the roles and positions that women should occupy. These roles were predominantly linked to Victorian ideas about possession. For Maori women and girls, the disestablishment of their own power-bases both historically and contemporarily, can be directly linked back to colonial rule. Pakeha men dealt with Maori men. The roles proffered for Maori women were mainly those of servitude: either maidservants for Pakeha households or 'good wives and mothers' for Maori men:

What has been shown so far is that the position of difference for Maori is one that is identified and controlled by Pakeha. The saying that we as Maori women are more disadvantaged because of compounded oppression associated with being women and being Maori this is true – this is our reality. Maori girls and women have been made invisible through being written out of historical accounts. Colonisation has had, and continues to have, a major impact on the ways in which Maori women's realities are constructed.   (Johnston and Pihama, 1994, p. 86)

Colonial mechanisms constructed them as savages.

Ann Salmon in *Two Worlds* cites an example of Eurocentric perceptions placed on Maori women's actions:

The red ochre and oil which generally was fresh and wet upon their cheeks and foreheads (was) easily transferable to the noses of anyone who should attempt to kiss them; not that they seemed to have an objection to such familiarities as the noses of several of our people evidently shewed, but they were as great coquettes as any

European could be and the young ones as skittish as unbroken fillies.   (Salmon, in Banks, 1992, p. 166)

Ritual encounters for Maori women were read as sexual lasciviousness by Surville's French crew landing in New Zealand. Native women were interpreted as coquettish and lustful when the responses they were actually making were ones of extreme derision and contempt:

> The women now approached the sailors 'making all the gestures that are not made, especially not in public, going as far as drawing aside the bird skin that covers their nakedness and showing everything they have'. This behaviour was interpreted by the French as 'lasciviousness', but under the circumstances of extreme hostility it was more likely to have been the whakapohane, an expression of intense derision and contempt.   (Salmon, in Banks, 1992, p. 166)

This recalls Bradley's similar misinterpretations of Aboriginal women in Australia (see Chapter 9 – Bradley, 1788). Assimilation through the denial of rituals and roles in Pakeha schooling added to the racism and subordination, social ordering of the races defining Maoris as secondary in intelligence to Europeans:

> Colonial discourses related to Maori girls and women have, on the whole, been constructed by Pakeha anthropologists whose interpretations have been framed within both androcentric and eurocentric paradigms.   (Johnston and Pihama, 1994, p. 89)

Linda Tuhiwai Smith comments that:

> Fundamental to Maori women's struggle to analyse the present has been the need to reconstruct the past conditions of Maori women. Those who first wrote about Maori society at the time of early contact between Maori and European were not Maori, neither were they female. Consequently, Maori women were either ignored or portrayed as wanton, amoral and undisciplined creatures. Maori society was portrayed as a hierarchy based on gender and by being left out of the accounts, Maori women were portrayed as being excluded from participation and determining their policy.   (Smith, 1992, in Middleton and Jones (eds), p. 2)

For instance, the 1867 Native Schools Act alienated Maori women from decision-making processes within their communities. Male adults were part of the process for deciding the establishment of a school rather than women, who were denied access to the decision-making about schooling in their area. The discourses perpetuated within the schooling system successively wrote women out of history and decision-making processes. Smith notes:

> This process has turned Maori history into mythology and Maori women within those histories into distant and passive old crones whose presence in the story was to add interest to an otherwise male adventure. Women who were explorers, poets, chiefs and warriors, heads of families, founding tipuna or ancestors of various hapu and who have frequently been made invisible through processes of colonisation, such as education. (Smith, 1992, p. 2)

Maori women were expected to be assimilated. They were deemed to be inferior to Maori and Pakeha men and to Pakeha women, their roles not to be homemakers themselves but domestic servants for others, and for this they were educated in a limited fashion. Re-centring the Maori woman subject is a key contemporary project.

Keri Hulme, *The Bone People*

Keri Hulme's winning of the Booker Prize had a significant effect on the rest of the world's awareness of Maori writing. Part Maori, she taught herself the Maori language from childhood, and now lives on a beach, Okarito, on South Island, describing herself as a 'quintessential dweller on strands' (Bartlett, 1997, p. 83). She says '*The Bone People* is a *purakau* or fantasy story, part of an old Maori tradition of "tales told in winter" ... the merging of oral traditions and written forms was likely to take place in a country like this. It's a kind of realist writing, playful albeit' (p. 85). And, 'With its insertion of poetry and song, impressionistic (even pointillistic) interior monologue, mythological framework, verbal play, and shifting point of view, it stretches the bounds of realism to breaking point' (p. 220).

Rough, beer-drinking, lottery-winning Kerewin settles in a house on the beach, enjoying her isolation until the difficult, gifted, autistic child Simon visits and through him she meets his father, Joe, also of mixed-race Maori descent. The novel charts their relationships and experiences, using poetic language, imagery, stream of consciousness:

She's standing on the orangegold shingle, arms akimbo, drinking the beach in, absorbing sea and spindthrift, breathing it into her dusty memory. It's all here, alive and salt and roaring and real. The vast cold ocean and the surf breaking five yards away and the warm knowledge of home just up the shore.   (Hulme, 1985, p. 163)

Like Patricia Grace's novel *Potiki* (1986), and the collection *Te Haihau/ The Windeater* (1986), it is a story based on the myth of Maui, youngest child adopted from the sea, who fishes up North Island, slows down the sun to enable people to farm, steals fire to help people be warm and cook, and dies while trying to defeat death through crawling through the vagina and out through the mouth of the great woman of the night, Hine-nui-te-po. The everyday acceptance as real of such myths is a key feature of Maori work. The supernatural is taken as truth, and often Maori writing is highly polemical, 'the messages of the fiction match those of political figures with a closeness seldom found in the western tradition' (Barrowman, 1996, p. xxiii).

The establishment and continuity of Maori identity are central to Hulme's work, as are descriptions of the beauty and wildness of the sea and the landscape in which she lives. In the short story 'One whale singing' a mother humpback whale swims a parallel course with a ship carrying a pregnant woman. The sounds the whale makes, unheard by people, measure her contentment, until she accidentally strikes the ship, sending it down. In the water the woman, who felt trapped by her own pregnancy, feels released by the whale and in communion with it. It is a delicate, sensitive, strange story:

The humpback, full of her dreams and her song beat blindly upward, and was shocked by the unexpected fouling. She lies, waiting on the water-top.

The woman stays where she is, motionless except for her paddling hands, She has no fear of the whale.   (Hulme, 1986, p. 70)

Patricia Grace

Patricia Grace also uses Maori myths and is very experimental: 'Grace, too, uses [Maori] mythical elements together with a limited narrator and impressionistic styles, and in her more recent novels, a dramatically shifting point of view' (p. 220). The shifting point of view is particularly noticeable in *Cousins* (1993). She focuses on Maori identity and women's roles, using subtle ironies.

> Kui was beginning to cry again, her crying becoming a wail, 'Our daughters don't come back,' she was calling. 'Our children go, they never return.' (Grace, 1993, p. 134)

Patricia Grace's remarkable novel *Cousins* (1993) traces the lives of three girl cousins as they grow up, each taking different chapters with their own narrative points of view. Between them they represent very different choices and possibilities for Maori women. Mata's story, in the present, starts the novel, which later tracks back through her growing up. Her travels position her as outsider in a growingly urban and materialistic consumer society. There is no place for Mata, who wanders restlessly among the signs of this alien culture which itself removes and defeats the community and rural memories and values she and other Maoris have had. Her homelessness derives from her mixed-race background and her upbringing in a home where she was defined, largely because of her blackness, as ugly, a negative self image she internalised and which, combined with her sense that her family had no place for her, led to rootlessness and rejection. Her child's-eye view in the early part of the book vividly evokes the difficulties Mata has in recognising her own identity, coming to terms with her self. She is only once allowed to visit her grandparents' and aunt's house, and this rough and ready community of sharing, caring, dirt and food is contrasted with the neat homes of which she has been told, but which she does not visit. Her story oscillates between homelessness in an urban environment and recollections of a strict upbringing. She has only gaps and silences left as memories of her father's rejection and of her mother, Anihera, who was ejected from her family for her mixed-race relationship, left her daughter and died soon after. These combine to portray a vivid picture of a dispossessed Maori woman, victim of internalised and enforced Pakeha values; of the faceless rush of urbanisation and consumerism which leaves her, of mixed race, stranded without identity. As with Morrison's *The Bluest Eye* (1970), she has internalised a rejection of her own blackness, seen as:

> bad curls that had to be cut, cut, cut. Matron snapping with the scissors, pulling down hard with the comb. Bad. She had to flatten

her hair down with water every morning and slide her two long
clips in to try and stop it from springing.   (p. 30)

Mata's confusions and limited intelligence are portrayed in a narrative style with gaps and fissures, misunderstandings the reader
can fill in. In her first factory job all her wages are taken by the land-
lady/guardian charged with her care, but it is not until her friend
Ada intervenes to enable her to have some privacy and independence that it becomes clear Mata's wages are paying off a debt owed
by her father for her keep over the years, and her repayments would
eventually far exceed the debt. Her naïve innocence renders her a
social victim. Even her relationship and eventual marriage lead to
loss and loneliness.

The stories interweave and circle round in oral fashion. Makareta's tale from the point of view of Polly, records some of the
same family incidents as Mata's. Makareta, more intelligent and
attractive, is central to the continuance of ancestor values, and
family responsibilities to a matrilineal, matriarchal household, the
respect of elders, and continuation of ritual. Through her life,
we hear of the young Maori men enlisting in a war which marginalised and then destroyed them. Makareta's life is about continuities:

I realise now that all her life she has been prepared for this time
as she travelled about with the old ones whenever they went to
tangihanga. She has a deep understanding of death as part of our
lives.   (p. 144)

The third tale is that of Missy, told most innovatively from the
point of view of her dead twin brother who, as a very close, and
dead, family member (though his presence is not acknowledged),
records his sister's and others' experiences of a very direct racism
which obliterates their language, mores and features, defining as
secondary and to be hidden/denied their names, family background, culture, and beliefs: ' "And any kids talk Maori to you",
Manny said . . . "You got to run away. Headmaster hit you with a big
strap" ' (p. 160). What the children are 'supposed to have' (p. 169)
are raincoats and right answers, instead they have complicated
extended families, some subsistence living, flour bags for raincoats
and different versions of the world and the answers (all designated
wrong).

Makareta, as spokesperson for the continuance of Maori culture, brings Mata back into the family. She inherits the rituals of the elders, whom she respects, and whose language and rituals she can continue despite her education and beauty:

> It was a night of singing and talk and stories, one of many such nights, because it was from that time that I began to be involved in the many activities and movements of the people in our determination that our existence, culture and values be recognised – that we as a people survive and have authority over our lives. (p. 207)

Her white husband Mick is wary, as are other white friends, of her growing activism, her 'exotics' (p. 207) less attractive when support for the traditions and community of her people become uppermost and a challenge to naturalised ideologies of Pakeha primacy and Maori subordination, if not erasement. Hers is a powerful testimony to the period of Maori identity and land rights revival, and to the difficulties of coping with the internal and social conflicts when a dispossessed and subordinated people demand recognition of their rights and equality:

> There were some among us too, building their own empires, who postured and posed and traded on the mystique of being Maori, and there was, therefore, a need to challenge, expose, confront – the way that women often do, not that women were always the blameless ones. As a people we had our own convoluted mindsets to straighten out, our own anger to deal with, our own proprieties to set, and our own hakihaki.   (p. 209)

She is insightful, recognising the collusion, pretence and contradictions within the Maori movement and among women, but none the less continually asserting rights, informing people. At this point the book, through the voice of Makareta, becomes quite polemical:

> There is work to be done because people need to know of the tactics that were used to destroy the economic base of the people, of the weight of legislation by which land and resources passed from their control. They need to know what the yardstick is that they have been measured by in schools and workplaces, which found them always wanting. They need to know that there is a

health system that endangers them, sometimes puts them in risk of their lives, an education system that withholds knowledge, blinds understanding, erodes self-esteem and confidence. They need to know that people have fought bravely in the past and that they can fight bravely too.   (p. 216)

Racism and injustice are pointed out, rights and the breaking of silence asserted. This is a powerful, imaginative book which weaves the factual and historical – Maori loss of land and of life in the war, disinheritance and subordination, dispossession in the twentieth-century urban worlds and the development of land rights, and a new outspoken, politicised, activist voice. It also interweaves the fantastic and the imaginative – the voice of a dead twin forming that of one of the narrators, all the dead and dispossessed somehow finding a symbolic space through the paradigmatic role of that voice.

The spiritual is as real as the factual: at the time of Makareta's death, Mata, rescued and staying with her, sees Kui Hinemate, the grandmother, and many other dead ancestors standing shadowy round her bed. Like her earlier *Potiki* and *Mutuwhenua: the Moon Sleeps*, *Cousins* is an elegant mix of factual, historical, first-person narrative, and spiritual, imaginative, powerful, individual and community record of the lives of the three cousins in a changing Maori world.

NEW WRITING – THE 1980s

The 1980s saw a real explosion of fiction from New Zealand women writers, Pakeha and Maori. Keri Hulme's *The Bone People* (1984) had great difficulty at first finding a publisher. Then she won the Booker Prize, which challenged the secondary position of Maori women. The establishment of the New Women's Press in 1982 played a part in the legitimating of women writers of fiction as did the university presses. Fiona Kidman wrote her controversial *I a Breed of Women* in the 1970s and two further novels in the 1980s, her reputation being mainly established with *The Book of Secrets* (1987). Sue MacCauley published her first novel in 1982, Rachel MacAlpine, in 1986. Some writers, including Frame, have been using metafiction and some turned to magic realism although the predominant form was initially psychological or social realism.

Laurel Bergmann in *Hecate* (20: 2, 1994), an Aotearoan edition, talks of a notable Maori playwright, Renée, and the lesbian Pacific Islander Cathie Dunsford whose work includes *Cowrie* and several anthologies. Other lesbian writers have also appeared including, for example, Te Awekotuku whose short story collection *Tahuri* is 'a verbally rich and vibrant study of what it means to be Maori and lesbian' (*Hecate*, p. 220). The 1998 *Australian Women's Book Review*, vol. 10, features a number of new writers including Emily Perkins, Sarah Quigley and Tina Shaw, who write of the younger generation – sex, drugs, rock 'n' roll and a search for meaning. Jennifer Fulton also features, as does the well-established feminist Beryl Fletcher.

While New Zealand could still be claimed to be colonial, rather than post-colonial, the women writers, Pakeha and Maori, are burgeoning in their creative expression of identity, race and gender.

11

Canadian Women's Writing

He stood, a point
on a sheet of green paper
proclaiming himself the centre
   ...
For many years
he fished for a great vision,
dangling the hooks of sown
roots under the surface
of the shallow earth.

It was like
enticing whales with a bent
pin

(Atwood, 1996 [1972], in Thieme, pp. 356–7)

Our stories are likely to be tales not of those who made it but of those
who made it back, from the awful experience – the North, the snow-
storm, the sinking ship – that killed everyone else. The survivor has no
triumph or victory but the fact of his survival; he has little after his
ordeal that he did not have before, except gratitude for having
escaped with his life....A preoccupation with one's survival is
necessarily also a preoccupation with the obstacles to that survival.

(Atwood, 1996 [1972], in Thieme, p. 360)

INTRODUCTION

This chapter sketches in some of the background against which
Canadian women write, noting the cultural differences of Canada,
its history and myths of wilderness, its US dominance. It looks largely
at work by Alice Munro, Margaret Laurence, Margaret Atwood, and
Carol Shields, and also indicates some of the more experimental, the
indigenous, or First Nations writing, particularly that of Jeannette

Armstrong and the migrant writing of Joy Kogawa and Suniti Namjoshi, among others. The Canadian is a 'settler-invader' culture, like the Australian with which it is often compared. Somewhat culturally schizophrenic, it is split between French and English influences and aware of constant potential overshadowing by the power and vulgarity (as it is seen) of the USA (see New, 1989). 'Canada . . . has tended to see herself as the undervalued orphan in the imperial family' (Brydon and Tiffin, 1993, p. 63), a 'Cinderella' country awaiting her moment, seeking identity and suffering national disputes engendered by the Free Trade Agreement with the USA, and the problems generated by the failure of the Meech Lake and Charlottetown Accords:

> Canada's origins of settlement in an age preoccupied with what A. B. McKillop terms 'the moral imperative', developed a ruling 'myth of concern' that sought to reconcile differences to assure a common good, a communal, synthesizing mentality rather than an oppositional one.   (Brydon and Tiffin, 1993, p. 68)

Despite indigenous dispossession, and internment of the Japanese during the Second World War, Canada still sees itself as a peaceable kingdom, maintaining survival myths. It imported English institutions, cultural values and writing traditions, adding further Caribbean influences. An increasingly sensitive issue for settler-originated writers has been the concern with finding an appropriate language in which to write. Canadian writers often feel they use 'alien' words in a 'colonial space' (Brydon, 1981):

> It was a situation in which the perceived 'inauthenticity' of the spoken New World/Word became the site of investigation and expression – not as the preliminary to a possible 'adaptation', but as a continuing dynamic of the use of 'alien' words in 'colonial space'.   (Ashcroft, Griffith and Tiffin, 1989, p. 140)

Kroetsch goes further:

> At one time I considered it to be the task of the Canadian writer to give names to his experience, to be the namer. I now suspect that, on the contrary, it is his task to un-name . . . there is in the Canadian word a concealed other experience, sometimes British, sometimes American.   (1974, p. 43)

The issue of finding appropriate language is also one which concerns Canada's indigenous writers, who similarly fail to find their experiences represented in the forms and expressions of English or US literature. Canada had almost entirely ignored its indigenous (or First Nations) people's writing until, in 1973, Maria Campbell's *Halfbreed* became the first contemporary published book by a First Nations writer. Lenore Keshing-Tobias, Lee Maracle, Ruby Slipperjack, Beatrice Culleton and Jeannette Armstrong, who directs the En'owkin School of International Writing, are all notable Native Canadian women writers.

Canadian literature, or 'Can lit', as an established canon for study, has only really emerged since around 1980 when, as in many postcolonial contexts, scholars and teachers wished to free Canadian academe from the influences and domination of both US and English literary canons, and in so doing work towards defining a Canadian literature. Looking back into earlier writings helps to establish a sense of history for national literatures, but it also often helps to reinforce myths and stereotypes, and this has certainly happened with Canadian literature as with several others. The myth which circumscribed more radical representations of women in Canadian literature has been traditionally that of the hardy settler woman living a tough life in great hardship, walking through the snow to help sick neighbours, ploughing, raising children and suffering from the cold and isolation with grit and determination. The Australian bush legends of the drover's wife (see Chapter 9) are very similar to this Canadian version of woman. Part of the origins of the figure arise from the real, fictionally enhanced (through fictionalised autobiographical writing) figure of Susannah Moodie, writing in the 1850s. Hers, like that of her contemporaries, was a harsh life. Moodie records tales of losing children in childbirth or through their wandering off into the seemingly endless bush, and bravery in supporting other settlers' wives in harsh conditions. Some of the lives of such hardy settlers in isolation recur in more contemporary writings by Canadian women. In the work of Margaret Atwood, in particular, they are re-written in order to critique stereotypes perpetuated by Susannah Moodie's followers.

Much women's writing from Canada also concentrates on the pioneering, small town or impoverished suburban lives of women whose constrained Edwardian existences derive from the colonial inheritance of old-fashioned paternalistic/patriarchal behaviours and beliefs. Often these women's restricted lives culminate in stalled love affairs, dull marriages, and an inability to gain freedom through paid work because of their geographical and cultural isolation. More recent work is likely to cross traditional genre boundaries and to intermix French and English language and forms.

Lola Lemire Tostevin's poetry concentrates on women's bodily and linguistic construction in *Color of her Speech* (1982), *Gynotext* (1983), and *Double Standards* (1985). Daphne Marlatt writes a free verse/ journal in *Touch to My Tongue* (1984) and a poetic novel, *Ana Historica* (1988). Other writers to explore include Aritha van Herk who questions the established form of the romance, and Jane Rule who writes on representations of women's sexuality. Kristjana Gunnar's lyrical novel *The Prowler* (1989) considers ways in which exploitative imperialism affects her family through successive generations. Writing by experimental women writers, as those above by immigrant, lesbian and indigenous writers, has flourished since the latter part of the 1980s:

A formerly unidirectional awareness of gender and colonialism has been explored in part by an interrogation of degrees of complicity in various forms of colonization of others, but in greater part by the proliferation of the voices of indigenous women. (Palmateer Pennee, 1994, p. 633)

This includes among others, Marlene Nourbese Philip (see Chapter 5). Dionne Brand's poetry, for example, *Primitive Offensive* (1982), *No Language is Neutral* (1990), short stories, *Sans Souci* (1988), and criticism, investigates racism, colonialism, lesbianism and her own identity. Poetry by Asian Canadians such as Joy Kogawa is growing. Others, including Carol Shields and Janette Turner Hospital, write in a more realist tradition.

Alice Munro

Alice Munro's stories (1997) circle round obsessions and frustrated passions; the stuff of rural and small town lives. Munro depicts lives of hope and constraint in wry, carefully wrought vignettes. Women alone, women whose one love disappears, returning married – leaving them to face a barrage of clichés about devaluing yourself, missing your chance, being on the shelf – the stuff of restricted minds and places are her subject matter. She tells of women unable, losing children, trapped in small homes as family servants, spinsters, widows, daughters working for parents, the paucity of available jobs and the gossip. Many of her women imagine themselves part of a grander, more ladylike world where tea parties require best hats and best manners. These women have transported in their minds a version of Englishness no longer easily current back home. They flounder in alien cultural soil. There is a great deal of poverty and family-based violence. With a series of wry, ironic short stories treating obsession, Munro captures details of clothing and mannerisms, seeing into the hopes and hearts of the people she depicts.

A piano teacher ('Dance of the Happy Shades') still produces an embarrassing party and show each year for the mothers, their off-spring repeating the same tunes the mothers once played. Each holds onto some sense of social position until the triply awkward final party. Upstairs the sick sister is dying, flies festoon the sandwiches, and the only really talented child performer is part of a mentally handicapped school group, thus highlighting the lack of talent of both children and mothers. Comments are pointed: 'The deceits which her spinster's sentimentality has practised on her original good judgement are legendary and colossal; she has this way of speaking of children's hearts as if they were something holy' (p. 17). Poignant moments and cruel vignettes identify each of Munro's characters as individuals: small people in small towns.

Margaret Laurence

Similar constraints dominate characters in Margaret Laurence's writing. *A Bird in the House* (1994 [1970]) is her semi-fictionalised autobiography as Vanessa, the lonely child and growing author who listens into the lives and debates of her elders. The bible is the most available book, and pioneer myths the most available subjects, both of which she mimics then critiques. Vanessa's first written pioneer story in her scribbler, 'Pillars of the Nation', is abandoned upon discovering that her tyrannical grandfather was himself a pioneer. An autocrat, he does irreparable damage to the lives of the women and men around him, thwarting and dominating them. Vanessa, supposed to take after him, measures her own stoicism with a different kind of imagination, heroic and mythic, a romantic intermixing of pioneering spirit and the everyday.

Women's lives are harsh, or dull and constrained. Edna, the unmarried aunt, cannot find work as a stenographer and lives out of town, doing housemaid's work, her possibilities of finding a partner dwindling as each male visitor is subjected to the grandfather's scrutiny and singeing critique, the bigotry of which changes in accordance with his moods and the responses given by each young man. Her gentle grandmother tries to keep the peace, provides meals and rarely asks for anything for herself as the thwarted grandfather paces the house like a caged beast, criticising the timing of all arrivals, clothes, behaviours, jobs, and the way his hardware business has been handled by his successor. The rocking chair creaks in the basement with his anger. Vanessa's child-consciousness, untampered by the adults' later interpretations, merely records this constrained, tortured lifestyle in which meals, in particular, are family occasions of power and control.

The limitations of women's lives in rural areas and town outskirts are fully explored through the lives of Vanessa's family, but theirs is also part of a larger frustration. Her gentle, imaginative cousin Cliff boards with Vanessa's family, treats her as an equal, and escapes the tyranny of the grandfather through cutting out mentally and retaining a fantasy world of fleet-footed horses and beautiful settings into which Vanessa buys. His own plans are thwarted by the grandfather's meanness, and a series of jobs selling inventions lead nowhere. Eventually, the escape dream of active service also collapses and so does he, retiring into mental illness; Vanessa's visit to his home up North confirms her sadness at the real limitations of dreams. Grandfather's anger can constrain Vanessa's life less than others' because of her intelligence and her mother's determination to invest in her education. Insights into family passions and thoughts, and into the developing writer in Vanessa, are delicately wrought and compelling reading. This is a tale of a growing author, but also of the thwarted lives of middle-class colonial and post-colonial women who cannot escape the constraints of their families, their class, their culture or their location.

Carol Shields

Carol Shields also explores pioneering and restricted lives. In *Mary Swann* (1987), the poetry of a working-class, relatively uneducated, rural woman has been discovered by the literary intelligentsia of California and New York, largely through the aid of her librarian friend who has ensured that the work was delivered to the local printing press and published. The worlds of the poverty and deprivation of Mary Swann and the appropriating activities of the literati are strongly contrasted, although the woman publisher from New York becomes more closely embroiled and eventually decides not to write Swann's biography. The novel deals with versions of fictionalising, representing and publishing.

Shields's *The Stone Diaries* (1993) is an award-winning novel (Booker), concentrating on the lives of a harsh Scottish settler and his daughter. The novel opens with her birth and the death of her mother, circling back to recount her parents' courtship, and her reticent father's great sorrow at her mother's death. His construction of a huge stone edifice to mark her death is a local marvel, but ultimately rather pointless. His stone-work is the only emotional outpouring this stony man can manage:

> He had thought himself alone in this world, but in fact he is a child of this solid staring rainbow, and of the persevering forms of light and shadow, of substance and ephemera. A child of the earth.   (Shields, 1993, p. 59)

The ephemeral and delicate are consistently linked and expressed through the solid and permanent; outward signs replacing expressions. Tragedy, understated, strikes in passing. Daisy Goodwill, the daughter, loses her excessive husband Harold on honeymoon when he falls from their window. The 'misalignment between men and women' (1993, p. 121) explains most things. The novel is a family saga written in first-person narratives, diaries, letters, lists and confused, inaccurate recollections, monitoring the relationships, tragedies, and developments of individuals in a wry, almost offhand way. The peculiarity of each is marked by the tone and detail of the record, reality never quite collated or touched, always a little too transient and dependent on the individual to be a monument in stone. The monument constructed by her father to mark his love for Daisy's mother is itself ironically vulnerable to destruction.

Margaret Atwood

Arguably Canada's greatest writer, Margaret Atwood consistently critiques pioneering myths and the everyday cultural myths which constrain women's lives. In 1970 she re-wrote Susannah Moodie's *Roughing it in the Bush, or Life in Canada* (1988 [1852]), challenging the stereotype of the tough settler woman Moodie initiated, which had dominated Canadian literature. In *The Journals of Susannah*

Moodie (1970) Atwood writes a modern work of consciousness rather than a realistic diary, highlighting themes made popular by Moodie and those who followed her: absent husbands, tough surviving wives, lost children, frustrations. This character is more of a twentieth-century woman in so far as we are invited into her consciousness, which registers the paradox of her situation. Atwood both brought Moodie to life for a twentieth-century readership, and enabled a critique of the representation of women she had initiated. In 1972 *Survival* followed, a critical piece beginning to define the character of Canadian literature in relation to, and apart from, that of the US and UK. Her novel *Surfacing* (1972) is a powerful tale using a survival theme, as does her critical work, but essentially investigating and challenging stereotypes of Canadian womanhood, positioning the US and US ways as destructive, hypocritical and superficial. In *Surfacing*, the woman rejects American men, offspring of popular culture and precursors of tourists seeking a 'modified wilderness experience':

> It wasn't the men I hated, it was the Americans, the human beings, men and women both. They'd had their chance but they had turned against the gods and it was time for me to choose sides. (Atwood, 1972, p. 154)

In her writing, 'American' denotes a homogenising imperialism that cannot tolerate difference, 'a tendency that can characterise American feminism as well as American imperialism' (Brydon and Tiffin, 1993, p. 94). She aligns herself away from the Americans' technologically adept invasiveness, and towards the native gods of place, but by doing so she 'places herself squarely within the Tory myth of Canadian identity as an alternative way of being North American' (Brydon and Tiffin, 1993, p. 94), leaving indigenous peoples out of the picture. The issue of hunting animals just for the kill is central. Canadians, too, can be hunters but not, she suggests, in the name of over-indulgence or fun: a superficiality inherent in the American way. Central to this argument is the image of the heron, who appears beautiful in flight and, later, crumpled and dead. In denying her name, 'I no longer have a name. I tried for all these years to be civilised but I'm not and I'm through pretending' (Atwood, 1972, p. 168), she also rejects the limitations of the need to name wild creatures and places, a link between naming, language and civilisation's limitations. The heroine's personal crisis causes a breakdown which is also a breakthrough, a familiar 1970s theme in women's writing. It is a powerful, sensitive, rather 'green' novel, which helped to establish Atwood.

Other novels use humour and irony to critique Canadian ways of life and women's representation and stereotyping. *The Edible Woman* (1969) indicts relationships which figuratively devour women, focusing on Marion who, about to marry Peter, realises her role is so dependent upon his version of her that she equates his engulfing and devouring of her personality with a form of cannibalism. Once she has identified herself with food she becomes acutely aware of the disgusting nature of people eating, enhanced by her pregnant friend Ainsley's delight in eating for two and self-identification with food and baby production. Like Katherine Mansfield's *In a German Pension* stories, the equation between birth, marriage and engulfment/engulfing, and digesting food is made revoltingly clear. Marion can eat nothing. Her cathartic moment comes when she manages to shake off the oppressive relationship with Peter, offering him a grotesque, cake version of herself. Having exterminated her sense of imminent consumption as part of someone else's, self-enhancing, staple diet, Marion returns to normality and eating. The book is funny and topical, equating issues of eating with identity, and critiquing the oppressive containment of stereotypical relationships. *Lady Oracle* (1976) is also amusing, while *Bodily Harm* (1981) again utilises the food metaphor, directly equating it with an oppressive sexual relationship. Laura, in trading her body, becomes like a consumable.

The Handmaid's Tale has received a great deal of feminist critical attention for its imaginative projection into a distopian future of some of the problems and possibilities which affect women (in the 1970s). The narrator is Offred, religiously garbed 'handmaid' because of her potential to bear children in a post-holocaust, infertile world of strict, tyrannically enforced patriarchy and gendered class system. Her taped story is discovered by future historians, in an archive. Offred's complete, enforced, subservience to the body, procreation and a subordinate role within a household containing a military male, a non-procreative, cosmetic companion Wife, and drudges or 'Marthas', is a terrifying potential future for women. Language is coded, thoughts seem policed, all sexual freedoms have been lost. While past films depict 'take back the night' marches and illustrate the vulnerability and inequalities of women in the latter part of the twentieth century, these freedoms are preferable over the tyranny and lies of the future state. It is a terrifying, polemically powerful, feminist, sci-fi novel.

Atwood takes cultural myths and investigates their roots, turns them around and exposes and undercuts them. Her use of irony and a mixture of the rich detail of everyday life with the equally rich detail of myth and metaphor make her works both realistic and fantastic.

The Robber Bride (1993) derives from a fairytale, 'The Robber Bridegroom', featuring a dominant male robber who tricks a series of hapless brides into coming home with him to his dreadful family, then hacks them to pieces and devours them. It is a Gothic marriage tale highlighting the pleasures and dangers of male/female relationships and sisterhood. Atwood's version removes the robber bridegroom and replaces him with a robber bride, Zenia, who consistently manages to infiltrate the relationships of those around her by investigating and getting them to trust and confide in her, then turning their weaknesses against them. In each case she then steals the male partners for herself. But this theft is always based, too, on the weakness of the relationship, its basis in fantasy and deception, and a certain stage in the development of each of the other women – Charis, Tony and Roz. Identity is a theme. The characters' identities are formed of each other, marked off against the 'Other', the predatory Zenia – herself a construction of their own fears, grown from tales they tell her, which she proceeds to realise. Arriving like the wicked witch in the Wizard of Oz, on a wind, Zenia is vampiric, feeding on the fears of others, predatory when invited in: 'people like Zenia can never step through your doorway, can never enter and entangle themselves in your life, unless you invite them' (p. 114).

A macabre Gothic fantasy, the novel investigates versions of sexuality, gender roles, male/female relationships and female/female relationships, the power of language, memory and history, its charting and control. Zenia, a master of disguises, produces lurid versions of herself and her history for each woman: a Russian, a refugee, a child prostitute. As in Tony the historian's lectures, versions unravel and history, seen as a construct, pinned down by military tactics, none the less evades real comprehension.

The book starts when Zenia returns from the dead, provoking each woman to tell her own tale. It sets up versions of time, of reality and of the woman at the core whose personality and stability of self changes and invents itself. As a mystery Zenia is folk tale and legend completed by readers and characters alike. The order of the narrative is also questioned. Reality, history and self are shown as constructs, memory undependable, 'memory divides, into what she wanted to happen and what actually did happen' (p. 153). The three words by which the women define Zenia illustrate their natures: inoperational (Tony), peaceful (Charis), kaput (Roz). Twinning is a motif which explores Otherising and coming to terms with versions of self and reality. Charis's repressed Other is the more violent abused Karen who returns when she is destabilised. Tony reverses words to control them following a disturbed childhood, the death of her mother; and Roz has twins, Erin and Paula, who themselves tell different versions of fairytales, construct life differently. The reversal of Tony's words, a language which gives her ritualistic power, compares with the others' alter egos or their mirror image/opposite, Zenia, who threatens each differently: 'she makes me sick of myself' says Charis (p. 33); 'what is she doing here on this side of the mirror?' (p. 34). For Tony, Zenia's influence means 'menace, chaos, cities, flame, towers crashing down, the anarchy of deep water' (p. 35).

The women are 'types'. Roz, businesswoman, flamboyant dresser with a loud voice, is always trying to control her size, aware of dressing and creating certain effects. Tony, the historian, needs another kind of control: 'she believes that the dutiful completion of pre-set tasks will cause her to be loved' (p. 140). Charis, earth mother and mystic, loves plants, gardens, feeding people; loses Billy who had drifted into and grafted onto her life. When Zenia moved in she took him away across the water on a barge as if passing into the other world, entering death like water. And indeed Zenia removes men from all three women. Her exact status in the novel is problematic. Psychoanalytically, she could be a mother or daughter figure against whom they must develop their individuality, a vampire, an Other, or like a corn god who must be dismembered for there to be new life. The women empower Zenia by believing in her existence. She is hard to erase despite vampire and cops 'n' robbers threats: 'Zenia you're history. You're dead meat' (p. 39). Charis believes people don't die anyway: 'Zenia was loose, loose in the air but tethered to the world of appearances' (p. 50).

These three tricked, finally self-assured women resemble the fairytale of the three little pigs, re-written in feminist form by Roz's twin daughters. The novel highlights mother/daughter relationships, the nature of friendships, self-constructs and women's roles, and plays with language, memory, history, versions of life/versions of tales (Zenia's end has several versions). The culturally derived stories by which women control their lives are merely constructs and could be shaken off.

Alias Grace (1996), in true post-modernist form, enables us to question the nature of fictional representations and records of events. Grace, a housemaid and possible (probable?) murderer of housekeeper Nancy and house-owner Mr Kinnear, tells her own tale of the events which cause the police to capture her and her (perhaps) lover, putting him to death and placing her in an asylum. There are a medley of other records, witness reports (one from Susannah Moodie), journalist and medical reports, legal records and an image or two, each pulling together a complex, contradictory picture, contradicting Grace's version and preventing readers from discovering which is fabricated. As such, then, the novel is partly about ways in which women are misrepresented, and partly about ways in which all methods of recording and re-telling history and experience are themselves flawed, fictive. The novel deals with identity and truth, testimony and history, fictions and records, and it asks which alias is real? Where is Grace?

The constrictions of women's lives are exemplified both by Grace, brought up in deprivation in Ireland, shipped across with her family to Canada and there farmed out on the death of her mother into more deprivation, as contrasted with pampered middle-class women. Thinking of the Doctor who psychoanalyses her, Grace comments on women's clothing and contemporary views of their frailty:

At least he isn't a woman, and thus not obliged to wear corsets, and to deform himself with tight lacing. For the widely held view that women are weak-spined and jelly-like by nature, and would slump to the floor like melted cheese if not roped in, he has nothing but contempt. While a medical student, he dissected a good many women – from the labouring classes, naturally – and their spines and musculature were on the average no feebler than those of men.   (p. 73)

Grace's story is a critique of romantic fictions. If she has indeed gone along with the murders on the insistence of her lover, her guilt could be punishable by death. But her story is also one of women and madness, aligned with 1970s tales of women's breakdown and breakthrough, and contemporary (late nineteenth-century) interest in psychoanalysis, in doctors' and patients' relationships (one thinks of Freud and Dora: in his psychoanalysis of Dora, a patient, Sigmund Freud interpreted her response to him through his sexually based psychoanalytical methods, finding that she transferred her affections to him, the analyst). Grace is seemingly a fit subject for study as a potentially violent, potentially innocent woman whose word is suspect. She says, 'Perhaps I will tell you lies' (p. 41). Young doctor Simon Jordan stimulates her mind and their conversation with food and flowers, so she plays a game for him. He becomes so involved and fascinated with her that he relinquishes objectivity. Definitions of madness and sanity, of truth and of lies circle this relationship. One main issue is the question of whether there are such things as alter egos or doppelgangers. Equally topical is the representation of, and investigation into, Victorian supernatural occurrences such as table-tapping and mediumship. While Grace's doctor explains her actions as symptoms, she and her accomplice use the contemporary dependence on the supernatural to suggest that any evil was the result of her possession by a dead friend, Mary Whitney.

Different versions of her tale derive from different peoples' prejudices. Ballad, newspaper and the governor's wife's scrapbook of the lives and horrors of criminals illustrate the translation and stereotyping of cases and a late nineteenth-century fascination with guilty, evil minds.

Margaret Atwood's work seeks to question the representation and construction of women's lives in different contexts through her employment of the imaginative scrutiny of what has been called 'Canadian Gothic'.

Aritha van Herk

Like Atwood, van Herk dispels the illusions of traditional romance even as she undercuts representations of passive virginal women, asserting:

> I come from the west, kingdom of the male virgin. . . . To be female and not-virgin, making stories in the kingdom of the male virgin, is dangerous. . . . Try being a writer there. Try being a woman there.   (van Herk, 1984, p. 15)

In *No Fixed Address* (1989 [1986]) her protagonist, Arachne, takes sexual pleasure where she finds it, subverting traditional constructions of women as marriage-seekers. She is a sales rep in ladies underwear and a series of different coloured panties trail her across Canada. Arachne moves into the wilderness to start to suggest alternative women's freedoms 'not at present attainable' (Alexander, 1998, p. 82), finding the rock shape of a Wild Woman high up, and lying down in its form:

> And there they find the Wild Woman, her stone outline spread to infinite sky, to a prairie grassland's suggestion of paradise, a woman open-armed on the highest hill in that world. They trace her outline: arms, amulet, hair, teeth, skirt, breasts, feet. Arachne stands between her legs.... She stretches out inside the woman, lies within the stones on her back beneath that wheeling sky, arms outflung like the woman's, her head cushioned on a circle of breast.   (In Thieme, 1996 [1986], pp. 446–7)

In her earlier *Judith* (1978) the Persephone/Pluto myth operates as Judith attempts to find her new identity. Avoiding a cosmeticised self, re-establishing contact with a childhood self, finding a union with the notion of female divinity in her work in the pig-barn:

> Judith entered the barn's loomy redolence eagerly. She was whole heartedly a part of their tumescent sanctuary of female warmth.... Transformed and spellbinding they surrounded her like priestesses of her creed.   (van Herk, 1978, p. 48)

'Aritha van Herk seeks to restore to women a sense of the numinous through reshaping traditional myths of female divinity' (Jones, 1994, p. 417). She reclaims women's mythical power and active sexuality.

FIRST NATIONS WRITERS

Maria Campbell

The semi-fictionalised autobiographical novel *Halfbreed* by Maria Campbell (1974) was the first novel published by a Canadian First Nations or indigenous Indian writer (see Chapters 7 and 9 on South Africa and Australia for semi-fictionalised autobiography). *The Book of Jessica: A Theatrical Transformation* (1986) followed, a play Campbell wrote with Linda Griffiths, inspired by an adaptation of Campbell's novel. She experienced the separation of living in native communities and the stigma of being of mixed or 'M'tis' identity (M'tis means *mestizzo*, or 'in the middle', of mixed race – and the term we would use today in a positive sense would be bi-racial) but she learned self-reliance and self worth from her pipe-smoking grandmother Cheechum. At the end of her novel Campbell expresses her sense of having found herself and her community again: 'I have brothers and sisters all over the country, I no longer need my blanket to survive' (Campbell, 1974, in Vizenor, 1995, p. 75). Of her work Kate Vangen says that the

> world the half-breed inhabits is the same world in which Euro-Canadians live; yet, the frustrations and heart-breaks they experience, even today, arise from the invisibility which is culturally and legally imposed upon them. By owning the term 'half-breed' and defiantly claiming its full history and sprinkling it with a good measure of humor, Campbell becomes one of the leaders of her people who Cheechum predicted would one day come.   (Vangen, in Vizenor, 1995, p. 75)

The reclamation of the term 'half-breed' is a powerful linguistic move, similar to that reclaiming of the initially abusive term 'queer' now transformed with pride into 'queer politics' and 'queer criticism' etc.

Initially 2,000 pages long, the book was cut to remove libellous material against the Canadian Mounted Police, a piece Cambell said she would like to restore. It contains recurrent, positive images of love, nature, beauty, and peace which mitigate against the harshness of Maria's life. She feels it difficult to fit in anywhere because she is neither an Indian nor a European Canadian but a mixture, a half-breed. 'We all went to the Indians' Sundances and special gatherings, but somehow we never fitted in' (Campbell, 'The Little People', in Vizenor, 1995, p. 82). But she learns the meaning of the special days when taken to meetings by her relatives. Speaking out and questioning rituals and power structures causes criticism of her, however, based on gender and ethnic hierarchies:

> When I expressed my opinion in these matters, Kokum would look at Mushroom and say: 'it's the white in her'. Treaty Indian

women don't express their opinions, Halfbreed women do. Even though I liked visiting them I was always glad to get back to the noise and disorder of my own people. (Campbell, in Vizenor, 1995, p. 82)

Jeannette Armstrong

Jeannette Armstrong is a children's writer and novelist, now director of the En'Owkin School of International writing in the Okanagan, British Columbia. Her children's novels are *Enwhisteetkwa: Walk on Water* (1982) and *Neekna and Chemia* (1984). Her novel *Slash* (1985) concerns a young man involved in the struggle for aboriginal rights. In 'This is a Story' (in Thieme, 1996, pp. 428–33) she tells a tale within a tale, a Trickster tale of Kyoti, one of the Okanagan who returns to his home area when things have deteriorated and the salmon runs are blocked up by the invaders. He recognises these 'Swallow' people as different from his own folk, dirtier and less respectful, not 'People'. Kyoti uses natural magical powers to restore the salmon runs. In oral-storytelling modes of simple factual phrases and dialogue, Armstrong evokes the magical moment, asserting its authenticity as a way of reading the situation:

> You shoulda seen Tommy's face, when he saw Kyoti and the rainbow ribbons hanging on the staff.
> That story happened. I tell you that much. It's a powerful one, I tell it now because it's true.
> (Armstrong, in Thieme, 1996, p. 432)

Her work is engaged, utilising Native Canadian Indian mythology and dealing with issues of equality and land rights.

Emma Lee Warrior

Emma Lee Warrior, a Peigan Indian, was born in Alberta, raised on a Peigan reserve and then studied for a BA in education and an MA in English. She now develops curricula in Blackfoot on a Blackfoot reserve. Telling the story of her birth in 'How I came to have a man's name' she talks of the desertion of her mother by her father, and learning how to pray to the Sun, Moon and Stars from her grandparents. On a sled through the snow, Yellow Dust took her mother to hospital for the birth:

> They bundled up bravely in buffalo robes,
> their figures pronounced by the white of the night;
> the still distance of the Wolf trail greeted them
> > (Warrior, 1988, in Niatum, p. 153)

In another poem, 'Reginald Pugh, the man who came from the Army', she berates the meanness of a social worker who cannot recognise cross-tribal marriages, or ways of living and values which differ from his own. He

> became the problem
> of all Indians
> sentenced to his files.
> He berated us
> for being Indians
> but his harangues
> were as useless
> as my curses
> > (Warrior, 1988, in Niatum, pp. 154–5)

Joy Kogawa

A third-generation Canadian of Japanese ancestry, Joy Kogawa writes poetry and novels, including *Obasan* (1981). Her work has been described as 'rich with small ephemera and an understated sometimes discontinuous voice' giving real shape to the geography and her take on it (Shikatani, 1996, in Chang, p. 136). *Obasan* reacts against imperialist technological culture, mourning the loss of a community – the East Coast Japanese Canadian. It

> enacts a dialogue that is never resolved between those who confront injustice through adopting the strategies of silent endurance and those who would try to change the world for the better through 'lobbying and legislation, speech making and storytelling' (*Obasan*, p. 199). Implicitly through its own storytelling, it moves from silence into voice, but paradoxically into a voicing that includes the enigma of silence.   (Brydon, 1994, p. 466)

Obasan reminds us of the complexities that race, class and gender bring. The novel does not locate the future in an English Canadianness but in a recognition of the value of difference, challenging Canadians to rethink their versions of Canada and society.

Suniti Namjoshi

Another migrant writer, from India, Suniti Namjoshi is a highly talented intellectual whose work re-writes myths for a feminist readership in an ironic and metaphorical way, much reminiscent of Angela Carter, Fay Weldon, Emma Tennant, Alice Walker and Toni Morrison. Born in Bombay 1941 and educated at the Universities of Poona and Missouri, she gained a doctorate at McGill in the USA in 1972. Her witty collection of fables consists of *Feminist Fables* (1981) first, then *The Conversations of Cow* (1985) and most recently *Because of India* (1989). There is a great deal of imaginative, dreamlike and ironic writing in her work, which argues about issues of women's misrepresentation in myth, religious and social injustices, and prejudices. She critiques and reappropriates all types of inherited knowledge, myth, literary allusions, nursery rhymes etc. from Indian and European sources.

Namjoshi re-writes gendered myths and fables into a feminist form. In 'Perseus and Andromeda' (1981) the role reversals free up the princess, while 'The Badge-Wearing Dyke and her Two Maiden Aunts' (1981) explores issues around the recognition of lesbianism. The two spinster mice have always been lesbian but never used the badge, while their niece needs to be political, polemical, and badge wearing. When she realises there is no need to *emphasise* lesbian identity, she feels rather better about the aunts. In 'Look Medusa' (1987, p. 114) Namjoshi uses irony to reverse the story of the arch-patriarchal figure, Perseus (again), whose mission this time is to cut off the head of Medusa, condemned through her sexual activity (making love in a goddess's temple) to be a snaky, fearsome monster representing the vagina dentata of men's horror and nightmare. Perseus is so demanding of attention and full of his image that he dies of it. Medusa troubles no-one living naturally, ignoring Perseus upon his arrival, but:

> . . . at last the hidden hero burned
> to be seen by her whom he had come to kill.
> 'Look, Medusa, I am Perseus!' he cried,
> thus gaining recognition before he died.
> (Namjoshi, 1987, p. 114)

In *The Conversations of Cow* (1985) a radical lesbian Brahmini cow provides homilies and critiques of racial, religious and gendered prejudices, and much humour (she is not an easily acceptable restaurant companion, for instance). It is a contemporary, radical, mythic piece of writing which dramatises practices of coping with differences of race, gender and sexuality. Suniti and Bhadravati, the cow, meet friends and conformity is an issue:

> 'I'm Suniti,' I say.
> 'Su? What?'
> I tell them again. They get it wrong.
> 'Well, we'll just call you Sue for short, just as we do Baddy here.' Her real name is Bhadravati. I look at Cow, who looks away.
> Later she says to me, 'Well, you have to adjust'.
>
> (Namjoshi, 1985, p. 18)

This moment illustrates issues of conformity, appropriation, Other-ising, misrepresentation, and challenges to accepted cultural and gendered myths which preoccupy Canadian women writers, as they do many of the other post-colonial women writers we have discussed here.

12

Black British Women's Writing

Observers with beady eyes and without Anglo-Saxon attitudes
(Rushdie, 1982, p. 8)

I have crossed an ocean
I have lost my tongue
from the root of the old one
a new one has sprung
(Nichols, 1984, Epilogue from 'I is a Long
Memoried Woman', p. 64)

This chapter looks initially at the history of writing by Black British women writers, at issues of identity and location, labelling and invisibility. Black British writers often write from more than one culture, some writing in the diaspora, between the country of their origin (or their parents' origin) and the UK. They concentrate on a variety of issues including race, gender, identity, relationships, and women's roles. The writers considered here include Jackie Kay, Maud Sulter, Barbara Burford, Grace Nichols, Merle Collins, Valerie Bloom, Amryl Johnson, Joan Riley, Meera Syal and Moniza Alvi.

ROOTS AND DIFFERENCES – HISTORICAL AND CULTURAL IDENTITIES

Professor Stuart Hall from the Open University has characterised Britain as the last colony in the British Empire – a last outpost of the Empire (Open University's *Literature in the Modern World* television programme, A316, 1991). In so doing he defines the kind of ideological, political and cultural struggles experienced by Black and Asian

273

people living in the UK, many of them second- or third-generation. Defining identity and recognising that race is itself a social construction has been part of the project of UK Black and Asian women writers. They write against racial and gender stereotypes, reclaiming a cultural identity both British, and connected to family roots in the Caribbean, Africa, India, Pakistan, etc. Their work is not always about race and identity, of course. They write of everyday living, family and relationships, lesbianism, sisterhood, topics chosen by other women writers, culturally inflected by their diasporan existence.

Caribbean and other writers comment on their invisibility in the literature and imaging of their home countries. This is exacerbated in the UK, where a traditional absence of representation has led to a sense of isolation, alienation and cultural confusion. Many writers speak of the rush to the television when an Afro-Caribbean or Asian commentator or star appears, because of the rarity value. Black or white, we all suffer from this constructed cultural hegemony which denies the existence of such a proportion of our community.

> To be Black and British is to be unnamed in official discourse. The construction of a national British identity is built upon a notion of a racial belonging, upon a hegemonic white ethnicity that never speaks its presence. We are told that you can be either one or the other, black or British, but not both. But we live here, many are born here, all 3 million of us 'ethnic minority' people as we are collectively called in the official Census surveys. (Safia Mirza, 1997, p. 3)

Britain has traditionally been a country of emigration and immigration. Just looking at the history of the arrival of Anglo-Saxon, Norman, French Huguenot, Jewish, Polish, Italian, Irish, Caribbean and Asian peoples testifies to this. And the British have also migrated to all parts of the world. But the chief visible signifier which seems to elicit racial discrimination and abuse is that of colour, the marker singling out people as Other, so for many this is turned into a politicised sense of identity:

> What defines us as Pacific, Asian, Eastern, African, Caribbean, Latina, Native and 'mixed race' 'others' is not our imposed 'minority' status, but our self-defining presence as people of the post colonial diaspora. At only 5.5 per cent of the population we still stand out, we are visibly different and that is what makes us 'black'.

This being 'black' in Britain is about a state of 'becoming' racialised; a process of consciousness, when colour becomes the defining factor about who you are. Located through your 'otherness' a conscious coalition emerges: a self-consciously constructed space where identity is not inscribed by a natural identification but a political kinship. (Sandoval, 1991, in Mirza, 1997, p. 3)

Recognition of the prolonged difficulties of people living in Britain is important when considering writing by women of colour and when, Black or white, we consider our own representation and our own lives in any multicultural society. Racism experienced by indigenous people, for example in Australia, New Zealand, southern Africa, is a related but not identical issue (to put it bluntly, they are unlikely to be asked why they don't pack up and go home).

Now living is submerged in whiteness, physical difference becomes a defining issue, a signifier, a mark of whether or not you belong. Thus to be black in Britain is to share a common structural location; a racial location. (Safia Mirza, 1997, p. 3)

As Salman Rushdie notes (above), the particular perspectives of writers who have immigrated to the UK make a significant contribution to the different ways in which we all see ourselves, whether hidden, misrepresented, constructed as stereotypically British or stereotypically Other. What we must remember is that the stereotypical construction of white Britishness is hugely problematic for all of us as individuals – does it make us all football hooligans, silenced housewives, or suited men with umbrellas? All labels homogenise those whom they label, but Black and Asian-originated British women write from a variety of experiences:

These differences are themselves reflective of the divisions amongst the various constituencies of Black women. Indeed, though our starting point has been to stress the historical link between us of colonialism and imperialism, we have also been concerned to recognise the divisions and contradictions amongst us ... generated and reproduced by the contemporary circumstances in which we find ourselves. (Grewal et al., 1988, p. 6)

Some diasporan writers appear in the chapters on their countries of origin: Jean Breeze in the Caribbean, Chapter 5; Buchi Emecheta in Africa, Chapter 6, etc. Others, who have largely settled in the UK or whose work concentrates on the British experience, appear here, but for some the decisions are fairly arbitrary. Emecheta settled in the UK in 1962 and her *Second Class Citizen* (1974) is about, and set in, Britain, considering the life and conflicts of Adah (based on Emecheta), a wife with five children, who has moved to the UK and finds herself considered as good only for childbearing and rearing, caught up in the in-fighting between Igbos and Yorubas in London. Emecheta's *Gwendolen*, considered in Chapter 6 on Africa, looks at a Caribbean girl's London upbringing. There are many Asian women writers, some of whom write from the Asian women's writing collective(s)/workshops/networks, and there are Chinese, Pacific and African American women writing, some with colonial or post-colonial backgrounds, others without, having been born in the UK. Strictly speaking, all are post-colonial as their work responds to and writes against the influences of colonialism and imperialism. Asian women born in India, Pakistan, Bangladesh, Sri Lanka, etc., but living in the UK or the US are considered in Chapter 8 in the part of that chapter on the diaspora. There are many for whom there is no space here, but I hope readers will seek them out.

One other point, however, is that there is probably much writing, the publication of which has been stalled or prevented because of the particular, often subtle, often covert, contexts of racism and sexism in which Black women writers work everywhere. While some writers are published, available, others are silenced: complacency is dangerous. Many UK contexts and outlets have, in fact, disappeared through lack of funds since the 1980s when some of the critical work accompanying the creative work was produced. The mid-Eighties saw a plethora of feminist bookshops providing opportunities for book signings, readings and writing groups. The magazine *Spare Rib* and the feminist presses were active, visible and publishing Black and Asian women's writing. Perhaps some of the political critical edge has gone out of women's writing, one might argue, because some of the cases for equality have been won or, as Jackie Kay (below) argues, it is time to turn to other themes, freed from the need to argue back and assert identity. It would take a longer survey than this to decide. But my gut reaction is that the reality is far from this Utopian belief. There are established writers now, but there are many whose first steps into publication have been prevented by the lack of nurturing and of those outlets. The late Nineties are a very different political context – not so much of suppression but of complacency, and of post-feminist backlash.

THE DIASPORAN EXISTENCE

> The diasporic writer cannot shake off the colonial legacy as it is manifest in metropolitan racism, cultural and linguistic superiority and a constant sense of being marginalised. (Ranjana Sidhanta Ash, 1995, p. 47)

The very word diaspora suggests a space between two places, and two places themselves. This emphasises both the dual sense of belonging, or half-belonging, felt by women writers in the diaspora, and a gulf, cultural, historical and geographical, between the two or more locations from which they and their work spring. On the one hand, they wish to represent and recognise their differences, their experiences and those of others in all/both of these spaces/places. On the other hand, they also try bridging these differences, recognising similarities and then allowing them to coalesce in themselves as writers. This is a necessary step to understanding one's identity as a migrated subject, or as any subject. In many ways the diaspora is effectively a double dispossession for women, involving colonial oppression and dispossession, and subjugation of women by men. A third, economic divisiveness also operates. Second- and third-generation women of Afro-Caribbean, African and Asian descent are often high achievers in both the educational and professional systems, but their mothers are more commonly less well economically positioned, often ghettoised by their hesitancy with the English language. Both wider cultural isolation and community-based cultural identity result from living in specific ethnic communities.

There is a particular burden of representation for writers living in the diaspora to relate to their/their family's roots in their countries of origin, including the UK, when there are conflicting ties and demands, confusions and distances involved. Replacing one stereotype with another, ghettoisation or tokenism must be avoided, as Yasmin Alibhai argues:

> In a society that still thrives on a colonial relationship with its own non-white populations, the dangers of black artists being flattered, appropriated and used are great, on the other hand,

when you come from a group of people denied even the basic human rights, their expectations of you are high and political. (Alibhai, 1991, pp. 17–18)

Silence continues the sense of absence, disabling attempts to join in the arena of changing discourses and representations of the multicultural society: 'An immigrant writer inevitably finds him/herself in the position of representing the marginalised immigrant community to the dominant one through his/her fiction' (Jena, 1993, p. 3).

Some second-generation writers are discovering roots, imagining homelands, visiting for the first time. The 'New Generation' poet Moniza Alvi writes of an imagined Pakistan and the entry of her father, Tariq, into a cold England of washing lines, long before she first visited Pakistan. Others, like Debjanee Chatterjee, commute between family in India, England, and the USA. Theirs are complex, split lives.

FEMINISM AND BLACK AND ASIAN WOMEN IN BRITAIN

Throughout the 1970s and 1980s, as Black women in Britain moved from invisibility to visibility, there began a dialogue between modernist feminist discourse and Black women's lives and experiences. On the one hand, one major element of the feminist enterprise called for the recognition of a 'universal' woman subject, but universalisation of the experience of women blatantly excluded Black women's diversity of experience, and acceding space in discussions about family and motherhood, economic conditions, etc., to the 'difference' made by women of colour was only a token gesture. Pratibha Parmar and Valerie Amos (1984) see white feminist discourses around the family, economy, etc., as subversive only in the cause of white feminism; an attempt to render white feminist experience as universal. In one sense this is a first step. A homogenised difference is asserted of women, set against patriarchy, and all differences are submerged in this. In the Harlem Renaissance period, for example, African Americans asserted their difference against WASP (White Anglo-Saxon Protestant) Americans (see Chapters 2 and 4), and women speaking out about gender were considered to be troubling political solidarity. Black and Asian feminists argued throughout the 1980s against being 'named' and marginalised by white feminism's universalising powerhouse. In *Feminist Review* (1984) for instance,

Black feminists write about the variety of their lives in their own contexts. Channelling energy into defining difference from white feminists enables a powerful political awareness of racial, and gendered, identity but can be an all-consuming subject. For Jackie Kay this has involved a move from 'So you think I'm a mule' (1984), to being able to ignore the 'white woman in your head' (Kay, 1989) and write about other things, the issue neither forgotten nor dominating. As Heidi Safia Mirza puts it:

> By the end of the 1980s, the black feminist critical project to excavate the dynamics of racial power and the silences it produces within white feminist discourse left black feminists exhausted and in need for self recovery. The flattening out and reduction of difference and diversity which had been assigned to interrogated whiteness within the feminist movement had outlived its purpose. The homogenising of black women, that empowering act of collectivity rooted in racism, began to erode black feminist theoretical legitimacy.   (Safia Mirza, 1997, p. 11)

In the late 1990s post-modernism has produced, for feminists, what can be seen as a liberating sensitive space, the recognition of 'difference'. 'Mapping' the difference has become a popular term. There are several problems inherent in this, however. One is that difference, as such, is always something constructed against a notional even if hidden 'norm', and this is most likely to be white, middle-class and, if we are talking about women, female, but as we move into wider spaces, male. Everything is constructed as different set against this notional norm. Its licence to speak is just that, a potentially temporary licence. Difference also dissipates strength in coming together. Even the term 'mapping' is problematic, denoting structures imposed upon the natural world by imperialists carving lands out, naming rivers, laying stake to ownership of vast tracts of hitherto (it was assumed) unnamed, uninhabited space. Mapping confines and limits. However, without maps and labels, though with edges left hazy and blurred, ever-changing, recognised as temporary ways of understanding space and difference, we could not speak. Names limit but enable discourse. Discussion implies some ownership and control (as with a book, carving authors up into geographical spaces), but it enables introduction and discussion. Asserting identity and confronting racism are issues in the work of many Black, Asian and white British writers, as are discussions of being female, of relationships, of families, and a concern with dispelling stereotypes in the representation of women of all ages and kinds.

Jackie Kay and Maud Sulter

Jackie Kay and Maud Sulter, both Glasgow-born, both argue that white feminists need to realise Black women have their own specific experiences.

> Before this night is over and before
> this new dawn rises we have to see
> these particular changes speak to
> our guarded uncertain before singing
> Sisterhood is Powerful.
> (Kay, 'We are not all sisters under
> the same moon', 1984, p. 58)

Jackie Kay has written of the need, initially, to address the white woman in her mind and her life in order to assert her own identity against that notional woman's prejudice.

> 'Where do you come from?'
> 'I'm from Glasgow'
> 'Glasgow?'
> 'uh huh, Glasgow.'
> The white face hesitates
> the eyebrows raise
> the mouth opens
> then snaps shut
> incredulous
> yet too polite to say outright
> liar
> she tries another manoeuvre
> 'And your parents?'
> 'Glasgow and Fife'
> (Kay, 'So you think I'm a mule?', 1984, p. 53)

This attempt to register difference is 'snookered' by the speaker's own sense of comfort with her identity, her origins and her colour. The poem is a direct confrontation, in dialogue, against racism in its everyday appearance. It also indicates an important stage in the work of Kay and other Black women writers, when the address to such racism dominates their writing (or prevents it). In time, however, cultural self-assertion develops into a secure identity, a place from which to speak of all manner of issues.

Kay's *Adoption Papers* (1991) is a powerful collection recording a story of adoption (her own), taking three voices, in three type-faces: the birth mother, the adoptive mother and the daughter. Identity, tracking down relations, fantasies of reunions, and fear that the adoptive mother might disappear because she was not 'real', predominate.

> After mammy told me she wisnae me real mammy I was scared
> to death she was gonnie melt
> or something or mibbe disappear in the dead
> of night and somebody would say she wus a fairy
> godmother ...
>
> (Kay, 'The Telling Part', 1991, p. 22)

This poem sequence queries origins, identity and relationships as the different experiences of the three women involved are expressed.

In Jackie Kay's poetry, women's roles, loving, identity, sexuality, motherhood, child theft, AIDS, fear of death and loss, the celebration of lesbian love, and hiding homosexuality, are persistent themes. One poem explores daily experiences related to sexual choice. It deals with a family where the lesbian partners ponder on how their child will cope with his identity in the harsh wider society. The boy, on his first day at school, finds ways to tell and understand his story. Unlike his friend Tunde, he has no father at home:

> ... I said I don't have a daddy;
> I have a mummy and a donor and a Deirdre
> (Kay, 'Mummy and Donor and Deirdre', 1991, p. 54)

The boy's story is interspersed with the mother's and Deirdre's wondering how to manage fitting into the constraints of conventional situations such as a parents' evening. The more immediate adjustment is managed by their son. Initially rejected in confusion by his friend, then reunited, he settles down, as does Tunde, to recognise that there are differences and different relationships, but everyday normality.

Sometimes Jackie Kay uses Glaswegian speech and rhythms. She adopts personae to articulate the delusions, hopes and fears of various women in their roles; everyday details of conversations, food, smells and tastes bringing the scenes vividly to our senses. Most recently Jackie Kay's novel *The Trumpet* (1998, The Guardian Fiction Award) concentrates on the relationship between 'reality' and 'performance'; it has a Glaswegian context and airs concerns with adoption (her own experience) and being of mixed race. In its consideration of the life of Glasgow trumpeteer Joss Moody who is revealed on his deathbed as a woman, Jackie Kay says that she was interested in the relationship between one person (the wife, Millie) knowing the secret and one not (the adopted son, Colman). Her engagement with this character relates to 'passing' (see Nella Larsen Chapter 2):

> I love African-American literature you know. I've read Nella Larsen's *Passing*. That notion of passing has always intrigued me as well. I find it is very, very interesting the idea of living your life as something that you are not. Racially or sexually, they are both equally fascinating.   (Kay, 1999, interviewed by Maya Jaggi, p. 53)

The book engages with the constructedness of identity. Hers is a highly articulate and powerful voice speaking about being a woman, and being Black, in the UK today.

Maud Sulter

The first Black British woman writer I ever actually met (early 1985) and spoke with was Maud Sulter, part of a younger generation of Black women artists and writers. She is a talented activist, highly articulate about the race, class and gender politics surrounding living, writing and publishing as a Black woman, some comments on which are articulated in her *As a Black Woman* (1985).

Maud Sulter was born in Glasgow in 1960. She is a journalist and photographer who writes fiction and poetry, and gives readings and seminars internationally. Her first work, *As a Black Woman* (1985), won the Vera Bell Prize. Maud Sulter takes an explicitly political stance, campaigning for civil rights, and gender and racial equality:

> as a black woman creativity is central to my existence. It is a means of survival, covering a spectrum as diverse as singing, sculpture,

hair braiding and childbearing. Our art demands participation. (Sulter, 'Passion', 1990, p. 9)

Her political work appears in *Through the Break, Women and Personal Struggle* (1986), with London's Women's Resource Centre, and in editing *Spare Rib*'s Black women's edition (1985) and *Feminist Art News*. She actively supports and encourages Black women's texts, films, and artwork, herself supported by, for example, Grace Nichols. Her writing has appeared in *Watchers and Seekers* (ed. R. Cobham and M. Collins, 1987) and her *Zabat: Poetics of a Family Tree* (1989):

> Daughters, she cries
> learn the tongues
> of this world voices
> teach the children
> of their wonder
> love as only a woman can
> take up the pen, the brush
> explosive,
> and name
> yes name
> yourself
> black
> women
> zami
> proud
> name yourself
> never forget
> our herstory.

('Full Cycle', in *Zabat*, 1989)

Other publications include *Passion: Discourses on Black Women's Creativity* (1990) with Ingrid Pollard, and *Echo: Works by Women Artists 1850–1940* (1991) for Liverpool Tate Gallery.

The occasional racism she experienced in Glasgow as a teenager silenced her. She recognised her resulting hostile response as demeaning, making her a victim:

I had to reassess my position as a black woman in a hostile society. Part of that reassessment was a stronger commitment to my writing. Identifying with other black people's experience brought me

relief. I was brought closer to them individually, collectively, politically, and I was no longer alone. I had a responsibility to help
other black people realise the importance of their own experience
and challenge that internalised (self) hatred that eats away at the
soul.   (Sulter, in Ngcobo, 1987, p. 61)

Maud Sulter facilitated workshops for Black women writers,
worked within the Greater London Council and ILEA-funded
Women's Education Resource Centre on the 1984–6 Black women's
creativity project, and enabled others to publish and feel pride in
their work:

> as a black woman
> every act is a personal act
> every act is a political act
>   ('As a Black woman', 1985)

Like Grace Nichols she explores the experience of Black women in
many contexts and the strength to reclaim self and power.

In her work she challenges the appropriation of women's voices
and critical comment by white feminists, an appropriation which
led in the mid-1980s to many articulate and talented black women
striving and succeeding in getting published so that they could
speak about their own experiences of being women and feminists
and Black. This led to a complete issue of *Feminist Review* being
produced by a Black women's group (1984), and to Black women
writers' readings at the feminist book shop *Sisterwrite*. Quite rightly
she has questioned the use of her work in critical publications,
seeing this as simply attributed appropriation. As discussed earlier
(Chapter 1), as readers, Black, Asian or white, we need to avoid
appropriation even as we also enjoy and attempt to understand
expressions which in some instances might exclude us, surprise us
or seem hostile to us (especially if we are white), but we should not,
as Spivak insists, allow ourselves to be silenced.

Joan Riley

Born in Jamaica, Riley studied in the UK and has written four
novels, chief of which, *The Unbelonging* (1985), has been made into a
film by Channel 4. Each of her novels deals with a stage in life, and
The Unbelonging focuses on the experience of Hyacinth Williams, a

young Jamaican girl who travels to the UK to live with her father and his family and tries both to come to terms with racism and sexism, and to develop a sense of her own identity. She is abused from childhood and fights to retain control of her body, but is punished by her father:

> She knew he would keep her standing there until her nerve went; knew he would wait for the tears to slip out, the shaking to start. She could feel her eyes burning, misery and self-pity swamping her, and she fought back the tears determinedly.   (1985, p. 13)

It is a very painful novel to read. Its treatment of the body, however, interestingly aligns itself with some of the arguments of the French feminists (Cixous, Kristeva and Irigaray), as has been noted by Gabrielle Griffin (Wisker, 1992, pp. 19–27). Hyacinth is alienated from her body, experienced as a site of oppression by her father both because of her terrified incontinence and latterly because of her sexual maturity. She experiences her isolation and pain as a child even when mature: 'As the scream echoed in her mind, the tears seeped out and Hyacinth knew she would never be free until that child had healed' (1985, p. 143).

BLACK BRITISH CARIBBEAN POETS

Black British/Caribbean women poets use a linguistic mixture of the varieties of English spoken in the Caribbean. They entertain and explore issues of race and identity, male and female relationships and the difficult pleasures of living in the diaspora, using irony and wit, everyday street language, puns, and well observed colloquialisms.

Merle Collins

Both Merle Collins and Christine Davis from Grenada were galvanised into writing by the revolution, and their poems often act like chants, involving others. An intellectual who lived in London and is now in the USA, Merle Collins is a very powerful performance poet. She involves her audience in her performance, encouraging them to repeat back 'crack' to her 'crick' in the poem 'Crick Crack Monkey', which explores the lies told about Black history or the lack of it. The poem differentiates these lies from those of childhood, part of

'Ananci Story Time' when the twist in the tail, the lie, was indicated by the sound of the branch cracking under the monkey. The biggest, but unacknowledged lies involve the 'discovery' of America, the freeing of slaves, and an end to apartheid. In each situation there was no logical need for theft and suffering in the first place.

Merle Collins, acclaimed for her novel *Angel* (1987) and her poetry collection *Because the Dawn Breaks* (1985), has worked closely with the group 'African Dawn', incorporating traditional oral, dramatic and musical forms into her performance. Like other performance poets (see Chapter 5), her work is like a musical score, brought to life by performance.

'Chant Me a Tune' charts the Middle Passage (taking slaves from Africa to America or the Caribbean), urging support and strength:

> move with me across the weeping Atlantic
> through the blood tears death pain and hurt
> . . . .
> i need you
> to remind me
> that i am
> the oceanic roar of angry strength
> that never dies
> that never dies
> that will never die
>
> (1985, p. 50)

She needs to be reminded of her strength and importance, though, like Mary Seacole, her strength is hidden behind white stories – Florence Nightingale, in Mary's case.

In 'She was so quiet', Mary, the cleaner from Nigeria, dies, and her connections with mother and son at home need to be remembered. Ordinary women gain a presence, remembered, although:

> just another faceless person
> unseeing and unseen
> on the streets of London
>
> (1985, p. 52)

Merle Collins uses Jamaican English to challenge the hypocrisy and racism of poetry-competition selections which rule out 'dialects'. She recalls the war effort and the transportation of slaves in ships from

Liverpool. Her own Jamaican English is empowering. The poem confronts racism head on, undercutting its premises:

NO DIALECTS PLEASE!
WE'RE British!
Huh!
To tink how they still so dunce and so frighten o we power
dat dey have to hide behind a language
that we could wrap roun we little finger
in addition to we own!

(Collins, 1987, p. 119)

Valerie Bloom

Valerie Bloom has carried on the work of Caribbean performance poet Louise Bennett (Miss Lou; see Chapter 5) as folklorist, lecturer and teacher with works such as her collection *Touch Mi, Tell Mi* (1983). Maggie Humm comments on her language that:

> Bloom's Black British dialect is a technical and rhythmic innovation. It is a self-conscious attempt to subvert the traditional language of poetry and insist on a merciless difference. These poets refuse embellishment or camouflage. They are linear poets who write free and open verse which works directly from example to example to make designs upon the world.   (Humm, 1991, *Border Traffic*, p. 59)

Performance and community response are important in her work:

> Such literature derives its power not only from the message of the craft but also from the personality of the artist. It depends a great deal on the flair of the performer, and the audience are participants while being informed and entertained. Its 'rapping' rhythm involves the listeners emotionally in the performance; the language of the ghetto encourages them to embrace this poetry as their own. In it they see themselves and laugh, for it gives vent to humour as well as social protest.   (Ngcobo, 1987 p. 3)

Born in Jamaica, Valerie Bloom studied English, African and Caribbean Studies at the University of Kent. Published in several anthologies, she produced her first book of poetry, *Touch Mi, Tell Mi*, in 1983. Her form is often like Miss Lou's: with four-line rhyming stanzas, dramatic personae addressing other characters through speech or letters about everyday experiences, and an ironic manner of exposing inequities, oppression and social foible, for example in 'Yuh Hear Bout?' and 'Wat more could she want':

> She is me woman yes!
> but she is old time thing
> me no must have
> another little young thing
> to rub up me jaw
> And make me feel young and sprucy
> What a wicked dreadful and unreasonable woman, eh.
>
> ('Wat more could she want', p. 25)

She is critical of men, too, through oppressed women's voices. Bloom performs in a riveting way, first teaching the audience about how to pronounce Jamaican words, Jamaican grammar and syntax; an activity which both changes the power base of coloniser/colonised and causes the audience to be involved in a community experience. She sings, and in one poem goes into a version of a fit. In 'Yuh Hear Bout?' (1987) her irony explores the absence of news of Jamaican and other Black suffering. Her poetry appeals to young and old alike, covering such issues as Jamaican village life, and political activities in the Caribbean and the world. Irony enables cutting comments to be absorbed by the whole audience.

Amryl Johnson

Amryl Johnson writes poetry and prose recording her experiences in the UK and the Caribbean. Julie Pearn says of her work:

> Amryl's earlier poems are full of a sense of bleakness and cold which is spiritual as much as physical. The British environment offers her images of thorns, dead leaves and brackish waters. These are not abstract images but reflect the hostility she feels from the society towards herself and all black people, and a general absence of love and creativity. (Pearn, 1988, p. 46)

Like many Black Caribbean women writers living in England, she travels between the two, writing of her journeying. The first return journey was the most surprising: she became aware of how much England had changed her, and how much she did or did not belong to the land of her roots. Caught up in steel band performances and enjoying the atmosphere, she was aware that much of this was a tourist attraction. On one memorable occasion on a boat, Amryl Johnson looked at the bobbing tourist heads and thought of the slave crossing, the thousands of Africans who suffered and died at sea. The collection *Long Road to Nowhere* (1985) was inspired by her second trip to the Caribbean and her return to the UK, which brought enjoyment, suffering, and the need to begin anew her understanding of her own diasporan position. The Caribbean has flaws: 'The Caribbean isn't all exotic fruit, white sands and coconut palms against a blue sky. The gulf between those who have and those who do not is too blatant to be ignored' (in Ngcobo, 1987, *Let it be Told*, p. 38).

> Whitewash the face of hunger
> When all the features have been removed
> Paint on the smile, the laughing eyes
> Show the tourists what they want
> But not too close
> Behind the grinning facade are slums
> Which rob the people – of all dignity
> ('Blowing in a Random Breeze' [1985],
> in Ngcobo, 1988, p. 38)

Other carnival poems celebrate her joy at rediscovering her own culture, and use the calypso beat, for example:

> Dis abandon to pleasure is drawin' we
> to one conclusion of unity
> Freedom was bought wit' dis in min'
> a full expression ah liberty
> ('J'ouvert' (We Ting) [1985], in Ngcobo, 1988, p. 38)

Her poems of market life are vibrant and amusing, and seeing her perform 'Granny in de market place' or 'The Peanut Vendor' transports the audience to a mixture of Kingston and Brixton where Granny acts as all canny grannies, testing the fruits and vegetables, giving back as much talk as she receives. The peanut vendor, a market 'wide boy', tries to woo his customers with promises and charm, all related to peanuts. Granny tests everything, pinches it, complains, and points out inconsistencies in the promises of the market seller, probably putting other customers off at the same time. The poem, a dramatic dialogue, like Jean Breeze's (see Chapter 5), utilises the dialect and colloquialisms of everyday street language:

> Yuh fish fresh?
>
> Woman, why yuh holdin' meh fish up tuh yuh nose?
> De fish fresh. Ah say it fresh.
> A ehn go say it any mo'
>
> Hmm, well if dis fish fresh den is I who dead an' done
> De ting smell like it take a bath in a lavatory in town
> It here so long it happy.
> Look how de mout' laughin' at we
> De eye turn up to heaven like it want tuh know e' fate
> Dey say it does take a good week before dey reach dat state.
>
> (Johnson, 'Granny in de market place',
> [1985], in Ngcobo, 1988, p. 42)

Grace Nichols

Grace Nichols grew up in Guyana and emigrated to the UK in 1977. A diasporan poet, she engages with the history of Black slave transportation, settlement, colonisation and immigration/emigration, with the everyday Caribbean and domestic magic of women, and differences between England and the Caribbean. She uses a mixture of everyday English and versions of Jamaican English, wherever appropriate, to suggest roots or the persona of a more naive, earthy Caribbean woman coping with UK aloofness and coldness. Her poem sequence 'I is a long memoried woman' (1984) won the Commonwealth Poetry Prize. Like elements of Toni Morrison's *Beloved* (1987) and Alice Walker's *The Temple of My Familiar* (1989), she imagines and re-enacts the Middle Passage from Africa, thinking back through her female ancestors, recalling, recording and reclaiming the crossing to the Caribbean:

> 'I is a long memoried woman' in fact owes its inspiration to a dream I had one night of a young African girl's swimming from Africa to the Caribbean with a garland of flowers around her.

When I woke up I interpreted the dream to mean that she was trying to cleanse the ocean of the pain and suffering that her ancestors had gone through in that crossing from Africa to the New World.   (Nichols, 1984, p. 298)

Grace Nichols's 'Home Truths' (1989, p. 296) reclaims the crossing, noting the hidden strength of women who bear this memory within them. They make something from nothing, unsung and silent. The poem sequence is in free verse, breath, movement and the body deciding the length and strength of lines, so that, for instance, the sequence about sugar cane is tall like the cane itself. Gabrielle Griffin comments of the language and form used in the poem sequence as a whole that:

the body of the text is only very sparingly marked by signs that come from a written tradition of language usage, such as commas, question marks, dots. In fact, nothing comes to an end with a full stop: there is no stopping the revolution. It is not over.   (Griffin, 1993, p. 26)

The poem is divided into five separate sections charting the woman/ every black woman's movement from capture in Africa, being sold into slavery, crossing the ocean to the Caribbean, becoming a slave in the sugar cane plantations and bearing the white man's children, while mourning the loss of her earlier life and her home. Her positive dreams of a whole self keep her from nightmares of disintegration: 'I must construct myself a dream / one dream, is all I need to keep / me from these blades of hardness / from this plague of sadness' ('One Dream', 1989, p. 39).

Called into the plantation owner's house to be his mistress and bear his children, she never loses her dignity, having her revenge for this humiliation: 'She enters into his Great House / her see-far looking eyes / unassuming' but thinks of the master who wants to 'tower above her' and the mistress wife spending her days in 'vacant smiling'. Gradually she 'slowly stir the hate / of poison in' ('Loveact', 1984, p. 54).

In 'Skin-Teeth' she speaks as a slave striking back: 'Not every skin-teeth / is a smile "massa" ' (p. 55). She will 'rise and strike again'. 'Out of Africa' traces the journeying from Africa to the Caribbean and England, dealing with the myths and stereotypes of each: mother Africa and exhaustion; the startling glare of the blue sea, coconuts and 'happy go lucky' air of the Caribbean, both of which emanate poverty; then Britain's coldness, where precision and restraint produce fruit and birds equally restrained: the budgie and the strawberry. A typical English 'gent' returns a lost umbrella. This rhythmic, repetitive poem lends itself to performance. 'Out of Africa', 'Into the Caribbean' or 'Into England' are repeated three times in each of their verses.

In another poem she enacts and explodes the male coloniser's myths of the highly sexed Black woman, a dumb female Caliban over-awed by the white imperialist's stunning civilised gifts. The poem works by using a naive point of view, exaggerating the achievements of the coloniser, a contemporary Columbus who conquers the girl, claiming the kudos of European civilisation, including plutonium. In the exchange, she gives him all the white coloniser's fantasies of highly sexed, obedient native women. 'He does a Columbus' flinging himself on her shores. But the Anansi-wise Black woman mocks power in an initially exciting sexual act, making 'a stool of his head'. The double reading of stool (to sit on, faeces, excreta) shows her subtle triumph.

Like Toni Morrison, Grace Nichols revives the importance of magic in the everyday. 'Twentieth-Century Witch Chant' is powerful, rhythmic and repetitive, calling on an entourage of historical women of strength, prophetesses and witches, who have been hidden and denied:

> Resurrect the ashes of the women burnt as witches
> resurrect the ashes
> mould the cinders
> stir the cauldron
> resurrect those witches
>
>   (1985, p. 117)

The poem demands a re-empowerment and resurrection of silenced and marginalised women of power. 'Resurrect' is repeated the magical three times, a chant building up until it turns into a spell against boys: 'As for the boys playing with their power toys / entoad them all' ('Twentieth-Century Witch Chant', 1985, p. 117).

Nichols's collection *The Fat Black Woman's Poems* (1984) was one of the first Virago titles. Her first adult novel, *Whole of a Morning Sky*, set in Guyana, came out in 1986. As oral performance poetry her work is powerful and magical. The stereotypical/mythical Black woman on the islands turns into the fat black woman who cannot fully fit into the coldness and austerity of England. 'The fat black woman goes shopping' (1984, p. 11), a very popular poem with students and women readers, explores the experiences of the fat black woman trying to shop for colourful and bright clothing, as out of place as such clothing in London during winter. The cold of the climate is echoed in that of the mannequins who show their distaste at her difference and size, 'exchanging slimming glances' (1984, p. 11). The 'accommodating' clothes she searches for are as rare as acceptance and accommodation in England. Her movement from shop to shop compares with her travel to England, 'all this journeying and journeying' leading her nowhere (1984, p. 11). Amusing and politicised in terms of race and gender, the poem shows the celebratory fat black woman refusing hostile, restrictive glances and defining herself positively. Over the series of poems she emerges as a kind of trickster figure watching from the sidelines as different values refuse and deny her. She toasts her size against a skinny Miss World contest: 'fat is a darling . . . fat speaks for itself' ('Looking at Miss World', 1984, p. 20). Faced with political choices she will refuse them ('The fat black woman versus politics', 1984, p. 22) 'to feed power crazy politicians a manifesto of lard / To place my X against a bowl of custard' and finally ('afterword') 'the fat black woman will emerge / and tremblingly fearlessly / stake her claim again' (1984, p. 24).

The colourfulness and generosity of the islands are replaced by the cold of England in 'Winter Thoughts':

> I've reduced the sun
> to the neat oblong of fire
> in my living room.
>
> (Nichols, 1985, p. 122)

But, returning shows her the limitations as well as the spell of the islands. Seeing young men in the streets rocking to dub rhythm she speaks to her brother, in Jamaican English to represent her own homecoming:

> An ah hearing dub-music blaring
> an ah seeing de many youths rocking
> hypnosis in dih street

> rocking to de riddum of dere own deaths
> locked in shop-front beat
> ('Walking with mih brother in Georgetown',
> 1985, p. 118)

Her brother merely remarks that she has been away for too long (seven years). She wonders whether she too is dying, to be disillusioned in this way. It is an insightful poem, noting that the sacrifice of Jamaican youth to poverty and the hypnotic beat of music, drug culture and unemployment is not an ideal, despite the sunshine. This is the insight of the diasporan writer. Through her persona, Grace Nichols highlights the benefits and limitations of both Caribbean and English lives, climates and cultures. With wry amusement, and magical insight, she overturns stereotypes, always aware of women's roles, oppressions and celebrations.

Barbara Burford

Born in the UK in 1946, Burford broke new ground in Black British women's writing by bringing out the first anthology, in 1984, *A Dangerous Knowing: Four Black Women Poets*. An active feminist and mother, she is committed to medical research, writes science fiction, poetry, prose and plays, such as 'Patterns', commissioned by the Changing Women's Theatre and performed in 1984. In 'Women Talking', she expresses the power of Black women together:

> And we are mistresses
> of strong, wild air,
> leapers and sounders
> of depths and barriers.
> (Burford, 1984, p. 3)

Her work challenges and refuses stereotypes of Black women as victims, celebrating energies, love and lesbian relationships. Her short stories in *The Threshing Floor* (1986) follow women's lives in Canterbury, UK, exploring lesbian relationships and creativity. Other stories appear in *Everyday Matters: 2* (Burford, 1984). In 'Miss Jessie' (Burford, 1984) a seemingly exhausted, kindly, maternal station cleaner 'invisible to the great mass of people', misnamed and ignored, takes home a Norwegian student to (ostensibly) care for, bath and feed him. Inheriting her Priest father's roles, she treats the young man (one of many?) as a sacrificial bullock. This is a culture-laden piece of horror.

ASIAN WOMEN WRITERS' COLLECTIVE

Initially a group of ten or so core members and others who met in London to write, listen and critically support each other's writing efforts, the collective produced their first publication, *No Right of Way*, in 1988, followed by *Flaming Spirit* (1994). Most are in full-time work with family responsibilities and have difficulty finding time to write, but are aided by collaborative effort. They debate issues of critical reception, whether to adopt critical techniques of the largely white, male, middle-class critic and publishing world, or to fall into the potential trap of publishing everything Black women produce on the grounds that they should be heard because of their marginality (issues which have dogged women's writing and publishing since the early days); asking

who formulated these criteria, and are they relevant to us, as Asian women writing in a country where writers are recognised as great on the terms of white middle-class male critics? How do we evolve our own standards without falling into the trap of venerating every word written by Black women purely because their disadvantaged position has reduced to a marginality? (Asian Women Writers' Collective, 1990, p. 151)

Some time has been spent finding publishing outlets, supporting each other in their writing, finding and sustaining their own voices, coming as they do from different origins within Asia and England:

Did it take that long for 'immigrants' to feel settled and strong enough to want to express, re-order and interpret their reality for themselves and society at large? We were also working in a vacuum; there seemed to be no precedents to which we could refer. (Asian Women Writers' Collective, 1990, p. 150)

Sometimes squeezed out of Black women's writing groups because not Afro-Caribbean, they determined to relate closely to such groups but establish their own, honing works for the anthology differently from those tried out at collective readings, making them more complex.

Since the late 1980s, GLC funding and special arts grants have disappeared, making it increasingly difficult for new groups to form and publish, while the few individuals who have made a name for themselves, also struggling with publishers, are more identifiable. The tales told in the various Asian Women Writers' Collective collections (*No Right of Way*, 1988; *Flaming Spirit*, 1994) trace the histories of individual Asian girls and women living and growing up in the UK, moving from India and Bangladesh, facing suspicion about their births and their passports, their relationships and their right to be living in the UK (for example, Sibani Raychaudhuri's 'Sisters' in *Flaming Spirit*, pp. 16–28). They face the cold, hostile neighbours and racial abuse ('Rebecca and the Neighbours', Tanika Gupta in *Flaming Spirit*). They also form friendships with Black, Asian and white friends, old and young, go out into the world and succeed at school, care for relatives, succeeding in a different society, their mothers isolated at home. Caught in England between two cultures, they miss the version of their own culture in their country of origin, although with time this grows more fanciful and idealised, more remote.

Many of the stories are written from the first-person narrative, either explicitly the author or another 'I' testifying figure, and all mark difference. As Vayu Naidu says in 'Cultures of Silence', 'she moves between geographies' (1994, p. 60).

Ravinder Randhawa

Born in 1953, Ravinder Randhawa is an Indian short-story writer concentrating on issues to do with British Asian immigrants, and the social and cultural imperatives placed upon Asian women. A founding member of the Asian Women Writers' Collective, her best known work is *A Wicked Old Woman* (1987), exploring difficulties for a second-generation Indian girl, Kulwant, in literally 'trying on' a series of possible identities created by the diasporan existence into which she is born. She moves through a series of stereotypes, initially rejecting the confinement of her role as either the victimised, poor Indian of media representation or the glamorous 'Indian Princess' of myth. Kuli (her alternative name) rejects her Indian upbringing, choosing education and a white boyfriend, Michael, but, overburdened with the revolutionary act and its consequences, reverts determinedly to a stereotypical Indian role, insisting on an arranged marriage, leaving Michael and education behind. Not surprisingly, the conflicts and contrasts of life in the UK, not to mention her own internal turmoil, militate against success. Blamed by her sons, and alone, she becomes old and homeless. In this last phase of her life, she reverts to victim Indian status, another stereotype. Other characters in the book choose differing versions of Asian or British stereotypical lifestyles, their names changing with context. C. L. Innes considers issues of multiple, conflicting cultural identities as explored here:

> Ravinder Randhawa's novel does not conceal the complexities and difficulties that confront Asians who seek to be productive members of the larger community, to live in England rather than merely survive on the margins. Assimilation is shown to be neither desirable nor possible but neither is it desirable to retreat into an artificial Indianness.   (Innes, 1995, p. 33)

What is not sought is the safe haven of an Oxfam-derived, missionary re-created version of a home from home in the Asian centre, which Kulwant defines as:

> a simulation sub-continent patched together with a flotsam of travel posters, batik work, examples of traditional embroidery, cow bells and last but not least woven baskets that you knew were from Oxfam. It was supposed to be inviting, user friendly: a home from home for the Asian woman trapped in the isolation of her house; a helping hand for the Asian man shell-shocked from dealing with the revolving door racism and vagaries of white bureaucracy.   (Innes, 1995, pp. 30–1)

Other examples of Randhawa's work appear in collections of short stories, including *More to Life than Mr Right* (1985) and *A Girl's Best Friend* (1987).

Sunetra Guptra

Guptra's work is part of the development of the second-generation younger Asian women's writing. Her two novels, *Memories of Rain*, (1992) and *The Glassblower's Breath* (1993), focus on displacement and the lives of young Asian women. In the former novel, a young Bengali woman cannot cope with the infidelity of her once-loved English husband and prepares to leave. In interior monologue combining Bengali translation and Asian English, it reflects the bilingualism and diasporan existence of Guptra, herself. The second novel considers the life of a Bengali girl in London involved in several relationships and sexual exploits. Each deals with women questioning their traditional roles and seeking sexual liberation, coping with conflicting representations and internal voices because of their diasporan existence.

Meera Syal

Syal is a novelist, actress (BBC2's *Goodness Gracious Me*) and film maker; 'Bhaji on the Beach' (1995) is much acclaimed. *Anita and Me* (1997) presents a marvellously funny, lively picture of growing up in an Asian community near Wolverhampton. Syal combines the exploration and enactment of the awkwardness of adolescence with her own assertion of individual identity, set against the overwhelming constriction of 'The Aunties', Indian women whose views help rule girls' lives, and provide a community comment on everything. Gossip and commentary remind us of women's family groups in Nwapa's *Efuru* and Toni Morrison's communities, notably in *Beloved* and *Paradise*.

The form is politicised and gendered. Syal explores a whole community through Meena's development and negotiation of small girl/ adolescent stereotypes. But this is fiction, and Meena identifies with various cultural myths, pointing out that 'I'm not really a liar, I just learned very early on that those of us deprived of history sometimes need to turn to mythology to feel complete, to belong' (p. 10). Meena is characterised by her over-heated, over-dressed life, and her rather adventurous and wicked spirit. Her community initially has no difficulty incorporating and responding sensitively to its first Asian family, but produces ugly moments when (it seems inevitable) the local wild boy, Sam Lowbridge, becoming a skinhead, taunts Asian people, unaware that Meena identifies with this. Nationalist and racist in his disruptive need to upset local attempts to spend donated money in a global help venture, Sam is the familiar voice of fascism and ignorance:

> 'You don't do nothing but talk, "Uncle". And give everything away to darkies we've never met. We don't give a toss for anybody else. This is our patch, not some wogs' handout.'
> I felt as if I had been punched in the stomach. My legs felt watery and a hot panic softened my inside to mush. It was as if the whole crowd had turned into one huge eyeball which swivelled slowly between me and pap.
>
> (Syal, 1997, p. 193)

Anita, rough local girl and radical friend, cannot ally herself with Meena in this situation, which is divisive, painful and poignant. Overt racism is luckily a rarity in her life; however, stereotyping and cultural crassness is an everyday occurrence. Sandy, Anita's mother, says generously: 'You're so lovely. You know, I never think of you as, you know, foreign. You're just like one of us' (1997, p. 29). This is amusing when related to friends and relatives, as is Meena's awareness of the (unspoken) stereotypical responses local people have to the trail of 'aunts' and 'uncles' (friends, elders) who visit their home, wickedly pointing out, 'I could see our neighbours shift uncomfortably, contemplating the apparent size of my family and the fact that we had somehow managed to bring everyone of them over here' (1997, p. 29).

Asian writers feel a responsibility to represent their society for their own community and the rest of British society, of which they are a part. Rushdie's own comments about beady-eyed observers is true for Meera Syal. As she experiences, watches and re-creates her own experiences and those of her community, she is well aware of returning to white British society a mixed version of Asians. Invisibility, a common problem of Asian diasporan writers, is a serious issue in Meena's and her family's life. As in Toni Morrison's *Jazz*, Black or Asian news is not considered news, a measure of covert racism, silencing and rendering absent:

> According to the newspapers and television, we simply did not exist. If a brown or a black face ever did appear on TV, it stopped us all in our tracks. 'Daljit! Quick!' papa would call, and we would crowd round and coo over the walk-on in some detective series, some long-suffering actor in a gaudy costume with a goodness-gracious-me accent. ('So Mr Templar, you speak fluent Hindustani too! But that won't stop me stealing the secret formula for my countrydom where I will soon rule the world. Heh heh heh . . . ') and welcome him into our home like a long-lost relative. (Syal, 1997, p. 165)

Humorous critiques of English and Asian stereotypes mix with an individual's growing up. Meena's identity starts to settle when her link is forged with her mother's mother, her 'Nanima', whose earthiness is different from her mother's educated responses. Nanima recognises Meena as a 'junglee' (1997, p. 200), a wild girl. She is not, she realises, totally without precedent: there is a place for her kind of rebellion in the family and culture. Meena's tale is filled with rites of passage, by water, accident, loss, meetings with strangers and recognitions. A major one is the arrival of a baby brother she finds she cares for. Another is a summer-holiday broken leg. These events take her from the claustrophobia of her lost friendship with Anita, into secondary school and beyond the book.

Black and Asian women writers in Britain write of women's lives, of racism, identity, their communities, difference. As 'Observers with beady eyes' they create a rich, powerful, humorous and articulate comment on a changing Britain.

Part III
Emergent Women's Writing

13

South-East Asia: Singapore and Malaysia

I read terrible stories –
Hate, rage, futilities of will –
And look for women, the small
Sufficient swans, showers of stars

(Geok-lin Lim, 1996, p. 1)

INTRODUCTION AND BACKGROUND

South-East Asia is taken to include Malaysia and Singapore, the Philippines and Thailand. Following this book's concern with writing from locations which once were under British colonial rule, this chapter concentrates on women's writing in Malaysia and Singapore, looking at the ways in which women writers deal with tensions between town and rural, or kampong, life, how they view the importance of conventional family structures and the increasing contemporary demands of the rapid consumer materialism of the region, particularly of Singapore, and how they represent the lives of women. Education is viewed as a route to improvement but against this striving are set the very real difficulties of stress, artifice, hypocrisy and a sense of the superficiality of materialistic values. Many women writers both deal with these tensions, and revive the importance of the supernatural, of superstition and myth in understanding the legacy of the past and current values. The work of Catherine Lim and Shirley Geok-lin Lim is of particular importance here.

HISTORY AND CONTEXT

The emergence of women's writing in South-East Asia parallels political and social change, and the improvement and extension of education for women. Both Malaysia and Singapore weave together a fascinating mixture of cultures, a legacy of their two hundred years of British rule, and Chinese, English and Tamil Indian immigration. Malaysia comprises mainland Malaya and, since 1963, British Borneo. At the same date Singapore also joined the newly formed Malaysia, but left in 1965 to become independent. Since then the two countries have developed rapidly, along largely similar but, in terms of values, somewhat different lines. Singapore, under the rule of Lee Kwan Yew, has turned into a fast-moving testimony to capitalism and materialism, but also to the value of education, in which there is much investment.

In Malaysia the national language is Bahasa-Malay, and until recently (1997) government policies have favoured and rewarded the education of Malays over Chinese and Tamils, whose tertiary education has been largely private as a result. The national literature is in Malay and funding has followed its production, but there are some writers who write also in English, or whose work is translated. English and Chinese are the most popular languages in which women write in Singapore. A more highly consumerist society, Singapore invests in education, awarding book prizes to new and established authors to encourage writing. Women were absent from publication in both countries prior to the 1960s, and have benefited in both from increased emphasis on education at home, and abroad. Many successful writers have studied in the UK, the US or Australia and several have settled abroad, writing of their homelands in the diaspora, returning occasionally to visit family and friends.

Malaysia

For women writers, magazine publishing was the first major encouragement with the development in 1930 of *Bulan Melayu* (*The Malay Moon*) by the Malay Women Teachers Association, founded by Hajjah Zainon Sulaimon (Ubu Zain). It insisted on the education of women as a key to the improvement of the wider society, the old adage 'educate a women and you educate a nation' carrying weight here. Education is a key theme in Malay women's writing, as also is the tension between traditional cultural values and the demands of the later twentieth century. Clashes emerge in issues such as arranged marriages, expected behavioural deference to the father (involving some silencing), and highly educated career women returning to the home and domestic responsibilities. One of the characteristics of subsequent writing has been noted by Koh Tai Ann (1992, p. 228) to be:

> a strongly missionary and didactic character to much of the women's prose fiction, the modern form most South-East Asian women writers adopt, partly because magazines and newspapers facilitated the publication of short stories and partly because female education in South-East Asian societies tended like the short story and the novel (and the mass media) to come in the wake of modernisation and Westernisation.

In the early days prior to and after independence, writing remained largely activist and nationalist in character and was mostly by men. After independence in 1957, women travelled to seek education abroad and education and literacy rose as part of the drive towards an increasingly industrialised and capitalist culture. Women's opportunities for publication grew similarly, although until the 1960s there was little published writing by women, not just because of lack of education but because of early marriages and economic hardship. A generation of students have gained in experience and confidence through studying at the University of Malaya, and abroad in the UK, the US and Australia and now write in English as well as Malay and Chinese, although rarely yet in Tamil. In Malaysia most women write in Malay (and so lie beyond the bounds of this study). The most recent writing, energised by Islamic writing contests, tends to concentrate on reinforcing traditional beliefs and behaviours, religious beliefs and social conformity among women. Although Koh Tai Ann (1992) reported that no Malaysian women novelists had written in English, emigration and a growing diaspora are obviously helping to redeem this problem somewhat. Australian writers with Malaysian origins, such as Beth Yahp (see Chapter 9), have benefited from increasing international interest in South-East Asian women writing abroad.

Singapore

Singapore, 'the bastion of capitalism' (Sessor, 1994, p. 28), has been ruled by Prime Minister Lee Kwan Yew since the 1950s. It outlaws public nuisances such as chewing gum and dropping litter, enforces road and social laws fiercely, thrives on the imposition of rules and regulations, and prospers, a lively mixture of old-fashioned, magical, spiritual family ways and naked capitalist values. Demonstrations, including public assemblies of more than five people, need police permission. Flourishing on contradictions, Singapore is a country of surveillance and investment, industrialisation and professionalism, yet it also carries remnants of the values of village lives, large families, Chinese medicine and traditional beliefs.

In Singapore writing by women is mostly in English or in English and Chinese, the two language cultures which have huge international potential readerships, usually entirely separate, although with the increased Western interest in Chinese and Chinese American women's writing (Maxine Hong Kingston, Amy Tan etc.), interest is growing Singapore Chinese women's writing in English, especially the work of Catherine Lim and Shirley Geok-lin Lim.

AUTOBIOGRAPHICAL WRITING

The first women's writing was autobiographical rather than fictional and charts contradictions in women's lives, some reflecting their lives as bond-servants suffering hardship, and social rising, for example Janet Lim's autobiography *Sold for Silver*, about her rise from being a bondmaid to a matron in a Singapore hospital. Others chart lives in very wealthy Chinese families (Yeap Joo-kim's *The Patriarch*, 1975; Queeny Chang's *Memories of a Nonya*, 1981) or as daughters of successful English-educated professionals from the colonial period (Ruth Ho, *Rainbow over my Shoulder*, 1975; Joan Hon, *Relatively Speaking*, 1984; Aisha Akbar, *Aisha Bee at War*, 1990; Bonnie Hicks, *Excuse me, are you a model?*, 1990).

NOVELS, SHORT STORIES, POETRY AND DRAMA

The first novel to be published in English by a Singapore woman writer was *Sing to the Dawn* by Minfong Ho, who has now emigrated to the US. Her writing concentrates on a popular theme, the rise of women from an impoverished immigrant past. Women's poetry began to be published in the 1960s, with Lee Tzu Pheng writing on private issues, and Shirley Geok-lin Lim who displays an acute awareness of her heritage, her position of difference, the changing times, and feminism in her own and other cultures. Other women poets include Geraldine Heng, *White Dreams* (1976); Angeline Yap, *Collected Poems* (1986); Hilary Tham, *No Gods Today* (1969); and Leong Liew Geok, *Paper Boats* (1987) and *Love is not Enough* (1991).

Emily of Emerald Hill

Among the rising women dramatists, the most famous and influential has been S. Kon whose *Emily of Emerald Hill* (1983) chronicles the life of a Singaporean Nonya (a Straits-born Chinese matriarch), Emily Gan, beginning in 1950 in her middle age, in a turn-of-the-century mansion, but moving backwards and forwards in time. Modelled on S. Kon's own domineering, formidable matriarch of a grandmother, Emily is the only character to appear on stage but many others are conjured up as we see her rise from bride to hostess, interfering matriarch and mother grieving for her son. Her days also chart the changes in Singapore, from the old mansions off Orchard Road in their heyday, to huge new hotels, apartment blocks and shopping plazas.

CONTEMPORARY WOMEN WRITERS

The work of contemporary women novelists and short-story writers concentrates on similar themes of convention versus change, autobiographical charting of their own and their families' histories, and the supernatural. Catherine Lim, the most notable amongst these writers, deals with the everyday and the supernatural, casting an ironic eye on the losses and paradoxes of such rapid commercialisation and dependence upon the material.

Much of the fiction-writing by women has been supported by the government's commitment to literature, the rise of the National Book Development Council and their awards of literary prizes, particularly the Singapore Literature Prize. Suchen Christine Lim, a writer with the Curriculum Development Institute of Singapore, published *'Rice Bowl'* (1984); *The Amah: A Portrait in Black and White* (1990), a short play co-authored with Ophelia Oi, which won a merit prize in the NUS–Shell short play competition; *A Gift from the Gods* (1990); and *A Fistful of Colours* (1992), which won the Singapore Literature Prize. She describes herself as: 'a Southeast Asian writer which is a third generation descendant of illiterate Chinese immigrants' (book blurb).

In her *Fistful of Colours* she explores three strong, defiant women, one Malaysian, one Chinese and one Indian Tamil, who reject the repressive lives offered by their societies and their parents' choice of future jobs and husbands. Suwen, the central character, suffers incest and abuse, which the traditional family structure absorbs and covers up. She exorcises her pain and anger through powerful painting which causes moral outrage (not ladylike enough, too erotic and personal, too passionate and powerful). Suwen leaves Singapore and her expatriate boyfriend. Nica Sivalingam, exploring her artwork in a small Malaysian village, defies her doctor father and pursues art rather than medicine, living with rather than marrying her Chinese boyfriend Robert Lim. Janice Wong wishes to escape a destiny dependent on her father's Chinese heritage, leaves home and marries Zul, a Malay journalist educated in English. All three concentrate on the complexities and contradictions of women's lives in contemporary Singapore, and the conflicts between the appeal of consumerism and of art or spirituality, between convention and women's new freedoms.

Another Singapore Literature Prize winner is Tan Mei Ching, a University of Washington graduate whose *Beyond the Village* (1994) interweaves myths of the mountain and the experience of the village for an abandoned mysterious child, Shi Ying. Tan Mei Ching has written numerous short stories, and her short play, *Water Ghosts*, won the NUS–Shell short play contest in 1992. Tan Mei Ching's concentration on storytelling and myth is allied with first-person narrative and a character growing in sensitivity and self-awareness.

Education abroad and literary prizes at home are a consistent pattern in the work of many of the contemporary women writers in Singapore.

Shirley Geok-lin Lim

Born in Malaysia and now living in the US, Shirley Geok-lin Lim was the first woman and Asian to win the Commonwealth Poetry Prize. Her *Crossing the Peninsula and other Poems* (1980) concentrates on exploring a multicultural identity. Lim, as a diasporan writer, negotiates her experiences and representations of Singapore, Malaysia and the US, writing of difference, travel, women's lives and mother–daughter relationships. She writes fiction, poetry and critical work. Speaking partly of her own relationship to language and that of Third World writers she says:

in the process of our discovering what we share with others, our tribal boundaries can become unstuck, our ancient or recent national identities can be shaken. This is the risk that Third World English language writers take, the risk that all explorers come up against in travelling too far, the possibility of alienation from their native cultures, of losing one's way home. The child who leaves home, seduced by a stranger's tongue, and never returns is to be mourned for. (Geok-lin Lim, 1988)

Her poetry conjures up the sights, sounds and smells of Malaysia, as both a visitor and one who was born there. She describes everyday behaviour, decay and change, commenting on women's roles:

> The woman who smuggles her hair
> in beige cloth poses on stiletto
> heels under a long black sateen skirt
> ...
> ...They are tearing down
> the South Seas Chinese shop fronts,
>
> and
>
> I had forgotten how dense the country.
> Layers of vegetation: padi
> kangkong ubi sugarcane banana
> thickets of mango rambai duku durian
>   (Geok-lin Lim, 1994, 'Tropical Attitudes', p. 108)

Catherine Lim

The most established Singaporean woman writer, Catherine Lim's own outspoken criticism of the hypocrisies and repressions of the state in her journalistic writing produced thinly veiled government threats. Reviewing her early volume *Little Ironies of Singapore* (1978), Austin Coates notes Catherine Lim's observant eye on Chinese mores and everyday life: 'she exposes men and women with a mixture of complacent ruthlessness and compassion' (Coates, 1978, p. 2). Those around her are guilty of complacency, having dangerously imbibed the false promises of a consumer society. Lim's characters seek success, material wealth and power, judge others by their belongings, and sacrifice their children to an educational conveyer belt which demands high success, ignoring emotional needs and individual difference. These are shrewd stories, and her tone is that of the objective recorder, who misses nothing and refuses to openly condemn. They indict hypocritical and destructive social and cultural practices and pretences through light descriptive touches, and their little ironies.

'Paper' focuses on the dominating obsession of Tay Soon and his wife Yee Lian for a 'big beautiful house'. The house is consistently described as a 'dream home' and a 'consuming passion' and these are the keys to Tay Soon's downfall. Sold on the materialistic images in *Homes* and *Modern Living*, he turns this fantasy into a nearly-within-reach concrete reality. Lim uses a mixture of conditionals, 'it would be a far cry from the little terrace house', and future tenses, 'was to be carpeted', to establish its near-achievement, matching the conviction and obsession of the family, who work relentlessly to achieve their 'peak of earthly achievement' (Catherine Lim, 1978, p. 7), the house. The story is set in the 1970s but is tellingly topical given the recent collapse of the so-called 'tiger economies' of South-East Asia. As the stocks start to rise, Tay Soon and Yee Lian start to invest, sure that their dream home is getting closer. Lim echoes their false conviction, which troubles the reader: 'and now there was to be no stopping' (1978, p. 8); 'I'll never sell now he vowed' and then, ominously, 'it's just paper gains so far' (1978, p. 9). They invest in their dream and when (as we know it inevitably will) the stock market collapses, they lose all. The fragility of paper and the similar fragility of paper money is something which the people of East and West have all experienced. Paper money is itself only a sign for wealth and worth, and only worth its exchange value in hard goods, but we invest our trust in it.

The old traditional Chinese culture merges with the Westernised as prayer papers are burned to try and reverse their bad monetary luck and Tay Soon's mind collapses with the horror of the loss. The dénouement is specifically built on Chinese cultural practices – the burning at death of paper replicas meant to signify objects and achievements in this world, to be taken to the next. Tay Soon's only dream house made solid is ironically an expensive, rather absurd, decorative carnival one, not quite the shape he would have wanted but marvellously showy. Perhaps another twist is that the old mother who refused any such flutters on the stock market but assiduously plied her own trade, gives all her own savings to send the paper house up in flames. Old and young, old values and new, are affected by this, materialistic, paper moon/dream of a house so grand it would show the world the earthly achievements and gains of Tay Soon and his family. Presumably the afterlife appreciated the burned show. The story refuses to back this reading – there are no emotional or philosophical rescues – both the traditional and the Westernised beliefs are in question. The dream house 'burned brilliantly, and in three minutes was a heap of ashes on the grave' (Catherine Lim, 1978, p. 12).

'The Teacher' and 'Adeline Ng Ai Choo' each deal with adolescents who seek death rather than face their failure at school. Far from being supportive, the teachers criticise the students' spelling, ignoring their poverty and the pressures on them to succeed, and they can rarely tell the students apart: 'I wonder why most of them write like that?' (Catherine Lim, 1978, p. 13) is one all-embracing comment, and 'Ah, they're all like that' (p. 14). Spelling corrections are focused on, ignoring pain and a girl's clear cry for help in her composition about her father:

> 'He canned me every time, even when I did not do wrong things still he canned me' – she means 'caned' of course – 'and he beat my mother and even if she sick, he wallop her'. This composition is not only grossly ungrammatical but out of point. I had no alternative but to give her an F straight away.   (Catherine Lim, 1978, p. 15)

The girl jumps from the eleventh floor. The teacher's complacent comment, ironically, is 'such a shy, timid girl. If only she had told me of her problems' (p. 15). Ai Choo's well-educated father also dominated her life – she too jumped from the flats and died, because her results were one mark short of passing.

Other stories deal with marriages based on wealth; love sacrificed for material prospects; old mothers trapped, dying, considered a real imposition in the spare bedrooms of materialistic daughters-in-law; oppressive fathers who prevent their daughters from going out with their friends, and the worthlessness of girl children in a society which inherits through the male line. Generations of women's lives are drawn in short tales of different families whose traditional ways clash with modern society. Girls are considered worthless, so in 'Male Child' Chuan Poon agonises that each time his wife produces, 'it was a girl child. Was this a punishment for sin?' (Catherine Lim, 1978, p. 31).

They do return...but gently lead them back (1983) is one of Lim's short story collections that features the supernatural, although it is the complex, contradictory web of behaviours and beliefs in which people enmesh themselves in order not to offend one spirit, please another, counteract this or that bit of potential bad luck, with which Lim deals with her deft touches of irony. Again, there are stories of girls considered worthless, boys precious, such as the tale of 'A Boy Named Ah Mnooi'. The boy, the only and really valued son, is given a girl's name and laden with clothes and amulets all his young life in order to ward off bad spirits who would be jealous of him because of his gender. He survives, but his peer Ah Khooi, whose mother is similarly superstitious, does not. In feeding him the prayer herbal powders prepared by the priest over the years, to protect him, she contributes to his early death: they contain arsenic. *The Serpent's Tooth* (1982) explores the stresses of a family and particularly the influence of the old mother, who tells remarkable stories, interweaving Chinese myths and placing herself at the centre, interpreting life through these myths/stresses of generational responsibilities and misunder-standings, the demands on mothers and mothers-in-law, the cos-seting of sons – these are all explored here in a novel laced through with culturally acute description, storytelling, superstition and irony.

Treatments of such clashes are also to be found in the Chinese American writers Maxine Hong Kingston and Amy Tan who each deal with the interlacing of the everyday, Westernised pressures on family and work and the traditional, superstitious family ties and pressures, and two differing world views and interpretations.

Lim's novel *The Bondmaid* (1997) charts the life of a wretchedly poor girl, Han, whose once-beautiful mother married at sixteen and produced a child a year until she wore herself out and wasted away. Han is moved from the tumble of siblings because of her beauty and ability to charm, and placed as a bondmaid in a rich Chinese house-hold where she and the young grandson and heir fall in love. But a house filled with patriarchal and matriarchal power and a great deal of class distinction can hold no happiness for her, and working in the 'House of Flowers', a brothel, seems the only way she can maintain some independence. The story intersperses the daily life and trials of Han with godlike interventions, and squabbles more obscene and unpleasant, filled with problems, misunderstandings, and confusions – it is an equal reality. The difficulties of young women in poverty in the class-ridden society of Singapore in the early 1950s are clearly portrayed through Han's own difficulties:

'Come here', bondmaids were used to hearing the order, prelude to punishment, to dalliance. Their bodies would gather together into tight knots of resistance but they had no choice, Go there, go there to be scolded, punched, caressed. (Catherine Lim, 1997, p. 263)

Her life is always in the power of others: 'the girl's body was an endless territory for his pleasurable roaming' (p. 265), thinks the Reverend of one of his bondmaids. Han advises the girl Peipei to put him off his fondling by smearing her breasts with faeces. Her more obedient sister, Pop, advises she ignore Han's wilful rejections of what is a woman's daily lot when working in a good family:

'Look at me', said Pop. 'Look at me and my good life with my family. If I had made a fuss and something bad had happened, would I be like this today?' and she held up her lucky male baby by way of reinforcing her point, Endurance. If women endured enough, a good life would eventually come to them. (Catherine Lim, 1997, p. 271)

Pregnant with the child of the grandson of the house, Han is painfully aware of economic differences and her own vulnerability in loving him. She none the less thinks that 'this man has a future that stretches before him like a golden road: mine is a deep dark pond whose waters will close over my head' (p. 274). His wife, LiLi, when presented with the statement of their love, is overwhelmed with jealousy and anger and blames witchcraft. No sisterhood here, but how could there be? Ironically, the old ways of first and second wives as a norm might have solved the problem, but the times of the 1950s changed what could and could not be done, and the later years of more and different job opportunities for intelligent, beautiful women like Han had not yet arrived. She was a victim of her culture and her historical moment – as well as her gender in a society obsessed by the importance of men and the subordination of women. LiLi argues 'you have been put under a spell by that demonic woman. She has used her secret blood on you ... the young master Wu bewitched by a common servant girl!' (p. 304). LiLi engineers a political meeting with the dying grandfather, but even that does not deter Wu in his life and duty, only her fall, and the subsequent saving of her and the child heir, cause him to reject Han. The worlds of the supernatural and the real join – Han becomes as a goddess; Wu, his family dying and leaving, spends the rest of his life tending her shrine until it burns up, and the heavily protected hut guarding it, on the central Singapore road in the middle of a development area, can be replaced by a Petroleum company. The myth has been unearthed – begun at the beginning and packed away again at the end of the book, the story is enlightening about a period and women's roles in it.

South-East Asian women writers engage with the contradictions faced by their contemporaries, particularly concentrating on the pressures to conform and succeed which can traumatise and confuse young girls and women. Catherine Lim's ironic tales, Suchen Christine Lim's alternatives and Shirley Geok-lin Lim's observations are lively, critical comments testifying to women's increasing freedom to speak out and challenge both repressive traditions and destructive contemporary tensions in women's lives.

14

Oceania – Pacific Rim Writing

She wears red feathers and a huly huly skirt,
she wears red feathers and a huly huly skirt,
she lives on just coconuts and fish from the sea,
. . . with love in her heart from me.

(Popular song of the 1940s)

> *she wears lei*
>   *around Gauguinesque*
>   *blossoming breasts*
>   *sweeping brown*
>   *round and around*
>   *looping above*
>   *firm flat belly button*
>   *peeking over*
>   *see-thru hula skirt*
> (not from her island – but what does it hurt?)
> . . .
> 'Lovely hula hands' (this line to be sung to the tune of the
> popular song which it appears in)
> *always understands*
>   *make good island wife – for life – no strife*

(Tusitala Marsh, 'Statued [stat you?]
Traditions', 1997, p. 52)

These quotations demonstrate both popular media images and the kinds of engaged responses contemporary Pacific Rim women writers have developed to counter cultural stereotypes representing them as sexually pliable, noble savages. This chapter concentrates on women's writing from Oceania, the Pacific Rim area, looking at

315

colonial history and cultural stereotypes, exploring conditions which enable writing and publication. It considers work by several women, particularly Marjorie Crocombe, Konai Helu Thaman, Momo von Reiche, Jully Sipolo, Teresia Teaiwa, Grace Mare Molisa, and Vanessa Griffen, all of whom deal with issues of cultural identity, the roles and representation of women.

INTRODUCTION: KEY ISSUES AND INCIDENTS, GEOGRAPHY AND HISTORY OF WOMEN'S LIVES AND WRITING IN THE PACIFIC

Denigrated, inhibited and withdrawn during the colonial era, the Pacific people are again beginning to take confidence and express themselves in traditional forms, that remain part of a valued heritage, as well as in new forms and styles reflecting the changes within the continuity of the unique world of our island cultures. (Crocombe, 1980, p. xiii)

The hilariously romantic through the pseudo-scholarly to infuriatingly racist; from the 'noble savage' literary school through Margaret Mead and all her comings of age, Somerset Maugham's missionaries, drunks and saintly whores and James Maicheer's rascals and godless people, to the stereotyped childlike pagan who needs to be steered to the Light. (Wendt, 1980, p. xiv)

The Pacific region includes Papua New Guinea, Vanuatu, the Solomon Islands, Tuvalu, Tokelau, Kiribati, Western Samoa, Fiji, Neuie, the Cook Islands and Tonga. It is an area also referred to as 'Oceania' and sometimes as Polynesia, but this final name could be misleading as not all the writers are of Polynesian descent; others are Fiji Indian, for example. There are over 1200 indigenous languages, and written literatures are relatively recent, but there is a long-standing oral tradition, in which women have played an important part.

The lives of Pacific women vary according to the islands or island group on which they live, for there are different customs and practices. But a consistent factor is the degree of illiteracy and women's subordination even though they carry out a large variety of essential tasks from work in the home to fishing, agriculture, etc.

When we start to read about Pacific women, to read their work and their representations of themselves, we are confronted by their rejection of exotic disempowering stereotypes (see the popular song above). These stereotypes are the result of interpretations based on European culturally determined ways of knowing, as Bernard Smith points out (1985, p. 5) 'European observers sought to come to grips with the realities of the Pacific by interpreting them in familiar terms.' The imaging of the Pacific is laced with power. Subramani characterises the popular image of the South Pacific woman as:

> amorous, nymph-like, with almost a childlike disposition to love. Such an image has continued to circulate in the West in order to pander to the taste of a reading public which wants women to be presented in a romantic light. (Subramani, 1992 [1985], p. 84)

This is a romanticised light, allowing little space for women to express their own identity and emotions and, after colonialism, to throw off the ridiculous bondage of being a fetishistic fantasy for European Western men – an exotic escape, a silent, loving, sensual, dark-skinned beauty who is like the earth, natural, not fussy like a Western woman. Women writers considered in this chapter all critique this image – some more assertively than others (see Teresia Teaiwa and Momo Von Reiche below). Maugham's version of a South Pacific woman gives us a good idea of the artificial, disempowering and heavily colonised stereotype against which they assert their articulate, lively, intelligent and individualised selves:

> You cannot imagine how exquisite she was. She had the passionate grace of hibiscus and the rich colour. She was rather tall, slim, with the delicate features of her race, and large eyes like pools of still water under the palm trees; her hair, black and curling, fell down her back and she wore a wreath of scented flowers. (Maugham, 1921, p. 130)

Her enchanting natural beauty is comparable with the natural abundance of the islands' palm trees, still pools and hibiscus flowers. Like the natural blooms, it suggests, she is ready to be picked and celebrated by Westerners. She does not, of course, speak for herself. In *The Moon and Sixpence* (Maugham, 1919) Ata, an example of this stereotype, 'leaves me alone...she cooks my food and looks after her babies.... She does what I tell her.... She gives me what I want from a woman' (p. 280). Strickland, the protagonist, denies that women have souls, claiming that they always 'get you' eventually. Man is helpless against woman the enchantress. This age-old dichotomous version of woman as virgin and whore, *femme fatale* and exotic ideal, can never result in an empowered woman, in any fiction or culture. One of the central jobs for women writers of the region is to debunk these fantasies, and question the traditions of their own origins which would render them subordinate to all the men in their families, unable to inherit, and in many cases sold off with a bride price. With deft linguistic play and full-frontal assault the women writers of the islands have taken the destructive denigrating results of these stereotypes to task, and also found time to write about everyday life, change, themselves and relationships, from their own points of view. Among others, Konai Helu Thaman has directly reacted against the stereotypes in European *writing*.

WRITING AND PUBLISHING

'Oceanian literature is a literature governed by the connections between identity, culture, politics and gender', and women's writing is affected by the oral literature in the region such as Polynesian legends and matriarchal tale telling. (Buck, ed., 1992, p. 181)

The contemporary writing of Pacific women has largely been enabled by the development of the University of the South Pacific's Institute of Pacific Studies, from where most of the poets and prose writers have at least initially been published and from where much research derives for this chapter.

The major novelist of the region is Albert Wendt. Wendt described being told stories or '*fagogo*' by his grandmother every evening (in Crocombe, 1980, p. 45). Early twentieth-century women writers include Florence Frisbie (*The Frisbies of the South Seas*, 1916; *Miss Ulysses From Puka Puka*, 1948), which are both autobiographical, and Tom and Lydia Davis's *Doctor to the Islands* (1955).

Writing by Pacific women, like that of men, began appearing in the late 1950s, encouraged in the University of Papua New Guinea and then the University of the South Pacific writing groups. Vanessa Griffen and others set up the University of the South Pacific Arts Centre (UNISPAC) with the aim of promoting creative writing, and in 1973 Marjorie Crocombe set up the South Pacific Creative Arts Society. They published in *The Pacific Islands Monthly* and eventually in their own journal, *Mana*, founded in 1973 ('*Mana*' means power or force concentrated in objects and persons).

The origins of the literature of the region are in the writings and encouragement of the missionaries:

> The new South Pacific literature coincides with the desire for independence. The literature drew sustenance from wide-spread anti-colonial sentiments in the region.... Colonialism will not be an easy subject to abandon.... Colonialism also means the negation of the writer's individuality; his efforts to free himself of his colonised self is part of the real process of becoming a person. Paradoxically in this process he also frees himself of his ancestral culture.   (Subramani, 1992 [1985], p. 76)

Anna Balakian (1962, p. 30) has advanced the notion of 'negative influence', the response against the creation of views of Polynesian Islanders by expatriate writers (from Melville to Maugham, etc.):

> It is apparent that the portrait of the islands in much of the European fiction seldom matches the reality known to Pacific islanders. There are idealised metaphors of South Seas paradise, romantic portrayals of Polynesian Adam and Adonis, on the one hand, and racial stereotypes of cannibals and Calibans on the other. These are all distorted images. But they have had a great influence in the region as well as outside.   (Subramani, 1992 [1985], p. 7)

Victims of the European need to believe in primitivism and lost innocence, in organic communities and the simple innocent life, all affect versions of the Pacific Islanders, particularly the women, onto whom have been loaded Europeans' desires and fears for the exotic and the innocent – and a sense of guilt.

FIJI

Of women in Fiji, Jessie Tuivaga says:

> Traditionally women are seen and not heard despite their contribution to the family's welfare and economy. While women are responsible for the cleanliness of the home and cooking and the general comfort of the family, they are also involved in wage

employment for the financial maintenance of the family. Sometimes they are the sole income earners.   (Tuivaga, in Tongamon, 1988, p. 1)

When the missionaries arrived in 1835 they abolished polygamy and regulated customs so that women worked the land and assumed domestic and medical responsibilities whilst men were decision-makers. Although missionaries introduced education for all, girls were not encouraged to pursue it into further and higher levels. Domestic violence ('wife-bashing') is a serious problem. In 1984 the Women's Crisis Centre opened, helping with counselling and informing the community about violence against women. The Women's Wing, established in 1984, has the central objective of equality between men and women in the workplace, both large factories etc., and cottage industries. While women's contribution towards the overall economy has been publicly acknowledged, more women are needed (the book concludes) in decision-making processes.

Teresia Teaiwa

Teresia Teaiwa is one of the younger generation of women poets in Fiji. Her work covers issues of islander travel, hybrid cultural identity, feminism, anti-colonialism, identification with nature and the elements, love, language and play. One of her most recent sets of poems plays on the word 'niu'. She says (in e-mail discussion, 12 January 1998) 'in most Pacific languages "niu" refers to the coconut, so in these poems I am exploring the possibilities of rethinking "nudity" (the bane of our existence as Pacific islanders) a richer, more subversive kind of "nudity"'. Rather like the modernist poet HD, Teresia is taking conventional, usually rather disempowering images and reversing them, seizing them for herself, exploring their implications. HD recuperates and transforms flower images conventionally connoting women's gentle, ornamental, natural delicacy, and absence of intellect. Teresia transforms the image of the coconut (niu), and that of niu/nudity. The play on words with 'niu', which sound like 'new', enables her to make it new, to critique the colonialist and tourist constrictions of Islander women as pretty, natural, exotic playthings. The development of the word 'nudity' from 'niu' rejects the construction of women positioned as objects in an exchange system whereby they are the consumed. The idea of being turned into a coconut was negative in myth, but she seizes it as an escape, a metamorphosis which enables the individual to avoid disempowering roles. Being turned into a coconut allows a mask, and an escape, rather than construction and consumption under an imperialist male gaze. In a prose poem, Teresia rescripts and redefines 'nudity' for a potential forthcoming edition of the *Penguin Dictionary of Oceanic Verse*.

'Nudity 111' (1999)

Nudity – n.

1.   A state of being turned into a coconut, and not being recognised as oneself; as distinct from being naked, in which case one is without clothes and is immediately recognised as oneself; for example 'Neither the hero nor the evil sorcerer recognised the heroine because of her nudity'. (And because the hero had been nude, the heroine had a hard time recognising him, too, at first, but she did in the end.)

2.   A form of clothing, a disguise or filter mask or husk; for example 'And so, since they didn't recognise her, the heroine in her nudity went on her merry way and left the evil sorcerer and the hero to their own devices'.

3.   A song, often an expression of joy or relief; for example 'And as she went she sang a sweet nudity...a nudity of freedom, of liberation from men, a nudity of independence, and of being single...a nudity for singular women wherever they may be'.

In 'Searching for Nei Nim'anoa' (1995) she wishes to link up with her people and her origins, using imagery of journeying, sailing, and personal response:

> I will pick up the pieces
> of my broken Gilbertese.
> Gather the remnants of
> my broken heart.
> And use them to chart my course.

Vanessa Griffen

Griffen is known for her critical work and short stories, frequently about women. They are 'distinguished by a conscious grasp of the social and economic pressures which govern their lives' (Subramani, 1992 [1985], p. 85), and in considering the everyday details of peoples' lives and emotions, she addresses the conventional stereotypical versions of women's lives in the Pacific as represented in European texts by Maugham etc. In her short story 'The Concert', her character, Miss Renner, takes her Fijian students to a concert in town, which they do not enjoy. However, when they break into Fijian song on the homeward journey she cannot fully enjoy the song for itself because it is Fijian – viewed as second-rate: 'Miss Renner realised that their singing was beautiful. But then, she thought, again with the same feeling of regret, they're only Fijian songs' (Griffen, 1973, p. 12). Subramani characterises her short stories as lyrical, relying on subject and tone rather than plot. She avoids first-person narrative, withdraws behind her fictional world and captures fleeting moments. Suva, the Fijian capital, is her usual setting and she concentrates on Fijians and Europeans or part-Europeans. In her story 'The New Road' Griffen depicts a place resonating with past beauty. An outsider looking into a departing culture, she captures it in fleeting moments, particularly in the early tales 'Marama', 'The Conscript', 'The Concert' and, more latterly, 'The New Road', 'Candles Glowing Orange' and 'One Saturday Morning'. Her work initially appeared in the magazine of the University of South Pacific (*UNISPAC*) from 1972 onwards.

THE SOLOMON ISLANDS

Much the same pattern of life for women as in Fiji is found in the Solomon Islands; however, there is a different attitude. While daughters are not allowed to answer back to fathers, and paternalism operates within an overall patriarchy, none the less an information source written by women, *Pacific women*, can show an interesting lack of feminist awareness when it celebrates this status quo:

> In fact, Solomon Island women do not see their role as degrading and never consider their status as inferior nor do they consider themselves subservient to men. Instead a Solomon Island woman is proud of herself and her supportive role because the success of husbands and men in general reflects the success of wives and women in general.   (Pollard, 1988, p. 42)

On marriage, women exchanged for a price are valued as an economic asset, and perform domestic duties for the husband's family. Men, as elsewhere, make the final decisions.

The first Solomon Islands publication to print creative writing was the *Kakamora Reporter* from 1970 onwards, and the first poet to be published in his own editions was John Suanana, followed by the first anthology of Solomon Islands poetry, in 1975:

Nostalgia for a vanished, idealised past and the search for identity in the present are themes with which Solomon Islands poets are still concerned. This hints at an ambivalence which infuses almost all published writing to date – the dilemma of an elite uncomfortable with its place in the vanguard of change. (*Pacific Writers' Pacific Islands Communication Journal*, vol. 14, no. 1, 1986, p. 15)

The first woman writer to be published was Jully Sipolo whose collection *Civilised Girl* came out in 1981, the first text to comment seriously on the lot of women in the Solomon Islands. It is 'powerful, piquant and poignant', forming the first feminist statement in Solomon Islands writing. Novels started to follow poetry, and then drama, one of the great successes being the Lukluk Wantok Drama Group who performed improvisations, wrote plays and tapped a creative vein in the performing arts.

They noticed a difficulty of resources preventing the publication of further issues of a Solomon Islands journal, and the interest of ex-patriots only in publishing and recording the traditions of old people:

Fundamentalist Christianity has left a residue of deep-seated shame and deprecation of traditional culture as something which has to do with a dark and sinful heathen past. This, perhaps allied with a reluctance to divulge too much to outsiders, and among younger people, difficulties in appreciating its relevance has conspired so far to dissuade Solomon islanders from writing about things which outsiders so easily assume they should be concerning themselves with. (*Pacific Writers*, 1986, p. 20)

Solomon Islanders do not want to write about traditions passing, but ex-patriots collecting and enquiring are more interested in those themes. There is no state patronage, commercial publishing or affluent book-buying public (and no bookshops outside the capital Honiara). Broadcasting does take place and the University of the South Pacific has encouraged writing and publishing with writers' workshops, as well.

Jully Sipolo

Her collection *Civilised Girl* (1981):

> broke new ground not only because it was the first published work of a woman writer, but also because, in content, it was the first attempt by any writer to comment seriously on the lot of women in the Solomon Islands. Her collection, powerfully piquant and poignant, forms the first feminist statement in Solomon Islands writing. (Maka'a and Oxenham, 1985, p. 5)

Jully Sipolo looks at the plight of women and men. In 'Sister's Lament' she addresses a woman whose promise has dissolved in drink, arguing that not only she, but all those who pinned their hopes on her have also lost:

> You were our hope.
> Our dreams were centred on you.
>   'Intelligent
>   Gifted
>   Talented
>   a genius'
>   ...
> You threw it away,
> The dream of a lifetime;
> All this
> For a sip of beer.

The engineer with his caravan and white Suzuki is clearly a colonialist in power in 'The Engineer'. The influx of Okinawa fishermen bringing strange music:

>   Clad in woollen jerseys
>   And track-suit trousers
>   Expensive radios

causes division, and intermixing: 'but there are half-castes now' (chanted by the Okinawa fishermen).

Of her own life as a working mother, her voiced loss is that 'my children don't know me'. 'Working Mother' and other poems examine the violence and hypocrisy hidden behind pleasant seeming local men, so in 'The Hypocrite' she notes that:

> He looked so innocent, so quiet and humble
> ... (in church) but then
> You showed your true self after the wedding
> Fangs bared, claws exposed
> a wolf in sheep's clothing

She comments on the discrepancy between men and women in terms of status and behaviours. Women are expected to be secondary to men and silent in the face of the men's empowered speech. In 'A Man's World' she comments that:

> My brother can sit on the table
> I mustn't
> He can say what he likes whenever he likes
> I must keep quiet
> He can order me around like a slave
> I must not back-chat

She must walk behind him, go round the back of the house to enter, and 'carry out [her] love affairs behind his back', knowing he has absolute power. She even has to pay compensation when she gets pregnant out of marriage.

The poems are sensitive and thoughtful testimonies to inequalities, love, family relations and the changing cultural world of the Solomon Islands.

TONGA

Tonga is a kingdom of 169 scattered islands, and a patrilineal society. Women do not inherit, and the complex extended family networks tie a range of children to relations. Women are absent from the modern political arena. More women have education at the primary level with a higher literacy rate generally, but only men proceed to tertiary education. In a society in a transitional stage between subsistence and a developing economy, social change is inevitable and some women have moved away from the dependence and responsibilities of the extended family and achieved, within a wage economy, a new status: 'the new status and the role of women is markedly influenced by the degree of economic freedom' (Tuivaga, 1988, in *Pacific Women*, p. 74). Tonga has a high literacy rate. Wood block – 'kupesi' – was its first printing system, but the absence of a Tongan alphabet delayed the use of printing as a dissemination of information (arriving with the missionaries in the early 1800s).

Konai Helu Thaman

Konai Thaman's poetry 'Marks a critical stage in the region's emotional history. It represents a shift towards a more open consciousness where traditional culture is no longer an immutable reality' (Subramani, 1992 [1985], p. 57). Her poetry, including *You, the choice of my parents* (1974), *Langakali* (1981), and *Higano* (1987), shows an ambivalence towards traditions and to colonial and post-colonial change, interrogating conventional assumptions of women's roles and Pacific Islander behaviours:

> I see myself dying slowly
> To family and traditions;
> Stripped of its will and carefree spirit,
> Naked on the cold and lonely waters
> Of a strange family shoreline
> Alienated from belonging truly
> ('You, the choice of my parents')

Konai Thaman writes of personal relationships and permanence. 'You, the choice of my parents' is a long poem, engaging with the double oppression of race/colonialism and gender. In 'My Blood' she writes:

> No Brother...
> My problem is not 'exploitation'
> Or unequal pay, or unawareness;
> My problem is that I

have been betrayed and tramped on
By my own blood.

Her poetry 'represents the place of women in traditional culture as one that is no longer unchallenged' (Buck, ed., 1992, p. 181).

There are a host of writers at the University of the South Pacific, Konai Thaman and Teresia Teaiwa among them, leading to the creation of a Pacific writers' forum within the literature and language department, headed by Arlene Griffen, and the success of 'Niu Wave' Dynamic Writers' Group.

Interviewed by Briar Wood, Konai Thaman says that in America she was not reading feminist but anti-colonial literature. Latterly she has become aware that her upbringing by her mother and two maiden aunts was not feminist and that the relationships between men and women in Tonga are 'complementary':

Even though Tonga was and still is a patriarchal society it never occurred to me that there was anything the boys could do that I couldn't do.... Our vernacular language itself isn't sexist ... my grandaunts were feminists before the word feminist became part of my vocabulary.   (Thaman, 1997, Interview with Wood, p. 7)

Briar Wood notes that her comments in poems are often about the difficulty of asking questions: 'the way the social structures are organised you can ask questions in particular contexts' (p. 7). One colleague working with women in a workshop found that she couldn't get them to raise questions about gender relations. Thaman suggests that facilitation to get them to raise these amongst themselves without her there is important:

Women talk a lot among themselves. There are things they would never talk about in mixed company, which again is something that development workers could pay more attention to. Because they're usually foreigners, they go in there and they see with their foreign eyes using their foreign observation tools and what they see is women who are subordinated, who cannot say anything, when in fact it isn't like that.   (Thaman, 1997, Interview with Wood, p. 8)

The line between the elders and children is breaking down. Tonga is a spiritual place based on the beliefs of hierarchies, knowledge and the chiefly ones – in Tongan society they were felt to have souls, and

Christianity gelled with this view. The women were always making garlands, a process called *'tui'*, of flowers divided into two types: *kakala hingoa* – the chiefly kakalas – and the more recently introduced non-fragrant *kakala verde*. In a layered garland you get both sorts and everyone wears *heilala* (garlands). Preservation of established ways is important, particularly now with nuclear families split off from elders, and so culture – Tongan studies – is taught in schools:

> culture changes but I think what I'm trying to do with the curriculum is to get students to be conscious that they have a culture, that it is not something you just discard, because one day it might come in handy.   (Thaman, 1997, Interview with Wood, p. 9)

She also acknowledges that, like the tradition of metaphorically clowning and putting on a mask, she adopts a persona in her poetry to speak out. Konai Thaman's poetry looks clearly at the realities of post-colonialism, mourning the loss of vitality of the past overcome with the imagery and popular culture of the late twentieth century. 'Island Fire' takes up these themes vividly with a mixture of images:

> Embers
> Of a once blazing
> Fire
> Sleep through an
> Endless night
> fraught with the din of
> billiard balls
> Hollywood violence
> Rock 'n' roll music
> And the slow turning of
> Foreign text book pages
> The embers wait
> Perhaps never to be
> Rekindled by
> Dry coconut leaves
> ... kerosene is easier.

A foreign culture's music, easy access to kerosene, and imported language have taken over from the once-blazing fire of the community and the past (in Subramani, 1992 [1985], p. 56).

VANUATU

Vanuatu is different again. There is a pyramidal pattern of population with a ratio of men to women much higher than elsewhere in the world, many women dying young, at around the age of 35, a result of carrying very heavy loads from the gardens, having to work harder than men, and in some cases due to violence inflicted by men. 'Whereas in most of the world women live longer than men, in Melanesia their lives are about six years shorter' (Kathleen Rarua, 1988, in *Pacific Women*, p. 79). The South Pacific is a region isolated from the rest of the world. Western civilisation and the development of culture and power are important and influential. Women's roles are being questioned: it is not enough to be seen as merely housewives and mothers, as well as victims of domestic violence in a patriarchal society where they are often breadwinners; however, there will need to be both economic change and governmental change to reflect and encourage development.

Vanuatu has many languages, some of which are disappearing. Publishing there is difficult. With the main languages English, French and Bislama (pidgin), financing publications with small print runs proves a difficulty and there is a problem about the cost of books so an unfair situation results whereby Vanuatu and other Pacific Islanders, giving their knowledge and time to foreign researchers, are unable to buy the books or read them in libraries. There are some writers' groups in the holidays. Vanuatu also has a comparatively large number of bookstores, some church-run and, previously, Co-operatives. There are public libraries in main towns and schools but few local writers, partly because of the need to publish everything in both French and English and in Bislama – but not in the whole 110 languages spoken in Vanuatu (van Trease, 1985, pp. 24–9).

Grace Molisa

'Grace Molisa's poetry is polemical and political, arising as it did directly out of her work for the Vanuatu Party which came to power after Vanuatu's independence in 1980' (Griffen, 1997, p. 23). She began writing by accident with her first poem, 'Vatu invocation', a response to a government document on tourism. She says that:

poetry actually is for me a personal way of filing away subjects that have weighed on my mind, issues that take a lot of thinking

about.... There are many, many different ways in which one copes
with frustration. (Griffen, 1997, p. 23)

'Hers is a personal use of language to wage war with words against
injustices that words help to produce and perpetuate' (Griffen, 1997,
p. 23). She uses words for anti-colonialist and feminist purposes
against language which oppresses. Arlene Griffen finds Grace
Molisa's poetry without aesthetic 'flights of fancy' or metre but quite
a straight attack – but I find much of it is in the relation between the
oral and scripted traditions – repetitive, see 'Custom':

Custom   inadvertently
is an English word   misappropriating
English   'custom'
a confluence   misapplied
of streams of words   bastardised
is a reservoir   a frankenstein
of every shade   corpse
nuance and hue   conveniently
sharply   recalled
contrasting   it intimidate
Melanesia's   women
limited vocabulary   the timid
supplementing   the ignorant
non-verbal   the weak.
communication.

(*Black Stone*, 1983, p. 24)

She is outspoken about the enforced self-effacement of Vanuatu
women, the ways in which foreign women and feminism elsewhere
are lauded but denigrated at home ('Delightful Acquiescence', 1983,
p. 24). Men, including her own partner, insist on children and marriage, then refuse the responsibilities and fail to support the pain
and the upbringing ('Coming of Age', 1989). In 'Delightful Acquiescence' she notes that:

Everybody loves
a self-effacing
submissive woman

Vanuatu men and women
love self-effacing

acquiescing women
...
Any woman showing promise
is clouted
into acquiescence.
Vanuatu loves
self-effacing, acquiescing
submissive slavish, women

(1989, p. 24)

Each line is transient except the last three, which start with 'a time of . . .' to build up an oral rhythm exploding finally into:

A time for taking
that step
ever forward
with Confidence.

(1989, p. 25)

In 'Village Women' she pays homage to the variety of hard work carried out by Vanuatu women. They work endlessly, are honest with no illusions or hypocrisy:

Vanuatu
village
women
carry
their country
on their shoulders.

(1989, p. 29)

She celebrates children in 'Children' as:

my pride
my pearls
of great price
measures
of my being
and potential

(1989, p. 28)

Talking of colonialism and racism using the phrase 'the isle of illusion', she points out the hypocrisy of white men who insisted that local people were ignorant and 'beasts of burden' but were happy to 'copulate / like others / and procreate / all hues' so that:

> Could
> it
> be
> that the
> wild
> and woolly
> tropical
> fruits
> of the Isles
> of Illusion
> be Sour grapes?
>
> (Molisa, 1989, p. 31, 'In the Eye
> of the Beholder')

The theme of this and 'Women', which follows it, is the exotic, erotic illusion peddled to and by Europeans about the islanders and women of the islands as backward, 'virile fruits' ready for harvesting.

SAMOA

Samoans have historically produced '*fagogo*', which are oral stories:

> The speakers were different, the story tellers different. But the stories, the way in which they were told, coupled with the closeness of the evening as family members lay together cocooned in the *false* security, helped create the Samoans' love of story, admiration of the storyteller's art, and fascination with the power of words: or 'telling it the *fagogo* way'.   (Dunlop, 1985, p. 41)

Oratory is strong and listeners are well aware of appropriate format in relation to occasion. Allusions to past historical events and traditional sayings add support and beauty to the stories: 'The love of words, building up into logical argument and woven into intricate plots, allusion and innuendo are all here' (Dunlop, 1985, p. 41), but parents do not usually encourage children to read and write unless it is for school – so oral literature, in effect, is strong. Books were a *'palagi'* thing for early Samoans, sometimes rejected because introduced by foreigners representing power and correctness. Students travelling abroad to study brought back ideas and the 1960s' challenges fuelled desires for nationhood and a national identity, reflected in literary works. This also included the alliances with Black Power movements. Fanaafi Maiai had previously published *Stories of Old Samoa* in New Zealand readers, and she and her brother Semisi began translating materials in the Samoan language. She tried to recapture the Samoan *fagogo* in translation, and translated European stories into Samoan for others to read, particularly *The Black Tulip*, and *Treasure Island*, among others featuring 'the South Seas'. Semisi moved on to try and find out the characteristics which ensured a story was being told in an interesting swaying *'fagogo'* way in Samoan. *Fagogo* tales were 'set pieces',

> dealing with universal themes of acceptable or unacceptable behaviours, with the right behaviour always conquering in the end. The suffusion of the supernatural element through the tales, may also have served to distance the action/moral from present reality. Bad things afar were not so personally threatening. The listeners could sit spellbound, in the knowledge that 'they were not like that' – a valuable defence mechanism.   (Dunlop, 1985, p. 49)

This derives from an oral history where the *pièce de résistance* of the orator in traditional society was always the *'pe'e'* (ancient historical song), and its status remains high in today's society (Taipo, p. 83, in *Pacific Writers*).

In the 1960s Albert Wendt, Samoa's foremost writer, began to be published, his work resembling that of a *fagogo* artist: swaying people, myth making. He worked to promote the creative talents of others. In the 1970s writers produced more work in the vernacular in poetry and story form, encouraged by the University of the South Pacific, and an annual short story competition was started, published in *Mana*, edited and published by the Samoan Writers' Association and read over the radio, taking the stories into homes to let people hear what became 'the *fagogo* of the air'. Children preferred to listen to radio, and many didn't want to hear the old repetitive traditional plots with supernatural intervention and blurring of real and unreal elements. These listeners lapped up the new short stories, many of which were highly topical, some very critical of everyday life and events: 'the story writers' response was shown in broader plot development and character reactions, instead of the mere chronicling of events' (*Pacific Writers*, pp. 60–1). The family of one writer, Dunlop tells us, were forced to carry out a forgiveness ceremony because she had overstepped the mark.

Momoe von Reiche

The work of Momoe von Reiche similarly questions cultural conflicts and the loss of tradition. Her poetry tends to be autobiographical and to mourn a lost Samoan way of life. She captures moments of anger and compassion, tenderness, loneliness and jealousy in personal poems. She also writes explicitly feminist poetry, often concerned with male infidelity. This initially met with hostility because of the subject matter. Sex was not considered appropriate for poetry. As Subramani comments: 'the men in her poetry are egotistical, self-absorbed. . . . The feelings of the persona explode in defiance and hostility' (Subramani, 1992 [1985], p. 85):

> I'm tired of wearing my soul out
> For the tall young man
> With penis vanity
> That hangs out of his mouth.
> His pride sits between
> His balls and views the world
> Through underwear eyes.
>   ('To Keri', in Subramani, 1992 [1985], p. 85)

It is not surprising that a poem so very explicit should cause a furore in an area where women were usually unlikely to speak out, and certainly not for publication. Momoe von Reiche represents a nostalgia for the loss of Samoan ways of life. She avoids anti-colonial sentiments, instead celebrating the earth:

> . . . the mountains of
> Solaua have more
> Warmth than
> His brown eyes
>   ('Solaua' in Subramani, 1992 [1985], p. 58)

COOK ISLANDS

Arthur Taipo says of writing in the Cook Islands that:

> Three well-defined periods shape the Cook islands writing: the missionary era, the colonial era and the era of self-government. The vernacular blossomed during the missionary era but waned during the colonial period. Lately, it shows signs of resurgence. Very little could grow during the colonial era but a contemporary well-spring has developed in the twenty years since self-government was attained. ('Writing in the Cook islands', *Pacific Writers*, p. 78)

The first printing press came from Tahiti and people wrote in Maori until the annexation by New Zealand where, after the turn of the century, it became a sin to speak Maori well into the twentieth century until teacher Taira Rere, a prolific writer, revived it. Work by the Frisbies (see pp. 000–0) appeared during the colonial era, and with self-government political writing appeared (well established even in the nineteenth century).

Oceanic/Pacific Rim women writers tackle exotic stereotypes and reflect on their lives and their islands' beauty, many aided and influenced by the University of the South Pacific.

15

Writing by Women from Cyprus

O cursed pair of breeches
Which rustle like taca-taca,
Who now is going to wash my breeches
In the lake?
And who will put them
On a line to dry?

O my lady from Yeroskipos,
Where are your promises now?

(A song/poem from 'The Strong Man'
quoted by Colin Thubron in *Journey into Cyprus*)

The rich poetry of Cyprus, well established since ancient days (twenty-seven centuries ago), is flourishing again now. One of its features is a love of the countryside, another is a rather romantic response to relationships (or in the case of the quotation above, an equally conventional, conservative response: a sense of loss at the removal of domestic service!):

> Two of the basic ingredients of Cypriot poetry are myth and history. And if we identify myth with the lyrical aspects of poetry, history lies behind the tragic aspect. Light and darkness, life and death, joy and sorrow, dream and harsh reality mark the course of this outpost of hellenism. These are the poles around which the circles of this island's fate have been carved out since ancient times.   (Kouyialis, 1983, p. 1)

This chapter looks at a variety of poetry mostly by Greek Cypriot women, including Niki Ladaki-Philippou, Niki Marangou, Nayia Roussou and others. One Turkish woman poet, Nesie Yasin, is also discussed and the travel and 'local diary' kind of writing by British residents in Cyprus is mentioned. Much poetry by women is politicised, the love of the island expressed through images of relationships, and vice versa with, ironically perhaps, very little feminist response to the kinds of gender-politics assumptions of the poem above. Women's writing has gradually developed with education and independence. On the island of love and machismo, it tends to deal with political partition, identity, the landscape and natural beauty of the country, motherhood, marriage and relationships.

Cyprus is a beautiful island at the edge of the eastern Mediterranean. This geographical location largely explains its divisions. It is relentlessly modern and consumerist, and dependably traditionalist. An ex-British colony (independent since the 1960s), Cyprus is currently planning to join the European Union, but is also geographically very close to Middle Eastern countries such as Turkey, Israel and Egypt. Some of the highly committed literary expression of national identity springs from its politically troubled history, and its continuing natural beauty. Cyprus has been invaded and owned by the Venetians, the Romans and the English among others; sometimes used tragically as a pawn in tussles for power between supernations; granted independence from Britain in 1960, and divided after the 1974 war following the power moves of the Greek Junta and the Turkish invasion.

The island, once relatively peacefully housing Turkish and Greek Cypriots side by side in towns, villages and businesses, became bitterly and bloodily split and as the North came under Turkish rule so Greeks lost their homes and fortunes, and Turks were removed from the South. Cyprus, now a very popular tourist location, was filled with refugees from both sides. But they are resilient, stubborn, hard-working and independent and each side has built homes, restaurants, businesses and farms back up again. Poetry from the Greek side of Cyprus is far more accessible than that from the Turkish side, especially that of women poets, but I did not want to confine myself to that of the Greek Cypriot women writers alone so there are also examples here from a Turkish woman poet, Nesie Yasin, who has collaborated with Greek and Turkish artists and poets. There is also writing from British ex-patriots who have settled there and now write of the natural beauties and the cultural vagaries of the place, an island rich in machismo and philosophy, tourism and the maintenance of certain traditions in relation to women's roles, family relationships, and male dominance.

Historically, Cypriot poetry began with hymns and religious poetry, then folk songs from individuals and anonymous sources, taking from idioms and forms found in Homer, and adapting and incorporating forms from the various and many conquerors of the island whose poetry seems to have influenced it even as have their cooking habits. In the late nineteenth century the printing press encouraged publication and Greek influence grew, so that we see poetry written in at least three versions of Greek: in the literary language Katharevousa, in Panhellenic or Demotic Greek, and in Cypriot dialect. Latterly there has been much poetry written in or translated into English.

Education is in Greek, or Turkish, but many students in secondary school learn English, and because of Cyprus's international contacts and history everybody speaks some English. It is not surprising, then, that much of the poetry is in English, but also that there is an issue of national pride and identity about writing in Cypriot dialect, a claiming of identity we can also find in many other post-colonial countries. Poets can choose to be read internationally should they write in English but to be able to catch more sensitively the lilt of their own tongue and relate to national identity and awareness, to make a statement about their origins and represent the lives of their own people, they need to write in their own language.

There is a long history of oral poetry and still, yearly, there is in May (during Pentecost or Whitsuntide), on the coast, a week-long festival, 'Kataklismos', at which oral poets deliver up their works to large audiences in the Greek Cypriot dialect. This sometimes involves 'public bantering with rhyming couplets usually verging on a heated argument' (Nadjarian, 1998, p. 61). These kinds of dialogue poems resemble the choice of dialogue in poetry by Caribbeans Amryl Johnson and Jean 'Binta' Breeze. This kind of oral performance poetry is much more of a male activity than a female one (such performance being frowned on as unladylike, perhaps) but testifies to the established importance of orality on the island. One singer/ song-writer described by Nadjarian (1998) as caught up in the largely male activities is 61-year-old Kyriakou Pelagia dubbed 'the singer of our roots', who has revived the Cypriot folk song, and also writes her own, initially disapproved of by her father because 'it was not a suitable profession for a girl in those days' (Nadjarian, 1998, p. 62). Although there is education for men and for women, and a university now in Nicosia, as well as universal secondary education, there are entrenched gender divisions and expectations.

The island has moved rapidly into the late twentieth century with regards to videos, tourism, fast cars and fashionable clothes, but fathers are fiercely protective of daughters (who were chaperoned even in the 1960s). Weddings, christenings and other family gatherings are enormous and highly traditional, and women play conventional (pre-feminist critique) domestic roles as well as holding down jobs, and donning black for life (or almost) if their husbands die. It is an island of village and town, where extended families live in mountain villages, visited by their cosmopolitan offspring on Sundays and for holidays, and everybody decamps to the hills in the boiling summer as the tourists flock to the seashores.

Women in the capital, Nicosia, run bookshops, write poetry and lead intellectual lives and it is here that the Cypriot women poets can be found, or, like Niki Ladaki-Philippou, some have emigrated to Greece, the USA, the UK or Australia, for there are many more millions of Greek and Turkish Cypriots abroad than at home.

Not surprisingly, the political division of Cyprus is a cause of many poems recording pain, the absence of loved ones, and memories of loss. Niki Ladaki-Philippou talks of 'Strolling on the walls / of Nicosia' and recalling the permanent destruction of such division:

> Your memory
> a whispering shadow
> a sword falling heavily
> on our life.
>
> Ever present
> the line
> dividing our city.
>   (Ladaki-Philippou, 1994, 'Preface: VII')

Kyrenia, a particularly lovely part of Northern Cyprus, is mourned by many and in the poem of the same name it is seen to remain in the memory, and imprinted on the movements and clothing of the poet:

> Kyrenia
> your jasmines
> have sprung up in our hearts and your beaches
> still clap against
> our children's heels. . . . Crumpled
> in the palm

> of Pentadactylos.
> Kyrenia
> ravished flower
> on the embroidered skirts
> of the girls of Cyprus
> (Ladaki-Philippou, 1994, p. 123)

She writes of her relationship with her mother and the mothers of the whole of Cyprus: 'The amalgamation of religion and country, the nature and life of Cyprus, as well as folk-song rhythms constitute the nucleus for the poetry of Niki Ladaki-Philippou' (Stephanides, 1994, p. 29). She writes of love, the Virgin Mary, mothering, and loss and relates these to the pain of Cyprus and that of the mothers of Cyprus.

Nayia Roussou, Head of Public Relations at the Cyprus International Broadcasting Company, writes from her position in the media and mass-communications particularly in her *Memories of War* (1975), containing poems and articles, *Testimony from Beyond the Borderland* (1988), a collection of poems, and *Transit* (1982). This was followed by *The Channels of Ariadne* (1985), which contains marks of personal grief for the transitory and the unseen, for 'lost communication' and 'plentiful moments of national and sometimes of universal concern about the change and the threat to man's intellectual values, about the threat to our own cultural values and roots in Cyprus and about the bitter metamorphosis generally, of the cultural and intellectual interior of our planet' (Theocharous, 1994, pp. 11, 12).

Enraged and tender, her poems are testimonies to the changes in Cyprus and the world, and are politically and ecologically charged. In the collection *Testimony on the Borderless Line: Along the Attila Line*, about villages in the Turkish-occupied North, in the prologue she notes:

> Light feather
> heavy feather,
> the barbed wire persists.
> The Word does the same
> (Roussou, 1988, in Theocharous, 1994)

As with many other Cypriot women poets, Nayia Roussou uses the imagery of gardens, orchards, fruits and flowers, of bread ovens and domestic settings, to testify to the loss she and others feel about the partition and the more widespread destruction in the world, over which many people simply respond with distanced lethargy (see *The Channels of Ariadne*, 1985). In the Epilogue from 'Ayios Sozomenos' and from *Testimony on the Borderless Line* she notes:

> And the blossoming lemon-tree
> the fruitful olive tree
> phantoms of Absence. . . . The oven cold,
> for years,
> is now filled with snakes.
> Where is the bread of life?
>
> (Roussou, 1988, in Theocharous, 1994)

In her 'Rage of Second June', Excerpt no. 1 ('Second June' is the Cypriot word for July) she conjures up a powerful mixture of the main imagery of fruitfulness, and destruction which is both real and surreal:

> I hold joy in my eyes,
> an armful of citrus fruit
> from Morphou
> and a bag of bullets.
>
> (Roussou, 1994, p. 38)

Morphou is now part of Turkish-occupied Northern Cyprus. 'Cyprus, / a cyclamen / deflowered' is how Klairi Angelidou (1994, p. 808) views Cyprus, using a mixture of natural imagery and the language of destruction and loss.

As her own personal reminder, another Nicosia-born woman poet, Niki Marangou, plants her garden with roses from around the world and so celebrates both the transitory and history:

> In company with the aphid and the grasshopper
> I have planted roses in the garden this year
> instead of writing poems
> the centifolia from the house in mourning at Ayios
> Thomas
> The sixty-petaled rose Midas brought from Phrygia
> The Banksian that came from China
> cuttings from the last mouchette that survived
> in the old town,

    but especially Rosa Gallica, brought by the Crusaders
    (otherwise known as damascene)
    with its exquisite perfume.

                                         (Marangou, 'Roses', 1998, p. 56)

The various histories and legacies of Cyprus are entwined in this poem.

Writing about Niki Marangou, Andriana Ierodiaconou and Nasa Patapiou, the latter two from the Karpas region, now occupied by the Turkish, Stephanos Stephanides (1994/5) comments that their work focuses on loss and change but also transcends history, looking to the quality of life:

> Each of the poets, in her particular voice, style, and feeling, inspires reflection – in a dialectic of death and regeneration – on the meaning of our familial and communal relations, and on the thread of identity and life in the images, rhythms, myths, dreams and rituals of our world, our natural environment, in the acts and habits of our everyday life, and in our historical and geographic dispersion. Each writes in a style that can be identified with modernism and its aftermath.   (Stephanides, 1994/5, p. 796)

There is a specific historical location for these writers, whose work post-dates the nationalism that sprang from the version of modernism developing in Cyprus poetry after the 1974 invasion and division. Stephanides translates the poems, but so do women. Andriana Ierodiaconou was born in Nicosia in 1952 and studied science at Oxford then Berkeley, California. Her poetry looks at her family, history, the division in 'Aishe', she imagines the lives of those living in her house in the occupied North – hosted by the family who pre-dated them. The house and courtyard are beautifully described:

> At the hour when the rose bush ceases its small white song at the yard's edge when the last artichoke dies with a small weeping.
> ('Aishe', in Stephanides, 1994/5, p. 807)

At this moment the bewildered stranger 'who lives in our old house' awakens and asks 'Aishe, who is beating the child', hearing a ghostly sound of loss. At that moment too, others implicated notice change and disillusionment:

The new solder outside the village suddenly notices the paint fading on the new sign. ('Aishe', in Stephanides, 1994/5, p. 807)

Her sense and expression of loss and change recalls the early twentieth-century poet Charlotte Mew. In 'Ballad of the Young Son' the sense of loss and personal pain is strong, concerned with families internalising the pain of loss caused by war.

That man's son they killed.

Since then his hair's got white or perhaps he's aged
he only sits in clubs like a broken sentence
he doesn't speak of death
('Ballad of the Young Son', in Stephanides, 1994/5, p. 808)

He seems too to have died, as it seems perhaps his wife, disappeared since their loss, might also have died. The emptiness echoes around the cafés and village. The parallels between popular culture, enjoyed but ignored, and the politics on their doorsteps are clearly defined:

Ordinary folk sit on chairs
drinking KEO, eating souvlaki, watching
and saying 'politics don't concern me'
while at the cinema
the old man John Wayne kills his enemies
('Summertime Poem', in Stephanides, 1994/5, p. 810)

Vines, almond blossoms, pomegranates, souvlaki, beer, sunshine, villages, cafés – the colours and descriptions of Cyprus evoke continuity, as well as loss. Mothers mourn, aunts pack up, children play – life continues but with loss.

Nasa Patapiou from the Karpas region relates her poems of identity to the beauty of the landscape, integrating the everyday contemporary with the mythical, positioning the unusual, chunky-tailed Cypriot mountain sheep, the Moufflon (sometimes used as a symbol of the island and largely living in the Cedar Valley, which was heavily bombed in the 1974 war), as her myth-inspired companion – a kind of permanent natural reminder of Cyprus and its history. In 'Solace' the Moufflon travels with her, friendly or wild, a reminder of death and loss, history, myth, her roots and self-definition, like a lover and a beloved country 'It tortures me / And it caresses' (in Stephanides, 1994/5, p. 831). Unusually, she has also produced a poem written from the body – equating herself with the landscape and with fecund nature, in 'Woman without Boundaries' she says:

> As I traverse
> the Gardens of
> Aphrodite
> And my body
> Bends
> My succulent fruits
> Drip milk
> Hope for
> The newborn.
>
> (1994/5, p. 832)

Nesie Yasin, a Turkish poet, also writes of loss and of Nicosia, particularly in a beautifully illustrated volume, *Nicosia* (1995). In 'Unseen Letters' Yasin uses the extended metaphor of lovers separated and the splitting of the city of Nicosia so that each reference to 'access', 'commanders', 'independent federal', 'betrayal', relates to the betrayal of the divided city which she loves, and her own lover:

> I will come barefoot as everyone sleeps
> in the same city
> walls cut across my path
>
> (Yasin, 'Unsent Letters', 1995, p. 81)

Where 'love is a national traitor' she writes, in a series of letters, of being parted by the walls and checkpoints, wire and hostility (a comparison with the divisions of Berlin), which separate the Greek from the Turkish side of Nicosia and Cyprus. In 'Letter 7th' she makes a direct political statement reminiscent of the anti-positivistic, patriarchal world views which led to war, seen in the work of Virginia Woolf (*Three Guineas*), Olive Schreiner, and others:

> no force can unite the United Nations
> as long as nations exist
> I want peace
> between woman and man
>
> (Yasin, 'Letter 7th', 1995, p. 93)

But for her, consistently, there is 'no permission to cross' so she imagines she could gain 'access to love' if she were to dress as a cat and claim the freedom that form would allow (Yasin, 'Letter 19th', 1994, p. 99). A poem pairing the pain and loss of, on the one hand, a beloved harmonica, left in the north when fleeing to the south, and on the other an almond tree, left in the south when fleeing to the north, 'Refugee Children' develops into a greater sadness and loss when, in 'Dead Children', on each side a child victim asks the same question, 'People, why must I die / People I was still just a child' (Yasin, 1994, p. 105). They are politically charged, personal and emotional poems, historical, universal and also individualised.

Women's travel writing is a feature of that of visitors and settlers and much of it follows that alternative routing of women's travel writing, commenting not on the main attractions but on local events and local individuals, vividly describing the flowers in spring, the sunsets, small children and family gatherings, as well as the landscapes. British-born writers largely choose prose but also celebrate the beauties of the island. Sheila Hawkins has produced a short series of books and journal articles on settling on the island, commenting on, for instance, setting up home, owls nesting, local landscape (1997). Some of the richest writing by non-Cypriots was that of women travellers in the late nineteenth and early twentieth centuries, and right through the century. Friends of Lawrence Durrell visited the island prior to the 1974 division, and women travellers produced books on the island, such as those by Esme Scott-Stevenson, Lady Brassey, Agnes Smith and then Lady Elisabeth Amelia Lewis. In the Second World War period, the traveller Freya Stark wrote vividly of its landscapes and the surprise meetings with local peoples.

Love and the beauty of the countryside of Cyprus reverberate throughout the writing produced by Cypriot poets and visitors. Often nature imagery represents political strife, geographical and political divisions, and differences in relationships, as the sexual politics and wider politics of the island are expressed through women's writing.

Bibliography

Chapter 1 Introduction

Ashcroft, Bill, Griffiths, Gareth and Tiffin, Helen (eds) (1989), *The Empire Writes Back* (London: Routledge).

Astley, Thea (1987), *It's Raining in Mango* (Sydney: Penguin).

Bakhtin, Mikhail (1981), *The Dialogic Imagination*, ed. Michael Holquist, and trans. Carol Emerson and Michael Holquist (Austin: University of Austin Press).

Belsey, Catherine (1980), *Critical Practice* (London: Methuen).

Boehmer, Elleke (1995), *Colonial and Postcolonial Literature: Migrant Metaphors* (Oxford: Oxford University Press).

Burford, Barbara (1987), 'The Landscapes Painted on the Inside of my Skin', *Spare Rib*, no. 179 (July).

Busby, Margaret (1992), *Daughters of Africa* (London: Vintage).

Carr, Helen (1985), 'Woman/Indian, the American: and his Others', in F. Barker, P. Hulme, M. Iverson and D. Loxley (eds), *Europe and its Others*, vol. 2 (Colchester: University of Essex Press).

Childs, Peter and Williams, Patrick (1997), *An Introduction to Post-Colonial Theory* (Hemel Hempstead: Harvester Wheatsheaf).

Chrisman, Laura and Williams, Patrick (eds) (1993), *Colonial Discourse and Post-Colonial Theory* (Hemel Hempstead: Prentice-Hall).

Christian, Barbara (1985), *Black Feminist Criticism: Perspectives on Black Women Writers* (London: Pergamon).

Cixous, Hélène (1981), 'The Laugh of the Medusa', in Elaine Marks and Isabelle de Courtivron (eds), *New French Feminism* (Brighton: Harvester).

Cooper, Caroline (1993), *Noises in the Blood* (London: Macmillan).

Dabydeen, David (1991), *Literature in the Modern World*, A316, BBC and Open University television production.

Davis, Angela (1982), *Women, Race and Class* (London: The Women's Press).

Davies, Carol Boyce (1994), *Black Women, Writing and Identity* (London: Routledge).

Dirks, Nicholas B. (1992), *Colonialism and Culture* (Ann Arbor, Michigan: University of Michigan Press).

Dirlik, Arif (1994), 'The Post Colonial Aura: Third World Criticisms in the Age of Global Capitalism', *Critical Inquiry*, 20, 2 (Winter).

During, Simon (1991), 'Waiting for the Post: Some Relations between Modernity, Colonization and Writing', in Helen Tiffin and Ian Adam (eds), *Past the Last Post: Theorizing Post-colonialism and Post-modernism* (Hemel Hempstead: Harvester).

Eagleton, Terry (1991), *Ideology: An Introduction* (London and New York: Verso).

Evans, Mari (1985), *Black Women Writers* (London: Pluto Press).

Faludi, Susan (1992), *Backlash* (London: Vintage).

Fanon, Frantz (1952), *Black Skin, White Masks* (London: Pluto Press).

Fanon, Frantz (1963), *The Wretched of the Earth* (Harmondsworth, Middlesex: Penguin).

Fanon, Frantz (1990 [1961]), 'On National Culture', in D. Walder (ed.), *Literature in the Modern World* (Oxford: Oxford University Press).

Fieldhouse, D. K. (1982), *The Colonial Empires* (London: Macmillan).

Foucault, M. (1976), *A History of Sexuality: An Introduction*, trans. Robert Hurley (Harmondsworth: Penguin).

Gilman, Sander (1992), 'Black Bodies, White Bodies: Towards an Iconography of Female Sexuality in Late Nineteenth-Century Art, Medicine and Literature', in J. Donald and A. Rattansi (eds), *Race, Culture and Difference* (London: Sage Publications, in association with the Open University).

Henderson, Mae Gwendolen (1993), 'Speaking in Tongues: Dialogics, Dialectics and the Black Woman Writer's Literary Tradition', in Laura Chrisman and Patrick Williams (eds), *An Introduction to Post-Colonial Theory* (Hemel Hempstead: Prentice-Hall).

hooks, bell (1989), *Talking Back: Thinking Feminist, Thinking Black* (Boston, Mass.: South End Press).

Hurston, Zora Neale (1986), *Their Eyes Were Watching God* (London: Virago).

Irigaray, Luce (1985), *This Sex which is Not One* (New York: Cornell University Press).

Jameson, Frederick (1971), *Marxism and Form: Twentieth-Century Dialectical Theories of Literature* (Princeton: Princeton University Press).

Kaplan, Cora (1986), 'Keeping the Colour in *The Color Purple*', in *Sea Changes* (London: Verso).

Kiberd, Declan (1995), *Inventing Ireland* (London: Jonathan Cape).

Kristeva, Julia (1980), *Desire in Language: A Semiotic Approach to Literature and Art* (New York: Columbia University Press).

Kristeva, Julia (1991), *Strangers to Ourselves* (London: Harvester Wheatsheaf).

Lacan, J. (1977), *Écrits: A Selection*, trans. Alan Sheridon (London: Tavistock).

Loomba, Ania (ed.) (1998), *Colonialism/Post Colonialism* (London: Routledge).

Lorde, Audre (1984) interviewed in *Black Women Writers at Work*, ed. Claudia Tate (New York: Continuum).

McLintock, Anne (1992), 'The Angel of Progress: Pitfalls of the Term "Colonialism" ', in *Social Text*, 31/32, reprinted in Chrisman and Williams (1993).

Mignolo, Walter D. (1994), Introduction to *Poetics Today*, 215, 4 (Winter).

Minh-Ha, Trinh (1989), *Woman, Native, Other: Writing Postcoloniality and Feminism* (Bloomington, Ind.: Indiana University Press).

Mishra, Vijay and Hodge, Bob (1991), 'What is a Post(-)colonialism?' *Textual Practice*, 5, 3.

Mohanty, Chandra Talpade (1988), 'Under Western Eyes: Feminist Scholarship and Colonial Discourses', in *Feminist Review*, 30 (Autumn), pp. 65–88.

Mongia, Padmini (1996), *Contemporary Post-Colonial Theory* (London: Arnold).

Nasta, Susheila (ed.) (1991), *Motherlands: Black Women's Writing from Africa, the Caribbean and South Asia* (London: The Women's Press).

Ngcobo, Lauretta (1987), *Let it be Told: Black Women Writers in Britain* (London: Virago).

Parmar, Pratibha and Amos, Valerie (1997), 'Challenging Imperial Feminism', in Heidi Safia Mirza (ed.), *Black British Feminism* (London: Routledge).

Rutherford, Anna; Jensen, Lars and Chew, Shirley (1994), *Into the Nineties: Post-colonial Women's Writing* (Armidale, New South Wales: Kunapipi, Dangaroo Press).

Said, Edward (1978), *Orientalism: Western Conceptions of the Orient* (London: Penguin).

Said, Edward (1993), *Culture and Imperialism* (London: Chatto).

Sheshadri-Crook, Kalpana (1994), 'The Primitive as Analysis: Postcolonial Feminism's Access to Psychoanalysis', in *Cultural Critique*, 28 (Fall), pp. 175–218.

Slemon, Stephen (1990), 'Unsettling the Empire Resistance Theory', in *World Literature Written in English*, 30, 2.

Slemon, Stephen (1991), 'Modernism's Last Post', in Ian Adam and Helen Tiffin (eds), *Past the Last Post: Theorizing Post-colonialism and Post-modernism* (Hemel Hempstead: Harvester Wheatsheaf).

Smith, Barbara (1982), 'Towards a Black Feminist Criticism', in Gloria T. Hull et al. (eds), *All the Women are White, All the Blacks are Men, But Some of us are Brave: Black Women's Studies* (London: Feminist Press).

Spivak, Gayatri and Gunew, Sneja (1986), 'Questions of Multiculturalism', in *Hecate*, 12, 1/2.

Spivak, G. (1988), 'Can the Subaltern Speak?' in C. Nelson and L. Grossberg (eds), *Marxism and the Interpretation of Culture* (London: Macmillan).

Spivak, G. (1987), *In Other Worlds: Essays in Cultural Politics* (London: Methuen).

Spivak, G. and Suleri, S. (eds) (1989), *Woman–Nation–State* (London: Macmillan).

Spivak, Gayatri (1990), interviewed in *The Post Colonial Critic: Interviews, Strategies, Dialogues*, ed. Sarah Harasym (London: Routledge).

Suleri, Sara (1992), 'Woman Skin Deep: Feminism and the Post-colonial Condition', in *Critical Inquiry*, 18 (Summer).

Tate, Claudia (1984), *Black Women Writers at Work* (New York: Continuum).

Thieme, John (ed.) (1996), *The Arnold Anthology of Post-Colonial Literatures in English* (London: Edward Arnold).

Tiffin, Helen and Adam, Ian (1993), *Past the Last Post: Theorizing Post-Colonialism and Post-Modernism* (Harvester Wheatsheaf).

Tiffin, Chris and Lawson, Alan (1994), *De-scribing Empire: Post-Colonialism and Textuality* (London: Routledge).

Walder, Dennis (1998), *Post-Colonial Literatures in English* (London: Edward Arnold).

Wisker, Gina (1993), *Insights into Black Women's Writing* (London: Macmillan).

Chapter 2   African American Women's Writing

Allen Shockley, Ann (1988), *Afro-American Women Writers, 1746–1933* (Boston: G. K. Hall).

Angelou, Maya (1989), 'Rosa Guy and Maya Angelou', in Jeffrey M. Elliott, *Conversations with Maya Angelou* (London: Virago).

Angelou, Maya (1970), *I Know Why the Caged Bird Sings* (London: Virago).

Angelou, Maya and Chrisman, Robert (1977), in Jeffrey Elliott (1989), *Conversations with Maya Angelou* (London: Virago).

Bethel, Lorraine (1982a), in B. Smith et al. (eds), *But Some of Us Are Brave: Black Women's Studies* (London: The Feminist Press).

Bethel, Lorraine (1982b), ' "This Infinity of Conscious Pain": Zora Neale Hurston and the Black Female Literary Tradition', in Smith et al. (eds), *But Some of Us Are Brave* (London: The Feminist Press).

Brooks, Gwendolyn (1946), *A Street in Bronzeville*.

Brooks, Gwendolyn (1949), *Annie Allen*.

Brooks, Gwendolyn (1953), *Maud Martha*.

Brooks, Gwendolyn (1956), *The Bean Eaters*.

Brooks, Gwendolyn (1972), *Report from Part One: The Autobiography of Gwendolyn Brooks* (Detroit: Broadside Press).

Busby, Margaret (1992), *Daughters of Africa* (London: Vintage).

Chrisman, Robert (1977), in Jeffrey M. Elliott (ed.) (1989), *Conversations with Maya Angelou* (London: Virago).

Elliott, Jeffrey (1989), *Conversations with Maya Angelou* (London: Virago).

Evans, Mari (1985), *Black Women Writers* (London: Pluto).

Gates Jr, Louis Henry and McKay, Nellie Y. (1997), *The Norton Anthology of African American Literature* (New York: Norton).

Gomez, Jewelle (1991), *The Gilda Stories* (London: Sheba).

Greene, Gayle and Kahn, Coppelia (1985), *Making a Difference* (London: Methuen).

Hurston, Zora Neale (1934), *Jonah's Gourd Vine* (Philadelphia: J. P. Lippincott).

Hurston, Zora Neale (1990), *Mules and Men* (New York: Harper Perennial; [1935] Philadelphia: J. P. Lippincott).

Hurston, Zora Neale (1986), *Their Eyes were Watching God* (London: Virago; [1937] Philadelphia: J. P. Lippincott).

Hurston, Zora Neale (1986), *Dust Tracks on a Road* (London: Virago; [1942] Philadelphia: J. P. Lippincott).

Hurston, Zora Neale (1930), to Mrs Mason, 25 November 1930, Alain Locke Papers, Howard University Library, Florida.

Hurston, Zora Neale (*c*.1938), 'Folklore' typescript, Florida Federal Writers' Project.

Jacobs, Harriet (1861), *Incidents in the Life of a Slave Girl*, reprinted in Henry Louis Gates Jr and Nellie Y. McKay (1997), *The Norton Anthology of African American Literature* (New York: W. W. Norton).

Larsen, Nella (1928), *Quicksand* (New York: Knopf).

Larsen, Nella (1929), *Passing* (New York: Knopf).

Lorde, Audre (1985), in Claudia Tate (ed.), *Black Women Writers at Work* (New York: Continuum).

Marshall, Paule (1959), *Brown Girl, Brown Stones* (New York: Random House).

Marshall, Paule (1983), *Praisesong for the Widow* (London: Virago).

Morrison, Toni (1970), *The Bluest Eye* (London: Triad Grafton).

Naylor, Gloria (1982), *The Women of Brewster Place: A Novel in Seven Stories* (New York: Viking).

Naylor, Gloria (1985), *Linden Hills* (New York: Ticknor and Fields).

Perry, Margaret (1976), *Silence to the Drums: A Survey of the Literature of the Harlem Renaissance* (Westport, Conn.: Greenwood).

Petry, Ann (1946), *The Street* (Boston: Houghton Mifflin).

Petry, Ann (1947), *Country Place* (Boston, Mass.: Houghton Mifflin).

Roses, Lorraine Eleena and Randolph, Ruth Elizabeth (eds) (1997), *Harlem's Glory: Black Women Writing 1900–1950* (Harvard: Harvard University Press).

Russell, Sandi (1990), *Render me my song* (London: Pandora).

Shange, Ntozake (1983 [1977]), *Cypress, Sassafrass and Indigo* (London: Methuen).

Shange, Ntozake (1992 [1975]), 'for colored girls who have considered suicide when the rainbow is enuff', in *Shange Plays: One* (London: Methuen).

Shange, Ntozake (1995), *Liliane* (London: Methuen).

Smith, Barbara et al. (1982), *But Some of us are Brave: Black Women's Studies* (London: The Feminist Press).

Tate, Claudia (1985), *Black Women Writers at Work* (London: Continuum).

Terry, Anne Lucy (1746), 'Bars Fight August 28, 1746', from *The American Museum of Ancient and Modern Fugitive Pieces, etc. Prose and Poetical*, vol. 1, no. vi (June 1787), in Josiah Gilbert Holland, *History of Massachusetts* (1855).

Walker, Alice (1983a), *The Color Purple* (London: The Women's Press).

Walker, Alice (1983b), *In Search of Our Mothers' Gardens* (London: The Women's Press).

Wheatley, Phillis (1988 [1773]), *The Collected Works of Phillis Wheatley*, ed. John C. Shields (New York/Oxford: Oxford University Press).

Wilentz, Gay (1992), *Binding Cultures* (Bloomington, Ind.: Indiana University Press).

Wilson, Harriet E. (1859), *Our Nig: or Sketches for the Life of a Free Black* (Boston, Mass.: author).

Wisker, Gina (1993), *Insights into Black Women's Writing* (London: Macmillan).

Chapter 3   Toni Morrison

Bethel, Lorraine (1982), in Barbara Smith, Gloria Hull and Patricia Bell Scott (eds), *But Some of us are Brave: Black Women's Studies* (London: The Feminist Press).

Blackburn, Sara (1973), 'You Still Can't Go Home Again', in *The New York Times Book Review*, 30 December.

Burford, Barbara (1987), 'The Landscapes Painted on the Inside of my Skin', in *Spare Rib*, no. 179 (July).

Christian, Barbara (1985), *Black Feminist Criticism: Perspectives on Black Women Writers* (London: Pergamon).

Christian, Barbara (1984), *Black Women Novelists* (West Port/London: Greenwood Press).

Evans, Mari (ed.) (1985), *Black Women Writers* (London: Pluto Press).

Hurston, Zora Neale (1978), *Their Eyes were Watching God* (Champaign, Ill.: University of Illinois Press).

Jackson, Rosemary (1981), *Fantasy* (London: Methuen).

Kaplan, Cora (1986), 'Keeping the Color in *The Color Purple*', in *Sea Changes* (London: Verso).

Lorde, Audre (1984), in Claudia Tate (ed.), *Black Women Writers at Work* (New York: Continuum).

Morrison, Toni (1987 [1970]), *The Bluest Eye* (London: Triad Grafton).

Morrison, Toni (1980 [1973]), *Sula* (London: Chatto & Windus).

Morrison, Toni (1980 [1977]), *Song of Solomon* (London: Triad Grafton).
Morrison, Toni (1983 [1981]), *Tar Baby* (London: Triad Grafton).
Morrison, Toni (1985a), in Mari Evans (ed.), *Black Women Writers* (London: Pluto Press).
Morrison, Toni (1985b), interview in *Race Today Review*.
Morrison, Toni (1987), *Beloved* (London: Chatto and Windus).
Morrison, Toni (1988), *Spare Rib*, interview with Andrea Stuart, no. 189 (April), p. 15.
Morrison, Toni (1992a), *Jazz* (London: Chatto).
Morrison, Toni (1992b), *Playing in the Dark: Whiteness and the Literary Imagination* (Harvard: Harvard University Press).
Morrison, Toni (1994), Interview with Alice Childress, *Black Creation Annual*, 1974–5, pp. 90–2, reproduced in Danielle Taylor-Guthrie (ed.), *Conversations with Toni Morrison* (University Press of Mississippi).
Morrison, Toni (1994), Interview with Robert Stepto, in Danielle Taylor-Guthrie (ed.), *Conversations with Toni Morrison* (University Press of Mississippi).
Morrison, Toni (1998), *Paradise* (London: Chatto).
Russell, Sandi (1990), *Render me My Song* (London: Pandora).
Tate, Claudia (1984), *Black Women Writers at Work* (London: Continuum).
Turner, Darwin T. (1985), 'Rootedness: The Ancestor as Foundation', in Mari Evans (ed.), *Black Women Writers* (London: Pluto Press).
Walker, Alice (1983), *The Color Purple* (London: The Women's Press).
Walker, Alice (1989), *The Temple of My Familiar* (New York: Harcourt, Brace, Jovanovich).
Willis, Susan (1984), 'Eruptions of Funk: Historicising Toni Morrison', in Henry Louis Gates Jr (ed.), *Black Literature and Literary Theory* (London: Methuen).
Wisker, Gina (1992), Review of Toni Morrison's *Jazz*, in *Wasafiri*, p. 42.

Chapter 4   Alice Walker

Bethel, Lorraine (1982), in Barbara Smith et al. (eds), *But Some of us are Brave: Black Women's Studies* (London: The Feminist Press).
Boehmer, Elleke (1991), 'Stories of Women and Mothers', in Susheila Nasta (ed.), *Motherlands* (London: The Women's Press).
Christian, Barbara (1984), 'Alice Walker: The Black Woman Artist as Wayward', in Mari Evans (ed.), *Black Women Writers* (London: Pluto).
Hall, Christine (1993), 'Arts, Action and the Ancestors: Alice Walker's *Meridian* in its context', in G. Wisker (ed.), *Insights into Black Women Writers* (Macmillan: London).
hooks, bell (1981), *Ain't I a Woman?* (Boston, Mass.: South End Press).
Jacobs, Harriet (1861), *Incidents in the Life of a Slave Girl*, reprinted in Henry Louis Gates Jr and Nellie Y. McKay (1997), *The Norton Anthology of African American Literature* (New York: W. W. Norton).
Kaplan, Cora (1986), 'Keeping the Color in *The Color Purple*', in *Sea Changes* (London: Verso).
Light, Alison (1985), from 'Collected Papers of the Literature Teaching Politics Conference, Bristol'.

Marks, E. and De Courtivron, L. (eds) (1981), *New French Feminisms: An Anthology* (Hemel Hempstead: Harvester Wheatsheaf).

Morrison, Toni (1970), *The Bluest Eye* (London: Triad Grafton).

Morrison, Toni (1987), *Beloved* (London: Chatto and Windus).

Tate, Claudia (1984), *Black Women Writers at Work* (London: Continuum).

Walker, Alice (1970), *The Third Life of Grange Copeland* (London: The Women's Press).

Walker, Alice (1972), *Five Poems* (Detroit: Broadside Press).

Walker, Alice (1986 [1968]), *Revolutionary Petunias and Other Poems* (London: Women's Press).

Walker, Alice (1982 [1976]), *Meridian* (London: Women's Press).

Walker, Alice (1987 [1979]), *Good Night, Willie Lee, I'll See You in the Morning* (London: Women's Press).

Walker, Alice (1983), *The Color Purple* (London: The Women's Press).

Walker, Alice (1983a), *In Search of Our Mothers' Gardens* (London: The Women's Press).

Walker, Alice (1983b), 'The Black Writer and the Southern Experience', in *In Search of Our Mothers' Gardens* (London: The Women's Press).

Walker, Alice (1988), *Living By the Word* (London: The Women's Press).

Walker, Alice (1989), *The Temple of My Familiar* (New York: Harcourt, Brace, Jovanovich).

Walker, Alice (1992), *Possessing the Secret of Joy* (London: The Women's Press).

Walker, Alice (1998), *By the Light of My Father's Smile* (London: Random House).

Walker, Alice and Parmar, Pratibha (1993), *Warrior Marks* (London: Jonathan Cape).

Wilentz, Gay (1992), *Binding Cultures* (Bloomington, Ind.: Indiana University Press).

Chapter 5   Caribbean Women's Writing

Allfrey, Phyllis Shand (1953), *The Orchid House* (London: Constable).

Austen, Jane (1996 [1814]), *Mansfield Park* (Harmondsworth: Penguin).

Bennett, Louise (1966), *Jamaica Labrish* (Kingston: Sangsters Book Stores).

Bennett, Louise (1982), *Selected Poems* (Kingston: Sangsters Book Stores).

Bennett, Louise (1983), 'Jamaica Philosophy', in Mervyn Morris (ed.), *Focus* (Kingston: Caribbean Authors).

Bennett, Louise (1989), Interview with Dennis Scott, in E. A. Markham (ed.), *Hinterland* (Newcastle: Bloodaxe).

Blackman, Paul (1949), 'Is There a West Indian Literature?', *Life and Letters*, 59, 135, pp. 96–102.

Bloom, Valerie (1982), *Touch Me, Tell Mi* (London: Bogle L'Ouverture).

Brathwaite, Edward Kamau (1977), 'The Love Axe: Developing a Caribbean Aesthetic, 1962–1974 – I', *Bim*, 16, 61, pp. 53–65.

Brathwaite, Edward Kamau (1984), *The History of the Voice* (London: New Beacon).

Breeze, Jean (1992), *Spring Cleaning* (London: Virago).

Breeze, Jean (1988), *Riddym Ravings and Other Poems*, ed. Mervyn Morris (London: Race Today).

Breeze, Jean (1988), Interview with Andrea Stewart, *Marxism Today*, November, p. 45.

Brodber, Erna (1980), *Jane and Louisa Will Soon Come Home* (London: New Beacon).

Brontë, Charlotte (1985 [1847]), *Jane Eyre* (Harmondsworth: Penguin).

Brown, Lloyd (1978), *West Indian Poetry* (New York: Twayne).

Brown, Stewart (1987), 'Dub Poetry: Selling Out', *Poetry Wales*, vol. 22, no. 2, pp. 53–4.

Busby, Margaret (1992), *Daughters of Africa* (London: Vintage).

Butcher, M. (1989), *Tibisiri* (Sydney: Dangaroo).

Cobham, Rhonda and Collins, Merle (eds) (1987), *Watchers and Seekers: Creative Writing by Black Women in Britain* (London: Women's Press).

Collins, Merle (1988), 'Women Writers from the Caribbean', in *Spare Rib*, no. 194 (September).

Collins, Merle (1987), *Angel* (London: Women's Press).

Collins, Merle (1985), *Because the Dawn Breaks: Poems Dedicated to the Grenadian People* (London: Karia Press).

Cooper, Carolyn (1990), 'The Word Unbroken by the Beat: The Performance Poetry of Jean Binta Breeze and Mikey Smith', in *Wasafiri*, no. 11, pp. 7–13.

Cooper, Carolyn (1993), *Noises in the Blood* (London: Macmillan).

Dabydeen, David (1988), *A Handbook for Teaching Caribbean Literature* (London: Heinemann).

D'Aguiar, Fred et al. (1988), *The New British Poetry* (London: Paladin).

Decraires Nerain, Denise (1996), 'Delivering the Word: The Poetry of Lorna Goodison', in Alison Donnell and Sarah Lawson Welsh (eds), *The Routledge Reader in Caribbean Literature* (London: Routledge).

De Lauretis, Teresa (1986), 'Feminist Studies/Critical Studies: Issues, Terms and Contexts', in T. de Lauretis (ed.), *Feminist Studies/Critical Studies* (Bloomington: Indiana University Press).

Donnell, Alison and Lawson Welsh, Sarah (eds) (1996), *The Routledge Reader in Caribbean Literature* (London: Routledge).

Edgell, Zee (1982), *Beka Lamb* (London: Heinemann).

Fanon, Frantz (1952), *Black Skin, White Masks* (London: Pluto Press).

Fanon, Frantz (1967), *The Wretched of the Earth* (Harmondsworth, Middlesex: Penguin).

Ford-Smith, H. (1986), Introduction to Sistren Theatre Collective, *Lionheart Gal* (London: Women's Press).

Gilbert, Sandra and Gubar, Susan (1979), *The Madwoman in the Attic: The Woman Writer and the Nineteenth-Century Literary Imagination* (Yale University Press).

Goodison, Lorna (1986), 'I am Becoming my Mother', 'Guinea Woman', 'Nanny', 'My Father Always Promised Me', 'Universal Grammar', 'Adoption Bureau' and 'Cyclamen Girls', in *I am Becoming my Mother* (London: New Beacon Books).

Goodison, Lorna (1988), 'Heartease', in *Heartease* (London: New Beacon Books).

Hearne, J. (1950), 'Ideas on West Indian Culture', *Public Opinion* (Jamaica), 14 October, p. 6.

Hodge, Merle (1970), *Crick Crack Monkey* (Oxford: Heinemann).

Kincaid, Jamaica (1997 [1985]), *Annie John* (London: Vintage).

Markham, E. A. (ed.) (1989), *Hinterland* (Newcastle: Bloodaxe).

Morris, Ann and Dunn, Margaret (1991), 'The Bloodstream of Our Inheritance: Female Identity and the Caribbean Mothers' Land', in Susheila Nasta (ed.), *Motherlands: Black Women's Writing from Africa, the Caribbean and South Asia* (London: The Women's Press).

Morris, Mervyn (ed.) (1983), *Focus* (Kingston: Caribbean Authors).

Morris, Mervyn (1982), in the Introduction to Louise Bennett's *Selected Poems* (for use in schools).

Morris, Mervyn (1988), 'Gender in Some Performance Poems', *Critical Quarterly*, vol. 35, no. 1.

Nasta, Susheila (ed.) (1991), *Motherlands: Black Women's Writing from Africa, the Caribbean and South Asia* (London: The Women's Press).

Nettleford, Rex (1966), Introduction to Louise Bennett's *Jamaica Labrish*,

Nourbese Philip, Marlene (1989), 'Discourse on the Logic of Language' and 'Earth and Sound', in *She Tries Her Tongue Her Silence Softly Breaks* (London: The Women's Press).

Ong, Walter (1982), *Orality and Literacy* (London: Methuen).

Rhys, Jean (1966), *Wide Sargasso Sea* (Harmondsworth: Penguin).

Rhys, Jean (1981), *Smile Please: An Unfinished Autobiography* (Harmondsworth: Penguin).

Savory, Elaine (1989), 'Caribbean Women Writers', in Maggie Butcher (ed.), *Tibisiri* (Sydney: Dangaroo).

Schipper, Mineke (1985), *Women and Literature in the Caribbean* (London: Allison and Busby).

Scott, Dennis (1989), in E. A. Markham (ed.), *Hinterland* (Newcastle: Bloodaxe).

Senior, Olive (1987), *Summer Lightning and Other Stories* (London: The Women's Press).

Senior, Olive (1989), *Arrival of the Snake Woman, and Other Stories* (London: The Women's Press).

Sistren Theatre Collective (1986), *Lionheart Gal* (London: The Women's Press).

Thomas, Elean (1986), *Spare Rib*, no. 172 (November).

Walker, Alice (1983), *In Search of Our Mothers' Gardens: Womanist Prose* (London: The Women's Press).

Chapter 6   Women's Writing from Africa

Achebe, Chinua (1993), *Things Fall Apart* (London: Heinemann).

Aliyu, Sani Abba (1997), 'Hausa Women as Oral Storytellers in Northern Nigeria', in Stephanie Newell (ed.), *Writing African Women* (London: Zed Books).

Amadiume, Ifi (1987), *Male Daughters, Female Husbands: Gender and Sex in an African Society* (London: Zed Books).

Andrade, Susan Z. (1990), 'Rewriting History, Motherhood, and Rebellion: Naming an African Women's Literary Tradition', *Research in African Literature*, 21, 1, pp. 91–110.

Ata Aidoo, Ama (1977), *Our Sister Killjoy, or Reflections from a Black Eyed Squint* (Longman, Harlow).

Ba, Mariama (1980), *So Long A Letter*, trans. M. Bode-Thomas (London: Heinemann).

Bethel, Lorraine (1982), ' "This Infinity of Conscious Pain": Zora Neale Hurston and the Black Female Library Tradition', in Barbara Smith et al. (eds), *But Some of us are Brave: Black Women's Studies* (London: The Feminist Press).

Boyce Davies, Carole and Adams Graves, Anne (1986), *Ngambika: Studies of Women in African Literature* (Trenton, NJ: Africa World Press).

Brown, Lloyd (ed.) (1981), *Women Writers in Black Africa* (Westport, Conn.: Greenwood Press).

Bryce-Okunlola, J. (1991), 'Motherhood as a Metaphor for Creativity in Three African Women's Novels: Flora Nwapa, Rebeka Njau and Bessie Head', in Susheila Nasta (ed.), *Motherlands* (London: The Women's Press).

Busia, Abena (1984), in Oladele Taiwo, *Female Novelists of Modern Africa* (London: Macmillan).

Chipasula, Stella and Frank (eds) (1995), *The Heinemann Book of African Women's Poetry* (London: Heinemann).

Emecheta, Buchi (1974), *Second Class Citizen* (London: Heinemann).

Emecheta, Buchi (1980), *The Joys of Motherhood* (London: Heinemann).

Emecheta, Buchi (1982), *Destination Biafra* (London: Heinemann).

Emecheta, Buchi (1989), *Gwendolen* (London: Heinemann).

Emecheta, Buchi (1994), *Kehinde* (London: Heinemann).

Ezeigbo (1997), 'Gender Conflict in Flora Nwapa's novels', in Stephanie Newell (ed.), *Writing African Women* (London: Zed Books).

Frank, Katherine (1982), 'The Death of the Slave Girl: African Womanhood in the Novels of Buchi Emecheta', *World Literature Written in English*, 21, 3, pp. 476–97.

Frank, Katherine (1987), 'Women without Men: The Feminist Novel in Africa', in E. Durosimi, M. Jones and E. Palmer (eds), *Women in African Literature Today* (Trenton, NJ: Africa World Press).

Gwaram, Hauwa (1983), in Beverly B. Mack (ed.), *Zaria* (The Northern Nigerian Publishing Company).

Isamila, Rashida (1983), in Beverly B. Mack (ed.), *Zaria* (The Northern Nigerian Publishing Company).

Jones, Eldred, and Palmer, E. (1967), 'Locale and Universe', in *Journal of Commonwealth Literature*, 3, pp. 127–31.

Katsina, Binta (1983 [1980]), 'Wakar Matan Nigeria', in Beverly B. Mack (ed.), *Zaria* (The Northern Nigerian Publishing Company).

Kristeva, Julia (1981), *Desire in Language* (New York: Columbia University Press).

Mack, Beverly B. (ed.) (1983), *Zaria* (The Northern Nigerian Publishing Company).

Mack, Beverly B. (1986), 'Songs from Silence: Hausa Women's Poetry', in Carole Boyce Davies and Anne Adams Graves (eds), *Ngambika: Studies of Women in African Literature* (Trenton, NJ: Africa World Press).

Morrison, Toni (1977), *Song of Solomon* (London: Random House).

Mugo, Micere Githae (1972), in Stella and Frank Chipasula (eds) (1995), *The Heinemann Book of African Women's Poetry* (London: Heinemann).

Newell, Stephanie (ed.) (1997), *Writing African Women* (London: Zed Books).

Njau, Rebeka (1975), *Ripples in the Pool*.
Nwapa, Flora (1966), *Efuru* (London: Heinemann).
Nwapa, Flora (1970), *Idu* (London: Heinemann).
Nwapa, Flora (1971), *This is Lagos, and Other Stories* (London: Heinemann).
Nwapa, Flora (1975), *Never Again* (London: Heinemann).
Nwapa, Flora (1980), *Wives at War and Other Stories* (London: Heinemann).
Nwapa, Flora (1981), *One is Enough* (London: Heinemann).
Nwapa, Flora (1986), *Women are Different* (London: Heinemann).
Ogot, Grace (1966), *The Promised Land* (Nairobi: East African Publishing House).
Oha, G. (1997), 'Culture and Gender in Flora Nwapa's Poetry', in Stephanie Newell (ed.), *Writing African Women* (London: Zed Books).
Ong, Walter (1992), quoted in Wilentz, Gay (1992) *Binding Cultures* (Bloomington, Ind.: Indiana University Press).
Ogundipe-Leslie, Molara (1987a), p. 5 in Wilson-Tagoe (1997) p. 12.
Ogundipe-Leslie, Molara (1987b), 'African Women, Culture and another Development', *Présence Africaine*, 141, 1, p. 133.
Ruddy, Patricia (1994), 'Prostitution', unpublished essay quoted in Stratton, F. (1994) *Contemporary South African Literature & the Politics of Gender* (London: Routledge).
Savory Fido, Elaine (1991), 'Mother/lands: Self and Separation in the Work of Buchi Emecheta, Bessie Head and Jean Rhys', in Susheila Nasta (ed.), *Motherlands* (London: The Women's Press).
Schipper, Mineke (1984), 'Mother Africa on a Pedestal', in *Unheard Words: Women and Literature in Africa, the Arab World, the Caribbean and Latin America* (London: Allison and Busby).
Shelu, Hajiya 'Yar' (1986), in Beverly B. Mack, 'Songs from Silence: Hausa Women's Poetry', in Carole Boyce Davies and Anne Adams Graves (eds), *Ngambika: Studies of Women in African Literature* (Trenton, NJ: Africa World Press).
Smith, Barbara (1987), 'Towards a Black Feminist Criticism', in Gloria T. Hull, Patricia Bell Scott and Barbara Smith, *But Some of us are Brave* (New York: The Feminist Press) pp. 157–75.
Steady, Filomena Chioma (ed.) (1985), *The Black Women Cross-Culturally* (Cambridge, Mass.: Schenkman Books).
Stratton, Florence (1994), *Contemporary South African Literature and the Politics of Gender* (London: Routledge).
Spivak, G. (1988), *In Other Worlds: Essays in Cultural Politics* (London: Routledge).
Taiwo, Oladele (1984), *Female Novelists of Modern Africa* (London: Macmillan).
Umeh, Marie (1980), 'African Women in Transition in the Novels of Buchi Emecheta', *Présence Africaine*, 116, 4, pp. 190–201.
Walker, Alice (1983), *The Color Purple* (London: The Women's Press).
Walker, Alice (1983), *In Search of Our Mothers' Gardens: Womanist Prose* (London: The Women's Press).
Walker, Alice (1992), *Possessing the Secret of Joy* (London: Vintage).
Wilentz, Gay (1992), *Binding Cultures* (Bloomington, Ind.: Indiana University Press).

Wilson-Tagoe, Nana (1997), 'Towards a Theorization of African Women's Writing', in Stephanie Newell (ed.), *Writing African Women* (London: Zed Books).

Chapter 7   South African Women's Writing

Barnett, Ursula (1983), *A Vision of Order: A Study of Black South African Literature in English (1914–1980)* (London: Sinclair Browne).

Brown, Lloyd (ed.) (1981), *Women Writers in Black Africa* (Westport, Conn.: Greenwood Press).

Bryce-Okunlola, J. (1991), 'Motherhood as a Metaphor for Creativity in Three African Women's Novels', in Susheila Nasta (ed.), *Motherlands* (London: The Women's Press).

Clayton, Cherry (1984), writing about Bessie Head in *A Bewitched Crossroad* (Oxford: Heinemann).

Congress of South African Writers (COSAW) collective (1994), *Like a House on Fire: Contemporary Women's Writing from South Africa* (Johannesburg: COSAW).

Copland, G. (1978), in Lloyd Brown (ed.) (1981), *Women Writers in Black Africa* (Westport, Conn.: Greenwood Press).

De Ko, Ingrid (1997), 'All Wat Kind Is', 'Small Passing', in Denis Hirson (ed.), *The Lava of this Land: South African Poetry, 1960–96* (Evanston, Ill.: Triquarterly Press).

Dhlomo, R. R. R. (undated), *An African Tragedy* (Lovedale Press).

Driver, Dorothy (1996), 'Transformation through Art: Writing, Representation and Subjectivity in Recent South African Fiction', in *World Literature Today: South African Literature in Transition*, 70, 1 (Winter).

Gilroy, Paul (1987), *There Ain't no Black in the Union Jack* (London: Hutchinson).

Govinden, Betty (1995), 'Learning Myself Anew', in *Alternation*, 2, 2, pp. 170–83.

Head, Bessie (1969), *When Rain Clouds Gather* (Oxford: Heinemann).

Head, Bessie (1971), *Maru* (Oxford: Heinemann).

Head, Bessie (1974), *A Question of Power* (Oxford: Heinemann).

Head, Bessie (1977), *The Collector of Treasures* (London: Heinemann).

Head, Bessie (1981), *Serowe, Village of the Rain Wind* (Oxford: Heinemann).

Head, Bessie (1984), *A Bewitched Crossroad* (Oxford: Heinemann).

Head, Bessie (1989), *Tales of Tenderness and Power* (London: Heinemann).

Head, Bessie (1991), *A Gesture of Belonging: Letters from Bessie Head, 1965–1979* (London: Heinemann).

Head, Bessie (1993), *The Cardinals: With Meditations and Short Stories*, ed. M. J. Daymond (Cape Town: David Philip).

Head, Bessie, Papers, Khama Memorial Musem (BKMM), Serowe, Botswana.

Head, Bessie (1990), *Bessie Head: A Woman Alone – Autobiographical Writings*, ed. Craig Mackenzie (London: Heinemann).

Karodia, Farida (1986), *Daughters of the Twilight* (Oxford: Heinemann).

Karodia, Farida (1988), *Coming Home and Other Stories* (Oxford: Heinemann).

Kuzwayo, Ellen (1985), *Call Me Woman* (Johannesburg: Ravan Press).

Kuzwayo, Ellen (1985), *Part of My Soul Went With Him* (Johannesburg).

Jabavu, Noni (1960), *Drawn in Colour* (London: John Murray).

Jabavu, Noni (1963), *The Ochre People* (London: John Murray).

Kuzwayo, Ellen (1990), in *Bessie Head: A Woman Alone – Autobiographical Writings*, ed. Craig Mackenzie (London: Heinemann).

Larson, Charles (1973), *The Emergence of African Fiction* (London: Macmillan).

Lazarus, Neil (1990), *Resistance in Post-Colonial African Fiction* (New Haven and London: Yale University Press).

Lewis, Desiree (1996), 'The Cardinals and Bessie Head's Allegories of Self', in *World Literature Today: South Africa in Transition*, Winter, p. 77.

Malange, Nise (1986), 'I, the Unemployed', in Ari Sitas (ed.), *Black Mamba Rising* (Durban: Culture and Working Life Publications, University of Natal).

Makeba Muse (1977), Donga, Feb. 1977.

Mhlope, Gcina (1987), 'Sometimes When it Rains', in Ann Oosthuizen (ed.), *Sometimes When it Rains: Writings by South African Women* (London: Pandora).

Moyana, T. T. (1976), 'Problems of a Creative Writer in South Africa', in Christopher Heywood (ed.), *Aspects of South African Literature* (London: Heinemann).

Nchwe, Manoko (1986), in conversation with Buttomelo.

Ngcobo, Lauretta (1981), *Cross of Gold* (London: Longman).

Ngcobo, Lauretta (1994), Introduction, *Like A House on Fire: Contemporary Women's Writing, Art and Photography from South Africa* (Johannesburg: COSAW Publishing).

Ngcobo, Lauretta (1989), Introduction to Miriam Tlali's *Soweto Stories* (London: Pandora Press).

Ola, Virginia Ozoma (1994), *The Life and Works of Bessie Head* (Dyfed, Wales: Edwin Mellen Press).

Ravenscroft, Arthur (1976), 'The Novels of Bessie Head', in *Aspects of South African Literature* (Ibadan, Nairobi, Lusaka: Heinemann).

Reagon, Gail (1994), 'Ellen Kuzwayo and Ways of Speaking Otherwise', in *Like a House on Fire: Contemporary Women's Writing, Art and Photography from South Africa* (Johannesburg: COSAW Publishing).

Reddy, Jayapraga (1987), *On the Fringe of Dream-Time and Other Stories* (Johannesburg: Skotaville).

Reddy, Jayapraga (1994), 'The Unbending Reed', in *Like a House on Fire: Contemporary Women's Writing, Art and Photography from South Africa* (Johannesburg: COSAW Publishing).

Rowbotham, Sheila (1983), *Women's Consciousness, Man's World* (Harmondsworth: Penguin).

Sam, Agnes (1989), *Jesus is Indian and Other Stories* (Denmark: Dangaroo Press).

Schreiner, Olive (1923), *Thoughts on South Africa* (London: Unwin).

Schreiner, Olive (1911), *Women and Labour* (London: Unwin).

Schreiner, Olive (1883), *Story of an African Farm* (Harmondsworth: Penguin).

Slovo, Gillian (1990), *Ties of Blood* (London: Headline Book Publishing).

Stead Eilerson, Gillian (1995), *Thunder Behind her Ears* (Cape Town: David Philip).

Stead Eilersen, Gillian (1989), Introduction to edition of *Tales of Tenderness and Power* (London: Heinemann).

Temba Qabula, Alfred, Hlatshwaya, Mi S'Dumo and Malange, Nise (1986), *Black Mamba Rising: South African Worker Poets in Struggle*, ed. Ari Sitas (Durban: Culture and Working Life Publications, University of Natal).

Tlali, Miriam (1975), *Muriel at the Metropolitan* (Johannesburg: Ravan).

Tlali, Miriam (1980), *Amandla* (Johannesburg: Ravan).

Tlali, Miriam (1989), *Soweto Stories* (London: Pandora Press).

Vervoerd, Henrik, Minister of Native Affairs, on the creation of the Department of Bantu Education in 1958, following the Bantu Education Act 1953, ref. 20. Cited in William J. Pomeroy (1971), *Apartheid Axis* (New York) pp. 22, 19.

Vigne, Randolph (1991), *A Gesture of Belonging: Letters from Bessie Head, 1965–1979* (London: Heinemann).

Wicomb, Zoe (1987), 'A Clearing in the Bush' and 'Behind the Bougainvillea', in *You Can't Get Lost in Cape Town* (London: Virago).

Chapter 8   Writing by Women from the Indian Sub-Continent

Alexander, Meena (1991), 'Grandmother's Letters', in *Slate of Life* (London: Women's Press).

Alexander, Meena (1991), 'Sidi Syed's Architecture', and 'Hotel Alexandria', in A. Ayyappa Paniker (ed.), *Modern Indian Poetry in English* (New Delhi: Sahitya Akademi).

Ash, Ranjana (1991), 'The Search for Freedom in Indian Women's Writing', in *Motherlands* (London: Women's Press).

Asian Women Writers' Collective (1988), *Right of Way* (London: Women's Press).

Basham, A. L. (1971), *The Wonder that was India*, transl. from Sanskrit by A. L. Basham (London: Fontana).

Buck, Claire (ed.) (1992), *Bloomsbury Guide to Women's Literature* (London: Bloomsbury).

Chatterjee, Debjani (1989), *I Was That Woman* (Somerset: Hippopotamus Press).

Chew, Shirley (1991), 'Searching Voices: Anita Desai's *Clear Light of Day*', in Susheila Nasta (ed.), *Motherlands* (London: Women's Press).

Das, Kamala (1988), *My Story*, transl. from Malayalam by the author (Delhi: Sterling Publications).

De Souza, Eunice (1987), 'Remember Medusa', etc., in *Ain't I a Woman! Poems by Black and White Women*, collected by Illona Linthwaite (London: Virago), p. 115.

Desai, Anita (1980), *The Clear Light of Day* (London: Vintage).

Desai, Anita (1998 [1988]), *Baumgartner's Bombay* (London: Vintage).

Desai, Anita (1990), 'A Secret Connivance', in the *Times Literary Supplement*, September, pp. 14–20.

Deshpande, Shashi (1987/8), *That Long Silence* (London: Virago).

Deshpande, Shashi (1993), Interview with Lakshmi Holstrom, *Wasafiri*, 17 (April), pp. 23–4.

Forster, E. M. (1924), *A Passage to India* (Harmondsworth: Penguin).

Holstrom, Lakshmi (ed.) (1993), *The Inner Courtyard* (London: Virago).

Jaggi, Maya (1992), 'The Indian Subcontinent', in Claire Buck (ed.), *Bloomsbury Guide to Women's Literature* (London: Bloomsbury), pp. 220–5.

King, Bruce (ed.) (1987), 'Women's Voices', in *Modern Indian Poetry in English* (Oxford: India Paperbacks).

Mukherjee, Bharati (1979), *Wife* (New York: Fawcett Crest).

Mukherjee, Bharati (1988), *The Middleman and Other Stories* (London: Virago).

Nasta, Susheila (ed.) (1991), Introduction to *Motherlands: Black Women's Writing from Africa, the Caribbean and South Asia* (London: The Women's Press).

Prawer Jhabvala, Ruth (1975), *Heat and Dust* (Harmondsworth: Penguin).

Roy, Arundhati (1997), *The God of Small Things* (London: Flamingo).

Sahgal, Nayantara (1985), *Rich Like Us* (London: Sceptre).

Scott, Paul (1966, 1968, 1971, 1975), *The Raj Quartet* (London: Heinemann).

Spivak, Gayatri (1988), *In Other Worlds: Essays in Cultural Politics* (London: Routledge).

Spivak, Gayatri (1990), in S. Harasym (ed.), *The Postcolonial Critic* (London: Routledge).

Tharu, Susie and Lalita, K. (eds) (1992), *Women Writing in India*, vol. 1 (London: HarperCollins).

Tharu, Susie and Lalita, K. (eds) (1993), *Women Writing in India*, vol. 2: *The Twentieth Century* (London: Pandora/HarperCollins).

Walder, Dennis (1998), *Post-colonial Literatures in English* (Oxford: Blackwell).

Chapter 9 Writing by Women from Australia

Angelou, Maya (1970), *I Know Why the Caged Bird Sings* (London: Virago).

Astley, Thea (1987), *It's Raining in Mango* (Sydney: Penguin).

Bandler, Faith (1977), *Wacvie* (Adelaide: Rigby).

Bandler, Faith and Fox, Len (1980), *Marani in Australia* (Adelaide: Rigby/Opal).

Bellear Noonuccal, Lisa (1991), 'Women's Liberation', in *Hecate*, 17, 1/2.

Bellear Noonuccal, Lisa (1996), 'Souled Out', in *Dreaming in Urban Areas* (Brisbane: University of Queensland Press).

Bradley (1788), 'Voyage to New South Wales', 29 Jan. 1788, cited in Karen Jennings and David Hollingsworth, 'Shy Maids and Wanton Strumpets', *Hecate*, 13, 2 (1987–8), pp. 113–33, at p. 129.

Buck, Claire (ed.) (1992), *The Bloomsbury Book of Women's Literature* (London: Bloomsbury).

Caine, Darryle (1996), 'Predators' and 'The Inheritance', in Madeleine Kinhill (ed.), *Screams* (Sunnybank, Queeensland: Ironbark).

Clare, Monica (1978), *Karobran: The Story of An Aboriginal Girl* (Sydney: APCOL).

Couani, Anna and Gunew, Sneja (eds) (1988), *Telling Ways: Australian Women's Experimental Writing* (Victoria: Australian Feminist Studies).

Daniels, Kay and Murnane, Mary (1980), *Uphill all the Way*.

Dark, Eleanor (1986 [1959]), *Lantana Lane* (London: Virago).

Davis, Jack et al. (eds) (1990), *Paperbark: A Collection of Black Australian Writings* (Brisbane: University of Queensland Press).

De Lauretis, Teresa (1987), *Technologies of Gender* (Bloomington, Ind.: Indiana University Press).

Desai, Anita (1988), *Baumgartner's Bombay* (Harmondsworth: Penguin).

Devanny, Jean (1926), *Sugar Heaven* (Sydney: Modern Publishers).

Devanny, Jean (1926), *The Butcher Shop* (Sydney: Modern Publishers).

Evans, Raymond (1982), 'Don't you remember Black Alice, Sam Holt? Aboriginal Women in Queensland History', in *Hecate*, 11, 2.

Ferrers, Kay (1984), *A Time to Write* (Sydney: Penguin).

Ferrier, Carole (ed.) (1985), 'Aboriginal Women's Narratives', in *Gender, Politics and Fiction* (Brisbane: University of Queensland Press).

Franklin, Miles (1946 [1901]), *My Brilliant Career* (Melbourne: Georgian House).

Goolagong, Evonne (1973), *Evonne! On the Move* (Sydney: Dutton).

Grenville, Kate (1988), *Joan Makes History* (London: Minerva, 1989).

Hamilton, Paula (1990), Paper delivered to the *Shaping Lives* Conference, Humanities Research Centre, ANU (July).

Handel Richardson, Henry (Ethel Robertson) (1930), *The Fortunes of Richard Marhoney* (Sydney).

Hawthorne, Susan and Pausacker, Jenny (eds) (1994), *Moments of Desire* (Sydney: Penguin).

Hazzard, Shirley (1980), *Transit of Venus* (Harmondsworth: Penguin).

Hodge, Bob and Mishra, Vijay (1991), *Dark Side of the Dream*.

hooks, bell (1982), *Ain't I a Woman: Black Women & Feminism* (London: Pluto).

Huggins, Jackie (1987/8), 'Firing on the Mind: Aboriginal Women Domestic Servants in the Inter-War years', in *Hecate*, 13, 2.

Huggins, Jackie (1990), 'Questions of Collaboration: an interview with Jackie Huggins and Isabel Tarrago', *Hecate*, 16, 1/2.

Jolley, Elizabeth (1993), *The George's Wife* (Sydney: Penguin).

Keesing, R. (1989), 'Creating the Past: Custom and Identity in the Contemporary Pacific', *Contemporary Pacific*, 1/2, pp. 19–42.

Keeffe (1988) 'Aboriginality: Resistance and Persistence', *Australian Aboriginal Studies*, 1, 67–87.

Kennedy, Marnie (1985), *Born a Half Caste* (Canberra: AIS).

Kristeva, Julia (1984), *Revolution in Poetic Language* (New York: Columbia University Press).

Langer, B. (1990), 'From History to Ethnicity: El Salvadorean Refugees in Melbourne', *Journal of Intercultural Studies*, 11, 2, pp. 1–13.

Langford, Ruby (1988), *Don't Take Your Love to Town* (Ringwood: Penguin).

Langford, Ruby (1991), 'Singing the Land', *Hecate*, 17, 2, p. 36.

Labalestier, Jan (1991), 'Through Their Own Eyes: An Interpretation of Aboriginal Women's Writing', in Gill Bottomley (ed.), *Intersexions: Gender/Class/Culture/Ethnicity* (London: Allen and Unwin).

Memnott, Paul and Horsman, Robin (1984), Preface to Elsie Roughsey, *An Aboriginal Mother Tells of the Old and the New* (Ringwood: Penguin).

Meston, Archibald (1897), *First Report on Western Aborigines*, 16 June, col/140.

Modjeska, Drusilla (1981), *Exiles at Home: Australian Women Writers, 1925–45* (Sydney: Angus and Robertson).

Morgan, Sally (1987), *My Place* (Fremantle: Fremantle Arts Centre Press).

Morrison, Toni (1987), *Beloved* (London: Chatto and Windus).

Narogin, Mudrooroo (1965), *Wild Cat Falling* (Sydney: Angus and Robertson).

Narogin, Mudrooroo (1968), 'Guerilla Poetry: Lionel Fogarty's Response to Language Genocide', in Ulli Beier (ed.), *Long Water, Aboriginal Art and Literature*, *Aspect*, 34 (August), pp. 72–81.

Narogin, Mudrooroo (1985), in J. Davis and Bob Hodge (eds), *Aboriginal Writing Today* (Canberra: AIAS).

Narogin, Mudrooroo (1990), *Writing from the Fringe* (Melbourne: Hyland House).

Pettman, Jan (1992), *Living in the Margins* (New South Wales: Allen and Unwin).

Pritchard, Katherine Susannah (1929), *Coonardoo* (London: Jonathan Cape).

Roughsey, Elsie (1984), *An Aboriginal Mother Tells of the Old and the New* (Penguin: Ringwood).

Ryan, Tracey (1997), *Vamp* (Fremantle: Fremantle Arts Centre Press).

Smith, Shirley C. and Sykes, Bobbi (1981), *Mumshirl: An Autobiography* (Richmond, Victoria: Heinemann).

Somerville, Margaret and Cohens, Patsy (1990), *Ingelba and the Five Black Matriarchs* (Sydney: Allen and Unwin).

Somerville, Margaret (1991), 'Life(H)istory Writing: The Relationship between Talk and Text', *Women/Australia/Theory*, Special Issue of *Hecate*, 17, 1, pp. 95–109.

Stead, Christina (1940), *The Man who Loved Children* (Harmondsworth: Penguin).

Storer, D. (1985), *Ethnic Family Values in Australia* (Sydney: Prentice-Hall).

Sussex, Lucy and Raphael Buckrich, Judith (eds) (1995), *She's Fantastical* (Melbourne: Sybylla Press).

Sykes, Bobbi (1979), *Love Poems and Other Revolutionary Actions* (Brisbane: University of Queensland Press).

Thieme, John (ed.) (1996), *Post Colonial Literatures in English* (London: Edward Arnold).

Walker, Alice (1983), *In Search of Our Mothers' Gardens* (London: The Women's Press).

Walker, Kath (1964), *We Are Going* (Brisbane: Jacaranda Press).

Walker, Kath (1992 [1966]), *The Dawn is at Hand* (London: Marion Boyars; first published 1966, Brisbane).

Walker, Kath (1970), *My People: A Kath Walker Collection* (Brisbane: Jacaranda Press).

Walker, Kath (1972), *Stradbroke Dreamtime* (Sydney: Angus and Robertson).

Walker, Maureen (1991), in conversation with Bronwen Levy, *Hecate*, 17, 2.

Walker, Shirley (1992), in Claire Buck (ed.), *The Bloomsbury Guide to Women's Literature* (London: Bloomsbury).

Ward, Glenyse (1988), *Wandering Girl* (Broome: Magabala Books Aboriginal Corporation).

Ward, Glenyse (1991), *Unna You Fellas* (Broome, Western Australia: Magabala Books Aboriginal Corporation).

Willetts, Kathy (1990), 'In Search of the Authentic Voice', in *Hecate*, 16, 1/2.

Yahp, Beth (1992), *The Crocodile Fury* (Sydney: HarperCollins).

Filmography

Film Australia (1975), *Sister If Only You Knew*.

Tracey Moffat, *Nice Coloured Girls*.

Chapter 10   Aotearoa – New Zealand

Banks, K. (1992), *Two Worlds: First Meetings between Maori and Europeans 1642–1772* (Auckland: Penguin).

Bartlett, Rima Alicia (1997), 'The Wonder of Words Winds through all Worlds: Keri Hulme Interview with Rima Alicia Bartlett', in *Wasafiri*, 25, (Spring).

Bergmann Laurel (1994), 'Where to from Here? Contemporary New Zealand Women's Fiction', in *Hecate*, 20, 2.

Dunsford, Cathie (1994), *Cowrie* (Melbourne: Spinifex Press).

Evans, Ripeka (1994), 'The Imagination of Powerlessness: Maori Feminism, a Perspective', in *Hecate*, 20, 2 – paper initially delivered 10 August 1993 to Auckland University winter series.

Ferrier, Carole (1995), *The Janet Frame Reader* (London: The Women's Press).

Frame, Janet (1951), *The Lagoon and Other Stories* (Christchurch: Caxton Press).

Frame, Janet (1961), *Faces in the Water* (New York: Braziller).

Frame, Janet (1965), *The Adaptable Man* (New York: Braziller).

Frame, Janet (1982), *Owls Do Cry* (New York: Braziller).

Frame, Janet (1984), *An Angel at My Table* (London: The Women's Press).

Frame, Janet (1985), *The Envoy from Mirror City* (London: The Women's Press).

Frame, Janet (1988), *The Carpathians* (London: Bloomsbury).

Grace, Patricia (1986), *Potiki* (London: The Women's Press).

Grace, Patricia (1987), *Collected Stories*: *Waiariki* (1975), *The Dream Sleepers* (1980), *Electric City* (1987) (Auckland, New Zealand: Penguin).

Grace, Patricia (1993), *Cousins* (London: The Women's Press).

Hulme, Keri (1985 [1983]), *The Bone People* (London: Picador).

Hulme, Keri (1986), *Te Kaihau/The Windeater* (Brisbane: University of Queensland Press).

Hyman, Prue (1994), 'New Zealand since 1984: Economic Restructuring – Feminist Responses, Activity and Theory', in *Hecate*, 20, 2.

Johnston, Patricia and Pihama, Leonie (1994), 'The Marginalisation of Maori Women', in *Hecate*, 20, 2.

Kidman, Fiona (1971), *A Breed of Women* (London: Macmillan).

Kidman, Fiona (1987), *The Book of Secrets* (London: Macmillan).

Kirwin (1992), 'Towards Theories of Maori Feminism', in R. du Plessis et al. (eds), *Feminist Voices: A Women's Studies Text for Aotearoa* (Auckland: Oxford University Press).

McCauley, Sue (1989), interview with Sue Kedgley, in 'Our Own Country', p. 41, quoted in Claire Buck (ed.) (1992), *The Bloomsbury Guide to Women's Literature* (London: Bloomsbury), p. 179.

Mansfield, Katherine (1911), *In a German Pension* (Harmondsworth: Penguin).

Mansfield, Katherine (1921), *Bliss and Other Stories* (Harmondsworth: Penguin).

Mansfield, Katherine (1922), *The Garden Party and Other Stories* (Harmondsworth: Penguin).

Mercer, Gina (1995), in Carole Ferrier (ed.), *The Janet Frame Reader* (London: The Women's Press).

Middleton, S. and Jones, S. A. (ed.) (1992), *Women and Education in Aotearoa*, 2 (Wellington: Bridget Williams Books).

Morrison, Toni (1970), *The Bluest Eye* (London: Triad Grafton).

Munro, Alice (1987), quoted in Carole Ferrier (1994), *The Janet Frame Reader* (London: The Women's Press), p. 12.

Plath, Sylvia (1963), *The Bell Jar* (Harmondsworth: Penguin).

Smith, L. T. (1992), 'Discourses, Projects and Mana Wahine', in S. Middleton and S. A. Jones (eds), *Women and Education in Aotearoa, 2* (Wellington: Bridget Williams Books).

Salmon, Ann (1992), quoted in Banks, *Two Worlds: First Meetings between Maori and Europeans 1642–1772* (Auckland: Penguin).

Wever, Lydia (1992), in Claire Buck (ed.), *The Bloomsbury Guide to Women's Literature* (London: Bloomsbury).

The 1998 *Australian Women's Book Review*, vol. 10, features: Emily Perkins, Sarah Quigley, Tina Shaw, Jennifer Fulton, and Beryl Fletcher.

Chapter 11   Canadian Women's Writing

Alexander, Flora (1998), 'Feminist Critiques of Romance', in Lynne Pearce and Gina Wisker (eds), *Fatal Attractions: Rescripting Romance in Contemporary Literature and Film* (London: Pluto Press).

Ashcroft, B., Gryforth, G. and Tiffin, H. (1989), *The Empire Writes Back: Theory and Practice in Post-Colonial Literatures* (London and New York: Routledge).

Atwood, Margaret (1969), *The Edible Woman* (London: Virago).

Atwood, Margaret (1970), *The Journals of Susannah Moodie* (London: Virago).

Atwood, Margaret (1972), *Surfacing* (London: Virago).

Atwood, Margaret (1976), *Lady Oracle* (London: Virago).

Atwood, Margaret (1981), *Bodily Harm* (London: Virago).

Atwood, Margaret (1985), *The Handmaid's Tale* (London: Virago).

Atwood, Margaret (1993), *The Robber Bride* (London: Bloomsbury).

Atwood, Margaret (1996a), 'Progressive Insanities of a Pioneer', in John Thieme (ed.), *The Arnold Anthology of Post-Colonial Literature in English* (London: Edward Arnold).

Atwood, Margaret (1996b [1972]), *Survival: A Thematic Guide to Canadian Literature* (Toronto: Asanti), in John Thieme (ed.), *The Arnold Anthology of Post-Colonial Literature in English* (London: Edward Arnold).

Atwood, Margaret (1996c), *Alias Grace* (London: QPD).

Brand, Dionne (1982), *Primitive Offensive* (Williams Wallace).

Brand, Dionne (1988), *Sans Souci* (Williams Wallace).

Brand, Dionne (1990), *No Language is Neutral* (Coach House).

Brydon, Diana and Tiffin, Helen (1993), *Decolonising Fictions* (Sydney: Dangaroo Press).

Brydon, Diana (1981), 'Landscape and Authenticity', *Dalhousie Review*, 61, 2 (Summer).

Brydon, Diana (1994), '*Obasan*, Joy Kogawa's "Lament for a Nation"', in A. Rutherford, L. Jensen and S. Chew (eds), *Into the Nineties: Post-Colonial Women's Writing* (Armidale, New South Wales: Dangaroo Press).

Campbell, Maria (1995), 'The Little People', in Gerald Vizenor (ed.), *Native American Literature* (New York: HarperCollins), extract from Maria

Campbell (1973), *Halfbreed* (Toronto: University of Nebraska Press and McClelland and Stewart).

Gunnar, Kristjana (1989), *The Prowler* (Red Deer College).

Jones, Dorothy (1994), 'Restoring the Temples: The Fiction of Aritha van Herk', in Anna Rutherford, Lars Jensen and Shirley Chew (eds), *Into the Nineties: Post-Colonial Women's Writing* (Armidale, New South Wales: Kunapipi Dangaroo).

Kroetsch, Robert (1974), 'Unhiding the Hidden', *Journal of Canadian Fiction*, 3, 3, p. 43.

Kogawa, Joy (1981), *Obasan* (Harmondsworth: Penguin).

Laurence, Margaret (1994 [1970]), *A Bird in the House* (Toronto: McClelland and Stewart).

Lee, Dennis (1974), 'Cadence, Country, Silence: Writing in Colonial Space', *Boundary*, 2, 3, 1 (Fall).

Lemire Tostevin, Lola (1982), *Color of her Speech* (Coach House).

Lemire Tostevin, Lola (1983), *Gynotext* (Underwhich).

Lemire Tostevin, Lola (1985), *Double Standards* (Longspoon).

Marlatt, Daphne (1984), *Touch to My Tongue* (Longspoon).

Marlatt, Daphne (1988), *Ana Historica* (Coach House).

Moodie, Susannah (1988 [1852]), *Roughing it in the Bush, or Life in Canada*, ed. Carl Ballstadt (Ottawa: Carleton University Press).

Munro, Alice (1997), *Selected Stories* (London: Vintage).

Namjoshi, Suniti (1981), *Feminist Fables* (London: Sheba).

Namjoshi, Suniti (1987), 'Look Medusa!' in Illona Linthwaite (ed.), *Ain't I a Woman: Poems by Black and White Women* (London: Virago).

Namjoshi, Suniti (1985), *The Conversations of Cow* (London: The Women's Press).

Namjoshi, Suniti (1989), *Because of India* (London: The Women's Press).

New, W. H. (1989), *A History of Canadian Literature* (London: Macmillan).

Niatum, Duane (ed.) (1988), *Harper's Anthology of 20th-Century Native American Poetry* (San Francisco: HarperCollins).

Palmateer Pennee, Donna (1994), 'Canadian Women's Literary Discourse in English, 1982–92', in Anna Rutherford, Lars Jensen and Shirley Chew (eds), *Not the Nineties: Post-Colonial Women's Writing* (New South Wales: Dangaroo Press).

Shields, Carol (1987), *Mary Swann* (London: Fourth Estate).

Shields, Carol (1993), *The Stone Diaries* (London: Fourth Estate).

Shikatani, Gerry (1996), 'Here, not There', in Juliana Chang (ed.), *Quiet Fires: A Historical Anthology of Asian American Poetry, 1892–1970* (New York: The Asian American Writers Workshop).

Van Herk, Aritha (1979), *Judith* (London: Corgi).

Van Herk, Aritha (1984), 'Women Writers and the Prairie: Spies in an Indifferent Landscape', *Kunapipi*, 6, 2, p. 15.

Van Herk, Aritha (1989 [1986]), *No Fixed Address* (London: Virago).

Vizenor, Gerald (ed.) (1995), *Native American Literature* (New York: HarperCollins).

Vangen, Kate (1995), 'The Native in Literature', quoted in Gerald Vizenor (ed.), *Native American Literature* (New York: HarperCollins), p. 75.

Warrior, Emma Lee (1988), in Duane Niatum (ed.), *Harper's Anthology of 20th-Century Native American Poetry* (San Francisco: HarperCollins).

Chapter 12   Black British Women's Writing

Alibhai, Yasmin (1991), *New Statesman* and *Society*, 15 February.

Amos, Valerie and Parmar, Pratibha (1984), *Feminist Review*, special issue: 'Many Voices, One Chant', no. 17 (July), pp. 3–19.

Asian Women's Writers Collective (1988), *No Right of Way* (London: Women's Press).

Asian Women's Writers Collective (1994), *Flaming Spirit* (London: Virago).

Asian Women Writers Collective (1990), 'At the End of a Greenhouse Summer', in Maud Sulter and Ingrid Pollard (eds), *Passion: Discourses on Black Women's Creativity* (London: Urban Fox Press).

Bloom, Valerie (1983), *Touch Mi, Tell Mi* (London: Bogle L'ouverture).

Burford, Barbara; Pearce, G.; Nichols, G. and Kay, J. (eds) (1984), *A Dangerous Knowing: Four Black Women Poets* (London: Sheba Press).

Burford, Barbara (1984), *Everyday Matters*, 2 (London: Women's Press).

Burford, Barbara (1986), *The Threshing Floor* (London: Women's Press).

Cobham, R. and Collins, M. (eds) (1987), *Watchers and Seekers* (London: The Women's Press).

Collins, Merle (1985), 'Crick Crack Monkey', in *Because the Dawn Breaks* (London: Women's Press).

Collins, Merle (1985), *Because the Dawn Breaks* (London: Women's Press).

Collins, Merle (1987), *Angel* (London: Women's Press).

Griffin, Gabrielle (1992), 'Writing the Body', in G. Wisker (ed.), *Insights into Black Women's Writing* (Basingstoke: Macmillan).

Gupta, Tanika (1994), *Flaming Spirit*, in Asian Women's Writing Collective, (London: Virago).

Guptra, Sunetra (1992), *Memories of Rain* (London: Orion).

Guptra, Sunetra (1993), *The Glassblower's Breath* (London: Orion).

Hosain, Attia and Markanda, Kamala (1973), *The Nowhere Man* (London: Allen Lane).

Humm, Maggie (1991), *Border Traffic* (Manchester: Manchester University Press).

Innes, C. L. (1995), 'Wintering: Making a Home in Britain', in A. Robert Lee (ed.), *Other Britain, Other British: Contemporary Multi-cultural Fiction* (London: Pluto).

Jena, Seema (1993), 'From Victims to Survivors: The Anti-hero as a Narrative Strategy in Asian Immigrant Writing with Special Reference to *The Buddha of Suburbia*', in *Wasafiri*, 17 (Spring).

Johnson, Amryl (1985), *Long Road to Nowhere* (London: Virago).

Jones, T. (1993), *Britain's Ethnic Minorities* (London: Policy Studies Institute).

Kay, Jackie (1984), 'We are not all sisters under the same moon', in *A Dangerous Knowing* (London: Sheba).

Kay, Jackie (1984), 'So you think I'm a mule', in *A Dangerous Knowing* (London: Sheba).

Kay, Jackie (1989), 'The White Woman in your Head', Open University television programme.

Kay, Jackie (1991), 'The Telling Part', in *Adoption Papers* (Newcastle: Bloodaxe Books).

Kay, Jackie (1991), 'Mummy and Donor and Deirdre', in *Adoption Papers* (Newcastle: Bloodaxe Books).

Kay, Jackie (1998), *The Trumpet* (London: Picador).

Kay, Jackie (1999), in conversation with Maya Jaggi, *Wasafiri*, no. 29 (Spring), p. 53.

Mason, D. (1995), *Race and Ethnicity in Modern Britain* (Oxford: Oxford University Press).

Mercer, K. (1990), 'Welcome to the Jungle: Identity and Diversity in Postmodern Politics', in J. Rutherford (ed.), *Identity, Community, Culture, Difference* (London: Lawrence and Wishart).

Mirza, Heidi Safia (ed.) (1997), *Black British Feminism: A Reader* (London: Routledge).

Morrison, Toni (1987), *Beloved* (London: Chatto and Windus).

Morrison, Toni (1992), *Jazz* (London: Chatto and Windus).

Morrison, Toni (1998), *Paradise* (London: Chatto and Windus).

Ngcobo, Lauretta (ed.) (1987), *Let it be Told: Black Women Writers in Britain* (London: Virago).

Nichols, Grace (1984), 'Loveact', and other poems, in *The Fat Black Woman's Poems* (London: Virago).

Nichols, Grace (1985), 'Twentieth-Century Witch Chant', in *Purple and Green: Poems by Women Poets* (London: Rivelin Grapheme).

Nichols, Grace (1986), *Whole of a Morning Sky* (London: Virago).

Nichols, Grace (1989), 'Home Truths', in E. A. Markham (ed.), *Hinterland: Caribbean Poetry from the West Indies and Britain* (Newcastle: Bloodaxe Books).

Nwapa, Flora (1966), *Efuru* (London: Heinemann).

Pearn, Julie (1987), in Ngcobo (ed.), *Let it be Told* (London: Virago).

Randhawa, Ravinder (1987), *A Wicked Old Woman.*

Raychaudhuri, Sibani (1994), 'Sisters', in Asian Women's Writing Collective, *Flaming Spirit* (London: Virago).

Riley, Joan (1985), *The Unbelonging* (London: The Women's Press).

Rushdie, Salman (1982), 'The Empire Writes Back with a Vengeance', *Sunday Times*, 2 July.

Sandoval, Cheva, (1991), 'Deterritorializations: The Rewriting of Home & Exile in Western Feminist Discourse', *Cultural Critique*, no. 6, p. 187.

Sidhanta Ash, Ranjana (1995), 'Writers of the South Asian Diaspora in Britain: A Survey of Post-War Fiction in English', *Wasafiri*, 21 (Spring).

Shabnam Grewal et al. (eds) (1988), *Charting the Journey: Writings by Black and Third World Women* (London: Sheba).

Skellington, R. and Morris, P. (1996), *'Race' in Britain Today*, 2nd edn (London: Sage).

Spivak, G. (1987), *In Other Worlds: Essays in Cultural Politics* (New York and London: Methuen).

Storkey, M. (1994), *London's Ethnic Minorities, One City, Many Communities: An Analysis of 1991 Census Results* (London: London Research Centre).

Sulter, Maud (1985), *As a Black Woman* (London: Akira).

Sulter, Maud (1986), *Through the Break: Women and Personal Struggle* (London: Sheba).

Sulter, Maud (1989), *Zabat: Poetics of a Family Tree* (London: Sheba).

Sulter, Maud and Pollard, Ingrid (eds) (1990), *Passion: Discourses on Black Women's Creativity* (London: Urban Fox Press).

Sulter, Maud (1991), *Echo: Works by Women Artists, 1850–1940* (Liverpool: Tate Gallery).
Syal, Meera (1997), *Anita and Me* (London: Flamingo).
Walker, Alice (1989), *The Temple of My Familiar* (London: The Women's Press).

Chapter 13 South-East Asia: Singapore and Malaysia

Coates, Austin (1978), frontispiece to *Little Ironies* (Singapore: Heinemann Writing in Asia series).
Geok-lin Lim, Shirley (1980), *Crossing the Peninsula and Other Poems*.
Geok-lin Lim, Shirley (1988), 'Tongue and Root: Language in Exile', in Raana Gauher (ed.), *Third World Affairs* (London: Third World Foundation for Social and Economic Studies).
Geok-lin Lim, Shirley (1994), 'Tropical Attitudes', in *Skoob Pacifica Anthology no. 2: Post-colonial Writings of the Pacific Rim* (London: Skoob).
Geok-lin Lim, Shirley (1996), *Amongst the White Moonfaces* (Singapore: Times Books).
Hicks, Bonnie (1990), *Excuse me, are you a model?* (Singapore: Times Books).
Koh Tai Ann (1992), in Claire Buck (ed.), *Bloomsbury Guide to Women's Literature* (London: Bloomsbury).
Kon, S. (1983 [1989]), *Emily of Emerald Hill* (London: Macmillan).
Lim, Catherine (1978), 'Paper', 'The Teacher' and 'Adeline Ng Ai Choo', *Little Ironies of Singapore* (Singapore: Times Books).
Lim, Catherine (1982), *The Serpent's Tooth* (Singapore: Times Books).
Lim, Catherine (1983), *They do Return . . . but Gently Lead them Back* (Singapore: Times Books).
Lim, Catherine (1997), *The Bondmaid* (London: Oriel).
Lim, Suchen Christine (1984), *Rice Bowl* (Singapore: Times Books).
Lim, Suchen Christine and Oi, Ophelia (1990), *The Amah: A Portrait in Black and White* (Singapore: Times Books).
Lim, Suchen Christine (1990), *A Gift from the Gods* (Singapore: Times Books).
Lim, Suchen Christine (1992), *A Fistful of Colours* (Singapore: Times Books).
Mei Ching, Tan (1992), *Water Ghosts* (Singapore: EPB Publishers).
Mei Ching, Tan (1994), *Beyond the Village* (Singapore: EPB Publishers).
Sessor, E. (1994), 'Singapore: The Prisoner in the Theme Park', in *The Lands of Charm and Cruelty* (New York: Vintage).

Chapter 14 Oceania – Pacific Rim Writing

Balakian, Anna (1962), 'Influence and Literary Fortune: The Equivocal Junction of Two Methods', *Year Book of Comparative and General Literature*, 11.
Buck, Claire (ed.) (1992), *The Bloomsbury Guide to Women's Literature* (London: Bloomsbury).
Crocombe, Marjorie (1980), Introduction, in Albert Wendt (ed.), *Lali: A Pacific Anthology* (Suva: Longam Paul).
Crocombe, Marjorie (1973), see *Mana: Annual of Creative Writing*, interview (Suva, 1973), p. 12.
Davis, Tom and Davis, Lydia (1955), *Doctor to the Islands*, in Buck Claire (ed.), *Bloomsbury Guide to Women's Literature* (London: Bloomsbury).

Dunlop, Peggy (1985), 'Samoan Writing: Searching for the Written Fagogo', in *Pacific Writers' Pacific Islands Communication Journal*, 14, 1 (Suva: The University of the South Pacific).

Griffen, Arlene (1997), 'Women Speak Out in Literature: Pacific and Caribbean Voices', *Wasafiri*, 25 (Spring).

Maka'a, Julian and Oxenham, Stephen (1985), 'Writing in the Solomon Islands: The Voice in the Shadow', in *Pacific Writers' Pacific Islands Communication Journal*, 14, 1 (Suva: The University of the South Pacific).

Maugham, Somerset (1919), *The Moon and Sixpence* (London: Heinemann).

Maugham, Somerset (1921), *The Trembling of a Leaf* (London: Heinemann).

Molisa, Grace (1983), *Black Stone* (Suva: Mana).

Molisa, Grace (1989), 'Coming of Age' and 'In the Eye of the Beholder', in *Black Stone*, 11 (Suva: Mana).

Pollard, Alice (1988), in *Pacific Women* (Suva, Fiji: Institute of Pacific Studies of the University of the South Pacific).

Rarua, Kathleen (1988), in *Pacific Women* (Suva, Fiji: Institute of Pacific Studies of the University of the South Pacific).

Sipolo, Jully (1981), *Civilised Girl* (Suva: The South Pacific Creative Arts Society).

Smith, Bernard (1985; 2nd edn), *European Vision and the South Pacific* (Melbourne: Oxford University Press; 1st edn, 1960).

Subramani, (1992 [1985]), *South Pacific Literature: From Myth to Fabulation* (Suva: Institute of Pacific Studies of the University of the South Pacific).

Taipo, Arthur (1986), 'Writing in the Cook Islands', in *Pacific Writers* (Suva: University of the South Pacific).

Teaiwa, Teresia (1995), 'Searching for Nei Nim'anoa', *Searching for Nei Nim'anoa* (Fiji: Mana Publications).

Teaiwa, Teresia (1999), 'Nudity III', in A. and G. Wisker (eds), *Spokes Poetry Magazine*, 28.

Thaman, Konai Helu (1974), *You, the Choice of my Parents* (Suva: Mana Publications).

Thaman, Konai Helu (1981), *Langakali* (Suva: Mana Publications).

Thaman, Konai Helu (1987), *Higano* (Fiji: Mana Publications).

Thaman, Konai Helu (1997), Interview with Briar Wood, *Wasafiri*, 25 (Spring).

Tuivaga, Jessie (1988), Taiamoni Tongamon (ed.), *Pacific Women: Roles and Status of Women in Pacific Societies* (Suva, Fiji: Institute of Pacific Studies of the University of the South Pacific).

Tusitala Marsh, Selina (1997), 'Statued (Stat you?) Traditions', in *Wasafiri*, 25 (Spring), p. 52.

Van Trease, Howard (1985), in *Pacific Writers' Pacific Islands Communication Journal*, 14, 1, pp. 24–9.

Wendt, Albert (ed.) (1980), *Lali: A Pacific Anthology* (Auckland: Longam Paul).

Chapter 15 Writing by Women from Cyprus

Angelidou, Klairi (ed.) (1994), *Nayia Rousseau* (Nicosia, Cyprus: Pen Publications).

Hawkins, Sheila (1997), *Beyond our Dreams* (Nicosia: Cyprus Mail Publications).

Ierodiaconou, Andriana (1994/5) 'Aishe', in Stephanos Stephanides, 'Three Cypriot Women Poets', in Theofanis Stavrou (ed.), *Modern Greek Studies Yearbook*, vol. 10/11 (University of Minnesota Press).

Kouyialis, Theoklis (ed.) (1983), *27 Centuries of Cypriot Poetry*, trans. John Vickers et al. (Nicosia, Cyprus: Pen Publications).

Ladaki-Philippou, Niki (1994), 'Preface: VII', in *Anthology 1960–1992* (Nicosia, Cyprus: Pen Publications).

Marangou, Niki (1998), 'Roses', in A. and G. Wisker (eds), *Spokes Poetry Magazine*, 28.

Nadjarian, Nora (1998), in *Sunjet*, 3 (Autumn).

Patapiou, Nasa (1994/5), 'Solace' and 'Woman without Boundaries', in Stephanos Stephanides, (1994) 'Three Cypriot Women Poets', in Theofanis Stavrou (ed.), *Modern Greek Studies Yearbook*, vol. 10/11 (University of Minnesota Press).

Roussou, Nayia (1975), *Memories of War* in *Testimony on the Borderless Line*.

Roussou, Nayia (1981), *Transit* in *Testimony on the Borderless Line*.

Roussou, Nayia (1985), *Channels of Ariadne* in *Testimony on the Borderless Line*.

Roussou, Nayia (1988), *Testimony on the Borderless Line: Beyond the Borderland* (Nicosia: Cyprus Press).

Stephanides, Stephanos (1994/5), 'Three Cypriot Women Poets', in Theofanis Stavrou (ed.), *Modern Greek Studies Yearbook*, vol. 10/11 (University of Minnesota Press).

Theocharous, Themis (1994), 'Nayia Roussou', in *Literary Profiles* (Nicosia, Cyprus: Pen Publications).

Thubron, Colin (19), *Journey into Cyprus*.

Yasin, Nesie (1995), in *Nicosia*, work by (Michalis Hadjipieris, Nesie Yasin, Georgios Kepola and Niyazi Kizilyurek (Nicosia, Cyprus: published by the authors).

Index